Becoming

Television and Popular Culture
Robert J. Thompson, *Series Editor*

Select Titles in Television and Popular Culture

Bigger Than "Ben-Hur": The Book, Its Adaptations, and Their Audiences
    Barbara Ryan and Milette Shamir, eds.

*Black Male Frames: African Americans
in a Century of Hollywood Cinema, 1903–2003*
    Roland Leander Williams Jr.

*Captain America, Masculinity, and Violence:
The Evolution of a National Icon*
    J. Richard Stevens

Reading Joss Whedon
    Rhonda V. Wilcox, Tanya R. Cochran, Cynthea Masson,
    and David Lavery, eds.

Screwball Television: Critical Perspectives on "Gilmore Girls"
    David Scott Diffrient with David Lavery, eds.

Television Finales: From "Howdy Doody" to "Girls"
    Douglas L. Howard and David Bianculli, eds.

Watching TV: Eight Decades of American Television, Third Edition
    Harry Castleman and Walter J. Podrazik

Watching TV with a Linguist
    Kristy Beers Fägersten, ed.

Becoming

Genre, Queerness,
and Transformation
in NBC's *Hannibal*

Edited by
Kavita Mudan Finn *and* EJ Nielsen

With a Foreword by Janice Poon

Syracuse University Press

Copyright © 2019 by Syracuse University Press
Syracuse, New York 13244-5290

All Rights Reserved

First Edition 2019

19 20 21 22 23 24   6 5 4 3 2 1

∞ The paper used in this publication meets the minimum requirements
of the American National Standard for Information Sciences—Permanence
of Paper for Printed Library Materials, ANSI Z39.48-1992.

For a listing of books published and distributed by Syracuse University Press,
visit www.SyracuseUniversityPress.syr.edu.

ISBN: 978-0-8156-3618-2 (hardcover)
     978-0-8156-3636-6 (paperback)
     978-0-8156-5464-3 (e-book)

Library of Congress Cataloging-in-Publication Data

Names: Mudan Finn, Kavita, 1983– editor of compilation. | Nielsen, E. J.,
    editor of compilation.
Title: Becoming : genre, queerness, and transformation in NBC's Hannibal /
    edited by Kavita Mudan Finn and EJ Nielsen ; with a foreword by Janice Poon.
Description: First edition. | Syracuse, New York : Syracuse University Press, 2019. |
    Series: Television and popular culture | Includes bibliographical references and index.
Identifiers: LCCN 2019014419 (print) | LCCN 2019014696 (ebook) |
    ISBN 9780815654643 (E-book) | ISBN 9780815636182 (hardcover : alk. paper) |
    ISBN 9780815636366 (pbk. : alk. paper)
Subjects: LCSH: Hannibal (Television program : 2013–2015) | Homosexuality
    on television. | Homosexuality and television.
Classification: LCC PN1992.77.H336 (ebook) | LCC PN1992.77.H336 B43 2019 (print) |
    DDC 791.45/72—dc23
LC record available at https://lccn.loc.gov/2019014419

Manufactured in the United States of America

Contents

List of Illustrations   *vii*
Foreword, *Janice Poon*   *ix*
Acknowledgments   *xiii*

1. Introduction
   A Love Crime
      Kavita Mudan Finn and EJ Nielsen   1

2. The Hannibalization of America
   The Cannibal Gourmet as Promethean Gift Giver
      Andrew Owen and Leanne Havis   10

3. Hannibal Lecter's Monstrous Return
   The Horror of Seriality in Bryan Fuller's Hannibal
      Jessica Balanzategui, Naja Later, and Tara Lomax   27

4. "Adapt. Evolve. Become."
   Queering Red Dragon *in Bryan Fuller's* Hannibal
      Ellie Lewerenz   54

5. Monstrous Masculinities in Gothic Romance
   Will Graham, Jane Eyre, *and* Caleb Williams
      Evan Hayles Gledhill   74

6. "Whispering through the Chrysalis"
   Hannibal Lecter and the Poetics of Mentorship
      Gabriel A. Rieger   96

7. The Great Red Dragon
   Francis Dolarhyde and Queer Readings of Skin
   Evelyn Deshane   *124*

8. Hannibal and the Cannibal
   Tracking Colonial Imaginaries
   Samira Nadkarni and Rukmini Pande   *145*

9. Bedelia Du Maurier
   Hannibal's *Femme Fatale and Final Girl*
   Kara M. French   *169*

10. "Some Lazy Psychiatry, Dr. Lecter"
    Teacups, Narrative, and Hannibal's *Critique of Psychoanalysis*
    Karen Felts   *192*

11. "Do You See?"
    Clues, Reasoning, and Connoisseurship
    Michelle D. Miranda   *215*

12. Fannibals Are Still Hungry
    Feeding Hannibal and Other Series Companion Cookbooks as Immersive Fan Experience
    Amanda Ewoldt   *239*

13. *Hannibal*
    Adaptation and Authorship in the Age of Fan Production
    Lori Morimoto   *258*

14. Rei(g)ning Lecter
    An Interview with Series Writer Nick Antosca on Hannibal
    Matthew Sorrento   *283*

Appendix: Hannibal *Episodes*   *303*
Contributors   *307*
Index   *313*

Illustrations

4.1. Darkroom sign from ". . . And the Woman Clothed with the Sun" (3.09) 57

4.2. Will Graham and Hannibal Lecter in "The Wrath of the Lamb" (3.13) 70

9.1. Bedelia Du Maurier in "Tome-Wan" (2.12) 177

9.2. Bedelia Du Maurier in ". . . And the Woman Clothed in Sun" (3.10) 178

11.1. The observatory, a frequent setting in seasons 1 and 2 of *Hannibal* 219

11.2. A Bertillon print as seen in Hannibal Lecter's office in "Amuse-Bouche" (1.02) 229

14.1. Nick Antosca on the set of *Channel Zero*, 2016 284

14.2. Will Graham and Hannibal Lecter in "The Number of the Beast Is 666" (3.12) 291

14.3. Scene from Peter Greenaway's film *The Cook, the Thief, His Wife, & Her Lover* (1989) 295

14.4. Nick Antosca with Fiona Shaw and Craig William Macneill on the set of *Channel Zero*, 2016 297

Foreword

Sometimes in this stimuli-loaded life of dodging event horizons, navigating swirling sensations, and running against the clock, you experience something that compels you to stop. Breathe deep. Dive in. Explore.

As in the time you first met Hannibal.

As the food stylist for the NBC series *Hannibal*, I experienced that first moment—as you might have—as a glowing image on a TV screen, viewed with awe in a silent, darkened room.

We were shooting the very first episode of a new series. New crew, unfamiliar actors, new script. The previous week, we had shot Hannibal Lecter and Will Graham's first motel breakfast scene. It felt disjointed. On location and far from set, I couldn't see the action and had no way of gauging how the scene was playing. We were disconnected except for a walkie-talkie that broke silence only to squawk out demands for more eggs and smaller sausages. We were fresh Kholodets: a hot, fishy mess not yet gelled.

But a fragment of the day's dialogue locked in my mind:

WILL. I don't find you that interesting.
HANNIBAL. You will.

A prophecy soon made true. For the next shoot, I requested a TV monitor so I could see what was happening on set. My food-styling crew was juggling reset plates and trying not to run out of fake liver (for voracious Mads Mikkelsen's first eating scene) when director-producer David Slade asked me for a show-and-tell of assorted lungs, utensils, and cooking techniques (for Mads's first cooking scene).

When the gnarly topic of how to press the lungs arose, Mads joined us and suggested, "I could do it with my hands. . . ." Brilliant. The wardrobe girl took him away to choose an apron. David made a Very British joke and went off to block the scene with the director of photography. I placed the prettiest lungs on set and returned to my station. Watching my TV monitor, I saw the frame creep in tight on Mads's hotly lit back, then plunge over his shoulder to reveal those hands gripping the plump, pink lungs. It was perfect: a miraculous result of unexpected collaboration in this newly formed team. In that moment, I knew we had our Hannibal.

As each episode flowed into the next, I devoured every new script and found them full of impossibly complex dialogue, challenging images, obscure references, and strange emotions. Every time I came into the studio, there were new actors and characters to admire in iconic costumes and freshly built sets rich with decor that was layered in meaning . . . a wellspring of references for me to draw upon as I created Hannibal's food. Most importantly, our showrunner, Bryan Fuller, was on top of everything. His communications to us were powerful (yes, in CAPSLOCK). His notes were magical points of inspiration that guided but never dictated. Best of all, he never said, "No, that's too crazy," so I was never afraid to go beyond convention. This spirit infused every department from the writers' room to the sound stage to postproduction. Bryan fostered a higher level of creativity in all the departments, and we all fed off each other, going higher, deeper, and wider than was ever thought possible in network television. He never underestimated the audience—winkingly leaving little gems for the astute viewer to discover. We all followed suit, layering metaphors and allusions into our work, thus making *Hannibal* one of the most culturally and philosophically dense TV series ever broadcast across our milquetoast land.

As season 1 unfolded, the trickle of comments on my weekly behind-the-scenes blog, *Feeding Hannibal*, became a flood of insightful remarks and queries from a growing viewership. This made me realize that the show was gaining an audience overwhelmingly intellectual, analytical, inquisitive, unbiased, and appreciative. These self-styled

Fannibals were astonishingly talented, as quickly became apparent from their eye-popping fan art, sweaty fanfiction, hilarious videos, GIFs, charming Tumblr posts, and tweets. They were so hungry to engage in the *Hannibal* universe that they started cooking *Hannibal* dinners and posting photos of their meal-sharing meat-ups. I could see the rosy fingers of Fannibalism taking hold in academia when I began receiving requests for critiques of *Hannibal*-based design assignments and later for permissions to cite my bloggings in academic papers on Hannibal's unusual appetites.

So now it comes as no surprise to me to regard this superbly curated collection of academic papers—each one a deep dive into the complexity of *Hannibal*. Some of these thoughtful essays explore (Why, Hannibal . . . *why?*), explain (because he can), interpret (teacups and butterflies), and extrapolate (Hannigram); others pronounce (it's OK to be weird) or speculate (H4nnibal). Each in its turn may have you nodding in avid agreement or contentiously shouting retorts, but they all express a shared fascination for, understanding of, and deep connection to *Hannibal*.

This *Hannibal* story of ours continues to touch us on so many levels because although it is fictitious and fanciful, its essence rings true. Its mirroring facets can be scrutinized through many different lenses, but each examination of this rich work reveals the full-spectrum, morality-fluid, validating universe of *Hannibal* because each glittering bit of the series comes from the same place: formed under the pressure and the pleasure of working as a team under the inspired leadership of Bryan Fuller with the knowledge that our work is not invisible—that it is seen and appreciated by a fandom that understands deeply the *Hannibal* world within and without.

Nakama always,
Janice Poon

Acknowledgments

We wish to thank all of our contributors for their insightful analyses, hard work, and flexibility. Many are independent, unaffiliated scholars who took time from work and family to produce their chapters, and we as editors want to offer our sincerest appreciation. Thanks to Deb Manion, Kay Steinmetz, and Mona Hamlin at Syracuse University Press as well as copy editor Annie Barva for guiding us through the publication process and to the two anonymous peer reviewers for their suggestions. We also thank Nan King for proofreading assistance and Lori Morimoto for indexing.

A special thanks goes to Janice Poon both for her delectable food styling and for writing the foreword to this collection. And thanks to Claudia Gironi for letting us license her gorgeous fanart for our cover image.

We thank Bryan Fuller, Martha de Laurentiis, Mads Mikkelsen, Hugh Dancy, and everyone else involved in bringing *Hannibal* to life.

Last, one of us (EJ) is a graduate student, and the other (Kavita) is an independent scholar, so both of us are reliant on personal support networks for our academic work. Kavita extends special thanks to everyone who watched her children while she worked and to her children for sleeping long enough for her to work when other childcare wasn't available. EJ's cats offered invaluable assistance, but Kavita's dogs are excluded from these acknowledgments for reasons they—like many of the individuals who end up as main courses on Hannibal's table—well understand.

Becoming

I | Introduction

A Love Crime

Kavita Mudan Finn and EJ Nielsen

It is nearly impossible to have grown up in the United States today without having encountered Hannibal Lecter in one form or another. One may have first learned of Hannibal the Cannibal through Thomas Harris's series of novels—*Red Dragon* (1981), *The Silence of the Lambs* (1988), *Hannibal* (1999), and *Hannibal Rising* (2006)—all of which have been adapted for the screen. In addition to Jonathan Demme's Oscar-winning film *The Silence of the Lambs* (1991), *Red Dragon* has been adapted twice: first as Michael Mann's *Manhunter* (1986) and some sixteen years later as Brett Ratner's *Red Dragon* (2002). Harris's two most recent novels, *Hannibal* (2001) and *Hannibal Rising* (2007), were filmed by Ridley Scott and Peter Webber, respectively, though neither films enjoyed the critical or box-office success of Demme's initial cinematic foray into the mythos. No matter the medium of that first encounter, however, Hannibal Lecter, Clarice Starling, Will Graham, and other characters and quotations have been absorbed into our popular culture, adding lines such as "it puts the lotion on its skin" to our shared cultural language and the idea of an urbane, educated cannibal psychiatrist to our collective stable of monsters.

When one of us (Kavita), who had first seen *The Silence of the Lambs* as an impressionable teenager, found out that the other of us (her undergraduate roommate, EJ), lover of all things macabre, had not yet seen the film, it was decided that such ignorance must be rectified posthaste, and a viewing party was arranged. As the FBI agents on-screen pulled the cocoon from the decapitated head of Jame Gumb's victim and asked why the killer would do that, EJ chimed in, "It's a symbol of death and rebirth!" When asked how they knew that, having never seen the film, EJ explained, "I mean, it's why I'd have done it."

But we digress.

When it was announced in 2012 that Bryan Fuller, best known for the television series *Wonderfalls* (2004), *Dead Like Me* (2003–4), and *Pushing Daisies* (2007–9), was going to be the showrunner for a television adaptation of *Red Dragon* titled *Hannibal*, a precursor to the events of *The Silence of the Lambs*, many fans of the Hannibal Lecter franchise were skeptical. Was it just another cynical attempt, like the critically panned films *Hannibal* and *Hannibal Rising*, to generate revenue from a popular franchise? Was Fuller the right person to direct a horror series? How could Mads Mikkelsen, a relatively unknown (at least in the United States) Danish actor, compare with the iconic Sir Anthony Hopkins, who won an Academy Award for his earlier portrayal? How could the show maintain suspense and interest when the audience already knew Lecter's big secret? Moreover, how much would a series about cannibalistic serial killers be allowed to show on a mainstream network such as NBC rather than on a premium channel such as HBO (*Game of Thrones*, 2011–19) or Showtime (*Dexter*, 2006–13) or even on a cable network such as FX (*American Horror Story*, 2011–) or AMC (*Breaking Bad*, 2008–13)?

From the first episode, however, it was clear that *Hannibal* (2013–15) was a species apart from typical network fare. Although the innovative and beautiful cinematography could be found in other network series, including Fuller's earlier work, *Hannibal*'s juxtaposition of Grand Guignol violence and curated artistry set it apart. Nearly every episode features potentially stomach-turning crime scenes alongside Food Network–worthy cooking sequences styled by Janice Poon, and many include deeply unsettling dream sequences, inspiring immediate comparisons to genre-bending series such as

David Lynch's original *Twin Peaks* (1990–91). Over its three seasons, *Hannibal* developed into a strangely gothic melodrama unafraid to mine or alter the source material as necessary. As we have argued elsewhere, *Hannibal* also incorporates many elements from film noir, constantly implicating its viewers in new and troubling ways.[1] A number of characters from the books are no longer white men—psychiatrist Alan Bloom has become Alana (Caroline Dhavernas), and the tabloid journalist Freddy Lounds has become Freddie (Lara Jean Chorosteki), a young woman with a popular crime blog, while Harris's all-white, mostly male FBI now includes a Jack Crawford played by Laurence Fishburne; a female supervisor, Kade Prurnell, played by Cynthia Nixon; and a female forensic technician, Beverly Katz, played by Hettienne Park. Fuller made it clear in interviews that, unlike many showrunners, particularly within the crime-procedural genre, he wanted explicitly to avoid story lines that depended on rape and the aestheticizing of violence against women.[2] Given how many episodes of any *CSI* series open with the brutalized body of a young woman, this choice can only be seen as a major step forward within the genre, even taking into account the fact that one of the show's two protagonists is a cannibal.

Setting aside what has become a typical television concern about spoilers, *Hannibal* operates on the assumption that its viewers already know Lecter's big secret (spoiler: the meat is people), and the script plays with those implications while keeping the rest of the characters in the dark. In his landmark study *Complex TV*, Jason Mittell observes that *Hannibal*'s choice to embrace the "knowledge

---

1. See Kavita Mudan Finn and EJ Nielsen, "'Blood in the Moonlight': *Hannibal* as Queer Noir," *Quarterly Review of Film and Video* 35, no. 6 (2018): 568–82.

2. James Hibberd, "'Hannibal' Showrunner Criticizes TV's Rape Scene Epidemic," *Entertainment Weekly*, May 28, 2015. It is worth noting that the first serial killer presented in the show kills young women by impaling them on deer antlers; images of those women recur during the first several episodes in flashbacks and dream sequences, and photographs of them appear later in the series. However, these images are the exception rather than the rule for *Hannibal*.

differential" between viewers and characters creates "dark, ironic humor" and that "the effect is to highlight the operational aesthetic, calling attention to the storytelling's playful practices of both withholding information and relying on intertextual clues."[3] The opening episode, for instance, cuts from the line "He's eating them" (referring to a different serial killer) to a wordless sequence of Dr. Lecter cooking an unidentified meat while listening to Bach's *Goldberg Variations*, a piece associated with Lecter in Demme's *Silence of the Lambs*. These nods to the viewer, acknowledging their awareness of who and what Hannibal is, implicate them in Hannibal's crimes even as the other characters slowly discover the truth about everybody's favorite psychiatrist. At the center of this moral quagmire is Will Graham (Hugh Dancy), whose pure empathy and vivid imagination make him invaluable as a criminal profiler while also leaving him dangerously vulnerable—and deeply attractive—to Hannibal.

The obsessive, codependent relationship between Mikkelsen's Lecter and Dancy's Graham (a role played by William Peterson in 1986 and Ed Norton in 2002) proved especially popular among fans of the show as it evolved organically over the course of three seasons. In a media landscape plagued by fan accusations of "queerbaiting," *Hannibal* stands apart not just for its nuanced portrayal of LGBT characters and relationships—in sharp contrast to Harris's source material, which, as Evelyn Deshane argues in their chapter, is heavily homophobic and transphobic—but also for the showrunners' and producers' respectful treatment of fans. As Lori Morimoto discusses in her chapter, Fuller liberally pulls from and repurposes elements from all of Harris's Hannibal Lecter books; the original *Red Dragon*, *Manhunter*, and *Hannibal* films; FBI profiler John Douglas's original memoir *Mindhunter* (1995);[4] and even, if obliquely owing to copyright issues, both film and book versions of *Silence of the Lambs*.

---

3. Jason Mittell, *Complex TV: The Poetics of Contemporary Television Storytelling* (New York: New York Univ. Press, 2015), 174.

4. John Douglas and Mark Olshaker, *Mindhunter: Inside the FBI's Elite Serial Crime Unit*, with a new introduction (New York: Gallery Books, 2017).

This creative bricolage, rather than following the trend of other, more traditional reboots or prequels, instead more closely resembles the kind of fanfiction culturally associated with women writing pseudonymously. By thus drawing together the trappings of prestige television—the particular kind of serial storytelling that Mittell classifies as "narrative complexity"—with the *affective* engagement and emotional resonance of fanfiction, Fuller's *Hannibal* offers a very different kind of crime-procedural drama and has thus earned an especially devoted fan following.[5]

Bryan Fuller and Fannibals (as fans of the show are known) quickly formed a relationship through social media and convention appearances noteworthy not simply for the almost unprecedented amount of contact between them on Twitter but also because Fuller, in contrast with the many recent public missteps of showrunners, writers, and networks, seemed genuinely to *understand* and appreciate the show's fanbase. Breaking the traditional "fourth wall" of fandom, which relies on a separation between fanworks and the original material, authors, and actors, Fuller made significant monetary pledges to support Fannibal kickstarters (anthologies of fanart and fanfiction) and once appeared at an event wearing a shirt printed with fanart of Will and Hannibal kissing.[6] His popularity with the fanbase is, on some level, an inscription of the relatively recent "rise of the 'showrunner,'" a phenomenon that, according to Michael Newman and Elana Levine, makes "popular art forms become more amenable to intellectualization, a key strategy of cultural legitimation."[7] Fuller, however, has also embraced his status as

---

5. Mittell, *Complex TV*, 18. According to Mittell, narrative complexity "employs a range of serial techniques, with the underlying assumption that a series is a cumulative narrative that builds over time, rather than resetting back to a steady-state equilibrium at the end of every episode" (18). Although some crime procedurals do have ongoing story lines, they are definitely in the minority.

6. Split Screens Festival, May 30–June 3, 2018, New York City.

7. Michael Z. Newman and Elana Levine, *Legitimating Television: Media Convergence and Cultural Status* (London: Routledge, 2012), 9.

a *fan* author, setting himself apart from the auteurism of showrunners such as Joss Whedon (*Buffy the Vampire Slayer* [1996–2003]), *Firefly* [2002–3]) and Steven Moffat (*Doctor Who* [2005–], *Sherlock* [2010–]), both of whom have garnered criticism for their dismissive treatment of fans.

Unfortunately, despite Fuller's efforts and campaigns by Fannibals, NBC cancelled *Hannibal* in 2015 owing to low ratings. The end (or at least pause) of *Hannibal* after a three-season run makes this an ideal time to consider the show more formally, and the authors here are just some of the many scholars captivated by Bryan Fuller's vision. For the reasons discussed earlier and others, *Hannibal* represents a potential future direction for television fandom as well as for the medium more generally—Fuller's subsequent work on *American Gods* (2017–) for Starz certainly evokes a number of the narrative and aesthetic choices he made in *Hannibal* and has earned notable critical and viewer acclaim. That multiple platforms, including both Netflix and Amazon, have expressed interest in new episodes of *Hannibal* and that the show's stars are constantly asked about its renewal, even when they are publicizing other projects, speak to *Hannibal*'s enduring appeal, as do several forthcoming essay collections about it, including this one.[8] The essays in this volume emerge from and draw on a range of fields—literature, history, gender studies, film and media studies, criminology, forensic science, psychoanalysis, and sociology—offering a wide variety of perspectives on this multifaceted series that we hope will start a conversation between scholars, fans, and those who fall into both categories. In combining these many critical lenses, we hope to highlight the

---

8. See Kyle Moody and Nicholas Yanes, eds., *Eating the Rude: Hannibal Lecter and the Fannibals, Criminals, and Legacy of America's Favorite Cannibal* (Durham, NC: McFarland, forthcoming); Jessica Balanzategui, Naja Later, and Tara Lomax, eds., special *Hannibal*-focused issue of *Quarterly Review of Film and Video* 35, no. 6 (2018). These works are in addition to the collection that preceded Fuller's series: Benjamin Szuminskyj, ed., *Dissecting Hannibal Lecter: Essays on the Novels of Thomas Harris* (Durham, NC: McFarland, 2008).

multivalent complexity of *Hannibal*, not just in Mittell's sense of the word, but in the emotional response the series encourages from its viewers. It is no mere puzzle box to be opened week after week, but a meal to be savored both figuratively and—in the case of Fannibal "meat-ups"—literally.

In the opening chapter, Andrew Owen and Leanne Havis explore the significance of Hannibal Lecter's participation in cannibalism not merely for his own food but also for his seeming obsession with sharing such delicacies with those around him, linking it to larger sociological trends of food consumption in the United States. Building on the real-world implications of *Hannibal*'s characters, Jessica Balanzategui, Naja Later, and Tara Lomax consider how the serial format of television recursively reinforces the motif of seriality that is central to the monstrosity of Lecter as serial killer. Their chapter also explores the ways that fanfiction, both Fuller's reimagining of Hannibal Lecter and the fanworks it has generated, can be seen as "radically monstrous." Ellie Lewerenz's chapter expands on these ideas of permeable textual boundaries, discussing how Fuller, while choosing to be faithful to some aspects of the original novel, is also at pains to queer Harris's text, blurring lines between order and disorder, insider and outsider, crime and law. This queering is especially evident in the complex relationship between Will Graham and Hannibal Lecter.

Further focusing on the relationship between Will and Hannibal, Evan Hayles Gledhill explores how *Hannibal*, read as a gothic text, restages "themes of monstrosity and empathy through the genre of the gothic romance." Gabriel Rieger's chapter then offers a wider lens to explore Hannibal's highly questionable mentorship not just of Will but of Abigail Hobbs and Miriam Lass, all of whom he argues are surrogates for and parallels to the character Clarice Starling. Clarice is noticeably absent from Fuller's series owing to copyright issues and yet, as Rieger argues, quite present through these other characters.

A number of Fuller's adaptation choices have addressed some of the uglier and more problematic elements in Harris's source texts.

Evelyn Deshane's chapter focuses on the transformation of the main *Red Dragon* narrative through the transposition of queerness and the prioritization of emotional fidelity over narrative fidelity. Not all of these adaptational choices are fully successful, as discussed in Samira Nadkarni and Rukmini Pande's chapter addressing the ways in which *Hannibal*, although more diverse than its predecessors, still relies on the whiteness of its main characters to render their violence and cannibalism acceptable to audiences. Shifting the focus from race to gender, Kara French looks at the character of Bedelia Du Maurier, an original creation by Fuller, and the ways she both fulfills and subverts the tropes of Final Girl and femme fatale while, perhaps more importantly, acting as an audience surrogate. Next, Karen Felts considers the ways in which *Hannibal*'s critique of traditional psychoanalysis also functions as a rejection of the heteronormative, problematic tropes of many of the other genre shows dealing with criminal investigation.

The subsequent two chapters, by Michelle D. Miranda and Amanda Ewoldt, address two major aspects of *Hannibal* that are outside the scope of traditional textual or film analysis: the show's portrayal of forensic crime-scene analysis and the fandom's response to *Hannibal*'s striking displays of culinary excess. First, Miranda applies tools of forensic examination to explore how the series combines crime-scene analysis with art connoisseurship, in keeping with the series' overarching theme of murder as an art form. Ewoldt then discusses the complex relationship between Fannibals and food, which *Hannibal* serves up as seductive temptation and ultimate cannibalistic taboo, and explores how this celebration of food becomes another form of fan practice.

Coming full circle to the adaptational strategies discussed in the opening chapter, Lori Morimoto analyzes how looking at *Hannibal* not simply as an adaptation but specifically as *fanfiction* opens the text up as an archontic work that blurs the lines between fan and producer. Finally, in an interview with Nick Antosca, screenwriter of the episodes "Aperitivo" (3.04), "The Great Red Dragon" (3.08), and "The Wrath of the Lamb" (3.13), the horror scholar Matthew

Sorrento and Antosca discuss Antosca's writing experiences and background with the character of Hannibal Lecter.[9]

Fannibals still live in hope that *Hannibal* will be revived, perhaps by Netflix or Amazon, to allow Fuller to finish a narrative arc originally planned for seven seasons. When asked, Fuller, Dancy, and Mikkelsen have expressed an interest in coming back to *Hannibal*, despite their busy post-*Hannibal* work schedules. In the meantime, *Hannibal* continues to inspire scholars and fans to write, draw, and discuss the show, possibly over fava beans and a nice Chianti.

Bon appétit

Bibliography

Douglas, John, and Mark Olshaker. *Mindhunter: Inside the FBI's Elite Serial Crime Unit*. With a new introduction. New York: Gallery Books, 2017.

Finn, Kavita Mudan, and EJ Nielsen. "Blood in the Moonlight: *Hannibal* as Queer Noir." *Quarterly Review of Film and Video* 35, no. 6 (2018): 568–82.

Hibberd, James. "'Hannibal' Showrunner Criticizes TV's Rape Scene Epidemic." *Entertainment Weekly*, May 28, 2015.

Mittell, Jason. *Complex TV: The Poetics of Contemporary Television Storytelling*. New York: New York Univ. Press, 2015.

Moody, Kyle, and Nicholas Yanes, eds. *Eating the Rude: Hannibal Lecter and the Fannibals, Criminals, and Legacy of America's Favorite Cannibal*. Durham, NC: McFarland, forthcoming.

Newman, Michael Z., and Elana Levine. *Legitimating Television: Media Convergence and Cultural Status*. London: Routledge, 2012.

Szuminskyj, Benjamin, ed. *Dissecting Hannibal Lecter: Essays on the Novels of Thomas Harris*. Durham, NC: McFarland, 2008.

---

9. In these chapters, ellipses with brackets around them indicate the chapter authors' omission of text; ellipses with no brackets indicate pauses in speech or ellipses in the original text and are usually given in quotations from the television series, films, and works of fiction.

2 | The Hannibalization of America

The Cannibal Gourmet as Promethean Gift Giver

Andrew Owen and Leanne Havis

It's a grisly world across which our cannibal strides.

A grim tableau littered with the detritus of neoliberalist exploitation, its gutters choked with the discarded *disjecta membra* of plastic convenience, a desolate postindustrial landscape where urban decentralization has left nothing but wanton decay and across which a savage wind blows the waste of cheap convenience. The remains of fast food abound, a glaring admission of capitalist exploitation and testimony to the growing need of the economically marginalized for dollar menus and "Supersized" options.

By the beginning of the twenty-first century, Ray Kroc's vision of a fast-food franchise had become a reality, engulfing, consuming the world. The McDonald's restaurant has become an empire that has expanded to serve more than 70 million customers a day in more than 35,000 restaurants spread out over 128 countries—a neoliberalist symbol of capitalist imperialism in the late twentieth and early twenty-first centuries. Consider the power of neoliberalism in the latter decades of the twentieth century: if the franchise took from 1954 to 1994 to sell more than 99 billion burgers, its global dominance allowed it to surpass 300 billion by 2013.[1] The world

---

1. George Ritzer, *The McDonaldization of Society*, 8th ed. (Newbury Park, CA: Sage, 2014), 2.

we inhabit is increasingly becoming a global society dominated by fast food, by convenience, by speed. Documentaries, such as Morgan Spurlock's *Supersize Me* (2004), warn us of the detrimental effects of the product on our bodies, but seemingly to no avail. Culture jams scream at an ostensibly indifferent society, warning of the dangers of obesity, of early death—"Weight: I'm Gaining It," "20 Piece Spongy McCarcasses for 4.99"—warnings that remain unheeded, perhaps because they are aimed at the very audience already made lethargic by the diet that is the source of the pestilence.

But, then again, how could it be any other way? Consider the societal dynamics: in these early decades of the twenty-first century, the population of the United States, the capitalist global leader, has grown increasingly more polarized, with the richest 20 percent of its population controlling 90 percent of its total wealth, while its poorest 15 percent live below the official poverty line[2]—economic disparity that translates as a capitalist's wet dream, propelling profits to undreamed of heights and causing the economically marginalized to be forced into consuming the very product that economically consumes them. In 2013, McDonald's revenues were $28.1 billion, a figure that surpassed the gross domestic product of countries the size of Ecuador.[3] Other capitalist franchises, progenitors of the sprawl economy, have also profited from such a polarized societal dynamic; the Walmart store exists in twenty-seven countries, serving more than 245 million customers in any given week.[4] The society of the twenty-first century is a society of "bliss points," a formula constructed by the fast-food industry in which the correct combination of salty and sweet ensures that hunger, the desire to consume, is never fully satiated.

Economic inequality serves as the catalyst by which such capitalist "convenience" companies are able to exploit the masses, ensuring

---

2. Gregory Mantsios, "Class in America—2014," in *Race, Class, and Gender in the United States*, 9th ed., ed. Paula Rothenberg (New York: Worth, 2014), 182–97.
3. Ritzer, *McDonaldization*, 2.
4. Ritzer, *McDonaldization*.

their custom by promising that their limited dollars will be able to go further in the companies' stores than anywhere else. Surely, Henry Miller's metaphorical depiction of life as "the mad slaughterhouse" has never seemed more appropriate than it does now.[5] If culture jams try to warn us of heart disease and diabetes, what of it? Even if the pig in the slaughterhouse is aware of its fate, what can it do? The mechanisms of exploitation and dominance in this slaughterhouse are so well oiled and all-encompassing that even if the pig were to struggle, its ultimate destiny would not be changed in the slightest.

Such a capitalist exploitative dichotomy is surely the antithesis of what was once promised to the Western social populace. Consider the preceding decades, the latter half of the twentieth century. Then, in a climate of seemingly unrelenting economic optimism, leaders promised prosperity for all, an existence governed by true equality and freedom. Lyndon Johnson, speaking to the American people in 1964, stated, "In your time we have the opportunity to move not only toward the rich society and the powerful society, but upward to the Great Society."[6] This utopian dream of societal equality began to gain momentum with such legislation as the Civil Rights Act of 1964 and the Voting Rights Act of 1965. In October 1964, Martin Luther King Jr. won the Nobel Peace Prize for his ideology concerning nonviolent revolution. Such acts could surely be equated with the birth cries of Johnson's promise, a sound heralding an existence characterized by an "abundance and liberty for all," where there would be an "end to poverty and racial injustice," a society where each child would receive "knowledge to enrich his mind and to enlarge his talents."[7]

In the following years, such utopian dreams seemed composed solely of unrelenting naivety as visions of societal equality were

---

5. Henry Miller, *The Tropic of Cancer* (New York: Grove Press, 1994).
6. Lyndon Johnson, "The Great Society," remarks presented at the Univ. of Michigan, May 22, 1964, at http://www.presidency.ucsb.edu/ws/?pid=26262.
7. Johnson, "The Great Society."

engulfed by the "flames of inequity."[8] Assassinations of leading figures, symbols of this supposed societal freedom, seemed to be growing in abundance, reaped in a red harvest of televised destruction, signaling a season of unrelenting violence and oppression: Malcolm X in February 1965, King in April 1968, Bobby Kennedy two months later. The promises of racial equality were violently exposed as manipulative political rhetoric as race riots erupted in a number of American cities, beginning with Watts in Los Angeles in August 1965. The country became divided over the war in Vietnam as its napalm-drenched carnage could be witnessed over dinner on a nightly basis through the medium of television. Even music that had supposedly offered a moment of societal harmony, the peace and love of countercultural ideology, epitomized by the Monterey Pop Festival in 1967 and Woodstock in 1969, descended into the brutality and on-screen murder at Altamont in December 1969. Then there were the Manson family murders, culminating with the real-life homicide of film actress Sharon Tate on August 9 that same year.

Utopian equality, the Great Society, call it what you will, had died in the womb, and all that remained was exploitation; the weak were at the mercy of the strong. A terrible tableau dominated by greed, sustained by neoliberalist hypocrisy. The promise of the Great Society strangled in utero, reanimated and transformed into the trite dogma of equality, fed to the impoverished herd chained to the capitalist economic machine. A false ideology that proclaimed that "anything is possible in America, if you have the faith, the will, and the heart."[9]

This is the festering womb in which our cannibal has been grown and nurtured, born to brutality and duplicitousness by incestuous

8. Martin Luther King Jr., "I Have a Dream," speech given at the March on Washington for Jobs and Freedom, Aug. 28, 1963, at http://avalon.law.yale.edu/20th_century/mlk01.asp.
9. Ronald Reagan, "The State of the Union," address before a joint session of Congress, Feb. 6, 1985, at https://www.reaganfoundation.org/ronald-reagan/reagan-quotes-speeches/state-of-the-union-3/.

parents who, with all false sincerity, tell their children of the American Dream, a beautiful bedtime story designed to keep restless offspring quiet.

It is a womb that breeds arrogance and vulgarity within its inhabitants, a desire to pathetically proclaim your superiority to those around you—proclivities that are distasteful, socially embarrassing, rude, serving only to extenuate the disharmony and disunity created by this festering social existence. Such debased neoliberalist behaviors and attitudes are unpalatable; they must be challenged, transmuted. However, such a metamorphosis calls for, as the very foundation of the transformative process, that one truly comprehend—without doubt, without uncertainty, and above all without the querulous voice of so-called conscience bleating in one's ear—that the rules of this alleged civilized society are nothing more than a fragile synthetic overlay, formulated by simple superstitious beings whose own ignorance, fear, and greed have culminated in the generation of a contrived morality and who cling to the childish belief in the objective understanding of good and evil.

In order to elevate oneself above the confines of such a unpalatable existence, one must, like Nietzsche's Übermensch, become master of one's own tastes, enjoy the feast when it presents itself, and find the propensity for self-indulgence, for boorishness, and for hypocrisy to be repugnant, unpalatable.

This is what it is to be Hannibal, to be Cannibal.

To be born into a world where the potential for good has been corrupted into exploitative foulness, whose fetid breath reeks of consumerism, and where the remnants of the subjugated are ensnared in the teeth of monopolistic capitalism.

As an inversion of such a societal dynamic, our cannibal utilizes his gastronomic proclivities to reverse the process, to take something that has a propensity for baseness, for rudeness, or for ignorance and transform them into something that can, in both its figurative and its literal sense, be enjoyed, savored, and ultimately, perhaps with a little wine, digested.

Cannibalism, then, quite unapologetically becomes the process by which the individual (perhaps, for some, this should read "victim"), once a source of disunity and disharmony, emerges as the very fulcrum of social accord and celebration—a central dish in a meal where friends and like-minded sophisticates can gather and agree on the pleasing splendor and beauty that is the focus, the very reason for the social gathering. After all, a pig may possess a disagreeable disposition, but when a pig is served as a pork loin, meat eaters the world over can agree as to its tenderness.

Such an undertaking necessitates, by its very dynamic, a careful selection process. As a consequence, our cannibal must avail himself of a carefully maintained series of recipe cards that can be systematically perused and cross-referenced with an equally cultivated set of "meat selections," individuals whose distasteful demeanor make them perfect candidates to be transformed into tasteful hors d'oeuvres or entrees.

If one finds the ingredients of such a meal to be distasteful, well, then, let us consider the alternative: products of the industrial mechanized process, cheaply made, synthetically enhanced, canned or frozen, miscellaneous "foodstuffs." Does this sound more appetizing to the reader? Surely not?!

In the posthumously published *Grundrisse*, Marx envisions an industrial society where all institutions are controlled and manipulated to serve the economic base.[10] In such an environment, work is reduced to a series of individualized mechanical movements, an assembly line of simple specifics in which the construction of product is achieved dispassionately, without true appreciation or even contemplation of the final medium. In such a social dynamic, an appreciation for the skills of the artisan is lost, sacrificed at the altar of industry and the profit generator that is mechanization. Machines

---

10. Karl Marx, *Grundrisse: Foundations of the Critique of Political Economy* (Middlesex, UK: Penguin Books, 1993).

can ultimately replace the human worker, with ingenuity and artistry forfeited to serve the bottom line. Such assembly-line procedure has been allowed to infect the food-making industry, with the preparation of burgers or sushi or tacos being reduced to a simple set of mechanical tasks achieved by each individual within the process undertaking a simple mechanized movement.[11]

Is this condition purported to be civilization, a state of existence in which nutrition and camaraderie are replaced by bliss points and convenience?

We must strive to do better. To claw ourselves out of such pits of all-consuming despair. To achieve residence on a higher social and cultural enclave, where we can gaze down at such mechanized mundanity with distrust and revulsion.

A self-professed devotee of *kaiseki*, "a Japanese art form that honors the taste and aesthetic of what we eat" ("Kaiseki," 2.01), our cannibal argues, as a counter to the formula of the bliss point, that "taste is not only biochemical, it's also psychological" ("Œuf," 1.04) in the striving to ensure that the artistry of food preparation and presentation remains extant.

As one fan of our cannibal's cuisine enthusiastically states while attending the opera, "Have you seen him cook? It is an entire performance" ("Sorbet," 1.07).

Our cannibal is the artisan, and, like the true artist, he states to his audience, "I cannot force a feast; a feast must present itself" (1.07). He would remind us that the consumption of food is not some mundane mechanical process, but rather an organic social enterprise, an essential behavioral trait that enhances communal understanding, strengthens the social bonds of the populace, and thereby ensures the longevity of societal harmony and conviviality.

Our cannibal acknowledges the fastidiousness with which he approaches his self-care: "I am very careful about what I put into

---

11. Ritzer, *McDonaldization*.

my body, which means that I end up preparing most meals myself" ("Apéritif," 1.01). Surely such a proclivity in a society dominated by convenience foods, whose ingredients are typically ascribed the opposite of the nutritious elements that supposedly compose the essential predicate of food, can be conceived of only as good practice and common sense.

And remember, one should begin the day with a self-prepared protein scramble . . . (1.01).

But what of the conversation at the dining table while we are enjoying this fine meal?

It seems that our cannibal host often reveals a dry sense of humor: he is a purveyor of the language of the anthropomorphic innuendo; he delights in revealing to his dinner guests precisely the nature of the dishes that he serves. After all, "it's nice to have an old friend for dinner" ("Entrée," 1.06), to serve them, "a particularly energetic lamb" (1.06), or if a guest is unable to quite place the fish, to state simply, "He was a flounder" (2.01).

To the casual guest, perhaps their host seems a little eccentric, ascribing an anthropomorphic quality to an animal, but what of it? A little humor is said to be an aid to digestion.

Perhaps with such interactions our cannibal deigns to give a slight nod of acknowledgment to the traditional description of human meat, "long pig." Indeed, porcine themes sometimes dominate areas of conversation. One meal served to unwitting guests is the carefully prepared entrée of "an especially supercilious pig" ("Coquilles," 1.05). In addition, Will Graham, in discussing the copycat killing committed by our helpful cannibal, posits, "This girl's killer thought she was a pig" (1.01). Similarly, in analyzing the murders committed by the Chesapeake Ripper, Graham uses the term *sounders* because "it refers to a small group of pigs, [and] that's how he [the Ripper] sees his victims: not as people, not as prey—pigs" (1.07). He notes that the "Ripper kills in sounders of three or four" ("Futamono," 2.06) and even acknowledges that the Ripper eats his victims "because they are no better to him than pigs" (2.06).

This style of humor can often be erroneously equated with gallows humor.[12] However, the cannibal is not a member of some subordinate social group bolstering morale at the cost of his oppressors. Rather, his humor is that of the confessional, attributable to the dynamics of executioner's humor, as identified by Alan Dundes and Thomas Hauschild; he is the dominant using humor to acknowledge his proclivities, his actions, and, most especially, the composition of his cuisine.[13]

Such humor in its Freudian sense captures our cannibal "baring its teeth" in a socially agreeable way, acknowledging to all what he truly is and what he is in fact serving them to eat, even if they lack the foresight to comprehend it.[14]

The relationship between humor, in particular social satire, and cannibalism is long established, being utilized to explore the parasitic practices inherent within the capitalist system of oppressor and oppressed: the bourgeoisie recline in their mansions, fattened by the opulence created by the unrelenting efforts of their subjugated workforce; the proletariat, victims of capitalistic exploitation, retrogress in their urban hells, their homes described by Engels in 1844 as a "chaos of small one-storied, one-roomed huts [. . .] cattle-sheds for human beings."[15] The metaphor is given literal credence in several late twentieth-century films, with one social class actually feeding on another, among them Peter Richardson's *Eat the Rich* (1985) and Peter Greenaway's *The Cook, the Thief, His Wife, & Her Lover* (1989).

Such a symbolic conception is founded on Jonathan Swift's satire *A Modest Proposal* (1729), in which the poor social classes of Ireland are instructed to eat their babies and thereby simultaneously obviate

---

12. Antonin J. Obrdlik, "Gallows Humor—a Sociological Phenomenon," *American Journal of Sociology* 47, no. 5 (1942): 709–16.

13. Alan Dundes and Thomas Hauschild, "Auschwitz Jokes," in *Humour in Society*, ed. Chris Powell (New York: Palgrave Macmillan, 1988), 56–65.

14. Sigmund Freud, *Jokes and Their Relation to the Unconscious* (New York: Norton, 2002).

15. Friedrich Engels, *The Condition of the Working-Class in England in 1844* (New York: BiblioBazaar, 2007), 68.

two societal problems: first, the hunger derived from economic marginalization and, second, the related issue of finding adequate sustenance for both parent and child. Such symbolic metaphors are concomitant to the dynamic of social reality that Émile Durkheim predicted would manifest as humanity attempted to free itself from the confines of religious ideology.[16] Whereas such an institution provided a moral guide for humanity, its obviation leaves only rampant consumerism and an unchecked exploitation of the weak—a malformed social fabric in which people are linked to things rather than to other people, ensuring that "the solidarity that arises from this integration is wholly negative"[17] and creating a desire for consumerism that can never truly be satiated, as it is only through the acquisition of things that life can acquire a temporary meaning. "Inextinguishable thirst is constantly renewed torture. [. . .] [A] thirst arises for novelties, unfamiliar pleasures, nameless sensations, all of which lose their savor once known."[18] This is a dynamic commensurate to that of Dante's she-wolf, whose

> nature
> Is so malign and vicious she cannot appease
> Her voracity, for feeding makes her hungrier.[19]

Although such symbolic subversion of dominant economic strategy is sublime, one must also acknowledge that the very setting of the cannibal's dinner feast, complete with enthusiastic, if ignorant, consumers and gourmet anthropophagous host, is beautifully commensurate with the Grand Guignol tradition, effortlessly combining the twin deviant delights of humor and horror, giving the perfect *douche*

---

16. Émile Durkheim, *The Division of Labor in Society* (New York: Free Press, 1984).

17. Durkheim, *Division of Labor*, 73.

18. Émile Durkheim, *Suicide: A Study in Sociology* (New York: Free Press, 1979), 247, 256.

19. Dante Alighieri, *The Inferno*, trans. Robert Pinsky (New York: Farrar, Straus and Giroux, 1994), canto 1, ll. 74–76.

écossaise, the "hot and cold" shower first brought to fruition on the stage of Paris's original theater of the macabre and something that can truly be savored from the perspective of the viewer, the casual witness to such gastronomic proclivities and frivolities.

However, we must consider: What are our host's motives in serving such dishes to his ignorant guests? Can it be that this macabre practice merely serves as way of demonstrating to both himself and his audience of secret onlookers his dominance over all who surround him?

As a dynamic, the setting is more complex than that of a simple juxtaposition between revulsion and relish, bearing more than a passing resemblance to Tantalus's attempt to test the gods' omniscience by serving them a banquet made from the flesh of his own son, Pelops. Within the myth, Demeter, the only god who eats the flesh, does so because of her own preoccupation, driven to distraction over the disappearance of Persephone, who has been kidnapped and taken to the underworld by Hades. Such a structure is certainly in keeping with that of our cannibal's *douche écossaise* milieu, composing a scenario in which members of the social and cultural elite as well as those specialized in the various practices of law enforcement are invited to a dinner party in which they are served a dish that, perhaps owing to their own petty preoccupations, causes them not to recognize, in due deference to William Burroughs's foundational work,[20] what is truly on the end of their fork.

Obviously, such a dynamic is concomitant with that of the previously established metaphorical representation of cannibalism as capitalist consumerism. From such a perspective, Hannibal, like Tantalus, tests the inherent qualities of those who perceive themselves as his social and cultural equals. Moreover, by inviting members of law enforcement, those who would seek to ensnare our cannibal, to share a meal at his dining table, he proves through their oblivious

---

20. William S. Burroughs, *The Naked Lunch* (1959; reprint, New York: Grove, 2013).

consumption, their unadulterated enjoyment of the dishes he has prepared for them, that he is unequivocally their superior.

After all, in keeping with the economic realities of the United States, is not the ultimate form of dominance to command a form of stratification in which all those relegated to an inferior and therefore subjugated position remain wholly ignorant of their true social status, mistakenly believing that their existence, rather than being marked by subordination, is defined by unequivocal equality? The metaphorical consumption of Pelops continues unabated, driven by an unrelenting gastronomic false consciousness, serving as a lesson in the maintenance of societal and cultural dominance given to us by our host.

But perhaps such a reading of our cannibal's dinner parties is a little too ungracious; in our hurried efforts to comprehend and catalog his motivations, we rudely do his courtesy a disservice. After all, such an analysis merely presents his social tableau, even his cuisine, as a metaphorical dynamic of the monopolistic capitalist culture that breeds the very boorish qualities that he disdains so vigorously. Worse, it even lends credence to hospital administrator Dr. Frederick Chilton's observation that "cannibalism is an act of dominance" (2.06). And do we really want to side with this character? Even if only on a single point?

No? Then let us reconsider: Isn't it only right, moral even, for us to conceive of an evening of anthropophagous delight, lovingly prepared by our host, from another angle ... that of the liberating egalitarian? After all, the cannibal, like the perpetrators of incest in John Ford's play *'Tis Pity She's a Whore* (1633) or Vladimir Nabokov's Humbert Humbert in his pursuit of the alluring Lolita (1959), can be conceived of as the symbolic rejection of all that can be conceptualized as comprising the moral landscape—those values and rules (whether moral or legal) that, as Marx stipulates in *The German Ideology*, are merely the product of the most powerful,[21] the social

---

21. Karl Marx, "From *The German Ideology*," in *The Portable Marx*, 9th ed., ed. and trans. Eugene Kamenka (New York: Penguin, 1983), 162–96.

elite who mold the societal environment to benefit their own ends. Not for him is this fate; the moral landscape littered with the debris of convenience foods, chemically processed and devoid of the essential elements that would denote nutrition, is, like the other purveyors of cultural pestilence (reality television, celebrity culture, and the tabloid press, to name just three), the rotting offal oozing from the undead carcass of the neoliberalist monster. This plastic parody of life is its nightmare, and the practice of anthropophagy is the action by which this symbolic rejection manifests itself.

In Nietzschian terms, the cannibal, through the refutation of the confines of this form of moral conventionality, frees itself from the fate of gastronomic castration, assuming the guise of predator in a world populated by uncouth eunuch-sheep, bleating the formula of conformity. "God has died," Nietzsche proclaims. "It is only since he lies in his tomb that you have been resurrected. Only now the great noon comes; only now the higher man becomes—lord."[22]

This is the rallying cry of the cannibal!

However, make no mistake: this is not a rejection born of savage ignorance, a primordial devolution instigated by Western neoliberalist greed. This is its contrary. This is evolution, the conscious rejection of primitive cultural norms and values—that unbecoming greed-driven hive mentality, doomed by the heat of a capitalist inferno into the perpetual frenzied consumer swarm.

Cannibalism is rebellion against these rude chains, an unfurling of anthropophagous wings that denote the Übermensch.

However, to openly reveal such proclivities to a societal populous drenched in the night sweats of social convention is to be labeled "monster."

And to be ostracized is ultimately the fate of all monsters.

The monster is a figure constructed to epitomize our fears, something to be shunned, hated, despised—we must reject it, use

---

22. Friedrich Nietzsche, *Thus Spoke Zarathustra*, trans. Walter Kaufmann (New York: Penguin, 1978), 286.

the thought of the monster to strengthen our devotion to established social and cultural mores, to entangle, to ensnare ourselves deeper in its moral web.

The monster is the reason why we build walls—structures designed to protect us from evil, from the very infection that it spreads.

Worse: behind these walls, so-called altruistic heroes seek to plot the monster's downfall.

Remember the fate of Grendel, doomed to sit outside the great mead hall Heorot, isolated from the warriors within—those figures inferior in both prowess and skill who feast, laugh, and toast one another. Their ability to conform makes them seemingly secure within its confines—that is, until Grendel, denied the warmth of conviviality and driven by rage, seeks to destroy Heorot, to devour all those within, to slake its thirst for vengeance.

However, our cannibal offers an inversion of such a dynamic: instead of sitting outside, he builds his own mead hall. It is a modern-day Heorot, renowned for its opulence and style, its conviviality and cuisine. Grendel, in the form of our cannibal, invites those who seek to be good, conforming members of society within its walls—to take a seat at its table and to enjoy the meal that it has prepared for them.

And the meal? What is its function from this perspective?

If the monster symbolizes the rejection of societal convention, pointing a clawed finger at the artifice of its construction, the confining nature of its mores, what is the dinner guest who shares of its food? Is there something more to the meal than merely the dynamic of Tantalus, the simple desire to prove oneself superior?

For answers, let us turn to Dante and his adventures in the underground. In the thirty-third canto of *The Inferno*,[23] our narrator discovers, amid the second ring of the ninth circle of hell, Ugolino, an individual turned anthropophagous owing to vengeance, eating the flesh from the decapitated skull of Archbishop Ruggieri, who, when alive, condemned both Ugolino and his sons to a death from

---

23. Dante, *Inferno*, canto 33, l. 5.

starvation. For Ugolino, cannibalism is the act that enables him to stave off, to relieve, "a grief so desperate." Yes! The cannibal's action in this scene can be thought of as a continuation of the capitalist metaphor, complementing the symbolic representation of a societal populace's unrelenting consumerism of products deemed essential, imbuing their lives with some sort of short-lived artificial satisfaction. But surely there is more; there has to be. Consider the very nature of the meal that our cannibal's guests eat, created by a craftsman, made from the basest epitome of the very capitalistic essence of trite, smug, vulgar, fake superiority. The raw ingredients, as has already been commented upon, are capitalist pigs, culled from the herds of swine that infect society with their boorish natures.

For confirmation of such an analysis, consider our cannibal's lament that "cruelty is a gift humanity has given itself" (1.05). Humans, those with the power to subjugate, have created a world that functions for their own benefit; all others are ensnared by this social entrapment, bound to follow the mores that perpetuate their incarceration while relentlessly stimulating the very sense of despair that they try to sate with continual unrelenting consumerism—the very dynamic that ensures that the most powerful retain their societal position. This is the perdition of Sartre made flesh, a vicious circle of hell bound by an artificial sense of moral purpose, a despicable veneer that fates us all to a life of pitiful mediocrity.

This is Ugolino's dynamic: to follow the rules of artificial convention is to offer your throat to the very social classes who utilize it to subjugate those around them. To adhere to this convention's parameters is to be the docile, unhappy victim forever, ready to be ripped asunder when those who dominate decree it. The porcine metamorphosis frees the cannibal, and the sharing of the results of this transformation is intended as a gift. Surely we cannot reject it on the grounds of some belief that it is merely a game, a smug desire on the part of our cannibal to prove himself superior. What he offers is the very essence of cannibalism, that entity that has freed itself of the entrapments of artifice, the mores of this so-called social normality. It is the ambrosia that frees us from these confines. It is the cannibal's most sacred gift—the very substance that makes him what he is.

The morality of artificial convention is stripped away; this old god is dead, rendered base, pathetic, by the taste of this Promethean gift. If the essence of power and the opulence it generates is to feed off those who produce it through the chains of their subjugation, then, like Ugolino, you must feed from those who would feed on you, for within each bite there is freedom!

But our cannibal understands that the substance of the gift that it offers can never be revealed without the lens of humor. Social convention, that moral artifice, is too strong for the majority to bare. If they understood the true essence of their temporary liberation at the table of their cannibal's dinner party, they would sink farther into that social fakery's depths, and their host, like Aeschylus's tragic hero, would be fastened "in bands of bronze immovable to this desolate peak, Where you will hear no voice, nor see a human form,"[24] chained and tormented for his purported crimes. That is why such a gift must remain hidden until a time when the oppressed unite, freeing themselves of the chains of subjugation, rising up in the realization that they have a world of exotic cuisine to prepare!

Bibliography

Aeschylus. *Prometheus Bound and Other Plays*. New York: Penguin, 1961.

Alighieri, Dante. *The Inferno*. Translated by Robert Pinsky. New York: Farrar, Straus and Giroux, 1994.

Burroughs, William S. *The Naked Lunch*. 1959. Reprint. New York: Grove Press, 2013.

Dundes, Alan, and Thomas Hauschild. "Auschwitz Jokes." In *Humour in Society*, edited by Chris Powell, 56–65. New York: Palgrave Macmillan, 1988.

---

24. Aeschylus, *Prometheus Bound and Other Plays* (New York: Penguin, 1961), 21.

Durkheim, Émile. *The Division of Labor in Society*. Translated by Steven Lukes. New York: Free Press, 1984.

———. *Suicide: A Study in Sociology*. Translated by John A. Spaulding and George Simpson. New York: Free Press, 1979.

Engels, Friedrich. *The Condition of the Working-Class in England in 1844*. Translated by Florence Kelley Wischnewetzky. New York: BiblioBazaar, 2007.

Freud, Sigmund. *Jokes and Their Relation to the Unconscious*. Translated by Joyce Crick. New York: Norton, 2002.

Johnson, Lyndon. "The Great Society." Remarks presented at the Univ. of Michigan, Ann Arbor, May 22, 1964. At http://www.presidency.ucsb.edu/ws/?pid=26262.

King, Martin Luther, Jr. "I Have a Dream." Speech given at the March on Washington for Jobs and Freedom, Aug. 28, 1963. At http://avalon.law.yale.edu/20th_century/mlk01.asp.

Mantsios, Gregory. "Class in America—2014." In *Race, Class, and Gender in the United States*, 9th ed., edited by Paula Rothenberg, 182–97. New York: Worth, 2014.

Marx, Karl. "From *The German Ideology*." In *The Portable Marx*, 9th ed., edited and translated by Eugene Kamenka, 162–96. New York: Penguin Books, 1983.

———. *Grundrisse: Foundations of the Critique of Political Economy*. Translated by Martin Nicolaus. Middlesex, UK: Penguin, 1993.

Miller, Henry. *Tropic of Cancer*. New York: Grove Press, 1994.

Nietzsche, Friedrich. *Thus Spoke Zarathustra*. Translated by Walter Kaufmann. New York: Penguin, 1978.

Obrdlik, Antonin J. "Gallows Humor—a Sociological Phenomenon." *American Journal of Sociology* 47, no. 5 (1942): 709–16.

Reagan, Ronald. "The State of the Union." Address before a joint session of Congress, Feb. 6, 1985. At https://www.reaganfoundation.org/ronald-reagan/reagan-quotes-speeches/state-of-the-union-3/.

Ritzer, George. *The McDonaldization of Society*. 8th ed. Newbury Park, CA: Sage, 2014.

3 | Hannibal Lecter's Monstrous Return

The Horror of Seriality in Bryan Fuller's Hannibal

Jessica Balanzategui, Naja Later, and Tara Lomax

Hannibal Lecter's propensity for serial murder has always been central to the horrors of the numerous Hannibal texts, from Thomas Harris's novels, to film adaptations, and more recently Bryan Fuller's television series *Hannibal* (NBC, 2013–15). In the latter, seriality is foregrounded and embellished in ways that render the characteristics of serial form, such as repetition, liminality, and return, significant components of Lecter's monstrosity. *Hannibal* embeds the deviant seriality embodied by Lecter into the text's form and themes in a way that torments the viewer in tandem with Lecter's literal violence. This analysis examines the relationship between serial murder and serial narrative as it pertains to questions of monstrosity, cultural anxieties about repetition, and the aesthetic devaluing of seriality.

We build upon Philip Jenkins's contention that the serial killer emerged as a mythic embodiment of monstrous repetition in the 1980s, when "the seemingly harmless mathematical term 'serial' so vastly (and suddenly) expanded its rhetorical significance, to imply monstrous violence with a near-spiritual dimension." Jenkins also questions the immoral and culturally taboo connotations of seriality, asking, "How [. . .] did serial crime come to represent an ultimate evil? What is so dreadful about the mere act of repetition?"[1] We expand on this provocation to acknowledge the similar moral judgment and cultural anxieties directed toward the aesthetic dimensions of the term *serial* in narrative form, which is most overtly associated with television seriality. As Andrew Ng suggests, "Serial killing is a ceaseless act of brutality because fantasy cannot be culminated—like watching a television 'serial.' The only way to satisfy television consumption is by watching more of it."[2] Here Ng implicitly suggests cultural intersections between seriality, monstrosity, and aesthetic deviance. These connections are foregrounded in Fuller's series as the television medium's characteristic seriality and formal repetition become a source of both horror and threatening textual play. This process manifests in three key dimensions of Fuller's *Hannibal*: the repetitive violence of the serial killer, the serial narrative form of the television medium, and the "deviant" seriality of fanfiction. These aspects reveal how Lecter's monstrosity is located not only in his violent crimes thus far but also in the threat of his imminent potential for future violence, future episodes, and future adaptations, including transformative fanfiction.

Hannibal Lecter and the Emergence of "Serial" Violence

As one of the most potent and enduring manifestations of the serial-killer mythos, Lecter is an influential expression of serial violence in the late twentieth- and early twenty-first-century cultural imaginary. According to Abby Bentham, Thomas Harris's original Lecter novels "cemented the relationship between serial killing, law enforcement, and popular culture. [. . .] [Harris] established the template for serial killer fiction and brought serial killers, and the profilers who sought

---

1. Philip Jenkins, "Catch Me Before I Kill More: Seriality as Modern Monstrosity," *Cultural Analysis* 3 (2002): 1.
2. Andrew Hock-Soon Ng, *Dimensions of Monstrosity in Contemporary Narratives: Theory, Psychoanalysis, Postmodernism* (London: Palgrave Macmillan, 2004), 71.

them, into the mainstream."[3] Lecter's influence upon the conception of serial violence in the Western cultural lexicon suggests that, since his inception, he has functioned as a vehicle for the cultural examination of serial violence's conceptual potency.

Although the serial killer has become one of Western culture's most persistent models of criminal monstrosity, the term *serial killer* did not become commonplace in American culture until the 1980s.[4] Jenkins points out that although the concept appeared in criminological writings during the 1960s, the term was confined to a small group of specialists in psychology and criminology who studied multiple homicide. Prior to the early 1980s, the term *mass murder* was typically used to describe what we now define as serial murder.[5] According to Jenkins, the terminology changed after a US Senate Committee hearing in 1983 about "patterns of murders committed by one person with no apparent rhyme, reason or motivation."[6] Although the term *mass murder* appropriately quantified murder scale, it did not accurately express the repetitive behavior associated with serialized killing. Serial murder became one of the most significant moral panics of the 1980s, which led to what Jenkins describes as "a whole new taxonomy of violence"—a reclassification of multiple homicide dependent on whether the murders were committed at a single time in a single place or were spread across time and place.[7] As Jenkins suggests, "The essence of serial crime was that the offender had a 'cooling-off period' between acts, a chance to stop and think, and yet returned to commit evil once again." Therefore, core to the taxonomy of serial killing was the "singular evil of seriality itself."[8] This taxon-

---

3. Abby Bentham, "Fatal Attraction: The Serial Killer in American Popular Culture," in *Violence in American Popular Culture*, vol. 1, ed. David Schmid (Westport, CN: Praeger, 2015), 209.
4. Jenkins, "Catch Me Before I Kill More," 2.
5. Jenkins, "Catch Me Before I Kill More," 2.
6. US Senate hearing, 1983, cited in Jenkins, "Catch Me Before I Kill More," 2.
7. Jenkins, "Catch Me Before I Kill More," 2.
8. Jenkins, "Catch Me Before I Kill More," 2.

omy ultimately led to the emergence of the field of criminal profiling, driven in particular by the Behavioral Science Unit (BSU) at the FBI Academy in Quantico, Virginia.

The fictional Hannibal Lecter emerged during this period and became central to how this serialized taxonomy of violence was personified and mythologized as the "serial killer." Lecter first appeared in Harris's novel *Red Dragon* in 1981 and then in *The Silence of the Lambs* in 1988.[9] As Jenkins points out, the idea of serial violence derived from and was popularized by Quantico's BSU, which is heavily featured in *Silence* and at which Harris conducted extensive research in preparation for writing both *Silence* and *Red Dragon*.[10] Resulting in part from the alignment of Harris's texts with contemporary developments in criminal profiling and new definitions of mass murder, the emergence of a serial-killer mythos became characterized by a tangled reciprocal relationship between popular fiction and reality. As Jenkins suggests, "It sometimes requires genuine mental effort to recall which are the 'real-life' killers: Lecter or Dahmer, Micky [sic] and Mallory or Bianchi and Buono." Jenkins elaborates: "The concept of serial killing is formed by an elaborate process of interaction between the ostensibly 'real' world of criminal justice and the 'fictional' realm of popular culture. Ideas and images freely travel between the two."[11]

Illustrating this interaction between reality and fiction, one of the earliest criminal profilers, John Douglas—an influential proponent of the concept of serial murder and the inspiration for the character of Jack Crawford—has pointed out that Harris's fictional killers were heavily inspired by real criminals, whose profiles the author

---

9. Thomas Harris, *Red Dragon* (London: Arrow Books, 1981), and *The Silence of the Lambs* (New York: St. Martin's Paperbacks, 1988).

10. Jenkins, "Catch Me Before I Kill More," 4; John Douglas and Mark Olshaker, *Obsession: The FBI's Legendary Profiler Probes the Psyches of Killers, Rapists, and Stalkers and Their Victims and Tells How to Fight Back* (New York: Pocket, 1998); Woody Haut, *Neon Noir* (London: Serpent's Tail, 1999), 215.

11. Jenkins, "Catch Me Before I Kill More," 15.

studied at Quantico.¹² Another former FBI agent, Robert Ressler, who taught at Quantico in the 1970s and 1980s, is often credited with coining the term *serial killer*, observing that it "seemed a highly appropriate way of characterizing the killings of those who do one murder, then another and another in a fairly repetitive way, and so in my classes at Quantico and elsewhere I began referring to 'serial killers.' [. . .] [I]t was part of our overall effort in trying to get a handle on these monstrous crimes, of seeking ways of comprehending them."¹³ Like Douglas, Ressler also worked with Harris to "provide some facts on which his fertile imagination could work," showing him specific cases, including that of Ed Gein—the model for Buffalo Bill in *Silence of the Lambs*.¹⁴ In turn, by consolidating key currents in the new definitional model of serial murder, Harris's Hannibal Lecter texts strongly influenced thinking about serial crime both in the mainstream consciousness and within the FBI.

Lecter combines the key monstrous elements of infamous criminals who caused the serial-killer moral panic during the 1980s. Such figures include Ted Bundy, who—like Lecter—orchestrated many dramatic prison escapes. Another criminal who fueled the moral panic was Jeffrey Dahmer, also known as the Milwaukee Cannibal, and Ressler worked on Dahmer's case. So entwined is Lecter's mythology with these two real killers that, according to Jenkins, "some books and media accounts present Hannibal Lecter as an authentic criminal mastermind, who is listed alongside Bundy and Dahmer."¹⁵ Such cataloging exemplifies both Lecter's cultural prominence and his transgressive capacity beyond the boundaries of the fictional texts in which he is featured.

12. Douglas, *Obsession*.
13. Robert K. Ressler and Tom Shachtman, *Whoever Fights Monsters: My Twenty Years Tracking Serial Killers for the FBI* (New York: St. Martin's Paperbacks, 1992), 51.
14. Ressler and Schachtman, *Whoever Fights Monsters*, 365–66.
15. Jenkins, "Catch Me Before I Kill More," 15.

Reflecting one of Jenkins's key signifiers of serial monstrosity, Bundy and Dahmer's violence threatened to recur ad infinitum and imminently over long stretches of time: both killers were active for more than a decade.[16] Lecter stretches this cultural anxiety to almost supernatural limits, having been active as a killer potentially since the 1940s, depending on which origin story is read as canonical. In addition, Bundy and Dahmer moved fluidly across states and territories.[17] In an augmentation of these killers' mobility, the entire world is Lecter's playground for serial murder—his globe-trotting, geographical unfixity is a key component of his monstrosity. Even when he is behind bars, he finds ways to impel others to commit violence on his behalf. This spatial uncontainability and unpredictability therefore render serial killers a seemingly ubiquitous threat, setting serial violence apart from earlier ideas about mass murder. Serial killers are, as Jenkins describes, "rootless killers [who] lack any ties that could keep them in one place, any conventional sense of home or family. Their lives are defined by routes, not roots, and they thus symbolize the failure of traditional ideals of community in modern America."[18] This combination of repeated violence with geographic and symbolic rootlessness ensures that serial killers embody a form of repetition that simultaneously disturbs conventional assumptions about temporality and identity. Key to the horrifying nature of the serial killer is that he is motivated not by a quest for development according to a prewritten script of social and personal progress, but instead by a compulsion to restage the same violent and socially reprehensible act, seemingly enacting an infinite loop of brutal violence and deviation.

Lecter's Symbolic Uncontainability

Highlighting their fixation with such mythologies of serial violence, Hannibal narratives tend to be formally structured around dual

---

16. Jenkins, "Catch Me Before I Kill More," 7.
17. Jenkins, "Catch Me Before I Kill More," 3.
18. Jenkins, "Catch Me Before I Kill More," 9.

serial-killer plots: one focused on Lecter and another focused on a secondary serial killer whom the FBI is trying to capture, often with Lecter's assistance. Whereas the secondary killers can effectively be psychologically profiled and thus tracked down and eventually captured, Lecter resists profiling and containment. As a result, he looms over the plot as a larger and more threatening incarnation of the serial violence the FBI is attempting to contain. He embodies the perpetual threat that serial murder and thus serial narratives cannot ultimately be contained.

Hannibal texts thus intensify the typical structure of the detective and criminal-profiler narrative, which according to Slavoj Žižek functions cathartically "to resymbolize the traumatic shock of symbolic incoherence [caused by the criminal's seemingly 'impossible' crime], and reintegrate it into some kind of secure symbolic reality."[19] In criminal-profiler narratives, the serial killer represents this "traumatic shock of symbolic incoherence": Jenkins suggests that "the essence of serial murder is that it is irrational, 'motiveless' at least in the sense of lacking any motive that could be understood by the normal run of humans. [. . .] The act denied, defie[s] reason."[20] This preoccupation is reflected in Hannibal texts by the central focus on the FBI profiler's quest to unlock the serial killer's mind: to determine the irrational motive at the core of his compulsive desires in order to effectively profile, track, and capture him. The various FBI profilers across Hannibal texts work "to resymbolize the traumatic shock" of the serial killer's defiance of reason in two ways: by attempting to deduce a coherent symbolic pattern in the killer's madness and by attempting to map the killer's actions in temporal sequence and in geographic space. This dual psychic and spatiotemporal quest is visually represented by the elaborate pinboards that each text's criminal profilers construct as they seek to map out the killer's violence. These

---

19. Slavoj Žižek, *Looking Awry: An Introduction to Jacques Lacan through Popular Culture* (Cambridge, MA: MIT Press, 1992), 58.
20. Jenkins, "Catch Me Before I Kill More," 9.

pinboards—complete with maps, strings connecting the sites of each crime, and images of each victim—attempt to reform the serial killer's actions into coherent, linear patterns. Ultimately, the criminal profilers perform a cathartic cultural function by, in Jenkins's words, "ending what would otherwise be an infinite sequence of crimes—by writing a conclusion to seriality."[21] The secondary serial killers across the Hannibal franchise are eventually profiled, and their serial violence is logically mapped out. As a result, the symbolic shock of their actions can be resituated into a coherent pattern, allowing the profiler to conclude their seriality.

Lecter's serial violence, however, cannot be effectively profiled and thus contained. Although his motivations, like those of all serial killers, are incomprehensible to "normal" humans, it is not because he lacks reason or the capability to resist his compulsion to commit murder and cannibalism. Lecter's motivations are instead beyond the grasp of the "normal run" of humans, his actions driven by thoughts and concepts that normal humans cannot comprehend. In fact, Lecter understands the unconscious drives and motivations of others better than anyone. He thus inverts the usual assumptions about madness and mindless compulsion that enable the eventual symbolic redomestication of the secondary serial killer. He positions the act of serial murder as incomprehensibly horrifying not because it is "motiveless," but because it is driven by a motive that escapes conventional human intellectual capacities. Will Graham makes this distinction explicit in the book *Red Dragon*: "Dr. Lecter is not crazy, in any common way we think of being crazy. [. . .] They say he's a sociopath because they don't know what else to call him. [. . .] His electroencephalograms show some odd patterns, but they haven't been able to tell much from them."[22] Lecter's "craziness" cannot be contained by conventional human logic; his "odd patterns" cannot be deduced or coherently mapped out on a pinboard. As a result,

---

21. Jenkins, "Catch Me Before I Kill More," 12.
22. Harris, *Red Dragon*, 64.

Lecter is a particularly potent and threatening personification of monstrous seriality because no conclusion to his serial violence can be written. This threat is reinforced in the series *Hannibal* as Lecter slowly defiles the dichotomous relationship between the serial killer and the criminal profiler: the embodiment of monstrous deviance and the personification of the normal order. Jeff Casey, describing the relationship between Graham and Lecter in Fuller's *Hannibal*, suggests that as the series progresses, Graham's "selfhood is threatened by [Lecter's] influence." Therefore, "this [increasingly] destabilized detective character subverts the boundary between the normative self and the deviant other. As a consequence, the series runs against the grain of the detective genre's tendency to reinforce normativity."[23]

Furthermore, throughout the franchise Lecter actively defies an ending to seriality by encouraging and facilitating its perpetuation, using other serial killers as vessels even when he is behind bars. Lecter's seriality is thus an affront to linear, teleological progression wholesale: his actions follow no discernible pattern. He thus threatens to undo the teleology of the detective narrative by denying the promise of eventual symbolic reintegration and, thus, by disturbing expectations about classical narrative structure, resolution, and closure. As Casey suggests, "The pleasure of the traditional detective story is grounded in the inevitable epistemological clarity that comes at the end. [. . .] This clarity is ideologically satisfying because it reaffirms the stability and basic rightness of the social order and its institutions (the police and the courts) and reaffirms the power of reason to distinguish between innocence and guilt."[24] Yet Hannibal texts—in particular Fuller's series—unsettle this entwining of narrative closure with a reaffirmation of the normal order. Not only does Lecter embody the perverse perpetuation of seriality even after each secondary serial killer in the text has been apprehended, but he also

23. Jeff Casey, "Queer Cannibals and Deviant Detectives: Subversion and Homosocial Desire in NBC's *Hannibal*," *Quarterly Review of Film and Video* 32, no. 6 (2015): 552.
24. Casey, "Queer Cannibals and Deviant Detectives," 552.

draws out what Casey refers to as the "latent moral ambiguity of the detective figure" to the point that the "deviant detective [comes to represent] an inversion of the categorical opposition between the normative self and the deviant other."[25] In Fuller's series—which Casey refers to as the most "extreme example" of such a breakdown[26]—the disintegration of the detective narrative's foundational oppositional binary is drawn to its ultimate conclusion as the serial killer and the criminal profiler end the series in an implicitly queer relationship. This collapse of boundaries further augments Lecter's monstrous ability to resist containment in normative, classical narrative structures and systems of meaning.

Monstrous Serials and Dreadful Repetition

The subversive narrative form of Hannibal texts parallels Lecter's own embodiment of monstrous, criminal seriality. This parallel is key to an understanding of the Hannibal franchise's cultural significance, and in particular understanding how Fuller's show self-reflexively engages with the Hannibal mythos. In so doing, Fuller's show illuminates more broadly the cultural and mythological dimensions of seriality as a formal and structuring device in popular fiction. Indeed, Ressler links his conception of the term *serial killer* with the serial adventure films of the 1940s, realizing that "each week you'd be lured back to see another episode, because at the end of each one there was a cliff-hanger."[27] Thus, as the Hannibal franchise demonstrates, the perpetuating impulses of serial form are fundamental to the mythologizing of the serial killer. Jenkins attributes this blurring of boundaries between textual form and criminal monstrosity to the relationship between serial murder and serial mythology: "The popular construction of serial murder has involved [. . .] [the] key building blocks of the mythology of seriality itself. As we see the constant

---

25. Casey, "Queer Cannibals and Deviant Detectives," 554.
26. Casey, "Queer Cannibals and Deviant Detectives," 554.
27. Ressler and Schatman, *Whoever Fights Monsters*, 52.

creation and recycling of media accounts, the proliferation of texts and images, and above all the endless repetition of claims, it is difficult not to describe this process as compulsive, irresistible, obsessive, lacking any natural ending."[28] Jenkins implies here that seriality, as a formal and industrial strategy, underpins mythologies of serial violence. Taking this association as a point of departure, therefore, we propose that seriality has been traditionally undervalued as an aesthetic device, to the point that it is considered a monstrous textual form. Serial form is often regarded as culturally and aesthetically abhorrent owing to its disruptive temporality, uncontainable textual scope, fluid and variable boundaries, and resistance to closure—a resistance facilitated by textual devices such as adaptation, sequels/prequels, remaking, rebooting, and long-form serialization across literature, cinema, and television. These attributes parallel Lecter's diegetic serial monstrosity in each of the Hannibal texts. Beyond the iterative textual form of each individual Hannibal text, the proliferation of texts that surround Lecter exemplify the monstrous proportions of seriality, as the Hannibal franchise reflects the serial killer's mythological implications in its formal and temporal logic. Across the franchise, these devices amplify the uncontainable scope, repetition, and endless deferment of capture and closure inherent to Lecter's monstrosity. Working with the mechanics of serial form, Lecter not only manifests across multiple media, installments, and incarnations, but also inhabits the interstitial and liminal spaces between each installment; this further amplifies Lecter's transgressive defiance of textual boundaries and closure.

Seriality is thus a textual monstrosity that propels the mythological power of Lecter's criminal behavior. Like Lecter and the mythology of the serial killer, serial narrative is immense in its scope: its episodic form provides too much textual content (and thus too many murderous events) to be contained by the formal conventions of classical narrative. The Hannibal franchise spans three-and-a-half

---

28. Jenkins, "Catch Me Before I Kill More," 15.

decades and constitutes installments and creative expressions across multiple forms in its official capacity, as well as a diverse and vibrant body of fanworks. All of these incarnations work to textually formalize Lecter's boundary-defying monstrosity and resistance to narrative closure. Moreover, they embellish the possibilities of intermediacy, in which transmedial devices both augment Lecter's threshold-crossing capacities and establish intermedial spaces that facilitate threat. For Eric Freedman, serial texts facilitate monstrous liminality and in-betweens: "Horror, science fiction and fantasy are by their very nature connected to the semiotic operations of serial texts; riddled with contradictions, the genres play in the liminal terrain between the real and the fictive, making them open metaphoric vessels that have proven quite malleable and responsive to cultural change."[29] Serial fiction and serial killers, therefore, similarly disrupt the norms of "proper" convention, whether they be moral, cultural, or aesthetic, and thus draw attention to the monstrous dimensions and manifestations of textual expansion.

The monstrosity of seriality is attributable not only to its association with serial murder and uncontainable textual scope but also to its status as an insult to the tenets of "true artistry." As Omar Calabrese recognizes, seriality is "regarded as the exact opposite of originality and the artistic,"[30] and so critics often consider it to be aesthetically and culturally undesirable. Such disdain is attributable to the way seriality resists and complicates closure, fragments narrative coherence, and disrupts temporal cohesion: as Angela Ndalianis suggests, "the 'fractured' narratives typical of seriality have been perceived as reflecting a 'dispersal' or 'corruption' of meaning."[31]

29. Eric Freedman, "Television, Horror, and Everyday Life in *Buffy the Vampire Slayer*," in *The Contemporary Television Series*, ed. Michael Hammond and Lucy Mazdon (Edinburgh: Edinburgh Univ. Press, 2005), 178.

30. Omar Calabrese, *Neo-baroque: A Sign of the Times* (Princeton, NJ: Princeton Univ. Press, 1992), 27.

31. Angela Ndalianis, *Neo Baroque Aesthetics and Contemporary Entertainment* (Cambridge, MA: MIT Press, 2004), 57.

In determining the monstrous nature of seriality, Jenkins draws on the cultural disdain for as well as the psychological treatment of repetition as an indicator of clinical and creative disruption. He considers repetition fundamental to the horror of seriality in that "the idea of uncontrollable repetition has proven deeply frightening to many cultures because it denies the ability to choose that is essential to free will, and thus to full human-ness."[32] When associated with human behavior, seriality in the form of relentless, uncontrollable repetition becomes a mark of quasi-supernatural otherness. Therefore, in raising the question "What is so dreadful about the mere act of repetition?" Jenkins considers the horror of seriality in quantified terms. However, Lecter demonstrates that the threat of seriality and repetition is attributable not only to the *quantifiable* dimension of serial murder but also to the *qualifiable* variability of liminality that comes with the multiplication, expansion, and intensification of serial narrative and form.

Ugly Variables

Although Lecter's mythology has traversed multiple media forms, Fuller's series offers the most explicit display of how Lecter personifies seriality. Television facilitates a greater opportunity for a complex interplay between difference and repetition than film in that it "is marked by greater variations in serial form, [. . .] enabled by shifts in the television industry, technology, and viewing practices."[33] Certainly, the various expressions of Lecter across literature and cinema contribute to the magnified serial proportions of Lecter texts, and, similarly, seriality is not distinct to any specific medium, genre, or historical period.[34] Nonetheless, many television scholars emphasize

32. Jenkins, "Catch Me Before I Kill More," 1, 8.
33. Jason Mittell, *Complex TV: The Poetics of Contemporary Television Storytelling* (New York: New York Univ. Press, 2015), 41.
34. Roger Hagedorn, "Doubtless to Be Continued: A Brief History of Serial Narrative," in *To Be Continued . . . Soap Operas around the World*, ed. Robert C. Allen (London: Routledge, 1995), 27.

seriality as a distinctive attribute of the medium.[35] In the interests of this chapter, Lecter's television incarnation serves to realize more strongly, and to complicate, the already present (but previously less overt) formal aspects of Lecter's serial monstrosity.

Writing about horror, television, and the intertextual implications of larger supertexts (or franchises), Freedman explores how television has great disruptive capacities within more conventional intertextual structures. This point is particularly applicable to the role of Fuller's *Hannibal* within the larger Hannibal franchise (or "supersystem"): "The television serial complicates the standard concept of a seamless inter-textual commodity or 'supersystem.' The television text at the center of the system is not necessarily in harmony with the texts that circulate around it."[36] It can certainly be said that Fuller's *Hannibal* provides variations and reworkings of other Lecter texts in ways that create multiplicities, divergences, and deviations, often in simultaneity with attempts at adaptation fidelity and repetition. Thus, part of what makes seriality—this "mere act of repetition"—so frightening is the interplay between continuity and deviation. As Lecter tells Will Graham in the episode "Apéritif" (1.01), "The mathematics of human behavior: all those ugly variables." The dread of repetition comes from what is predictable and part of the killer's "design," but must also be attributed to the ugliness (and horror) of variability.

The driving force of variability in serial texts is the complicating and disrupting of teleological, linear temporality. Episodicity produces gaps, interruptions, and fissures in the temporal continuity of narrative form, which Roger Hagedorn suggests is instrumental in "multiplying the elements of time, space, and character [that] allow[] for infinitely greater narrative complication."[37] In Fuller's *Hannibal*,

---

35. Jason Mittell, "Narrative Complexity in Contemporary American Television," *Velvet Light Trap* 58 (2006): 29; Glen Creeber, *Serial Television: Big Drama on the Small Screen* (London: British Film Institute, 2004), 4.
36. Freedman, "Television, Horror, and Everyday Life," 168.
37. Hagedorn, "Doubtless to Be Continued," 28.

nonlinear temporality not only is implemented to enhance the narrative but also has murderous implications and significance. This is exemplified by the serialized disembodiment of one of Lecter's victims, Abel Gideon, across seasons 2 and 3, in which his body is both formally and temporally dismembered for consumption. In the episode "Futamono" (2.06), the elaborate presentation of Gideon's leg cooked in clay aestheticizes the formal aspects of seriality. The dissection of his body into different parts—and the further dissection of these parts into different subsections for consumption—monstrously expresses the excessive fragmentation and simultaneous sinuous connections of serial form in a corporeal way. Gideon's association with the monstrous capabilities of seriality is expressed in temporal terms at the beginning of the third season in the episode "Antipasto" (3.01), in which the dismemberment of his remaining leg is revealed through a flashback sequence. In this example, Gideon's body is *dis*embodied in tandem with the series' nonchronological narrative logic, so he slowly experiences death by seriality across multiple seasons. Furthermore, this embodied expression of monstrous seriality—that is, through the episodic fragmentation of human limbs—recurs in the series finale ("The Wrath of the Lamb," 3.13) with the amputation of Bedelia Du Maurier's leg. This scene recalls the temporal association between seriality, violence, and the body that is represented across Gideon's serialized disembodiment, but, as a concluding moment in Fuller's cancelled show, it also temporally gestures toward a speculative future.

The association between monstrosity and serial logic is central to the movement from classical to postmodern horror in which serialization is harnessed as a formal device for expressing the returning monster. Paul Budra contends that there is a direct association in hypersequelized horror franchises between serial return and monsters: "The sequelization of horror movies is indicative of the emergence of the postmodern horror film, a sub-genre that manifests frightening cultural uncertainty through formal innovations, while seducing the viewer through an alignment with the recurring monster."[38] This perspective not only conceptualizes the frightening cultural uncertainty of sequelization as an example of formal innovation but also points to the potential for viewing seriality as in itself the recurrent monster. As Budra puts it, "The threat in postmodern horror, then, is not the lurker on the threshold, but the very absence of thresholds."[39] However, as a long-form series that is "driven by the apparently contradictory impulses of simultaneously anticipating and postponing a narrative climax,"[40] Fuller's *Hannibal* relies on the liminality of thresholds to perpetuate Lecter's serial monstrosity. It is the obscuring and continually shifting thresholds of narrative form that make television an apt medium for textually realizing the monstrosity of seriality; as Lorna Jowett and Stacey Abbott argue, "the seriality of TV lends itself to moral complexity and the dystopian vision associated with paranoid rather than classic horror."[41] Film is thus not alone in its capacity to complicate and challenge the conventions of classical horror; indeed, television has a greater potential for obscuring thresholds and harnessing the unpredictable variability of serial monstrosity. In Fuller's *Hannibal*, the culminating force of such unfixed thresholds manifests in unpredictable narrative directions that perpetuate the threat of the monster's imminent return. To return to Jenkins's question, "What is so dreadful about repetition?," it is not repetition in itself that is so dreadful, but its capacity to produce infinitely variable and unfixed thresholds, giving monsters all the more potential to lurk in the shadows and return at any future moment.

38. Paul Budra, "Recurrent Monsters: Why Freddy, Michael, and Jason Keep Coming Back," in *Part Two: Reflections on the Sequel*, ed. Paul Budra and Betty A. Schellenberg (Toronto: Univ. of Toronto Press, 1998), 190.

39. Budra, "Recurrent Monsters," 191.

40. Maria Ionita, "Long-Form Televisual Narrative and Operatic Structure in Bryan Fuller's *Hannibal*," *CineAction* 94 (2014): 23.

41. Lorna Jowett and Stacey Abbott, *TV Horror: Investigating the Dark Side of the Small Screen* (London: I. B. Tauris, 2013), 280.

Futurity and Security

As Lecter's monstrosity develops outside the diegesis of each individual text and into the franchise's serial form, so does he exceed the limits of linear temporality. Just as serial form provokes a temporal logic constituting multiple unfixed thresholds, the serial killer embodies the uncanny temporal logic of the threshold between the present and the future. The irresistible terror of Lecter is fixated on the potential—through his compulsive repetition—to manifest imminently. This anticipation is key to the perpetuity of the serial killer in a cultural and political context. Terror flourishes *in potentia*: monsters are more powerful in the near future, an uncertain space between anticipation of their imminent presence and their actual manifestation.

Jenkins characterizes the ongoing and impending threat of the serial killer by emphasizing the connection between futurity and monstrosity: "A serial killer is a monster, a word that in its origins suggested not just something threatening, but also a figure that was a warning or sign, a *monstrum*."[42] In this understanding, monstrosity is a temporal threat: an uncertain being that endangers teleology by muddling past and future with its promise to return. The serial killer's earlier violence threatens to be repeated momentarily and more intimately: outside of popular fiction, this is a construct that, as Jenkins notes, served to justify a substantial ongoing budget for the BSU in the 1980s.[43] The uncanny, unquantifiable potential of repetition continually threatens the security and cohesion of *all* communities and institutions that rely on teleological structures for their conceptual power, not just those communities affected thus far. The serial killer's point of greatest power in the cultural imagination is *soon*.

In his examination of the societal underpinnings of monstrosity, Robin Wood positions the monster's mythological role as a

---

42. Jenkins, "Catch Me Before I Kill More," 14.
43. Jenkins, "Catch Me Before I Kill More," 4.

disruption to social convention. The monster threatens, defies, and deviates from hegemony: the serial killer in particular uses the tools of repetition and nonlinearity to these ends. The serial killer's imminent violence defies the hegemonic ending Wood describes, in which the monster is annihilated or assimilated and normality is thus restored. Wood argues that monsters are representations of the socially repressed, and he focuses in particular on how the monster may represent queer and female sexualities. As suggested earlier, the monster's threat to classical narrative structure and closure parallels a challenge to sociocultural normativity, which imbues monsters with a radical potential to deviate from and defy the status quo, especially as their narratives problematize normative temporality. Wood predicts "the return of the repressed" via the monster: this constant threat of "return" is key to Lecter's serial tendencies.[44]

In the seriality of the Hannibal franchise, the normative social institution's future—its continuity—is the construct that the monster radically defies. From the diegetic anxieties over Lecter and Graham's homoromantic partnership and their struggle to form an alternative family with Abigail Hobbs—a character who is precariously positioned as their surrogate daughter—to fans' anxieties over the show's future beyond network television after its cancellation, Lecter's continuity defies normative ideals about futurity and linear, teleological progression. His subversive interplay between continuity and repetition is particularly significant in this context. As Lee Edelman has suggested in his work on the ideological power of heteronormative "reproductive futurism," the genetic continuity of the nuclear family signifies the stability and reinforcement of the hegemonic social narrative.[45] In Fuller's series, Lecter's serial monstrosity is aligned with his desire—upheld throughout the show's three seasons—to form

---

44. Robin Wood, "An Introduction to the American Horror Film," in *Planks of Reason: Essays on the Horror Film*, ed. Barry Keith Grant (Metuchen, NJ: Scarecrow Press, 1984), 168, 169–70, 171, 164.

45. Lee Edelman, *No Future: Queer Theory and the Death Drive* (Durham, NC: Duke Univ. Press, 2005), 2.

an unconventional, queer family that defies the continuous logic of "reproductive futurism": thus, Lecter's disruption to linear narrative time via his serial monstrosity is explicitly associated with his defiance of conservative, heteronormative social structures. The disruptions to these kinds of continuity compound and work in tandem with the other aspects of radical monstrosity that may be read in the Hannibal mythos, such as the revelation that Lecter is bisexual. Lecter's narrative and the imminent futures of Hannibal narratives can thus be considered useful mechanisms for exploring monstrosity as a radical tool.

101 Antipastos

Illuminating the importance of "terror *in potentia*," works of fanfiction are imminent and potential narratives that have sprung from Fuller's *Hannibal*. Fans' creative interactivity is part of the anticipatory tension that fuels serial-killer narratives, as Richard Tithecott claims: "The reader is forced to 'write' the text, to assume authorship in order to anticipate what comes next. The signature is both a sign of the author's existence and an invitation into the mind of the serial killer which we show few signs of wanting to refuse."[46]

Fuller's *Hannibal* openly invites and acknowledges fanfiction as part of its canon, with Fuller stating that he considers the show to be his own fanfiction spun from Harris's *Red Dragon*.[47] These relationships demonstrate how fanfiction is also driven by serial logic, in which stories draw from existing texts to serve as sequels, prequels, interquels, reboots, retellings, alternate endings, and more. Although fanfiction is often considered outside the scope of formal analysis of transmedial texts, in the case of serial-killer narratives

---

46. Richard Tithecott, *Of Men and Monsters: Jeffrey Dahmer and the Construction of the Serial Killer* (Madison: Univ. of Wisconsin Press, 1997), 91.

47. Laura Prudom, "'Hannibal' Finale Postmortem: Bryan Fuller Breaks Down That Bloody Ending and Talks Revival Chances," *Variety*, Aug. 29, 2015, at http://variety.com/2015/tv/news/hannibal-finale-season-4-movie-revival-ending-spoilers-1201581424/.

and especially the self-reflexive, intermedial mythology of *Hannibal*, fanfiction considerably expands and enhances the monstrous and radical potentials of seriality.

The radical capacity of monstrosity is refracted in the transgressive possibilities of fanfiction. Although Fuller, like other fan authors, commits playful and alarming disruptions of continuity, his Lecter is ultimately annihilated in the final scene of the series finale. Yet even this annihilation, in which Lecter tumbles from the edge of a cliff with Graham in his arms, suggests the possibility of Lecter's return: after this climactic fall, the camera hovers over the edge of the cliff to show that there are no bodies in the water below. Every work of fanfiction is a harbinger of Lecter's serial return, expanding always in the potential future: the *soon* of *Hannibal*. The nonlinear temporality that propels and empowers seriality is fundamental to the premise of fanfiction, as each story disrupts continuity by repeating and revising the narrative possibilities of *Hannibal* anew. Fanfiction's experiments with serial logic may be read as a monstrous extension of the disruptive formal power rooted in the Hannibal mythology.

Fanfiction encapsulates the anxiety of seriality by enacting potential and perpetual deviations upon the narrative. Like the serial killer, it threatens and subverts social institutions in culturally monstrous ways. Wood's categories of repressed monstrosity may be found in *Hannibal* fanfiction: many stories focus on the queer romance between Lecter and Graham, and they are often written by women and nonbinary authors.[48] The moral panic surrounding fandom, in particular what is known as "slash" fanfiction about Lecter and Graham's romance, centers on the "deviant" behavior of characters in fanworks and fans' creative "deviance" from the

---

48. The popular fanfiction website Archive of Our Own compiled statistics after surveying archive users. Only 4 percent of archive users identified as male (although transgender and trans* were separate categories), and only 38 percent identified as heterosexual. See "AO3 Census Masterpost," centrumLumina, Oct. 5, 2013, at http://centrumlumina.tumblr.com/post/62816996032/gender and http://centrumlumina.tumblr.com/post/62840006596/sexuality.

official source texts. Thus, cultural anxieties about fans' deviance parallel cultural anxieties about the serial killer's social and formal deviance. These anxieties illustrate the power of monsters—and of those deemed culturally monstrous—to disrupt narratives of power and narrative conventions of closure. As Wood and Casey note, different groups suffering social repression may find intersectional and mutually empowering narratives in monstrosity.[49] The radical potential in fanfiction has been researched extensively by scholars such as Constance Penley;[50] however, in *Hannibal* fandom the eminence of the serial killer, serial form, and serial monstrosity complement this potential in unique ways.

Fanfiction functions on the power of imminence: the overwhelming sense that beyond the official narrative, more is sure to follow. It rejects the linear chronology of narrative by identifying and building from myriad splinter points in the source material. Each of these splinter points is open for abundant departures and repetitions as well: for instance, if one wishes to explore an aftermath of the *Hannibal* episode "Mizumono" (2.13) other than the subsequent episode "Antipasto," popular fanfiction website Archive of Our Own (AO3) offers more than one hundred stories that diverge from this episode in different directions.[51] This suggests there are a hundred *soons* in "Mizumono" alone—a hundred imminent potentials—and the moment following "Mizumono" is repeated in a hundred different ways. To consume these stories requires a consciously atemporal

---

49. Wood, "An Introduction to the American Horror Film," 171; Casey, "Queer Cannibals and Deviant Detectives," 552.

50. Constance Penley, "Brownian Motion: Women, Tactics, and Technology," *Technoculture* 135 (1991): 154.

51. Taken from AO3, where 101 works are tagged as "Post-Episode: s02e13 Mizumono." Various related tags include "Mizumono Spoilers," "Episode: s02e13 Mizumono," and "Episode Fix-It: s02e13 Mizumono," and simply "mizumono." See "1–20 of 101 Works in Post-episode: s02e13 Mizumono," Archive of Our Own, n.d., http://archiveofourown.org/tags/Post-Episode:%20s02e13%20Mizumono/works, accessed Jan. 31, 2017.

logic, in which "Antipasto" is merely one among a cluster of the potential futures of "Mizumono," each open to exploration.

In *Hannibal* fandom, writers pay meticulous attention to continuity—to show precisely how they will be disrupting it. Therefore, fanfiction functions as a disruptive practice that participates in the monstrous variability of both qualifiable serial textual form and quantifiable serial murder. Writers tag which episode their story splinters from while weaving elements from other episodes to be used in alternative contexts. The show offers this potential in part through its seriality, where breaks between episodes allow gaps to be filled, and protagonist Graham's unreliable narration allows considerable leeway to develop alternate narratives. Fan stories are serial in themselves, often written in chaptered form. The deviation from the "canon" in these stories extends into other deviances: from the totality of male auteurism, from the suppression of queer intimacy in television, and from a teleological ideology that rejects repetition.

The canonization of a text as hermetic and linear casts fanfiction as a violation and an act of violence upon the text. Fan authors repeat, with variation, the narrative, disturbing its linear continuity, enacting violence upon the hermeticism of the text and often writing diegetic violence in their stories. They thrive on the potentials of futurity, engaging in serial repetitions that metatextually build on the seriality of the killer's narrative. The anxiety that fans may be potentially violent mirrors the way *Hannibal* fan authors engage with the source material. Joli Jenson's study of the pathologization of fans cites research directly linking fans to serial killers, and Jenson notes that "the literature of fandom is haunted by images of deviance. The fan is consistently characterized [. . .] as a potential fanatic. This means that fandom is seen as excessive, bordering on deranged, behavior."[52] The narrative deviations that fan authors explore are

---

52. Joli Jenson, "Fandom as Pathology: The Consequences of Characterization," in *The Adoring Audience: Fan Culture and Popular Media*, ed. Lisa A. Lewis (1992; reprint, London: Routledge, 2002), 11, 9.

potentially radical and culturally monstrous, so that an affinity is created between the monstrous Lecter and the fans who rewrite him.

Fan deviancy applies particularly to fanfiction and more so to slash fanfiction, where cultural anxieties coalesce over gender and sexuality. Kristina Busse notes how fans' transformative practices are characterized as feminine and queer and how they intersect with gender as a source of cultural anxiety. She later argues that the excess, affect, deviation, and sexuality of transformative fandom are policed in ways "predicated on unruly sexuality and queer bodies."[53] The anxious containment of women's creativity and sexuality overshadows much scholarship that rereads fanfiction as powerfully transgressive. Slash fiction compounds these anxieties by bringing the queer intimacy in a work such as *Hannibal* over the threshold from subtext to text: most Hannibal fanfiction on AO3 foregrounds the affair between Graham and Lecter as textual. As Casey has noted, their queer relationship is specifically portrayed as a deviant transgression of hermetic personal boundaries:[54] Graham says in "Dolce" (3.06), "You and I have begun to blur." Lecter and Graham's potential to "become" one another looms imminently in the show, queering the anticipatory space beyond the show's textual present. Open expression of queer male intimacy compounds the anxieties surrounding women and gender-nonconforming writers taking control of the narrative. Fanfiction narratives are examples of the "return of the repressed" that Wood describes. Wood theorizes that the monster is a vessel through which the repressed may defy their repressors.[55] When the monster is a serial killer, as in Fuller's *Hannibal*, a significant element of intersecting monstrosity is nonlinear temporality, which must be repressed to ensure the continuity of

---

53. Kristina Busse, "Geek Hierarchies, Boundary Policing, and the Gendering of the Good Fan," *Participations: Journal of Audience and Reception Studies* 10, no. 1 (2013): 82, 76, 88.

54. Casey, "Queer Cannibals and Deviant Detectives," 552.

55. Wood, "An Introduction to the American Horror Film," 173, 192.

heteronormative reproductive futurism. When teleological continuity is understood as an intersectionally repressive ideology, the capacity for fanfiction to find power through narrative and social deviation is an exemplary use of a radical monster narrative that is particular to the serial killer.

The centrality of the serial killer in fanfiction and of seriality in fanfiction's narrative form highlights how fanfiction can be read as radically monstrous. Fan authors use the monstrosity of *Hannibal* to challenge textual and hegemonic order, expanding Lecter's ability to exert self-reflexive influence beyond the diegesis. Lecter's monstrosity extends into his own narrative, form, and even, as Jenkins has noted, social context,[56] allowing writers to inscribe radical monstrosity throughout the deviant seriality of fanfiction. Both fanfiction and serial-killer mythologies rely on the distinctive temporal logic of imminence, futurity, and repetition to achieve this inscription. The imminent future becomes a liminal space in which deviant, alternate, and radical narratives may be explored.

Conclusion

Initially emerging in Harris's texts as a monstrously amplified embodiment of the new concept of the "serial killer" in the 1980s, Hannibal Lecter became the crucible for the complex anxieties that drove and underwrote ideologies of serial violence (and counterhegemonic threats) during this period. As a result, Lecter became embedded in the cultural imagination as the personification of monstrous seriality. The monstrosity embodied by the character extends beyond the diegetic frame into the form of each Lecter narrative and into the rampant seriality that is characteristic of the entire Hannibal franchise. As a result, Lecter texts draw out the culturally threatening elements always latent within serial form, embellishing seriality's subversive play with narrative thresholds, fissures, and fragments.

---

56. Jenkins, "Catch Me Before I Kill More," 15.

This textual defiance of teleological narrative structure and classical narrative closure in turn invites further embellishments from fans, who have latched onto the narrative gaps of Fuller's *Hannibal* to enact their own modes of radical serial monstrosity via fanfiction. In these ways, the originally diegetic potential Lecter holds to threaten sociocultural order expands monstrously beyond textural thresholds, propelled by the power of seriality itself.

Bibliography

"1–20 of 101 Works in Post-episode: s02e13 Mizumono." Archive of Our Own, n.d. At http://archiveofourown.org/tags/Post-Episode:%20s02e13%20Mizumono/works. Accessed Jan. 31, 2017.

"AO3 Census Masterpost." centrumLumina, Oct. 5, 2013. At http://centrumlumina.tumblr.com/post/62816996032/gender and http://centrumlumina.tumblr.com/post/62840006596/sexuality. Accessed Jan. 31, 2017.

Archive of Our Own. Website, n.d. At http://archiveofourown.org/. Accessed Jan. 31, 2017.

Bentham, Abby. "Fatal Attraction: The Serial Killer in American Popular Culture." In *Violence in American Popular Culture*, vol. 1, edited by David Schmid, 203–22. Westport, CN: Praeger, 2015.

Budra, Paul. "Recurrent Monsters: Why Freddy, Michael, and Jason Keep Coming Back." In *Part Two: Reflections on the Sequel*, edited by Paul Budra and Betty A. Schellenberg, 188–99. Toronto: Univ. of Toronto Press, 1998.

Busse, Kristina. "Geek Hierarchies, Boundary Policing, and the Gendering of the Good Fan." *Participations: Journal of Audience and Reception Studies* 10, no. 1 (2013): 73–91.

Calabrese, Omar. *Neo-baroque: A Sign of the Times*. Princeton, NJ: Princeton Univ. Press, 1992.

Casey, Jeff. "Queer Cannibals and Deviant Detectives: Subversion and Homosocial Desire in NBC's *Hannibal*." *Quarterly Review of Film and Video* 32, no. 6 (2015): 550–67.

Creeber, Glen. *Serial Television: Big Drama on the Small Screen*. London: British Film Institute, 2004.

Douglas, John, and Mark Olshaker. *Obsession: The FBI's Legendary Profiler Probes the Psyches of Killers, Rapists, and Stalkers and Their Victims and Tells How to Fight Back*. New York: Pocket, 1998.

Edelman, Lee. *No Future: Queer Theory and the Death Drive*. Durham, NC: Duke Univ. Press, 2005.

Freedman, Eric. "Television, Horror, and Everyday Life in *Buffy the Vampire Slayer*." In *The Contemporary Television Series*, edited by Michael Hammond and Lucy Mazdon, 159–80. Edinburgh: Edinburgh Univ. Press, 2005.

Hagedorn, Roger. "Doubtless to Be Continued: A Brief History of Serial Narrative." In *To Be Continued . . . Soap Operas around the World*, edited by Robert C. Allen, 27–48. London: Routledge, 1995.

Harris, Thomas. *Red Dragon*. London: Arrow Books, 1981.

———. *The Silence of the Lambs*. New York: St. Martin's Paperbacks, 1988.

Haut, Woody. *Neon Noir*. London: Serpent's Tail, 1999.

Hock-Soon Ng, Andrew. *Dimensions of Monstrosity in Contemporary Narratives: Theory, Psychoanalysis, Postmodernism*. London: Palgrave Macmillan, 2004.

Ionita, Maria. "Long-Form Televisual Narrative and Operatic Structure in Bryan Fuller's *Hannibal*." *CineAction* 94 (2014): 22–28.

Jenkins, Philip. "Catch Me Before I Kill More: Seriality as Modern Monstrosity." *Cultural Analysis* 3 (2002): 1–17.

Jenson, Joli. "Fandom as Pathology: The Consequences of Characterization." In *The Adoring Audience: Fan Culture and Popular Media*, edited by Lisa A. Lewis, 9–29. 1992. Reprint. London: Routledge, 2002.

Jowett, Lorna, and Stacey Abbott. *TV Horror: Investigating the Dark Side of the Small Screen*. London: I. B. Tauris, 2013.

Mittell, Jason. *Complex TV: The Poetics of Contemporary Television Storytelling*. New York: New York Univ. Press, 2015.

———. "Narrative Complexity in Contemporary American Television." *Velvet Light Trap* 58 (2006): 29–40.

Ndalianis, Angela. *Neo Baroque Aesthetics and Contemporary Entertainment*. Cambridge, MA: MIT Press, 2004.

Penley, Constance. "Brownian Motion: Women, Tactics, and Technology." *Technoculture* 135 (1991): 135–61.

Prudom, Laura. "'Hannibal' Finale Postmortem: Bryan Fuller Breaks Down That Bloody Ending and Talks Revival Chances." *Variety*, Aug. 29, 2015. At http://variety.com/2015/tv/news/hannibal-finale-season-4-movie-revival-ending-spoilers-1201581424/.

Ressler, Robert K., and Tom Shachtman. *Whoever Fights Monsters: My Twenty Years Tracking Serial Killers for the FBI*. New York: St. Martin's Paperbacks, 1992.

Tithecott, Richard. *Of Men and Monsters: Jeffrey Dahmer and the Construction of the Serial Killer*. Madison: Univ. of Wisconsin Press, 1997.

Wood, Robin. "An Introduction to the American Horror Film." In *Planks of Reason: Essays on the Horror Film*, edited by Barry Keith Grant, 164–200. Metuchen, NJ: Scarecrow Press, 1984.

Žižek, Slavoj. *Looking Awry: An Introduction to Jacques Lacan through Popular Culture*. Cambridge, MA: MIT Press, 1992.

4 | "Adapt. Evolve. Become."

Queering Red Dragon *in Bryan Fuller's* Hannibal

Ellie Lewerenz

Fidelity to the source material is often the first measure of quality for fans and critics alike when it comes to films and serial television adapted from a novel. The more popular and well known the book, the more viewers will bring a set of expectations to the adaptation that often leaves them frustrated when the film or series deviates from its source. As Brian McFarlane notes, "Fidelity criticism depends on a notion of the text as having and rendering up to the (intelligent) reader a single, correct 'meaning' which the filmmaker has either adhered to or in some sense violated."[1] The term *violated* suggests a severe offense committed by the adaptor against the source text. Written several years later, Robert Stam's list of terms associated with moralistic fidelity criticism is equally harsh: "infidelity, betrayal, deformation, violation, vulgarization and desecration."[2] All of these words describe a transgression that results in a loss of value for the original text.

It is surprising, then, that in search of a paradigm to replace "fidelity" as the ultimate goal of adaptation, Stam proceeds to list

---

1. Brian McFarlane, *Novel to Film: An Introduction to the Theory of Adaptation* (Oxford: Oxford Univ. Press, 1996), 8.
2. Robert Stam, "Beyond Fidelity: The Dialogics of Adaptation," in *Film Adaptation*, ed. James Naremore (New Brunswick, NJ: Rutgers Univ. Press, 2000), 54.

"translation[], reading, dialogization, cannibalization, transmutation, transfiguration, and signifying" as alternative ways of defining adaptations that do not work toward a faithful reworking of their source material.³ Although all of these words suggest a transformation from one text to another, *cannibalization* is the only term with predominantly negative connotations. In connection to fiction, cannibalizing something is connected to the act of salvaging selected parts while disregarding others, which again sounds like a description of an unfaithful adaptation that is extremely selective about which parts of the original to neglect and which to utilize. In season 2 of the NBC series *Hannibal* (2013–15), Dr. Frederick Chilton suggests that "cannibalism is an act of dominance," which would mean that the phrase "cannibalistic adaptation" describes an act whereby the new text achieves supremacy over its source material. It seems to fit better with the principles of fidelity criticism, especially given cannibalism's association with perverse transgression and violence. But the fact that Stam puts the word *cannibalization* on the same level as other tropes that he sees as more adequate ways to talk about adaptation suggests that he finds something more productive in the cannibalization of fiction.

It seems only fitting that Bryan Fuller's *Hannibal* should be an example of this type of adaptation. Michael Fuchs has already described how "the show not only draws upon earlier entries in the Lecter franchise, but rather cannibalistically incorporates them."⁴ In this chapter, I focus on *Hannibal*'s cannibalistic adaptation of Thomas Harris's novel *Red Dragon* (1981) in the final six episodes of the third season, which combines fidelity to the source novel with substantial deviations from and criticism of it. The result is a queering of the source text that questions the binaries set up by Harris's novel and renders them more ambiguous, especially in regard to the relationship between Will Graham and Hannibal Lecter.

---

3. Stam, "Beyond Fidelity," 62.
4. Michael Fuchs, "Cooking with Hannibal: Food, Liminality, and Monstrosity in *Hannibal*," *European Journal of American Culture* 34, no. 2 (2015): 99.

Adapting *Red Dragon*: *Hannibal* and Fidelity

Since the early 2000s, adaptation theory has been increasingly critical of fidelity as the first measure of an adaptation's success. Although fidelity suggests the source text's priority, scholars such as Linda Hutcheon view an adaptation as "a derivation that is not derivative—a work that is second without being secondary,"[5] and they thereby turn away from the assumption that any adaptation is automatically inferior to its source. More specific to novel-to-film adaptations, Stam questions whether literal fidelity is even possible for a film and finds the concept to be essentialist for both media. For him, fidelity "assumes that a novel 'contains' an extractable 'essence,' a kind of 'heart of the artichoke' hidden 'underneath' the surface details of style." Because there is no such essential core, Stam views the source novel as an open rather than a closed structure that "forms a dense informational network, a series of verbal cues that the adapting film can then take up, amplify, ignore, subvert, or transform."[6] By theorizing that *Hannibal* is a cannibalistic adaptation of *Red Dragon*, I want to examine which cues the show takes up, which it transforms, and what effects these decisions have—or, in other words, which parts of the textual body it chooses to salvage and which it chooses to disregard.

Certain parts of *Hannibal*'s *Red Dragon* arc are very faithful to Thomas Harris's novel and appear in the series with only minimal changes. The scenes between Francis Dolarhyde and Reba McClane in *Hannibal* are among the most faithfully translated parts of the novel. Their first meeting in ". . . And the Woman Clothed with the Sun" (3.09) very closely resembles chapters 29 through 31 in *Red Dragon*. The attention to detail in adapting the scenes is apparent from a passage early on in the chapter and its equivalent in *Hannibal*. Harris describes Dolarhyde looking for Reba's workplace: "He found the door he wanted at the end of a labyrinth of halls. The sign

---

5. Linda Hutcheon, *A Theory of Adaptation* (London: Routledge, 2006), 9.
6. Stam, "Beyond Fidelity," 68.

4.1. Darkroom sign from ". . . And the Woman Clothed with the Sun" (3.09). (© NBC/Gaumont)

beside the door said: 'Infra-red Sensitive Materials in Use. NO Safe-lights, NO Smoking, NO hot beverages.' The red light was on above the sign."[7]

The sign is reproduced on-screen without alteration, which already shows the close fidelity *Hannibal* sometimes has in relation to its source material. More important, Reba and Dolarhyde's dialogue comes almost entirely from *Red Dragon*. From their initial encounter at the firm to their meeting over coffee and pie at Reba's house, the biggest changes from book to television are that some less-essential lines have been cut and others slightly rearranged. The only addition seems to be Reba's remark that Dolarhyde would be "better off shooting digital" and his reply, "Oh, I'm not a fan of that format," an acknowledgment that shooting on film has declined in popularity since *Red Dragon* was published. These scenes immediately indicate two things: first, *Hannibal*'s ability to be faithful to the

---

7. Thomas Harris, *Red Dragon* (1981; reprint, London: Arrow Books, 1993), 267.

source text when it chooses to be and, second, the deliberate decision to integrate the Reba/Dolarhyde relationship into the series relatively unchanged.[8]

But although there is a high degree of fidelity in some cases, *Hannibal* intentionally deviates from its source at other times. There are changes most prominently in some of the key characters' identity. *Red Dragon*'s male characters Dr. Alan Bloom and Freddy Lounds become female characters Dr. Alana Bloom and Freddie Lounds, respectively. Jack Crawford and Reba McClane are played by black actors Laurence Fishburne and Rutina Wesley despite both of these characters being described as white in the novel. This can be seen as a conscious choice to include more women and characters of color than Harris's novel and its subsequent adaptations. Furthermore, the scenes between Dolarhyde and Reba are the only ones adapted with such a high level of fidelity. *Hannibal* also makes major alterations to the plot by, for example, making Dr. Chilton and not Freddie Lounds the person who is kidnapped by Dolarhyde and completely replacing the original ending, which sees Lecter still institutionalized and Graham disfigured.

By closely adhering to Harris's *Red Dragon* in some regards while deliberately deviating from it in others, *Hannibal* falls somewhere between a faithful adaptation and a more transformative one. This shows that the series is very intentional in its decision when to aim for fidelity and when not to and confirms the cannibalistic approach of *Hannibal*'s adaptation process: only certain parts are incorporated, while others are transformed or ignored. In an interview prior to the release of the third season, Bryan Fuller described *Hannibal* as "very much fan fiction of these characters that I adore."[9] Much like fanfiction does with its source material, *Hannibal*'s cannibalistic

---

8. For a discussion of the *Red Dragon* arc's unusual chronology with respect to the rest of the series, see chapter 7 in this volume.

9. Ross Scarano, "Bryan Fuller Knows You're Reading into 'Hannibal's' Homoeroticism, and He Thinks It's Hilarious," *Complex*, Sept. 16, 2014, at http://www.complex.com/pop-culture/2014/09/bryan-fuller-hannibal-interview-slash-fiction.

adaptation treats *Red Dragon* as "not a closed but an open structure" that creates a strong basis for the series but is subject to extensive transformation as well.[10] I focus on the results of this mode of adaptation, especially in connection to the relationship between Will and Hannibal, in the next section.

Queering *Red Dragon*

Hannibal is a show that thrives on its characters and the connections between them; even the credits sequence specifies that the series is "based on the *characters* from the book 'Red Dragon' by Thomas Harris" (emphasis added) rather than on the novel itself. It is also on the level of characters and their relationships with each other that I would suggest *Hannibal*'s cannibalistic adaptation becomes a queering of the source text. *Queer* is a slippery term, often intentionally so. David Halperin, for instance, defines it as anything that is "at odds with the normal, the legitimate, the dominant," which underlines its defiant intention.[11] Michael Fuchs similarly finds that *Hannibal*'s treatment of its sources "transforms *Hannibal*'s text into a monstrous one that heeds no boundaries."[12] In this basic sense, *Hannibal* can be considered queer because of its disobedient stance against convention.

More specifically, the cannibal in fiction has historically been regarded as outside the normative, "the ultimate marker of difference in a coded opposition of light/dark, rational/irrational, civilized/savage."[13] In other words, as a cannibal, Hannibal Lecter is as far away from normality as anyone can be. This nonnormativity is evoked in the novel *Red Dragon* when Will Graham says that "Dr. Lecter is not crazy, in any common way we think of being

---

10. Stam, "Beyond Fidelity," 57.

11. David Halperin, *Saint Foucault: Towards a Gay Hagiography* (Oxford: Oxford Univ. Press, 1995), 62.

12. Fuchs, "Cooking with Hannibal," 99.

13. Robert Stam, *Literature through Film: Realism, Magic, and the Art of Adaptation* (Malden, MA: Blackwell, 2005), 321.

crazy."[14] He describes him as a monster that defies even pathological categories. This view is echoed in a conversation between Alana and Hannibal in the episode "The Great Red Dragon" (3.08) after he has been admitted to the Baltimore State Hospital for the Criminally Insane:

> ALANA. You've been long regarded by your peers in psychiatry as something entirely Other.
> HANNIBAL. What do you term me?
> ALANA. I don't. You defy categorization.

As a character, Hannibal falls not only outside of the legitimate but also outside of the known.

This inability to define identity is a continuing theme in *Hannibal*'s *Red Dragon* arc. For example, in ". . . And the Woman Clothed in Sun" (3.10), Hannibal tells his surrogate daughter Abigail, "Even if you know the state of who you are today, you can't predict who you will be tomorrow. You are defined up to now, not beyond." Hannibal Lecter signifies both through his character and through his dialogue that identity is fluid rather than fixed. This stance can be considered queer in the way that Madhavi Menon defines the word: queerness reveals "that coherence is a projection and not a truth."[15] Thus, Hannibal's defiance of existing categories is queer insofar as it goes against the idea that any identity is fixed or needs to adhere to external expectations of coherence.

Whereas Lecter is set up as a nonnormative character in both the novel *Red Dragon* and the *Hannibal* series, the role of Will Graham changes considerably from the novel to the series. As an investigator, he can be considered a liminal character in both versions because the detective in crime fiction traditionally "stands between the normative

---

14. Harris, *Red Dragon*, 63.
15. Madhavi Menon, "Introduction: Queer Shakes," in *Shakesqueer*, ed. Madhavi Menon (Durham, NC: Duke Univ. Press, 2011), 7.

'us' and the criminal, pathological, and deviant 'them.'"[16] In *Red Dragon*, Graham is described as being valuable to the FBI because he has a unique way of thinking that enables him to catch serial killers. Although this proximity to the minds of murderers is so distressing to Graham that he wakes up sweating after nightmares about Dolarhyde's victims, the threat that the situation poses to Graham's normativity is contained at the end of the novel, with Dolarhyde dead and Lecter still locked away in a psychiatric ward. Graham clearly has doubts about how well he understands criminal minds and is unsure what that indicates about himself, but he does not do anything morally ambiguous throughout the novel. So although there is some ambiguity about Graham's proximity to the criminally insane, he is still presented as the person in charge of containing the threats posed by the deviant rather than one of the deviant himself.

There is still a long distance between Graham and the killers he investigates, exemplified by the clear divide between him and Dolarhyde during the investigation at the Leeds' house early on in the novel. When Graham tries to understand the killer's actions, his internal monologue runs like this:

> Mrs. Leeds was lovely, wasn't she? You turned on the light after you cut [Mr. Leeds's] throat so Mrs. Leeds could watch him flop, didn't you? It was maddening to have to wear gloves when you touched her, wasn't it? [. . .] You took off your gloves, didn't you? The powder came out of a rubber glove as you pulled it off to touch her, DIDN'T IT YOU SON OF A BITCH. You touched her with your bare hands and then you put the gloves back on and you wiped her down. But while the gloves were off DID YOU OPEN THEIR EYES?[17]

---

16. Jeff Casey, "Queer Cannibals and Deviant Detectives: Subversion and Homosocial Desire in NBC's *Hannibal*," *Quarterly Review of Film and Video* 32, no. 6 (2015): 551.

17. Harris, *Red Dragon*, 23, full capitalization in the original.

In his monologue, Graham refers to the killer in the second person, and his primary reaction seems to be anger, judging from the insult to Dolarhyde as well as the use of full capitalization. During the same scene in *Hannibal*, Will re-creates the crime in his imagination and visually stands in for Dolarhyde, retracing his steps. More than that, his internal monologue also puts him in the killer's place. Standing in front of the dead Mrs. Leeds, Will takes off his gloves and says, "I have to touch her. This is my design." The killer goes from being an object (you) for Will in the novel to being the subject (I) in the series. For the duration of the scene, Will and Dolarhyde become indistinguishable.

Hannibal makes Will Graham more transgressive than his counterpart in the novel by putting him in closer proximity to the murderers he investigates. Since "queer sexuality, psychiatric illness, and other modes of social 'deviancy' became inextricably entwined with criminality in the American imagination,"[18] Will's close association with the criminally insane also makes him a deviant in a more general sense. Whereas the detective in crime fiction and film usually acts as a threshold between the normative and the nonnormative, this barrier is eliminated in *Hannibal*.

As a result, series characters can no longer easily be put into opposing categories such as "straight/queer," "mentally healthy/mentally ill," "good/evil." Because Will Graham does not function anymore as a limit between these divisions, characters tend to fluctuate between categories rather than being fixed to one or the other. This recognition of "the absurdity of limits" is another one of the defining aspects of queerness, according to Madhavi Menon.[19] So because Will's deviancy essentially breaks down binary divisions, his character stops being a marker of the normative and becomes an enabler of queerness instead.

18. Casey, "Queer Cannibals and Deviant Detectives," 553.
19. Menon, "Introduction," 7.

So far this analysis of Will Graham and Hannibal Lecter has focused on the ways their characters defy what is considered normative. But queerness also goes beyond issues of more general non-normativity and is associated largely with gender and sexuality. As Menon describes it, queerness indicates an interest in "the larger lived realities of desire."[20] *Hannibal* investigates desire through the relationship between Will and Hannibal. The queer dimension of their connection is already implied long before *Hannibal*'s *Red Dragon* arc. Prior to more explicit references that their relationship encompasses something other than friendship, Jeff Casey describes how the series frequently creates homoeroticism between Hannibal and Will "while providing plausible deniability to fans who may be uncomfortable with [their relationship's] homoerotic possibilities."[21] In "Nakachoko" (2.10), a sex scene between Hannibal and Alana Bloom is intercut with one between Will and Margot Verger. The scene can be understood in multiple ways because "narratively the sex scene recuperates both men as heterosexual, but visually the sequence blurs the erotic boundaries between everyone involved."[22] For the two women, these boundaries vanish completely in the following season, when they become a couple, marry, and have a child together.

As for Will and Hannibal, although there is still plausible deniability about their relationship in the second season, Hannibal's feelings are made clear in a conversation between Will and Bedelia Du Maurier in "The Number of the Beast Is 666" (3.12) about the way Hannibal has affected him:

BEDELIA. It excites him that you are marked in this particular way.
WILL. Why?
BEDELIA. Why do you think?

---

20. Menon, "Introduction," 9.
21. Casey, "Queer Cannibals and Deviant Detectives," 560.
22. Casey, "Queer Cannibals and Deviant Detectives," 560.

WILL. (scoffs) Bluebeard's wife. Secrets you're not to know yet sworn to keep.
BEDELIA. If I am to be Bluebeard's wife, I would have preferred to be the last.
WILL. Is Hannibal in love with me?
BEDELIA. Could he daily feel a stab of hunger for you and find nourishment at the very sight of you? Yes. But do you ache for him?

Bedelia's answer explicitly acknowledges the romantic aspect of Hannibal's feelings toward Will and renders any ambiguously homoromantic moments prior to this scene unambiguously queer. In her work on male homosociality, Eve Kosofsky Sedgwick prominently describes desire as "the affective or social force, the glue, even when its manifestation is hostility or hatred or something less emotively charged, that shapes an important relationship."[23] Throughout the series, the glue that keeps Will and Hannibal together changes its form repeatedly, from curiosity to a budding friendship to open hostility. But what Bedelia confirms is that whatever form it takes, Hannibal's desire for Will has long had a romantic dimension, and the look of realization on Will's face as the world around him goes black suggests that he feels the same.

Menon stresses that with respect to queer media, in addition to the focus on desire there has recently been "a shift in emphasis from sex acts to more wide-ranging issues of non-normativity."[24] As discussed earlier, the characters' nonnormativity is clear, but Bedelia and Will's dialogue also shows how queer desire and deviance are intertwined. Bedelia's phrasing that Hannibal could "daily feel a stab of hunger" for and "find nourishment at the very sight" of Will shows the complexity of Hannibal's emotions by relating love to food—and thus automatically to cannibalism and murder. Moreover, not only

---

23. Eve Kosofsky Sedgwick, *Between Men: English Literature and Male Homosocial Desire* (New York: Columbia Univ. Press, 1985), 1.
24. Menon, "Introduction," 15–16.

is the cannibal regarded as a marker of the nonnormative, but also, according to Caleb Crain, there is a perceived similarity between cannibalism and homosexuality: "it [cannibalism] offers to relieve the self of the burden of selfhood; it offers a chance to surrender the body, to consume or be consumed by another."[25] Bedelia's remark creates a feedback loop in which a declaration of love is associated with food, which is associated with cannibalism, which is associated with love and eroticism. Each link in the chain defies the normative and manifests *Hannibal*'s queer context.

The explicitly romantic desire between Will and Hannibal is one of the major changes from *Red Dragon* to *Hannibal*'s cannibalistic adaptation of it, but it is not the only instance where the series modifies the novel's engagement with queerness. Jeff Casey, among others, has noted that "Thomas Harris' novels, and to a lesser extent the film adaptations, are quite homophobic and transphobic."[26] Buffalo Bill, the serial killer in *The Silence of the Lambs* who murders women to put on their skin, is a prominent example of "the conflation of queerness, disability, and criminal violence."[27] Similarly, *Red Dragon* treats Dr. Bloom's suggestion that Dolarhyde "had an unconscious homosexual conflict, a terrible fear of being gay" as a serious diagnosis.[28] This is underlined during the kidnapping of Freddy Lounds: "[Dolarhyde] placed his hand on Lounds's heart and, leaning to him intimately as though to kiss him, he bit Lounds's lips off and spat them on the floor."[29] Just one page earlier, Dolarhyde asks Lounds if he thinks of him as a queer, so the kiss/bite is both a violent reaction to and an affirmation of Dolarhyde's suppressed homosexuality. As Evelyn Deshane argues in chapter 7 of this volume, Fuller's own identification as queer underpins his narrative choices in cannibalizing

---

25. Caleb Crain, "Lovers of Human Flesh: Homosexuality and Cannibalism in Melville's Novels," *American Literature* 66, no. 1 (1994): 34.
26. Casey, "Queer Cannibals and Deviant Detectives," 555.
27. Casey, "Queer Cannibals and Deviant Detectives," 560.
28. Harris, *Red Dragon*, 186.
29. Harris, *Red Dragon*, 205.

Red Dragon's plot and characters while discarding as many of the homophobic and transphobic elements as possible.

For instance, *Hannibal* gives to Frederick Chilton the theory that Dolarhyde dislikes the media calling him the "Tooth Fairy" because of "the homosexual implication of the word *fairy*," but Chilton's credibility as a psychiatrist has been in question since his introduction in season 1. Through rejecting or recontextualizing homophobic narratives and blurring the boundaries between "normal" and "abnormal" characters, *Hannibal* shows the subversive potential of adaptations. "By offering a revised point of view from the 'original' [and] voicing the silenced and marginalized,"[30] departures from the source can be seen as commentary and criticism rather than as violations of the source text.

Cannibalizing Fidelity

The faithful aspects of *Hannibal*'s adaptation process work together with elements of queer deconstruction to create new meanings. A closer analysis of the final scene in the series shows how this cannibalization of the source texts connects formerly unrelated parts of *Red Dragon* to each other so that even the most unmodified parts of the novel work toward a queering of the source. More specifically, I want to examine how the series links the relationship between Dolarhyde and Reba to the relationship between Will and Hannibal.

As already argued, the scenes between Dolarhyde and Reba are among the most faithful parts of *Hannibal*'s adaptation of *Red Dragon*. The theme that their relationship sets up in the novel and that the series preserves is the discrepancy between what Dolarhyde wants and what his serial-killer persona, the Dragon, wants. The beginning of the novel as well as of the *Red Dragon* arc in *Hannibal* is about Dolarhyde trying to fully become the Dragon. The very first scene of "The Great Red Dragon" (3.08) is a montage of Dolarhyde

---

30. Julie Sanders, *Adaptation and Appropriation* (London: Routledge, 2006), 19.

seeing William Blake's painting in a magazine and subsequently working out, getting a tattoo that makes his back look like the Dragon's in the painting, and buying special dentures. All of these actions indicate bodily transformation and Dolarhyde's aim of making himself and the Dragon indistinguishable.

But Reba's introduction seems to separate the two personas again, as this passage in the novel reveals: "This new twoness with the Dragon disorientated [Dolarhyde]. He first felt it when he put his hand on Reba's heart."[31] However, Reba and the Dragon are not diametrically opposed; their relationship is more complex than that. As Hannibal explains in ". . . And the Beast from the Sea" (3.11), the Dragon presents an opportunity and a hindrance for Dolarhyde at the same time: "If it weren't for the power of your becoming, if it weren't for the Dragon, you could never have had her." So although Dolarhyde takes the strength to talk to Reba from the Dragon, he is also afraid that the Dragon will view her as an obstacle in the course of Dolarhyde's becoming and so kill her. The conflict that Dolarhyde represents is one between self-realization (as the Dragon) and love for another person (as Dolarhyde).

Although this theme is limited to the Dragon in the novel, the series relates it to Will and Hannibal's relationship by drawing parallels between Will and Dolarhyde. The similarities between them become especially apparent in the last few episodes of season 3. As dialogue from ". . . And the Beast from the Sea" shows, Francis Dolarhyde and Will Graham are driven by the same impulse:

HANNIBAL. The Dragon likely thinks you are as much a monster as you think he is.
WILL. Is this a competition?
HANNIBAL. "Two souls, alas, are dwelling in my breast, and one is striving to forsake its brother." The Great Red Dragon is freedom to him, shedding his skin, the sound of his voice, his own reflection. The building of a new body and the othering

---

31. Harris, *Red Dragon*, 313.

of himself, the splitting of his personality, all seem active and deliberate. He craves change.
WILL. He didn't murder those families. He changed them.
HANNIBAL. Don't you crave change, Will?

The answer seems to be affirmative as Will makes a transformation of his own in the following episodes. In the final episode of the series, "The Wrath of the Lamb" (3.13), Will tells Bedelia about his plan to let Dolarhyde kill Hannibal. Bedelia seems to see right through him:

BEDELIA. Can't live with [Hannibal], can't live without him. Is that what this is?
WILL. I guess this is my becoming.

Becoming is the word that has been used to describe Dolarhyde's transformation into the Dragon throughout the *Red Dragon* arc, so the use of it in this exchange underlines the parallel between him and Will. Where Will has before now been very conflicted and anxious, he is now definitely drawn toward murder. As Hannibal says, the investigation has already changed Will so considerably that there might not be any point in his going back home to his wife and son. Will's transformation ultimately stands in the way of his love for his family. This suggests that the conflict is the same for both Dolarhyde and Will: their pursuit of self-realization (through murder) clashes with their pursuit of love (for Reba and for Molly and Wally, respectively).

But although their conflict is the same, the outcomes are vastly different for them. As in the novel, in the series Dolarhyde has to choose between Reba and the Dragon and decides on the latter. He would have to stop and reverse his transformation for a relationship with Reba, and so love and self-realization remain mutually exclusive. Will, in contrast, completes his transformation and achieves love *through* self-realization. However, the kind of love he finds is not the kind of love he was looking for before the transformation. To examine this claim in more detail, the final scene of "The Wrath of the Lamb" is particularly important because it shows the last necessary steps in Will's transformation before his union with Hannibal.

After Will has instructed Dolarhyde to kill Hannibal, Hannibal and Will go to Hannibal's cliff-side house. When Dolarhyde comes to look for them, Will expects him to assault Hannibal, but Dolarhyde instead attacks Will. Then, however, the opposition between Will as a participant in the crime and Hannibal as the victim becomes a collaboration when they together turn against Dolarhyde and manage to kill him.

In addition, after unexpectedly being attacked by Dolarhyde, Will turns from victim to killer. Out of his flesh, he pulls the same knife that Dolarhyde used to attack him and stabs Dolarhyde in return. Multiple close-ups on the knife underline its importance as a tool that transforms Will. The theme of transformation is further underlined by the focus on the blood being shed in the scene, often in slow motion. As Hannibal says several episodes earlier in ". . . And the Woman Clothed with the Sun," "Blood rituals involve a symbolic death and then a rebirth." Here, covering both Will and Hannibal as they hold on to each other at the edge of the cliff, blood marks the completion of Will's metamorphosis through murder.

The scene between Bedelia and Will has already established that Will's becoming is tightly linked with Hannibal—"Can't live with him, can't live without him." This connection is stressed in the final lines of the last episode, just before Will and Hannibal fall off the cliff together:

HANNIBAL. See? This is all I ever wanted for you. For both of us.
WILL. It's beautiful.

Changing Will has always been Hannibal's goal, and the completion of this process allows them to be more intimate than ever before. The murder of Dolarhyde negates their opposition: instead of hunting *for* each other as in previous episodes (Will hunting the Chesapeake Ripper, Hannibal nearly killing Will), they now have a chance to hunt *with* each other. Killing Dolarhyde puts them on the same level—neither of them at a disadvantage, neither of them the victim.

4.2. Will Graham (Hugh Dancy, *left*) and Hannibal Lecter (Mads Mikkelsen, *right*) in "The Wrath of the Lamb" (3.13). (© NBC/Gaumont)

In other words, the murder breaks down the boundaries between them and destabilizes the limit between what were formerly opposed parties, an investigator and a serial killer. More than that, it enables a romantic union between them. Through the turn to the queer and the nonnormative, the incompatibility between self-realization and love that Dolarhyde sets up becomes love *through* self-realization in Will and Hannibal's case.

But even the opposition between Will and Hannibal on the one side and Dolarhyde on the other is not clear-cut in this scene. In *Red Dragon*, Will describes Dolarhyde as "a man with a freak on his back,"[32] which underlines Dolarhyde's separation from the Dragon. *Hannibal* visualizes the distinction between them by repeatedly showing Dolarhyde with wings inspired by William Blake's Red Dragon paintings and thus separates Dolarhyde's natural body from

---

32. Harris, *Red Dragon*, 396.

the artificial extension of the Dragon. When Dolarhyde sinks to his knees in the final scene, the action happens in slow motion, and the wings are visible on his back. After the next cut, the slow motion stops, Dolarhyde falls down, and the wings are gone, suggesting that the fantasy of the Dragon dies with him. But a couple of shots later, Dolarhyde is shown from above, bleeding out, and his blood re-creates the Dragon's wings. This re-creation makes them for the first time just as natural as the rest of his body and calls the separation between him and the Dragon into question again.

The final scene of "The Wrath of the Lamb" demonstrates how even more faithfully adapted elements in *Hannibal*, such as Dolarhyde's character, are used to queer and cannibalize Harris's novel *Red Dragon*. Instead of adhering to "the fundamental narrative, thematic, and aesthetic features of [the series'] literary source,"[33] these elements are used not only to further develop Will and Hannibal's queer union at the end of the series but also to render clear-cut divisions more ambiguous.

Conclusion

As an adaptation, *Hannibal* displays a high degree of fidelity in some places but modifies and deconstructs in others. In the *Red Dragon* arc, primarily the scenes between Francis Dolarhyde and Reba McClane are transferred from Harris's novel with minimal changes, thus putting emphasis on the conflict between self-realization and love that the relationship represents. But especially when it comes to the relationship between Will and Hannibal, the series diverges further from the novel. In *Red Dragon*, there is a clear opposition between Lecter as a deranged if sophisticated serial killer and Graham as a good if self-doubting FBI agent. *Hannibal* deconstructs these binaries by emphasizing the similarities between the two men and by adding an ambiguously homoerotic dimension to their relationship. Although

---

33. Stam, "Beyond Fidelity," 54.

there is still some plausible deniability of this dimension in the first two seasons, the final episode makes the romantic attraction between them explicit.

In the final scene, killing Dolarhyde with Hannibal makes Will realize his full potential as a murderer, which in turn enables his union with Hannibal. The series suggests that Dolarhyde and Will share the same conflict between love and self-realization. For Dolarhyde, these categories remain mutually exclusive. But by turning toward the "abnormal," Will and Hannibal use self-realization as a means to love rather than as an obstacle to it. Through a combination of fidelity, critique, and alteration, *Hannibal* turns a source text that is structured around binary oppositions between straight and queer, mentally ill and healthy, and normative and nonnormative into a queer adaptation that is based on the blurring of the same boundaries.

Bibliography

Casey, Jeff. "Queer Cannibals and Deviant Detectives: Subversion and Homosocial Desire in NBC's *Hannibal*." *Quarterly Review of Film and Video* 32, no. 6 (2015): 550–67.

Crain, Caleb. "Lovers of Human Flesh: Homosexuality and Cannibalism in Melville's Novels." *American Literature* 66, no. 1 (1994): 25–53.

Fuchs, Michael. "Cooking with Hannibal: Food, Liminality, and Monstrosity in *Hannibal*." *European Journal of American Culture* 34, no. 2 (2015): 97–112.

Halperin, David. *Saint Foucault: Towards a Gay Hagiography*. Oxford: Oxford Univ. Press, 1995.

Harris, Thomas. *Red Dragon*. 1981. Reprint. London: Arrow Books, 1993.

Hutcheon, Linda. *A Theory of Adaptation*. London: Routledge, 2006.

McFarlane, Brian. *Novel to Film: An Introduction to the Theory of Adaptation*. Oxford: Oxford Univ. Press, 1996.

Menon, Madhavi. "Introduction: Queer Shakes." In *Shakesqueer*, edited by Madhavi Menon, 1–27. Durham, NC: Duke Univ. Press, 2011.

Sanders, Julie. *Adaptation and Appropriation*. London: Routledge, 2006.

Scarano, Ross. "Bryan Fuller Knows You're Reading into 'Hannibal's' Homoeroticism, and He Thinks It's Hilarious." *Complex*, Sept. 16, 2014. At http://www.complex.com/pop-culture/2014/09/bryan-fuller-hannibal-interview-slash-fiction.

Sedgwick, Eve Kosofsky. *Between Men: English Literature and Male Homosocial Desire*. New York: Columbia Univ. Press, 1985.

Stam, Robert. "Beyond Fidelity: The Dialogics of Adaptation." In *Film Adaptation*, edited by James Naremore, 54–76. New Brunswick, NJ: Rutgers Univ. Press, 2000.

———. *Literature through Film: Realism, Magic, and the Art of Adaptation*. Malden, MA: Blackwell, 2005.

5 | Monstrous Masculinities in Gothic Romance

Will Graham, Jane Eyre, *and* Caleb Williams

Evan Hayles Gledhill

The television show *Hannibal* (NBC, 2013–15) restages themes of monstrosity and empathy through the genre of the gothic romance. The gothic romance is often a tale of the recuperation or redemption of the monster through empathy and love. These monsters are usually male; through the "making monstrous" we see the unequal power granted them by patriarchal society, and through the romance we can see their recuperation, which, by extension, allows us to interpret them as damaged by patriarchy as much as enacting it. Marketed and consumed as a gothic text, *Hannibal* enters into a dialogue with this genre's traditions. In all these stories, the creators develop a great deal of sympathy for their monstrous characters, while the audience is encouraged to explore and understand the motives of both the monster and their victims. To achieve such ends, these fictions focus on an intense relationship between two individuals. In choosing to centralize a same-sex relationship in *Hannibal*, series creator Bryan Fuller's production denaturalizes the heteronormative model for interpersonal relationships to reveal the assumptions of normativity that structure not only our narrative expectations but also our expectations around the power dynamics that shape relationships. Like the high-powered microscopes the technicians in the FBI labs use to examine the evidence of the crimes they investigate,

Fuller's queer reading acts like a lens to focus attention on previously underexplored dynamics within an established genre.

The conventions of the gothic romance developed in the late eighteenth century, and this essay traces the genre's themes in one modern iteration through comparison to two of the most famous and long-standing examples from the past: William Godwin's novel *Caleb Williams* (1794) and Charlotte Brontë's novel *Jane Eyre* (1847). *Hannibal*'s plot structure follows the same pattern as Godwin's text, in which a rich and successful man with a role in local peacekeeping first befriends and then persecutes a less-powerful man who knows his violent past. *Jane Eyre*, like Thomas Harris's Hannibal Lecter novels, is a frequently adapted text, and every adaptation must balance the tension between romance and gothic terror in depicting how a powerless girl falls in love with an (initially) unrepentant abuser. The narrative of *Hannibal* develops over three seasons from a detective series, in which Will must discover that his friend is a cannibal through the traditional legal structures, to a sensational gothic romance that repeatedly suggests that Will's identity as an individual is being subsumed into his relationship with Lecter. Triangulating *Hannibal*'s gothic influences through representations of unequal relationships in its predecessors, this chapter explores gendered power dynamics in the central interpersonal relationships in these three texts.

Hannibal enacts a monstrous restatement of Godwin's themes of rationality and injustice, which it reexamines through an emotional love story with clear echoes of Brontë's Rochester-and-Jane dynamic. This framework, by historicizing *Hannibal*'s gothic heritage, enables us to bring to the fore narrative themes and aesthetic tropes that have long been present in this popular genre. In Bryan Fuller's adaptation, *Hannibal* does not simply restage older stories for a modern era, bringing out concerns that a new audience finds exciting and relevant, but also draws our attention to elements that have always been present in these narratives.

In Godwin's novel, the relationship between Caleb Williams and his employer becomes antagonistic after Caleb learns that Mr. Falkland has committed murder; Falkland subsequently pursues Caleb through legal and extralegal means in England and abroad. Caleb constantly compares himself to Falkland and foregrounds his feelings of empathy and love for a man he wishes were his friend. In *Jane Eyre*, Jane falls in love with her employer, Mr. Rochester. Discovering—in the church on her wedding day—that he is already married to a "madwoman" he has secretly locked up in his house, she flees and hides under an assumed name. Yet Jane cannot deny her love and returns to Rochester when she fears he is hurt. In *Hannibal*, Will Graham (Hugh Dancy) and Hannibal Lecter (Mads Mikkelsen) begin as colleagues and friends working in criminal profiling for the FBI, but when Will suspects that Hannibal might be a serial killer, their relationship becomes a complicated legal cat-and-mouse game. Will retreats but is drawn back into Hannibal's orbit and eventually into his murderous schemes. The modern update thus "queers" an established pattern, in which love leads the wronged party to forgive his or her tormentor, to reveal new aspects of the existing gender dynamics at work in these texts.

A Crimson Peak: Generic Apotheosis

The gothic romance is a genre popular with modern audiences, especially in the form of on-screen adaptations and glossy period dramas: new television and film versions of *Jane Eyre* are produced at least once every ten years. Yet, though this pattern might suggest a measure of nostalgic safety, the gothic has always been a genre with bite. Charlotte Brontë's novel took on the topical issues of women in the workplace, especially as domestic workers, and the lack of opportunities afforded to women. Elizabeth Rigby's review in 1848 addressed the awkward issue of the governess's social rank: "There is nothing upon the face of the thing to stamp her as having been called to a different state of life from that in which it has pleased God to place you; and therefore the distinction has to be kept up with a fictitious barrier."[1] Yet even this reviewer, who clearly saw the point Brontë was making,

---

1. Elizabeth Rigby, "*Vanity Fair*—and *Jane Eyre*," *Quarterly Review* 84 (Dec. 1848): 177.

could not agree with the proposed solution: that women should desire more educational and career opportunities. Rigby insisted "all this cannot be altered with us [. . .] all this must be continued as it is."[2] William Godwin was even more radical, an eighteenth-century writer opposed to the idea that men should hold power based solely on birthright or that social and economic class should allow certain men absolute power over others. *Things as They Are*, as Godwin subtitled his novel, was intended to be a critique: "It was proposed, in the invention of the following work, to comprehend, as far as the progressive nature of a single story would allow, a general review of the modes of domestic and unrecorded despotism by which man becomes the destroyer of man."[3] Both *Jane Eyre* and *Caleb Williams*, therefore, were created as overtly socially critical texts.

Though not produced by a sole author who expresses a clear political intent, *Hannibal* engages with the critical tradition of its genre. The series brings to the fore themes and issues that in the earlier texts appear to be incidental but are, I argue, in fact crucial to understanding the power dynamics at work between the monster and his victim(s). The "making monstrous" of individuals is an act of social power dynamics, but likewise the extension of empathy.

Godwin's novel sought to explore directly the fallibility in the established system of inherited patriarchal power by addressing class, and the latent queerness in the text is, it would seem, a by-product rather than an essential feature of the novel's discourse about interpersonal male relationships. Yet in the preface to his collected novels in 1831, Godwin himself suggested that his readers locate the relationship between Caleb Williams and his employer in the tradition of the gothic romance, making a reference to a famous fairy tale:

> Falkland was my Bluebeard [. . .]. Caleb Williams was the wife who, in spite of warning, persisted in his attempts to discover

---

2. Rigby, "*Vanity Fair*—and *Jane Eyre*," 178.
3. William Godwin, *Caleb Williams*, ed. Pamela Clemit (Oxford: Oxford Univ. Press, 2009), 312.

the forbidden secret; and, when he had succeeded, struggled as fruitlessly to escape the consequences, as the wife of Bluebeard in washing the key of the ensanguined chamber, who, as often as she cleared the stain of blood from the one side, found it showing itself with frightful distinctness on the other.[4]

Previous critics have also noted that Caleb uses the language of courtship to describe his relations with his patron.[5] Caleb's language suggests infatuation: "From the very first moment I saw him, I conceived the most ardent admiration. He condescended to encourage me; I attached myself to him with the fullness of my affection."[6] I argue that this queerness that Godwin encodes into his text enables a complex engagement with the way norms of gender and sexuality are reflections and products of social power relations.

In Brontë's story, the gender dynamics are central because the relationship is overtly and openly a heterosexual romance between a monstrous man and the woman who attempts to redeem him. In Rochester's manipulation of Jane and her rival for his affections, Blanche Ingram, as well as in his treatment of his wife, Bertha, the monstrous exploitation of gendered power relations within society is central to the novel's plot. The language used to frame the relationship between Caleb and Falkland prefigures similar language in *Jane Eyre*, as when Caleb claims there is a "magnetical sympathy between me and my patron," and they exchange a look "by which we told volumes to each other."[7] Jane, regarding Rochester, describes "that look which seemed to me so penetrating: [. . .] I understand the language of his countenance and movements: [. . .] I have something in my brain and heart, my blood and nerves, that assimilates me mentally

---

4. Godwin, *Caleb Williams*, 351.
5. See Alex Gold Jr., "It's Only Love: The Politics of Passion in Godwin's *Caleb Williams*," *Texas Studies in Language and Literature* 19 (1977): 135–60.
6. Godwin, *Caleb Williams*, 298.
7. Godwin, *Caleb Williams*, 109, 123.

to him."⁸ However, the dynamics that are central to each novel's critique—of heterosexual desire in Brontë's novel and of the overt class tension in Godwin's—are somewhat altered in *Hannibal*: in the modern iteration, it is the more powerful monster rather than his victim who both stresses the similarities and sympathies between the central characters and initiates a seduction. Thus, I argue, *Hannibal* explores the same themes of legal and social power as the older novels but uses an open acknowledgment of queer possibilities to examine gendered power relations in new and productive ways.

Fuller says his adaptation of Thomas Harris's novels works in the tradition of "slash fiction," a genre of fanfiction that has gained increasing mainstream attention in recent years.⁹ However, this practice has long been a creative output within specific communities and viewed as having liberatory potential. In an article exploring slash authors' modes and motives, one female writer of slash states her reasons for creating stories about male rather than female characters: "He is usually the main character [. . .] the one to whom the adventure happens and the one who makes it happen. [. . .] A woman, having internalised the values of our culture, might feel that women are devalued *per se* [. . .]. So you don't want to be her [. . .]. The male hero is easier to 'feel' the adventure with."¹⁰ The option for creating new works about female characters, to counter the dominance of

---

8. Charlotte Brontë, *Jane Eyre*, ed. Richard Nemesvari (Peterborough, Canada: Broadview Press, 1999), 253.

9. Ross Scarano, "Bryan Fuller Knows You're Reading into *Hannibal*'s Homoeroticism, and He Thinks It's Hilarious," *Complex*, Sept. 16, 2014, at http://www.uk.complex.com/pop-culture/2014/09/bryan-fuller-hannibal-interview-slash-fiction.

10. Quoted in Shoshanna Green, Cynthia Jenkins, and Henry Jenkins, "'Normal Female Interest in Men Bonking': Selections from the Terra Nostra Underground and Strange Bedfellows," in *Theorising Fandom: Fans, Subculture, and Identity*, ed. Cheryl Harris and Alison Alexander (New York: Hampton Press, 1998), 9–40, reprinted in *Fans, Bloggers, and Gamers: Exploring Participatory Culture*, ed. Henry Jenkins (Durham, NC: Duke Univ. Press, 2006), 67.

male-centric fictions, is deemed less attractive in that the "devaluing" of women not only is an emotional barrier to connection with a character, who is viewed as lesser in status, but also affects the power dynamics of social interactions and perception of characteristics. Thus, male characters can explore a range of emotional and physical experiences—for example, states of vulnerability—without negative preconceptions: as this same female writer puts it, "his weakness is not perceived as something that makes him in essence inferior or different [to another male character]."[11] I argue that Fuller is working from the same perspective; when a man like Will takes on the disempowered role traditionally assigned to heroines within gothic romance, the role signifies very differently. The central relationship in *Hannibal* can be explored as slash fiction and a critique of gendered power relations in contemporary society, but it is also a genre text that works with and through the codes and conventions of the gothic romance to critique this textual tradition.[12]

Murder Husbands: Critically Queering Patriarchal Power

That women are disempowered and femininity despised is not a new theme in gothic romance. Godwin was aware that gender as well as social class affected power dynamics within individual relationships—he was an early feminist campaigner, married to Mary Wollstonecraft—and he described the power imbalance between Caleb and Falkland in gendered terms.[13] Caleb's dependence on another man is presented as echoing the lack of power that women experienced in a

---

11. Quoted in Green, Jenkins, and Jenkins, "'Normal Female Interest,'" 68.
12. See Evan Hayes Gledhill, "Queer(y)ing Adaptation: Bryan Fuller's *Hannibal* as Slash Fiction Gothic Romance," in *Hannibal Lecter and the Fannibals, Criminals, and Legacy of America's Favorite Cannibal*, ed. Nicholas Yanes and Kyle Moody (Jefferson, NC: McFarland, forthcoming).
13. In *Jane Eyre* and *Caleb Williams*, frequent references are made to colonial trade and slavery with regard to power differentials; however, these racial allusions are not made with regard to interpersonal relationships between the central characters and thus largely fall outside the purview of this chapter. The lack of critical

society dominated by men. Caleb's relative lack of masculinity, in his disempowered position with respect to Falkland, is further suggested linguistically, as when he states that he is forced to act in ways that a "man, who never deserves the name of manhood" might.[14]

Godwin depicts some of these intersections of gender and class through the minor female character Emily, the niece of Falkland's rival landowner, Mr. Tyrell. She is hounded into a marriage she doesn't want with a man who is not her social or educational equal and threatened with rape because her "reputation" is her only bargaining chip in the arrangement. The dangers of a marginal social position are demonstrated by Emily's limited agency as a woman born into a high social status, but with no money and no reputable means of obtaining any except through marriage. Driven into a pauper's cell because her relatives refuse her room and board once she disobeys them, Emily dies of a fever. This is the fate that also awaits Caleb when he cannot escape his own role dependent on the good will of more powerful men; once he loses his reputation, he is confined to prison. Caleb is "feminized" in the social power dynamic, both by Falkland's persecution and by his regard for Falkland, thus prefiguring Jane's dynamic with Rochester and Will's experience with Lecter.

The precarity of the "feminine" role in society also governs the fate of Will Graham in *Hannibal*: Lecter uses his superior social position to ruin Will's professional standing and to manipulate Will's relationships with others until he agrees to accept Hannibal's courtship. Lecter is a clinical doctor with an aristocratic background, and he displays his finely cultured tastes in opera, food, and art. Will joined the FBI from a background as a police officer, and his social background is intimated to be working class and rootless. *Hannibal* thus seems to offer a critique of masculine structures of power

---

engagement with racial power disparity in these texts by white authors is another highly productive area of study.

14. Godwin, *Caleb Williams*, 230.

similar to the one given in *Caleb Williams*: Lecter escapes suspicion for a long time, as does Falkland, because he exploits a certain image of a powerful, white man and casts suspicion on a man of a lower social background. It is important not to fall into the patterns of previous queered readings of the relationships in Godwin's novel that often perceive characters as being "feminized" in their roles and behaviors without noting how this feminization describes a power dynamic as much as a gender dynamic.

The alignment of gender norms and power is signified in *Caleb Williams* and *Hannibal* through the deployment of the same cultural codes and conventions of queerness. Just as Caleb's disempowerment is signified through feminization, femininity is likewise suggested to be what threatens Falkland's hold on power. Previous critics have noted the ways that Caleb's aristocratic employer is coded as queer through his feminine attributes, including references to Falkland's "extreme delicacy of form and appearance" and manners that are "admirably in union with feminine delicacy."[15] Falkland is also described as a "foreign-made Englishman,"[16] who has spent extensive time abroad in Italy studying art, thus further blurring boundaries and categories of identity. Here we can see clear echoes of Hannibal Lecter, a foreign European on American soil, who spent his youth in the same city as Falkland: Florence, Italy. Robert J. Corber notes that both refinement and continental society held associations of queer desire in English society in the eighteenth century; he cites a pamphlet from 1749 stating that homosexuality was "imported from Italy amidst a train of other unnatural Vices."[17] Corber further suggests that Godwin recognizes an inherent queerness to an individual's identity, an "orientation" as we would term it in our own era, arguing that "Godwin's novel participates in a homophobic discourse in which

---

15. Godwin, *Caleb Williams*, 18.
16. Godwin, *Caleb Williams*, 19.
17. Quoted in Robert J. Corber, "Representing the 'Unspeakable': William Godwin and the Politics of Homophobia," *Journal of the History of Sexuality* 1, no. 1 (1990): 86.

the locus of guilt has already shifted from a specific act [sodomy] to particular individuals [men with certain recognizable traits]."[18] This Enlightenment-era shift in thinking about homosexuality, from codifying only the acts, such as sodomy, to recognizing an underlying sexual orientation in our current phrasing, also suggests that certain characteristics of behavior are inherent to certain bodies and bodily types, in particular behaviors that supposedly make a man "unfit" for a role in respectable society. Both Godwin's and Fuller's texts explore the idea that it is an inherent femininity that both makes women vulnerable and makes a man unfit to wield power.

I argue, however, that Godwin's use of homophobic discourse, which draws an equivalence between queerness of identity and social limitations, is not leveraged *against* homosexuality but rather offered as an example of the failures of a social structure that uses bodily characteristics as markers of worth above and beyond demonstrable ability. This use is demonstrated in the description of the character of Caleb, as Corber recognizes: "the very qualities that Falkland admires in Caleb make Caleb an unsuitable object for his patronage."[19] Caleb is, as Godwin describes, "ill-prepared for the servile submission [his patron] demanded"; he has even grown used to considering himself "much [his] own master."[20] Caleb is aware of a likeness between himself and Falkland and draws constant parallels between them despite the social barriers that separate them. Thus, Caleb might be a worthy partner for Falkland in personal or professional terms, but this position is not tenable under the existing patriarchal and class-based social structures owing to his lower-class birth and the stigma against same-sex pairings. And Falkland would be a worthy landlord, in comparison to the monstrous Tyrell, whose torments of his more refined neighbor lead to their joint downfall; Falkland kills Tyrell in a fight, setting himself on the path toward

---

18. Corber, "Representing the 'Unspeakable,'" 98.
19. Corber, "Representing the 'Unspeakable,'" 90.
20. Godwin, *Caleb Williams*, 139.

tyranny. Caleb and Falkland are equals in this one respect: both of them know the truth about the other's "nature"; they know that they are fitted for more than what society will allow them. Thus, Godwin critiques the idea of social judgment based on attributes of class and inherent bodily characteristics, both of gender and of sexuality.

Godwin further brings to the reader's attention that such judgment is not simply levied by individuals against other individuals but is also built into the structures and systems of society. As Caleb seeks to use the courts to prevent Falkland's continuing persecution, he recognizes that he is, in fact, aligning himself with the same societal power structures that acted against him in Falkland's hands. Caleb therefore does not relish the idea of taking his revenge: "What chance could I ascribe to new exertions of a similar nature; which, if undertaken at all, must be undertaken with infinitely more unfavourable auspices?"[21] Caleb's preference for a personal rather than a judicial resolution to the injustices perpetrated by the monster upon his victim again finds direct parallel in *Hannibal*. In their cat-and-mouse use of the legal system, Hannibal first seeks to frame Will, then Will seemingly conspires with Jack Crawford (Lawrence Fishburne) to frame Hannibal in turn before both undertake an extralegal pursuit across Europe. Femininity is shown to disempower individuals in both their private and public lives; when they are discredited in their workplace, their word carries less weight before the law. The movement of Hannibal and Will's interactions from the institutional offices of the FBI to the psychiatrist's office and then to the home reflects their relationship's increasing intimacy, just as the reverse movement from home to law court reflects the disintegration of the trust between Caleb and Falkland. However, the traditional idea that the home is a feminine sphere dominated by women, a zone of safety for them, is revealed in the gothic romance to be yet another space where power resides with men and masculine norms are venerated.

---

21. Godwin, *Caleb Williams*, 263.

"Totally Functional, and More or Less Sane":
The Boundaries of Personal Autonomy under Patriarchy

Caleb, Jane, and Will are positioned as socially "lesser" than their tormentors and, even though Godwin's text is specifically about class, power relations are coded in all three novels in particularly gendered terms. Brontë's novel presents an individual response to the problems of systemic power differentials, a "silent revolt" in Jane's term,[22] rather than addressing the wider systemic issues that Godwin explores through a depiction of the machinations of the legal system. Caleb and Falkland look to the judicial system to determine the nature of guilt and redemption, as flawed as the system is demonstrated to be, and it is individual empathy that is in the end the arbiter of worth. In *Jane Eyre*, the law of the land is from the outset supplementary to the individual's ethical and emotional responses: Jane's aunt, Mrs. Reed, is bound by her husband's promise to care for Jane as a child; though Mrs. Reed feeds and sends Jane to school, Jane judges her negatively for her lack of emotional engagement. The individual's ethical and emotional response is of primary importance in Brontë's novel as a means of foregrounding female agency; as a woman, Jane has little standing within the justice system, the government, or the church.

Jane's social position as an educated orphan is similar to Caleb's, and the central measure of her worth is her "reputation," which makes her employable (or marriageable) as judged by more powerful men. It is possible to read Godwin's text as solely about power struggles between men, relegating the subplot, in which Tyrell's niece Emily is persecuted and dies, to the position of a mere reflection on Tyrell's character rather than a central example of the alignment of femininity with disempowerment. In Brontë's story, however, the central relationship is overtly and openly a heterosexual romance between a monstrous man and the woman who attempts to redeem him. Jane's sole method of resisting co-option into men's schemes—whether

---

22. Brontë, *Jane Eyre*, 178.

Rochester's illegal bigamy or St. John Rivers's proposal of a loveless but worthy marriage—is through her dedication to following her own ethical and emotional inclinations.

Will Graham's and Caleb's physical and social worth is highlighted by their shared gender with their tormentors; the unequal division of power between these men is signified by *coded* femininity, not justified by femaleness. In Brontë's novel, the powerful Rochester is forced to acknowledge the differential between a woman's allotted social worth and her interior subjectivity: "I could bend her with my finger and thumb; and what good would it do [. . .]? If I tear, if I rend this slight prison [. . .] I could call myself possessor of its clay dwelling place. And it is you, spirit—with will and energy, and virtue and purity—that I want, not alone your brittle frame."[23] Rochester, who repeatedly demonstrates the control he can wield over women by virtue of his physical and social power, is forced to the realization that just because he can doesn't mean that he should. As Brontë stated in an introduction to the second edition of her novel, "Conventionality is not morality."[24] Jane is able to withstand Rochester's assaults on her morality, just as Caleb endures Falkland's persecution, and she is able to argue her case against his because she, unlike Will Graham, is confident of her own sanity and selfhood at all times.

The link between social ostracism and homosexuality in *Caleb Williams* is echoed in the link between insanity and improper sexual behavior in *Jane Eyre*. Rochester seeks to mediate the reality and experience of his partners; he expresses with confidence that it is his decision whether he can marry and his reasoning that Jane should follow, not her own: "Jane! Will you hear reason? [. . .] [B]ecause if you won't I'll try violence." Further, Rochester states simply of his first wife, "Since the medical men had pronounced her mad, she had of course been shut up." There is little description of

---

23. Brontë, *Jane Eyre*, 394.
24. Brontë, "Appendix A: Prefatory Material to Subsequent Editions of *Jane Eyre*," in *Jane Eyre*, 557.

Bertha's symptoms of madness, barring Rochester's own summary of her nature: "I had marked neither modesty, nor benevolence, nor candour, nor refinement in her mind or manners [. . .]. I found her nature wholly alien to mine, her tastes odious to me, her cast of mind common, low, narrow, and singularly incapable of being led to anything higher, expanded to anything larger [. . .]. [A] nature the most gross, impure, depraved I ever saw."[25] Rochester's verdict is moral, not medical, yet the language of both is intertwined throughout this passage. Despite their differences of approach, all of these texts clearly demonstrate the power held by white men over the bodies and minds of others—the power to decide who goes free, whose reputation is considered good, who marries whom, and who is considered "sane" and normal.

The parallels between Rochester's and Lecter's treatment of women and the objects of their seductions demonstrate their acceptance of and investment in the power they hold as (white) men. When Rochester contemplates Jane's judgment of his behavior toward Bertha, he attempts to reassure her that his wealth and power will be deployed for her benefit, not to control her: "Your mind is my treasure, and if it were broken, it would be my treasure still." Yet Jane has noted that in his behavior Rochester objectifies women and disregards her feelings: "Without seeming to recognize in me a human being, he only twined my waist with his arm and riveted me to his side."[26] Lecter likewise maintains that what he is doing is in Will's best interests, but always as determined by Lecter himself: "I only want what is best for you" ("Tome-wan," 2.12). Will's response addresses Lecter's use of power to center his needs and desires above all else: "You don't want me to have anything in my life that isn't you." Will notes that friendship demands equality but that the patient–psychiatrist relationship (subtextually the predator–prey dynamic) denotes a

---

25. Brontë, *Jane Eyre*, 392, 398, 396. This dismissal of Bertha Mason inspired Jean Rhys's celebrated postcolonial adaptation of Brontë's novel, *Wide Sargasso Sea* (1966), which reimagines *Jane Eyre* from Bertha's (Antoinette's) perspective.

26. Brontë, *Jane Eyre*, 391, 377.

power imbalance in their interactions ("Sakizuke," 2.02). This assertion echoes twentieth-century feminist arguments that there can be no such thing as a fully consensual heterosexual relationship under patriarchy because of the imbalance of power between the genders.[27] Is this not an argument made in *Jane Eyre* when the heroine and hero can be reunited only once he has lost his physical and social power? Jane returns to Rochester and marries him only after he is blinded and physically weakened in the fire that destroys his home, Thornfield Hall. He is unable to perpetrate the violence he once threatened or to communicate on paper, so Jane controls his social world—his finances, his household, and his access to culture—as he controlled his first wife. Lecter, likewise, gives up his power, submitting to incarceration, so that Will knows "exactly where I am. And where you can find me" ("Digestivo," 3.07). For the dominant man to relinquish power appears to be a staple of the romance of redemption.

Throughout *Jane Eyre*, Brontë depicts individual men privileging their desires over and above the needs and wants of women, noting that it is socially acceptable to do so; like Godwin, she demonstrates that the personal reflects the political. Jane records the power imbalance that exists between herself and Rochester, always referring to him as "master," even when they are about to marry. Jane outlines how few options she has available in escaping his household and thus how much power a man in a remote household could wield: "Jane Eyre, who had been an ardent, expectant woman—almost a bride, was a cold, solitary girl again: her life was pale, her prospects were desolate [. . .]. My hopes were all dead [. . .]. I looked at my love: that feeling which was my master's—which he had created."[28] Thornfield Hall is inhabited by many women, both servants and family, but it is a man's domain: Mrs. Fairfax, Rochester's housekeeper, keeps it in a state of constant readiness to receive its master:

---

27. Carole Pateman, "Women and Consent," *Political Theory* 8, no. 2 (1980): 149–68.

28. Brontë, *Jane Eyre*, 383.

"Though Mr. Rochester's visits here are rare, they are always sudden and unexpected; and, as I observed that it put him out to find everything swathed up, [. . .] I thought it best to keep the rooms in readiness."[29] Tellingly, it is as Rochester unfolds his history to Jane that we see the clearest exploration of patriarchal society in Brontë's novel; he considers his every action against Jane's and Bertha's own interests as "reasonable," all utterly justified to protect his (a man's) reputation.

Lecter, like Rochester and Falkland before him, is shown to exploit the normative assumptions of wider society rather than to act in an entirely oppositional manner. Although in their psychiatry sessions Will and Lecter are positioned on-screen as mirroring each other, suggesting that the key contrast highlighted in the series is between the two men, a telling comparison can be drawn between Will and Lecter's female patients. Lecter's refusal to allow Will bodily autonomy and acknowledgment is echoed in his treatment of Phyllis "Bella" Crawford (Gina Torres) and Margot Verger (Katherine Isabelle). In "Kō No Mono" (2.11), Lecter breaches Margot's confidentiality, alerting her brother to her pregnancy, knowing that the consequences will likely be domestic violence. Margot is collateral damage because Lecter's true target is the fetus fathered by Will—a potential rival for Will's attention and affection. Lecter similarly disregards Bella's right to medical confidence in "Mukōsuke" (2.05); after she attempts suicide in his office, trusting Lecter as her psychiatrist with her final words, Lecter revives her against her wishes. Although he determines his course of action by flipping a coin, demonstrating his lack of personal regard for Bella, he intimates that he places Jack Crawford's desires above those of his wife when he tells Jack, "I couldn't do that to you." This act blurs the boundaries between Lecter's monstrous real self and his "person suit" ("Sorbet," 1.08) and implicates both him and Jack in the same patriarchal systems of value that places men's desires above women's.

29. Brontë, *Jane Eyre*, 172.

The alignment of the monstrous man with the dominant norms of his society is as central to the social critique in all three texts as it is to their narrative progression. However, each of the earlier novels constructs the possibility for improvement, whether through the reformation of society along more equal lines to prevent future monstrous action or through the redemption of the individual monster who is forced to relinquish his excessive power. Rochester is not coded as extraordinary, as Lecter is in his role as serial killer or as Falkland is in his role as murderer; instead, it is Rochester's victims who are made extraordinary by his persecution. Though it is suggested that Rochester's behavior is monstrous—that Thornfield is an "accursed place," offering "a living death," and a "narrow stone hell, with its one real fiend, worse than a legion of such as we imagine"[30]— the text is ambiguous as to whether Rochester refers here to himself and his experiences or to his "mad" wife and hers. Rochester is redeemed, brought to embody the position of a better kind of masculinity, as Jane's willingness to love enables him to achieve the role of father, husband, and head of household that he always desired. This resolution does not disturb the wider structures of patriarchal power at work that enabled Rochester's monstrous actions in the first place.

At the end of *Caleb Williams*, Caleb gets his day in court and is vindicated but finds it a hollow victory to destroy the reputation of a man who had the potential to do good, and Falkland dies repentant. In an unpublished version, Godwin had the magistrate side with Falkland, suppress Caleb's testimony, and commit the increasingly mad hero to imprisonment. This version, where Caleb's gravestone reads, "Here lies what was once a man," offers a harsher social critique and restates the gendered nature of power dynamics.[31] The published version retains a measure of trust in the very system that

---

30. Brontë, *Jane Eyre*, 390.
31. "Appendix A: Manuscript Ending for *Caleb Williams*," in Godwin, *Caleb Williams*, 311.

is maintained and managed by such monstrous men as Tyrell and Falkland in their positions as magistrates and landlords.

In *Hannibal*, it is the "monster" who instigates a personal relationship beyond the central pair's connection through employment, and it is, arguably, not the monster who undergoes profound personal change in his habits and outlook.

"I Am of His Kind": The Monster Devours Its Victim

In the gothic romance, empathy for the "monster" is developed through the sympathy that exists between the monster and the hero/ine. Rochester's acknowledgment of the bond with Jane, in contrast to Falkland's seeming obliviousness to Caleb's feelings in the first volume of Godwin's novel, is vital to the interpretation of a heterosexual romance: "I believe you felt the existence of sympathy between you and your grim and cross master, Jane." Rochester further states, "I have for the first time found what I can truly love—I have found you. You are my sympathy—my better self."[32] This clearly echoes the language used in *Hannibal* for the affection expressed between men: "friendship can sometimes involve a breach of individual separateness" ("Kaiseki," 2.01). Similarly, Jane's declaration at the end of Brontë's novel, "I am my husband's life as fully as he is mine [. . .] bone of his bone, and flesh of his flesh,"[33] is made visible on-screen in *Hannibal*'s graphic interludes. The merging of Lecter and Will's personalities is suggested on-screen in "Dolce" (3.06) through images of inky line drawings blending together and shots that merge their reflections in glass to form a gestalt image. With the protagonists' final tumble over a cliff edge in "The Wrath of the Lamb" (3.13), this unified identity is fully realized visually and narratively: wrapped in each other's arms, Will and Hannibal are together—people who care for each other but also monsters who kill together.

32. Brontë, *Jane Eyre*, 405, 406.
33. Brontë, *Jane Eyre*, 554.

In the final season, Lecter comes closer to eating Will than at any previous point and the implications are profound: Will and Hannibal would become one in this act of violence, but only Will as an individual entity would cease to exist. Though this merging echoes and twists the language of romantic love, which is used not only in *Jane Eyre* but also in the wider cultural traditions of Anglo-American fiction, it also has a significant legal precedent. Rochester's ability to openly acknowledge admirable aspects in Jane that he wishes to acknowledge in himself—such as courage, moral fortitude, intelligent reflection, passion—enables a suggestion of equality, despite their different class backgrounds. However, Jane doesn't represent a threat to Rochester's power in the same way that Caleb is a threat to Falkland. When Rochester offers to elevate Jane socially through marriage, she is still under the law his inferior, as demonstrated by the position of Bertha, whose marriage was arranged so that Rochester might claim her money. Marriage consolidates the man's power rather than reducing it. Indeed, the plot of *Caleb Williams* would be resolved easily through marriage were Caleb a woman because a wife could not be compelled to testify against her husband in a court of law in the late eighteenth century. This legal loophole is in itself evidence of women's diminished status in society—under English common law, a wife was considered an extension of her husband as a legal entity rather than an individual in her own right.[34] The image of Caleb or Will as Bluebeard's wife, linking masculine norms of subjectivity and selfhood to gendered marriage customs and romantic modes, enables us to unpack both paradigms through a queer reading.

But the queer monster may be acting in the service of a patriarchal system that elevates men over women and masculinity over femininity, a system that will inevitably crush a feminine man. The tragedy of *Caleb Williams* is that an equal partnership is not possible between two men of unequal social status. All the violence meted

---

34. For a full explanation of this legal tradition, see Colin Manchester, "Wives as Crown Witnesses," *Cambridge Law Journal* 37, no. 2 (1978): 249–51.

out by Falkland centers on his inability to embody appropriate class and gender roles; the initial murder is inspired by the unjustness of Tyrell's power, meted out in response to mockery—the murder is the revenge of a queer masculinity against a bully. This maligned, feminized man cannot bring himself to trust other maligned men in this society, and he ends up perpetuating the very social structures of power he despises. The tragedy of *Hannibal* seems quite opposite; the representative of a powerful and corrupt white masculinity seduces others into a random violent order based solely on his whim: Lecter murders those who offend his sense of propriety. After the final credits of *Hannibal*'s final episode, a brief scene shows Bedelia Du Maurier (Gillian Anderson) apparently serving or being served her own leg as a roast dinner (3.13). The table is set for three. It is suggested that Lecter is bringing Will, his "final girl" and Bluebeard's last wife, back with him as a new monster. Is this consummation of Will and Hannibal's romantic pairing the revenge of a queered masculinity, the apotheosis of Lee Edelman's suggestion that the queer is inherently aligned with the destruction of normative society?[35] Or is it a glamorized representation of the ultimate toxic masculinity, which continues in the tradition of *Jane Eyre*, romanticizing a relationship of profound inequality that ultimately does nothing to counter the dominant social norms that create inequity?

Reader, I marry them: queerness and queer cultures are not immune to the effects of toxic masculine norms, as critics of Edelman have noted, and queering our reading of texts does not necessarily challenge normative gender assumptions within those texts or within the reader. Marketed and consumed as a gothic text, *Hannibal* enters into a dialogue with the traditions of the genre and its exploration of gendered social norms. This adaptation is not simply restaging older stories for a modern era, bringing out concerns that a new audience finds exciting and relevant, but is also drawing our attention

35. Lee Edelman, *No Future: Queer Theory and the Death Drive* (Durham, NC: Duke Univ. Press, 2004), passim.

to elements that have always been present in these narratives. The exploration of the gendered institutional power in the legal system and the revelation of the domestic space as fraught with power negotiations have a long history in the gothic romance. *Hannibal*, as stylistically fresh as it appears, is very much a genre show and highly typical in its themes and conclusions. In making space for an overt acknowledgment of queer potentiality, however, it also encourages us to query the links between embodiment and identity when considering the negotiation of interpersonal power.

Bibliography

Brontë, Charlotte. *Jane Eyre*. Edited by Richard Nemesvari. Peterborough, Canada: Broadview Press, 1999.

Corber, Robert J. "Representing the 'Unspeakable': William Godwin and the Politics of Homophobia." *Journal of the History of Sexuality* 1, no. 1 (1990): 85–101.

Edelman, Lee. *No Future: Queer Theory and the Death Drive*. Durham, NC: Duke Univ. Press, 2004.

Gledhill, Evan Hayles. "Queer(y)ing Adaptation: Bryan Fuller's Hannibal as Slash Fiction Gothic Romance." In *Eating the Rude: Hannibal Lecter and the Fannibals, Criminals, and Legacy of America's Favorite Cannibal*, edited by Nicholas Yanes and Kyle Moody. Jefferson, NC: McFarland, forthcoming.

Godwin, William. *Caleb Williams*. Edited by Pamela Clemit. Oxford: Oxford Univ. Press, 2009.

Gold, Alex, Jr. "It's Only Love: The Politics of Passion in Godwin's *Caleb Williams*." *Texas Studies in Language and Literature* 19 (1977): 135–60.

Green, Shoshanna, Cynthia Jenkins, and Henry Jenkins. "'Normal Female Interest in Men Bonking': Selections from the Terra Nostra Underground and Strange Bedfellows." In *Theorising Fandom: Fans, Subculture, and Identity*, edited by Cheryl Harris and Alison Alexander, 9–40. New York: Hampton Press, 1998. Reprinted in *Fans, Bloggers, and Gamers: Exploring Participatory Culture*, edited by Henry Jenkins, 61–88. Durham, NC: Duke Univ. Press, 2006.

Manchester, Colin. "Wives as Crown Witnesses." *Cambridge Law Journal* 37, no. 2 (1978): 249–51.

Pateman, Carole. "Women and Consent." *Political Theory* 8, no. 2 (1980): 149–68.

Rigby, Elizabeth. "*Vanity Fair*—and *Jane Eyre*." *Quarterly Review* 84 (Dec. 1848): 118–19.

Scarano, Ross. "Bryan Fuller Knows You're Reading into *Hannibal*'s Homoeroticism, and He Thinks It's Hilarious." *Complex*, Sept. 16, 2014. At http://www.uk.complex.com/pop-culture/2014/09/bryan-fuller-hannibal-interview-slash-fiction.

6 | "Whispering through the Chrysalis"

Hannibal Lecter and the Poetics of Mentorship

Gabriel A. Rieger

The Problem of Clarice

Shortly after the television series *Hannibal* debuted on NBC in April 2013, speculation among the series' avid fans turned to how writer-producer Bryan Fuller might reimagine Clarice Starling. Fuller had already reinvented the familiar characters of Thomas Harris's novel *Red Dragon* (1981) through innovative casting and writing, and the re-creation of one of the most iconic characters in the Hannibal canon presented tantalizing possibilities. Fuller's original intention, as expressed in an interview with the popular-culture web magazine *Assignment X*, was to create a seven-season arc in which "Season Five would be *The Silence of the Lambs* era, Season Six would be the *Hannibal* era, and then Season Seven would be a resolve to the ending of that book."[1]

I thank Ms. Heather Frazier of Ohio State University for her invaluable assistance in the development of this essay's argument.

1. Abbie Bernstein, "Exclusive Interview: *Hannibal* News on Season 1, Season 2, and beyond from Showrunner Bryan Fuller," *Assignment X*, June 13, 2013, at https://www.assignmentx.com/2013/exclusive-interview-hannibal-news-on-season-1-season-2-and-beyond-from-showrunner-bryan-fuller/.

The "ending of that book," *Hannibal* (1999), infamously unites Hannibal and his adversary/protégé Clarice as lovers and is controversial among both critics and fans, some of whom felt that Harris had betrayed Clarice.[2] Most prominent among them was Jodie Foster, who won a Best Actress Oscar for portraying the character in *The Silence of the Lambs* (Jonathan Demme, 1991) but declined to reprise the role in *Hannibal* (Ridley Scott, 2001) on the grounds that "people believed in Clarice's heroism and I don't want to betray her."[3] Writing for the *London Review of Books*, John Lanchester summarized the problem of the ending thus: "The moral algebra of *Hannibal*, which has hitherto been careful, is suddenly and spectacularly abandoned," delivering shock "at too high an aesthetic price."[4] Of course, viewed from another perspective, the ending of *Hannibal* constitutes neither a "betray[al]" of Clarice nor an "abandon[ment]" of the novel's "moral algebra." Rather, that ending serves to underscore one of the most prominent themes in the Hannibal canon: the theme of mentorship, specifically mentorship in relation to gender and power.

Although the aesthetic value of the novel's conclusion and the question of whether it constitutes a "betray[al]" of Clarice are necessarily subjective, Bryan Fuller's plan to resolve the ending of the novel *Hannibal* was never realized; the series was cancelled after only three seasons, before he was able to secure the rights to Clarice from Metro-Goldwyn-Mayer. Lacking the rights to the character, Fuller apparently made a virtue of necessity by mapping elements of

---

2. For a more detailed consideration of popular reaction to the novel's conclusion, see Stephen M. Fuller, "Deposing an American Cultural Totem: Clarice Starling and Postmodern Heroism in Thomas Harris's *Red Dragon, The Silence of the Lambs*, and *Hannibal*," *Journal of Popular Culture* 38, no. 5 (2005): 819–33.

3. Quoted in "Jodie Foster," *Guardian*, Dec. 29, 1999, at https://www.theguardian.com/film/1999/dec/30/1.

4. John Lanchester, "'Slapping the Clammy Flab,'" *London Review of Books*, July 29, 1999, at http://www.lrb.co.uk/v21/n15/john-lanchester/slapping-the-clammy-flab.

her character onto other characters in the television series, including Abigail Hobbs, Miriam Lass, and, perhaps most to the purpose, the protagonist Will Graham. Hannibal's interactions with Will and Abigail take the same form of mentorship as his interactions with Clarice in Harris's novels *The Silence of the Lambs* (1988) and *Hannibal*, where he seeks to create a companion for himself. The absence of Clarice Starling presents a lacuna in which Fuller can explore the dynamics of mentorship as well as the particular intimacies that those dynamics facilitate.

(En)Gendering Mentorship

Mentorship is a central theme throughout the Hannibal canon—in the books, the films, and the television series. In keeping with Hannibal's loosely defined psychopathy, his mentorship is fundamentally selfish: it serves to replicate him in other characters by building upon those elements he shares in common with them. From his first appearance in *Red Dragon*, Hannibal adopts the role of mentor, advising Will Graham on the search for the Tooth Fairy. Pointedly, upon realizing that Will has anticipated his advice, Hannibal taunts him, saying, "You just came here to look at me. Just to get the old scent again, didn't you? Why don't you just smell yourself? . . . The reason you caught me is that we're just alike." Hannibal's taunt effectively infects Will; after leaving the hospital, Will suffers "the absurd feeling that Lecter had walked out with him."[5] Compare this feeling to Clarice's reaction following her first interview with Hannibal in chapter 4 of *The Silence of the Lambs*. The encounter leaves her both "excited" and "depleted," feeling "an alien consciousness loose in her head, slapping things off the shelves like a bear in a camper."[6]

The theme of mentorship is central to Harris's character Clarice in both *The Silence of the Lambs* and *Hannibal*. In chapter 44 of

---

5. Thomas Harris, *Red Dragon* (1981; reprint, New York: Dell, 2000), 82–83, 86.
6. Thomas Harris, *The Silence of the Lambs* (1988; reprint, New York: St. Martin's Press, 2000), 26.

The Silence of the Lambs, Harris writes that "[o]f the two brightest people Starling knew, one was also the steadiest person she knew and the other was the most frightening. Starling hoped that gave her some balance in her acquaintance."[7] In each of the novels, Clarice is "balance[d]" between two mentors who speak to distinct (if perhaps analogous) aspects of her character. Jack Crawford, the agent-in-charge of the FBI Behavioral Science Unit, mentors her in the rigid methodology of investigation and the objective evaluation of forensic evidence; his mentorship speaks to her ordered, Apollonian reason. In contrast, Hannibal Lecter mentors her in the subjective realms of taste and personal trauma; his mentorship speaks to the chaos and the artistry of her Dionysian imagination.

The tension between those two psychic poles is resolved at the conclusion of *Hannibal*, when Clarice effectively embraces Hannibal's nature—or perhaps her own. Harris describes how "Clarice Starling's memory palace is building [. . .]. It shares some rooms with Dr. Lecter's own memory palace—he has discovered her there several times—but her own palace grows on its own. It is full of new things."[8] Throughout *Hannibal*, the Apollonian structure of the FBI, central to Jack Crawford's mentorship, is revealed to be fundamentally corrupt (Deputy Assistant Attorney General Paul Krendler uses it as a weapon to falsely incriminate Clarice), while Clarice's Dionysian sense of aesthetics ("housed in parts of the mind that precede pity," as Hannibal helpfully reminds her[9]), central to Hannibal's mentorship, evolves and strengthens.

In keeping with this novel's theme of gender, the corruption of the FBI is articulated in terms that speak to Clarice's gendered vulnerability. In chapter 67, Paul Krendler, plotting to sabotage Clarice, imagines her living in "some god-damned dyke den." As the fantasy progresses, "he picture[s] Starling as old, tripping over those tits,

---

7. Harris, *Silence of the Lambs*, 276.
8. Thomas Harris, *Hannibal* (New York: Delacorte Press, 1999), 483.
9. Harris, *Hannibal*, 466.

those trim legs turned blue-veined and lumpy. . . . He wanted to stand next to her after she was disarmed and say without moving his mouth, 'You're old to still be fucking your daddy, even for Southern white trash.'"[10]

Krendler's hatred of Clarice is rooted in an inverted erotic desire (he recalls an abortive sexual encounter with "a girl with Starling's coloring but not her sense"[11]) and is thus intensely gendered—not to mention homophobic. His fantasy builds on this inversion, transposing the physical expressions of Clarice's femininity, weaponizing her gender against her. His hatred is also exploitative (expressing a frustrated desire to use her), reflecting the exploitative foundation of her relationship with the FBI, which uses her and eventually discards her. If Hannibal's mentorship empowers her (giving her "all [she] need[s]" of her father and facilitating the construction of her memory palace), the FBI disempowers her (Krendler seeks to employ his most hateful invective "after she was disarmed").[12] Hannibal would employ her personal trauma to strengthen her, while Krendler (representing the FBI) would employ it to degrade her. In either case, however, mentorship is inextricably bound to gender.

By the end of the novel, through a process of intense psychoactive and hypnotic therapy, Hannibal has either transformed Clarice or facilitated her transformation, utilizing those elements of her psyche (e.g., her anger, her vulnerability, and her sense of taste) upon and within which he can build. In either case, he has replicated elements of himself in her to create a companion. By the final chapter, "their relationship has a great deal to do with the penetration of Clarice Starling, which she avidly welcomes and encourages. It has much to do with the envelopment of Hannibal Lecter, far beyond the bounds of his experience. It is possible that Clarice Starling could frighten him."[13] The sexual metaphor is a useful one. Sex requires exchange

10. Harris, *Hannibal*, 339.
11. Harris, *Hannibal*, 338.
12. Harris, *Hannibal*, 452, 339.
13. Harris, *Hannibal*, 483.

and suggests a measure of mutuality. Through his process of mentorship, Hannibal has created not only a companion but also an equal. Hannibal is "the most frightening" person Clarice knows, but it is now "possible" that Clarice "could frighten him." Clarice is no longer in danger; Hannibal's mentorship has achieved its purpose in creating a new and independent entity to be his companion. As Harris notes in chapter 99 of *Hannibal*, "With all his knowledge and intrusion, he could never entirely predict her, or own her at all. He could feed the caterpillar, and he could whisper through the chrysalis; what hatched out followed its own nature and was beyond him."[14]

To create this companion, Hannibal's mentorship builds upon those things the two characters hold in common, in particular their shared taste and their shared trauma of loss. Hannibal's initial plan is to re-create his lost sister, Mischa, in the space occupied by Clarice. He regards the "potential flexibility" she shows in killing the deputy Johnny Mogli as either a "hopeful sign" that there might be "room for Mischa *within* Starling" or "simply another good quality of the place Starling must vacate."[15] In either case, Hannibal seeks to replicate a part of himself within Clarice. His mentorship is effectively an infestation, and, in keeping with the theme of gender, it results in a kind of generation.

We see a similar infestation in Hannibal's interactions with Will Graham in *Red Dragon*, with similarly gendered implications. Hannibal makes another attempt to infect Will in chapter 36 of that novel when he sends a letter asking him, "When you were so depressed after you shot Mr. Garret Jacob Hobbs to death, it wasn't the *act* that got you down, was it? Really, didn't you feel so bad *because killing him felt so good*?"[16] Hannibal attempts to build on elements the two men share in common, but in *Red Dragon* Hannibal's attempt to replicate himself in Will is unsuccessful. Will ends

---

14. Harris, *Hannibal*, 465–66.
15. Harris, *Hannibal*, 454, emphasis in original.
16. Harris, *Red Dragon*, 348, emphasis in original.

the novel realizing that he has "all the elements to make murder," but he speculates that "awful urges are the virus that makes vaccine"; he will not be overtaken by those elements of Hannibal that infect him.[17] In the novel *Hannibal*, conversely, the replication is entirely successful; Clarice participates in the cannibalizing of Paul Krendler and ends the novel with her own memory palace "shar[ing] some rooms with Dr. Lecter's" even as it "grows on its own."[18]

This sense of infection and replication is central to Hannibal's threat. Beyond the threat of murder or the more intimate and degrading threat of cannibalism, Hannibal threatens infection. In chapter 7 of *Red Dragon*, Will Graham requires time to "brace himself" before interviewing Hannibal so that "if he felt Lecter's madness in his head," he could "contain it quickly, like a spill."[19] Hannibal is introduced in *The Silence of the Lambs* with Jack Crawford's admonition to Clarice to "tell him no specifics about yourself. You don't want any of your personal facts in his head."[20] In the film version, screenwriter Ted Tally amends the line to "Believe me, you don't want Hannibal Lecter inside your head," making the threat of psychic infection more explicit.

This notion of infection provides a useful point of entry to considering the character of Hannibal Lecter and the narrative and theoretical use to which Fuller and his writers put him in the television series. Reviewing the novel *Hannibal* for the *New York Times* in 1999, Stephen King declared Hannibal Lecter to be "a Count Dracula for the computer-and-cell-phone age," and the two characters evince significant parallels.[21] As King notes, both Dracula and Hannibal are iconic monsters in popular culture (Hannibal Lecter having been portrayed, as of this writing, by four different actors with four

---

17. Harris, *Red Dragon*, 454.
18. Harris, *Hannibal*, 483.
19. Harris, *Red Dragon*, 79.
20. Harris, *Silence of the Lambs*, 6.
21. Stephen King, "Hannibal the Cannibal," *New York Times*, June 13, 1999, at http://www.nytimes.com/books/99/06/13/reviews/990613.13kingct.html.

distinct performance styles). Beyond this, both characters are exotic aliens, eastern European social nobility (both are counts) set apart by their archaic manners from the modern world they inhabit. Most to my purposes, both are predators whose predations involve infestation. As Stephen Arata notes, "In *Dracula* vampirism designates a kind of colonization of the body. Horror arises not because Dracula destroys bodies, but because he appropriates and transforms them. Having yielded to his assault, one literally 'goes native' by becoming a vampire oneself."[22] This parallel is implied in the Hannibal canon as well, although Hannibal's colonization targets the mind rather than the body. Even Harris's physical descriptions of Hannibal echo descriptions of Dracula; Hannibal's eyes "reflect the light in pinpoints of red," and Harris notes the whiteness of his teeth when Hannibal considers Clarice's identification card.[23] Demme's film *The Silence of the Lambs* explicates this element of the character when Officer Murray asks Clarice, "Is it true what they're saying, he's some kind of vampire?"

Miriam Lass, Abigail Hobbs, and the Inadequate Mentee

Hannibal's implicit vampirism may serve to facilitate our understanding of the character because it underscores the predatory and infectious threat of his influence, manifest through his mentorship of Clarice in the novels and displaced onto her various surrogates in the television series. Perhaps the most explicit of these surrogates and thus the first to consider here is Miriam Lass.

Miriam Lass parallels Clarice in that both are young women who enter their respective narratives as FBI trainees, protégées of Jack Crawford sent to interview Hannibal Lecter. However, Hannibal's interaction with and mentorship of Miriam differs in its methods as well as in its objectives from his mentorship of Clarice and her other

---

22. Stephen D. Arata, "The Occidental Tourist: *Dracula* and the Anxiety of Reverse Colonization," *Victorian Studies* 33, no. 4 (1990): 630.
23. Harris, *Silence of the Lambs*, 16–17.

surrogates. These distinctions are telling. Hannibal never attempts to build a companion out of Miriam, and they seemingly share no traits in common. Nor does he facilitate Miriam's growth; he merely dominates her in order to weaponize her against Dr. Frederick Chilton. He does not "whisper through [her] chrysalis" because he has no interest in creating an independent entity emergent on the other side. Nothing in his mentorship of Miriam, to the extent that their brief interaction can be called a mentorship, seeks to re-create himself or to build on her existing personality. She thus operates more as a contrast with Clarice than as a proper surrogate for her.

A closer surrogate for Clarice is Abigail Hobbs. Clarice Starling and Abigail Hobbs parallel and invert one another in significant ways. Both characters are orphaned women of college age, a stage of life at which they might seek mentorship. Clarice is introduced as a recent graduate of the University of Virginia and an FBI trainee, whereas Abigail's plans to attend college are interrupted by the fact that her father "killed girls at all the schools [she] applied to" ("Œuf," 1.04). Both characters come from working-class backgrounds with connections to law enforcement; Clarice's father is a night marshal, and Abigail's father is a pipe fitter and serial killer whose crimes put her in Will and Hannibal's orbit. Significantly, Hannibal mentors both characters as they grow into their respective and implicitly hereditary (and thus natural) roles: Clarice trains to be an FBI investigator, whereas Abigail effectively apprentices (first to her father and then to Hannibal) as a murderer.

Abigail's inversion of Clarice is more than superficial; it proves fundamental to her relationship with Hannibal. In *The Silence of the Lambs*, Hannibal taunts Clarice throughout their mentorship, most famously and pointedly during their first encounter in chapter 3, when he observes,

> You're so ambitious, aren't you? Do you know what you look like to me, with your good bag and your cheap shoes? You look like a rube. You're a well-scrubbed, hustling rube with a little taste. Your eyes are like cheap birthstones, all surface shine when you stalk

some little answer. And you're bright behind them, aren't you? Desperate not to be like your mother. Good nutrition has given you some length of bone, but you're not more than one generation out of the mines, *Officer* Starling.[24]

Hannibal's taunting is central to his mentorship in that it establishes his dominance over her, even while she ostensibly has power over him. This dominance underscores their gendered positions. Beyond this, his taunting, even while it unsettles Clarice, also draws her toward a clearer understanding of herself, beginning the process of replication, or perhaps self-discovery, that will conclude in the third novel.

In Fuller's television series, Abigail Hobbs inverts this dynamic by taunting Hannibal. As presented in *The Silence of the Lambs*, Clarice Starling is extremely intelligent (the top quarter of her class, as Jack Crawford notes), but her training in psychology and the rigid methodology of forensic investigation do not prepare her for Hannibal; he overwhelms her both intellectually and emotionally. In "Potage" (1.03), psychologist Alana Bloom describes Abigail, conversely, as having "a penchant for manipulation"; she can "with[hold] information to gain information." Later in the same episode, once Abigail realizes that Hannibal has allowed her to return home from the hospital "to find evidence" in the Minnesota Shrike murders, she taunts him with her knowledge of his complicity in warning her father of the investigation, asking, "Are we going to re-enact the crime? You be my dad [indicating Will], you be my mom [indicating Alana], and you be the man on the phone [indicating Hannibal]." She looks Hannibal in the face as she speaks the line, and Hannibal, seemingly at a loss, looks away.

Hannibal taunts Clarice with her vulnerability, specifically her class position, whereas here Abigail inverts the dynamic, taunting Hannibal with his vulnerability, specifically her knowledge that he

---

24. Harris, *Silence of the Lambs*, 22, emphasis in original.

has sabotaged the investigation. In both cases, the taunting works as an exchange, forging a bond of intimacy between the two characters. At the close of "Potage," after Hannibal has induced Abigail to murder Nicholas Boyle, she tells him directly, "I think you called the house as a serial killer, just like my dad." She makes clear to him that just as he can blackmail her with the murder, she can blackmail him with obstruction of justice. When Hannibal responds by promising to "keep [her] secret," she replies, "And I'll keep yours." Her face, which has been anxious throughout their conversation to that point, contorts into a wry smile. Later in the season, in "Relevés" (1.12), tabloid journalist Freddie Lounds describes Abigail as "one of those very smart girls who hasn't quite figured out that very smart girls grow up and know all the moves that they're making."

Abigail's smile suggests that she believes she has achieved some measure of parity with Hannibal. Her "penchant for manipulation" makes her an excellent mentee and potential companion for him. She understands that she has been manipulated into murdering Nicholas Boyle (persuaded rather than coerced, as Hannibal's psychiatrist, Dr. Bedelia Du Maurier, will later specify), and she responds in kind. Her manipulation is a trait she shares with Hannibal, one he can exploit and build on.

Abigail's "penchant for manipulation" also facilitates another essential component of Hannibal's mentorship, both in the novel and in the series: symbolic death and rebirth. Clarice's symbolic death occurs in chapter 86 of the novel *Hannibal*, when she is shot twice with tranquilizer darts, and Tommaso says that she has had "maybe too much *narcotico*. She's maybe dead." Of course, Clarice does not die because Hannibal facilitates her recovery, "administering stimulant countermeasures" to the tranquilizer "with infinite care." She regains consciousness in "fresh-smelling semidark, knowing in some primal way that she was near the sea."[25]

---

25. Harris, *Hannibal*, 425, 435, 439.

The sea is a traditional symbol of birth from the earliest world mythologies,[26] and after her near-death experience Clarice is effectively reborn into Hannibal's sensual world, "waking in a pleasant room" amid "the smell of fresh flowers" and "faint chamber music."[27] Her death and rebirth are essential elements in her emergence as Hannibal's companion; her previous life is discarded, and she emerges as a new creature.

This process of symbolic death and rebirth is made more explicit in the *Hannibal* episode ". . . And the Woman Clothed with the Sun" (3.09) when Hannibal tells Abigail, "I'm sorry I couldn't protect you in this life, but I can protect you in the life we create for you." He draws blood from her to fake her death, noting as he does so that "blood rituals involve a symbolic death and then a rebirth. As with all things in the natural world, you'll adapt now and mutate later." As he prepares to spray the collected blood, he asks her, "Are you ready to die, Abigail?" and she replies in the affirmative. Like Clarice, she dies in order to be reborn.

Beyond her "penchant for manipulation," part of what makes Abigail such an attractive mentee for Hannibal is that she is already familiar with the process of murder. In "Trou Normand" (1.09), she confesses her involvement in the Minnesota Shrike murders, explaining to Hannibal, "I knew what my father was. I knew what he did. I knew. I was the one who met the girls, talked to them. Laughed and joked. Found out where they lived, where they were going, when they'd be alone. Girls who looked like me. They could have been my friends. I couldn't tell him no."

These qualities thus provide Hannibal with potential points of infection. Nevertheless, her experience was acquired against her

---

26. See especially the Enuma Elish, the Babylonian creation epic in which the earth is born of "primeval Tiamat," the primal ocean mother. The pattern persists in later mythologies as well, in which the sea is regularly associated with fertility goddesses (e.g., Aphrodite).

27. Harris, *Hannibal*, 439.

will, and it has traumatized her. She evinces powerful anxiety as she recounts the experience to Hannibal, and he comforts her with an embrace.

Abigail's anxiety may explain why Hannibal's mentorship of her never fully succeeds. Unlike Clarice, Abigail never proves to be Hannibal's equal. When she reemerges at the close of "Mizumono" (2.13), she hesitates in her role. She appears on the verge of tears as she prepares to attack Alana Bloom and even apologizes before shoving her through the window. When Will arrives at the scene shortly thereafter, Abigail sobs as she tells him, "I didn't know what else to do, so I did what [Hannibal] told me." She screams as she watches Hannibal eviscerate Will. In the "Mizumono" screenplay, the stage direction indicates that "Hannibal stands next to a terrified Abigail[,] who realizes she's made a bargain with the devil."[28]

Abigail never rises to the challenge of Hannibal's mentorship; she remains "terrified" of him to the end. She has some elements in common with him, but she merely follows his direction; she lacks the necessary sense of an independent self to ever really be his equal.[29] Hannibal cannot replicate himself in her because she remains fundamentally subordinate to him, just as she was to her father. To return to Hannibal's phrase, she adapts, but she never properly mutates. Whatever emerges from her chrysalis, Hannibal will always control it.

In keeping with Abigail's subordinate and gendered sensibility, Hannibal's mentorship of her is intensely paternal. He acknowledges

---

28. See Stephen Lightfoot and Bryan Fuller, "Mizumuno" screenplay, *Hannibal*, episode 2.13, Living Dead Guy Productions, 2015, at http://livingdeadguy.com/wp-content/uploads/2015/04/H213-Mizumono-Web.pdf.

29. Commentators have noted the significance of the etymology of the name "Abigail": it comes from the Hebrew term *abhigayil*, meaning "my father is rejoicing," but it can also refer more generally to a domestic servant. According to the *Oxford English Dictionary*, the earliest usage of the name as a synonym for *female servant* is 1616, when it appears in plays by Samuel Cowper and by Beaumont and Fletcher.

as much in "Œuf" when he comforts her by telling her "you're not your father's daughter, not anymore." The line in context is ambivalent, allowing for the suggestion that Hannibal may now fill that role, and he does come to fill it; Abigail transfers her filial bonds fundamentally intact from her father to Hannibal. Hannibal will make their relationship explicit in ". . . And the Woman Clothed with the Sun" when he tells her, "You accepted your father," and asks, "Would it be so difficult to accept me?"

Ironically, Abigail's clearest contrast with Clarice, her subordination, is underscored in a scene that features one of the most explicit parallels between the two characters. In ". . . And the Woman Clothed with the Sun," Hannibal confronts Abigail with the exhumed corpse of her father, replicating the intense psychotherapy he employed on Clarice in chapter 95 of the novel *Hannibal*. In the novel, the skeletal remains of Clarice's father provide her with a sense of closure, freeing her from the weight of his expectations; as Hannibal observes, "What you need of your father is here, in your head, and subject to your judgment, not his."[30] He repeats these lines almost verbatim to Abigail, Clarice's surrogate, in ". . . And the Woman Clothed with the Sun" when he presents her with the corpse of her father, but we know (because the scene is presented in flashback and we have already seen its effect) that the result is transferal rather than escape. In symbolically killing her father (slashing him with a hunting knife, "lov[ing] him the way he loved you," in Hannibal's phrase), Abigail effectively facilitates her transformation into Hannibal's daughter.

The paternal dynamic between Abigail and Hannibal is apparent throughout the series, but Hannibal speaks most explicitly to it in the first-season episode "Savoureaux" (1.13) when he tells Bedelia, "I never considered having a child, but after meeting Abigail, I understood the appeal, the opportunity to guide, and support, and in many ways direct a life." Hannibal directs Abigail in how to commit and conceal murder. She takes to the process, in part, but he is never

---

30. Harris, *Hannibal*, 452.

able to fully replicate himself in her because she is never sufficient to embody him. In her role as daughter, however, she does facilitate a bond between Hannibal and his primary mentee, the television series' primary surrogate for Clarice Starling, Will Graham.

Will Graham and the "Breach of Individual Separateness"

The relationship between Hannibal and Will is the richest in the series and has occasioned an extraordinary amount of commentary among the series' fanbase. Fuller notes in an interview for the website Bloody-Disgusting that, "as a gay man, I've always been fascinated with heterosexual male friendships, and seeing patterns of romance and devotion that are not sexualized, but are nevertheless very deeply felt. So, it was really about unpacking that in a way, and I think as it progressed, the lines became blurry."[31] In the absence of Clarice Starling, many of the gendered elements of her relationship with Hannibal, including their "patterns of romance and devotion," as well as many of their conversations are displaced onto Will.[32] The erotic relationship that provides the metaphor by which Thomas Harris presents the characters' mutuality and sense of exchange in the novel *Hannibal* is more muted in the series, although it nevertheless colors the characters' relationship.

From the outset of the series, Hannibal is explicitly a mentor to Will, murdering Cassie Boyle in "Apéritif" (1.01) to highlight the unique features of the Minnesota Shrike murders in relief, thus showing Will "a negative" so that he can "see the positive." Following the death of Garret Jacob Hobbs, the mentor relationship transforms and strengthens as the two men bond over the care of Abigail. They inhabit parental roles, with all of the gendered implications of those roles. Will and Hannibal's relationship is not explicitly erotic, but in

---

31. Kalyn Corrigan, "*Hannibal* Creator Bryan Fuller on Cannibalism, Diverse Representation, and the Unwavering Bonds of Male Friendship," Bloody-Disgusting (website), Dec. 8, 2015, at http://bloody-disgusting.com/interviews/3372394/3372394/.

32. Corrigan, "*Hannibal* Creator Bryan Fuller."

its evolving intimacy it mimics the structure of an erotic relationship, with Will functioning as a surrogate for Clarice.

In the series, Will and Hannibal fall, at least superficially, into archetypal masculine and feminine roles. Will wears a beard, while Hannibal's clean-shaven face highlights the delicacy and implicit femininity of his features. Will's clothing is drab and utilitarian; he favors khakis and flannel shirts in a palette of browns and tans. Hannibal's clothing, by contrast, is exquisitely colored and textured; in an interview with *Esquire*, Fuller describes the character as one "who appreciates the beauty in life, who [loves] color and pattern and stimulating fabrics."[33] When Will isn't lecturing or investigating, he relaxes by fishing or repairing engines; Hannibal, by contrast, spends his leisure time in traditionally feminine activities such as cooking, drawing, and reading.

Of course, the clearest contrast between the two characters appears in their fundamental natures. Will possesses the gift of perfect empathy, and so human interaction overwhelms him; as a result, he is intensely solitary. Hannibal, conversely, is sociable, continually holding dinner parties for his wide circle of friends. His divergence from the conventional tropes of masculinity is made explicit in chapter 49 of the novel *Hannibal* when Paul Krendler (caught in his own matrix of gendered and erotic torment) observes of Hannibal, "I've always figured he was a homo-sexual [. . .] [a]ll this artsy-fartsy stuff. Chamber music and tea-party food."[34]

That said, these gender associations are only superficial. In more fundamental ways, the characters' gender associations are inverted. Throughout the series, Will Graham is repeatedly forced into the kind of disempowered positions that are traditionally associated with women. He is unable to resist Jack Crawford, who effectively bullies him into investigating murders even as he suffers psychic agony in

---

33. Quoted in Jordan Porteous, "How the New Hannibal Lecter Became the Best-Dressed Man on TV," *Esquire*, May 15, 2013, at http://www.esquire.co.uk/culture/film/news/a3899/hannibals-style-mads-mikkelsen/.

34. Harris, *Hannibal*, 263.

doing so. Will is intensely sensitive to violations of his personal space, and yet that space is continually invaded throughout the series, not least by Hannibal, who engages him with aggressive and invasive (and "radically unorthodox," as Dr. Chilton notes ["Takiawase," 2.04]) forms of therapy. Jack leads Will into "dark places," and Hannibal ostensibly helps to lead him out, but in either case Will is led.

The gender inversion in the relationship extends to Hannibal as well. For all of his superficial associations with the feminine, he plays the masculine role of aggressor in his relationship with Will. He calls on Will at his home, brings him gifts (of food), and leads him in his investigation of the Minnesota Shrike murders. As previously noted, even Hannibal's preferred methodology of mentorship, penetration of his protégé's mind, allegorizes masculine coition. The gender dynamic of their relationship is complex, not to say fluid, and allows for considerable flexibility as Fuller maps the character of Clarice onto Will.

As is the case with Clarice, Will takes on the role of protégé to Hannibal, and he maintains that role even after he has become aware that Hannibal is the Chesapeake Ripper. In the television series, Hannibal applies his mentorship in a manner similar to his application in the novels: he seeks to re-create himself in Will through a process, at least initially, of infection. Speaking to Hannibal from his cell in "Kaiseki" (2.01), Will says, "I used to hear my thoughts inside my skull with the same tone, timbre, and accent as if the words were coming out of my mouth [. . .]. Now my inner voice sounds like you. I can't get you out of my head." Hannibal's reply reveals his methodology when he tells Will, "Friendship can involve a breach of individual separateness."

Hannibal breaches Will's "separateness" to re-create himself in Will's mind, effectively beginning the process of transformation that is eventually completed in the close of season 3. Significantly, whereas Abigail's sense of self is too weak to allow for Hannibal's re-creation of himself in her, Will's sense of self is too strong, at least initially. As in *Red Dragon*, in the series Will resists Hannibal's attempts at psychic infestation, and the process by which Hannibal re-creates himself in Will proves to be long and involved.

That process begins in the first episode of the series when Hannibal effectively traps Will into killing Garret Jacob Hobbs, forcing him to experience murder in a more intimate manner than even his hypersensitive imagination had previously allowed. He builds on this foundation by displacing his own crimes onto Will, making Will confront the dissonance of his two roles of investigator and apparent murderer. In season 2, when Hannibal re-creates the Ripper murders on the bailiff in "Hassun" (2.03) and sabotages the trial through his murder of Judge Davies (revealing justice to be "not only [. . .] blind" but also "mindless and heartless"), he releases Will from captivity and effectively facilitates the rebirth that is central to his mentorship, but penetrating Will's extraordinary sense of self will require a more profound rebirth.

Later in the second season, in "Su-zakana" (2.08), Will experiences another potential rebirth, although, unlike his previous ones, this one is prevented rather than facilitated by Hannibal. Hannibal prevents Will from committing a premeditated, nondefensive murder of Clark Ingram by blocking the hammer of Will's revolver. Having done so, he repeats narrative lines similar to those spoken about Clarice Starling in the novel *Hannibal*: "With all my knowledge and intrusion, I could never entirely predict you. I can feed the caterpillar, whisper through the chrysalis, but what hatches follows its own nature and is beyond me."

The murder of Clark Ingram would have marked Will as a murderer, transcending Jack Crawford's and the FBI's moral strictures to dispense justice in accordance with his own will. Read superficially, this action might be considered a replication of Hannibal in Will, although, as Hannibal points out, the act itself is misdirected. It is "not the reckoning [Will] promised [him]self." The reckoning that Will seeks must be personal and undertaken for himself alone. Nevertheless, Hannibal is obviously pleased with Will's progress, particularly with the independence of his judgment. Whatever Will becomes, whatever emerges from Will's chrysalis, it will "follow its own nature."

Will comes closer to that ideal in another symbolic death and rebirth in the murder of Randall Tier in the subsequent episode, "Shiizakana" (2.09), a monumental event in his mentorship that closes a circle of mutuality. Will acknowledges as much in "Naka-choko" (2.10) when he tells Hannibal, "This makes us even. I sent someone to kill you, you sent someone to kill me." Hannibal's reply makes the exchange explicit. He advises Will to "consider it an act of reciprocity. One positive action begets another."

The death of Randall Tier is a "positive action" for various reasons. It effectively completes Will's apprenticeship to Hannibal; at the end of "Shiizakana," Will displays the corpse like a work of art, which the master murderer Hannibal inspects with approval. It underscores the equality that is central to their relationship; they are able to exchange and to parry one another's attacks. Finally, the killing of Randall provides Will with another near-death experience that serves as a symbolic death to facilitate his rebirth. When Randall crashes through Will's window, Will envisions him as the ravenstag, which serves as Will's totem throughout the series. In short, Will attacks himself. As the fight begins, the ravenstag transforms into the Wendigo, which is Hannibal's totem, and as Will beats Randall to death, the Wendigo transforms into a bloody and grinning Hannibal. Will's and Hannibal's identities flicker in the scene, associating but pointedly never fully fusing.

As their relationship approaches its moment of crisis in the second season, Will, like Clarice, is split between two mentors, Jack and Hannibal. Also as in Clarice's case, the tension between these two mentors drives Will's actions. The direction of "Mizumono" explicates this split: Will's face is divided down the middle as he converses with Jack and Hannibal in their separate offices. Although Will ostensibly resolves this tension in favor of Jack (attempting to facilitate Hannibal's capture), he does call Hannibal to warn him of his impending arrest. Pointedly, this call consists only of the phrase "they know," the same phrase with which Hannibal warned Garret

Jacob Hobbs in the pilot episode. Even as Will betrays and breaks free from Hannibal, he effectively becomes him.

We see here in "Mizumono" the clearest evidence of Hannibal's mentorship in Will. Hannibal has infected Will and transformed him, but, as in Clarice's case, he can "never entirely predict [Will], or own [him] at all." As Hannibal notes at the close of the episode, "I wanted to surprise you. And you . . . wanted to surprise me." Preparing to kill Will, he asks, "Do you believe you could change me the way I've changed you?" and Will replies, "I already have." This is the clearest indication of the characters' mutuality that the series has presented to this point, although Hannibal has not succeeded in creating a companion for himself. Will remains, even at the point of death, Jack Crawford's creature and Hannibal's opponent.

Hannibal's attack provides yet another in what has become for Will a series of symbolic deaths. As Will bleeds out on the floor, he watches Abigail die and is in turn watched by the ravenstag, which, too, is dying, its sides heaving with gradually lessening force. In the aftermath of the attack, however, a kind of symbolic rebirth ensues. The house fills with an ocean of surging blood, an image that conflates the associations of birth and death, the life force and the death force that have surrounded Will and Hannibal's relationship throughout the series.

One might be tempted to see Hannibal's mentorship as complete in this scene; Will has effectively replicated Hannibal, speaking Hannibal's words as he sabotages Jack's intended arrest. He has achieved a level of equality with Hannibal in that the two men have changed one another. Finally, Will has been implicitly killed (although his fate is left unresolved at the close of the episode) and reborn in the ensuing gush of blood. The only element missing in the relationship, the single parallel with Clarice Starling that Will has failed to embody, is companionship. For all of the superficial connection between Will and Hannibal, no true "breach of individual separateness" has occurred.

That "breach" does not occur until the third season as the consequences of the "red dinner" (as fans of the series have taken to calling it) gradually emerge. Abigail, the chief external bond between Hannibal and Will, is revealed to be incontrovertibly dead, and Will begins the process of forging a new bond as he pursues Hannibal to Europe. Hannibal is not merely prey for Will; he participates in the forging of the bond, creating a spectacular tableau out of Anthony Dimmond in "Primavera" (3.02), which Will correctly interprets as "[a] valentine written on a broken man." Once Will has recognized the valentine, however, it transforms, breaking its bonds and disassembling itself to become a truncated human form from which emerge the antlers and hooves of the ravenstag, Will's totem. The valentine becomes Will because Will is the broken man onto whom Hannibal has projected his desire.

Nakama

As Will begins his pursuit, however, that desire is ambiguous; the relationship that the two men shared prior to "Mizumuno" has ended, and what will replace it remains in doubt. As with Clarice Starling, Hannibal associates Will with his dead sister, Mischa. In the series, it falls to Bedelia Du Maurier to make the connection explicit in "Secondo" (3.03) when she declares, "Whatever your sister made you feel was beyond your conscious ability to control or predict. . . . I would suggest that what Will Graham makes you feel is not dissimilar." Acknowledging this connection, Hannibal recalls that Mischa "would influence me to betray myself, but I forgave her that influence" and concludes that to forgive Will he must "eat him" as he ate Mischa.[35]

The implicit intimacy between Will and Hannibal is layered in this exchange. Will is associated with Hannibal's blood relative, and

---

35. In the novel *Hannibal*, the German soldiers (actually described as deserters) eat Mischa. In the subsequent novel, *Hannibal Rising*, the deserters are revealed to have been Lithuanian Waffen-SS, and we learn that they fed some of Mischa to young Hannibal Lecter, who was starving. In the television series, the timeline and narrative are adjusted so that it is Hannibal who ate Mischa, with no mention of the soldiers.

layered onto that intimacy is Mischa's "influence," which would lead Hannibal to "betray [him]self." The ultimate intimacy, the ultimate breach of "individual separateness" that he achieved with Mischa and that he seeks with Will, is to eat him. The companion whom Hannibal seeks to create not only must be his equal but must also effectively become him, sharing the same psychic and physical space. He achieves this synthesis with Clarice Starling in part through sex; Harris notes in the novel *Hannibal* that "their relationship has a great deal to do with the penetration of Clarice Starling [. . .] [and] the envelopment of Hannibal Lecter."[36] In the case of Mischa and potentially in the case of Will, the synthesis is achieved through cannibalism.

Hannibal's intention to cannibalize Will is superficially inconsistent with his desire for companionship because Hannibal employs cannibalism as an expression of dominance. As Will notes in "Futamono" (2.06), "The Ripper eats his victims because they're no better to him than pigs." If cannibalism is an expression of dominance, however, it makes sense that Hannibal would deploy it to contain the threat that both Mischa and Will present to him. Mischa "would influence [him] to betray [him]self," and Will would betray him to the FBI. The danger of an equal companion is that such a companion, like Clarice, "could frighten him." Equality allows the possibility of a threat, and cannibalism is a means of containing that threat.

Paradoxically, cannibalism can also be a show of respect. In the film *Red Dragon* (Brett Ratner, 2002), Hannibal follows his attempted murder of Will by declaring, "Remarkable boy. I do admire your courage. I think I'll eat your heart." In "Dolce" (2.06), Hannibal says of his intention to cannibalize Bedelia, "[It] would be a shame not to savor you." Hannibal's attempt to cannibalize Will fits neatly into both dynamics, dominance and respect, although it is not finally the means by which the two men "breach [their] individual separateness."

---

36. Harris, *Hannibal*, 483.

Of course, that "individual separateness" has arguably been breached well before the third season. When Will seeks out Hannibal at Lecter Castle in "Secondo" (3.03), he encounters the servant Chiyoh, who suggests that each is a *nakama* to the other, "a very close friend, someone you share with." Will concurs with her assessment and declares, "I've never known myself as well as I know myself when I'm with him." Also, despite his protestation that he is not "like Hannibal," his interactions with Chiyoh replicate Hannibal's interactions with her; in a manner somewhere between persuasion and coercion, he manipulates her into killing her prisoner. As Chiyoh observes in the same episode, "You said Hannibal was curious if I would kill. You were curious, too [. . .]. You were doing what he does. He'd be proud of you, his *nakama*." Hannibal has already replicated, or perhaps merely liberated, elements of himself in Will.

The two men are pointedly revealed in this episode to share a mutuality even beyond what Hannibal might have anticipated. When Will arrives at the Lecter estate, where Hannibal's memory palace began, he engages in a kind of psychic therapy with him, seated in office chairs on the castle grounds. As the two men speak, we find that their roles have reversed, with Will playing the role of therapist, interrogating Hannibal about his childhood trauma. The two have achieved a kind of synthesis, or at least an exchange. Will has entered Hannibal's memory palace and his mind, inhabiting Hannibal's role as therapist. Hannibal's mind is penetrated, and Will is enveloped in the memory palace in a tableau that calls to mind the mutuality Hannibal shares with Clarice at the close of the novel *Hannibal*.[37] That mutuality is made more explicit in "Dolce" (3.06) when Will finally meets Hannibal again and confides to him that "before you and after you . . . it's all starting to blur." Hannibal concedes in "Dolce" that "freeing yourself from me and me freeing myself from you, they're the same." The two men have achieved mutuality, but

---

37. Harris, *Hannibal*, 483.

neither is as yet willing to commit to it, as evinced by Will's attempt to murder Hannibal and Hannibal's subsequent attempt to cannibalize Will. Each man seeks escape from the other.

Hannibal's attempt to cannibalize Will suggests that he has not fully embraced their bond, but his attempt is thwarted when the two are captured and transported to Muskrat Farm, where their bonding process continues. While seated at Mason Verger's table in "Digestivo" (3.07), Will bites a piece of flesh from the face of Cordell Doemling, replicating the iconic image of Hannibal Lecter biting the nurse, as referenced in *The Silence of the Lambs*, the first explicit representation of Hannibal's violence. Hannibal responds to Will's attack with a smile of unmistakable pride. The two men share in this instance a single mind.

The connection, or perhaps the synthesis, is made explicit at the end of the episode as Hannibal tends to Will, declaring to him, "Your memory palace is building. It's full of new things. It shares some rooms with my own. I've discovered you there, victorious." Will rejects this connection, but his rejection is ambiguous as he tells Hannibal, "When it comes to you and me, there can be no decisive victory." The "breach of individual separateness" is complete, even if Will does not yet realize it. Hannibal is willing to wait for him, however, allowing himself to be captured by the FBI so that, as he tells Will, "[you will] know exactly where I am and where you can find me."

Will's moment of realization does not occur until the final episode of the series (thus far), aptly titled "The Wrath of the Lamb" (3.13), when, after an extended pursuit in which Will inverts the dynamic of the first two seasons by taking on Hannibal's former role of pursuer, the two men escape from captivity and prepare for their final battle with the Red Dragon. The scene is primal; the two men fight together with axe and knife and teeth, as if they share a single mind, attacking the Dragon in unison and finally killing him. At that moment, the fusion between Will and Hannibal is complete. Standing over the corpse of the Dragon, Will references Hannibal's famous line from the novel, repeated in the same context in "... And the Woman Clothed with the Sun": "Have you ever seen blood in the moonlight, Will? It appears quite black." Will's response in the finale, "It really does look black in the moonlight," speaks not only to their shared triumph but also to a shared aesthetic understanding, which is always central to Hannibal's mentorship. Similarly, in the final chapter of the novel *Hannibal*, Clarice shares a residence with Hannibal in "an exquisite Beaux Arts building" in Buenos Aires; our last image of the couple finds them "dancing on a terrace" in a shared experience of aesthetic bliss.[38] Will likewise "dances" with Hannibal on a terrace; their battle against the Dragon is presented in slow motion and scored with music, giving it the appearance of a dance.

The dance does not, however, conclude Will's narrative as it does Clarice's; one final death and rebirth remain for him. Standing on the terrace, overlooking the sea, Hannibal tells Will that "this is all I ever wanted for you," suggesting that the re-creation of himself in Will is complete. For a moment, the two men embrace, like lovers, until Will abruptly tackles Hannibal and plunges off of the cliff with him, both men plummeting into the primal womb of the sea.

Is this final death Will's or Hannibal's? It seems unlikely that either man can have survived the precipitous fall into the ocean, but of course miraculous survival is so common in the series as to be thematic. Following the closing credits, the camera pulls back to reveal Dr. Du Maurier, dressed for a formal dinner, with her own roasted leg displayed on a platter before her. She is implicitly Hannibal's victim, being forced to consume herself, as was Abel Gideon. Pointedly, however, the camera pans around the table to reveal, without lingering on them, two place settings. If Will and Hannibal have survived their fall and been reborn of the sea, they now prepare to share a communion, entered into willingly and with full consent.

---

38. Harris, *Hannibal*, 484.

One sees an echo here of Clarice's communion with Hannibal in chapter 100 of the novel *Hannibal*, when they share a meal of Paul Krendler's brains. In either case, the meal takes on the coloring of vengeance and underscores the couple's shared predation as they literally eat their enemy alive. By this point in the narrative, Hannibal and Clarice, like Hannibal and Will, have effectively fused their natures. Through a long process of infestation and careful nurturing, Hannibal's mentorship has produced a companion for himself, one who remains independent but who can share with him elements of his bliss.

Looking Forward

The rights to the characters from *The Silence of the Lambs*, including Clarice Starling, became available for purchase in August 2017, and Bryan Fuller has expressed interest in returning to his series for a fourth season should fan interest persist and circumstances permit. If so, he may yet have an opportunity to reimagine an actual Clarice, as opposed to her surrogates. In an interview for the website CraveOnline, when asked about the possibility of reimagining Clarice, Fuller replied,

> There's a couple of ways to go. There's the Ellen Page way, which I think would be fantastic and more kind of in line with the Clarice that we all know. But I know I would also like to explore who Clarice would be from a different racial background. There's something about being poor and white in the South but there's something else about being poor and black in the South, and I think it could be the necessary gateway into the character, to make Clarice as much our own signature character as we tried to make Will Graham.[39]

---

39. William Bibbiani, "Bryan Fuller Describes *The Silence of the Lambs* Season of *Hannibal*," CraveOnline, Aug. 30, 2015, at http://www.craveonline.com/entertainment/895949-exclusive-bryan-fuller-describes-silence-lambs-season-hannibal.

Whatever form Clarice may take, the shadow she casts over the canon will likely remain undiminished, and her fans will anxiously wait to see what emerges from her eventual chrysalis.

Bibliography

Arata, Stephen D. "The Occidental Tourist: *Dracula* and the Anxiety of Reverse Colonization." *Victorian Studies* 33, no. 4 (1990): 621–45.

Bernstein, Abbie. "Exclusive Interview: *Hannibal* News on Season 1, Season 2, and beyond from Showrunner Bryan Fuller." *Assignment X*, June 13, 2013. At https://www.assignmentx.com/2013/exclusive-interview-hannibal-news-on-season-1-season-2-and-beyond-from-showrunner-bryan-fuller/.

Bibbiani, William. "Bryan Fuller Describes *The Silence of the Lambs* Season of *Hannibal*." CraveOnline (website), Aug. 30, 2015. At http://www.craveonline.com/entertainment/895949-exclusive-bryan-fuller-describes-silence-lambs-season-hannibal.

Corrigan, Kalyn. "*Hannibal* Creator Bryan Fuller on Cannibalism, Diverse Representation, and the Unwavering Bonds of Male Friendship." Bloody-Disgusting (website), Dec. 8, 2015. At http://bloody-disgusting.com/interviews/3372394/3372394/.

Fuller, Stephen M. "Deposing an American Cultural Totem: Clarice Starling and Postmodern Heroism in Thomas Harris's *Red Dragon*, *The Silence of the Lambs*, and *Hannibal*." *Journal of Popular Culture* 38, no. 5 (2005): 819–33.

Harris, Thomas. *Hannibal*. New York: Delacorte Press, 1999.

———. *Red Dragon*. 1981. Reprint. New York: Dell, 2000.

———. *The Silence of the Lambs*. 1988. Reprint. New York: St. Martin's Press, 2000.

"Jodie Foster." *Guardian*, Dec. 29, 1999. At https://www.theguardian.com/film/1999/dec/30/1.

King, Stephen. "Hannibal the Cannibal." *New York Times*, June 13, 1999. At http://www.nytimes.com/books/99/06/13/reviews/990613.13kingct.html.

Lanchester, John. "'Slapping the Clammy Flab.'" *London Review of Books*, July 29, 1999. At http://www.lrb.co.uk/v21/n15/john-lanchester/slapping-the-clammy-flab.

Lightfoot, Stephen, and Bryan Fuller. "Mizumono" screenplay, *Hannibal*, episode 2.13. Living Dead Guy Productions, 2015. At http://livingdeadguy.com/wp-content/uploads/2015/04/H213-Mizumono-Web.pdf.

Porteous, Jordan. "How the New Hannibal Lecter Became the Best-Dressed Man on TV." *Esquire*, May 15, 2013. At http://www.esquire.co.uk/culture/film/news/a3899/hannibals-style-mads-mikkelsen/.

7 | The Great Red Dragon

Francis Dolarhyde and Queer Readings of Skin

Evelyn Deshane

Throughout the third season of NBC's series *Hannibal* (2013–15), show creator and producer Bryan Fuller hinted that there would be more queerness in the upcoming story lines. Most fans took his comments to mean that the main fan pairing, "Hannigram," a romantic pairing between Will Graham and Hannibal Lecter, would become officially sanctioned.[1] Although their union certainly warrants further examination and is discussed elsewhere in this volume, this chapter examines how Fuller's adaptation process for the *Red Dragon* story line situates him as both fan of the source material and a member of the LGBTQ community as he attempts to undo the prior negative associations with queer people in Thomas Harris's work. Throughout the latter half of the third season, he situates the characters and their surroundings, especially that of Francis Dolarhyde, in a landscape out of time and place, thereby queering them, as through Jack Halberstam's theorization.

In the book *In a Queer Time and Place: Transgender Bodies, Subcultural Lives*, Jack Halberstam develops what he dubs "queer time" and "queer place"; through his cultural analysis of various

---

1. Bryan Fuller, "I'M THINKING OF THE 10 EPISODES WE HAVE LEFT AND WHAT'S YET TO BE SEEN. #HANNIGRAM IS A THING AND IT'S COMING FOR THE #FANNIBALS!" @BryanFuller, @hoziered, Twitter, June 22, 2015.

popular artifacts, he demonstrates how these two frameworks affect "transgender embodiment."[2] For Halberstam, the concept of "queer" refers to "non-normative logics and organizations of community, sexual identity, embodiment, and activity in space and time," where "queer time" refers to "specific models of temporality that emerge within postmodernism once one leaves the temporal frames of bourgeois reproduction and family, longevity, risk/safety, and inheritance." Similarly, "queer space" becomes connected to "the place-making practices within postmodernism in which queer people engage and it also describes the new understandings of space enabled by the production of queer counterpublics." The queer temporal body, then, is one that exists and is "imagined according to logics that lie outside of those paradigmatic markers of life experience—namely, birth, marriage, reproduction, and death."[3] It is a body that is removed from the social order, made to look different, and, because of these facts, has a different future (or no future at all). All of these facets of place, time, and (re)productivity work together to form a movement in queer theory called "queer futurity," of which Halberstam's book is only one enduring text.[4] I argue here that the third season of NBC's *Hannibal*, especially the episodes following the three-year time jump (3.08 to 3.13), embodies this queer futurity more than any other part of the series[5] and that the character that

---

2. Judith/Jack Halberstam, *In a Queer Time and Place: Transgender Bodies, Subcultural Lives* (New York: New York Univ. Press, 2005), 1. Halberstam has published several books under different names owing to transgender status. I refer to Halberstam using the pronouns *he, his, him* and credit him as Jack Halberstam in the essay, though some of his books were published under the name "Judith Halberstam," as indicated in the bibliography.

3. Halberstam, *In a Queer Time and Place*, 5.

4. See the rest of Halberstam's work published after *In a Queer Time* and consider the works of Elizabeth Freeman, Leo Bersani, Lee Edelman, and Jose Esteban Munoz for more on queer futurity.

5. On this point, see also Aja Romano, "'Hannibal' Is Subverting Everything We Know about Male Relationships," *Daily Dot*, Aug. 27, 2015, at https://www.dailydot.com/parsec/hannibal-series-finale-hannigram-queer-subtext/.

becomes queered in this arrangement most of all is Francis Dolarhyde in his subsequent narrative arc.

These aspects of the physical body, place, and future are inherently linked to Francis Dolarhyde's character in all of his various adaptations. His facial scar makes him take a job where others cannot see his deformity, and he smashes mirrors in his home so he cannot see himself. His large home furthers his alienation from the social order, especially as he lives alone and without any family. Dolarhyde's traumatic memories disrupt his everyday activities, making him simultaneously an older man and a small boy. And because he is a killer, his life trajectory is associated with death and annihilation—not productivity and thriving. In the Harris novel *Red Dragon* (1981) and the two film versions, *Manhunter* (Michael Mann, 1986) and *Red Dragon* (Brett Ratner, 2002), the aura of failure surrounding Dolarhyde gives him a queer reading in negativity[6] and associates his villainous status with his queer sexuality.[7] However, Fuller's adaptation of Dolarhyde in the third season of the NBC show changes the dynamic of Dolarhyde's queerness. By using his position as a fan, show creator, and queer person to sympathetically portray Dolarhyde, Fuller employs in his adaptation what Patricia White dubs "retrospectatorship."[8] By doing both a "page-to-screen" adaptation[9] of the *Red Dragon* story line in some crucial areas and

---

6. On this view, see also Leo Bersani, "Is The Rectum a Grave?" *AIDS: Cultural Analysis/Cultural Activism* 43 (Winter 1987): 197–222.

7. See also Alex Pappadamas, "Q&A: Bryan Fuller on the End (for Now) of 'Hannibal,' the Future of Broadcast TV, and His Plans for Clarice Starling," *Grantland* (blog), Aug. 31, 2015, at http://grantland.com/hollywood-prospectus/qa-bryan-fuller-on-the-end-for-now-of-hannibal-the-future-of-broadcast-tv-and-his-plans-for-clarice-starling/.

8. Patricia White, *Uninvited: Classical Hollywood Cinema and Lesbian Representability* (Indianapolis: Indiana Univ. Press, 1999), 197, cited in Rachel Carroll, "Affecting Fidelity: Adaptation, Fidelity, and Affect in Todd Haynes's *Far from Heaven*," in *Adaptation in Contemporary Culture: Textual Infidelities*, ed. Rachel Carroll (New York: Continuum, 2009), 43.

9. Carroll, "Affecting Fidelity," 36.

completely diverting it in others,[10] Fuller chooses a new reading and new understanding of the queer characters in the Harris universe, thereby healing the prior wounds left by Buffalo Bill, Margot Verger, and other characters. Moreover, through the engagement of Halberstam's concepts of queer temporality, Fuller also manages to effectively queer Dolarhyde's body by presenting him as a potential transgender character. Dolarhyde's feelings of body dysphoria, as expressed through the creation of the Great Red Dragon, are meant to locate him in the current discourse of gender dysphoria and common tropes in transgender storytelling, such as the breaking of mirrors. By the end of the series, Fuller's depiction of Dolarhyde becomes the queerest of all—because even in death Dolarhyde manages to bring Will Graham and Hannibal Lecter together once and for all.

Past Trauma in Adaptation

Thomas Harris has been a contested author in the LGBTQ community for years.[11] In spite of his efforts to produce texts that contain queer characters, he often portrays them as stereotypical, associates their sexuality with previous abuse, or makes them the villain of the story. When the film *The Silence of the Lambs* (Jonathan Demme, 1991) was nominated for an Oscar, protestors gathered outside the red carpet to make their distaste known for Buffalo Bill.[12] Many other cultural theorists—from Marjorie Garber to Jack Halberstam—have written about the negative impact that Buffalo Bill's "gender dysphoria gone horribly awry"[13] has had on the public's perception of gay men, transgender women, and anyone else who is gender nonconforming. Building on this analysis, trans writer Julia Serano also

---

10. See Thomas Harris, *Red Dragon* (New York: Dell, 1981).
11. Pappadamas, "Q&A: Bryan Fuller."
12. Neal Broverman, "Violent Gay Protests at the Oscars: Could It Happen Again?" *The Advocate*, Feb. 27, 2016, at https://www.advocate.com/arts-entertainment/2016/2/27/violent-gay-protests-oscars-could-it-happen-again.
13. Marjorie Garber, *Vested Interests: Cross-Dressing and Cultural Anxiety* (New York: Routledge, 1997), 116.

notes how these conflicting images of gender transition have led to a larger cultural split in the representation of transgender people, trans women in particular; if a trans person appears on-screen, that person is represented as either a deceptive or pathetic character.[14] Over time, Buffalo Bill's cultural legacy has been his fulfillment of both of Serano's transgender tropes. In the 1980s and 1990s, Buffalo Bill was the villainous transgender person who struck fear into society because of the permeability of gender roles, thereby representing the trope of transgender deceptiveness. Since the early 2000s, however, the image of Buffalo Bill standing in front of a mirror with genitals tucked between legs and dancing to "Goodbye Horses" has become a joke, adapted into comedies such as *Family Guy*, thereby casting Bill as a pathetic character. Everyone knows Buffalo Bill's legacy—but that does not mean the legacy is good.

Bryan Fuller understands this. As both a fan of the Harris books and a member of the LGBTQ community, he has witnessed these debates about Buffalo Bill and Thomas Harris,[15] so he has used his position as fan and queer person to become a better adaptor of his source material.

In *The Silence of the Lambs*, Clarice Starling uncovers the storage locker owned by Jame Gumb (Buffalo Bill) and unearths the head of his lover Benjamin Raspail. Upon talking to Lecter, she discovers that Raspail was a former patient of his, which is how Lecter first came into contact with Jame Gumb. Because Fuller's adaptation is a prequel that takes place before Lecter's incarceration, Fuller needed to depict Hannibal's practice and therefore depict Benjamin Raspail and Jame Gumb before the skin suit was ever dreamed up. In the episode "Fromage" (1.08), Fuller takes the elements of Buffalo Bill that were not as politically charged or criticized as the "woman suit"[16]

---

14. Julia Serano, *Whipping Girl: A Transsexual Woman on Sexism and the Scapegoating of Femininity* (Berkeley, CA: Seal Press, 2007), 36–40.

15. Pappadamas, "Q&A: Bryan Fuller."

16. Thomas Harris, *The Silence of the Lambs* (New York: St. Martin's Press, 1988), 360.

and creates Tobias Budge, the cello player who makes his strings from the intestines of his victims and is in a close relationship with Franklyn Froideveux, an easy Benjamin Raspail stand-in. Although Budge can be read as effeminate, he is not portrayed in a stereotypical way, and his story line is over within the same episode.

In the second-season episodes "Shiizakana" (2.09) and "Nakachoko" (2.10), Fuller also attempted another re-creation of the Buffalo Bill lore with Randall Tier, a man who makes an exoskeleton suit to wear when he kills his victims. As I have discussed elsewhere, Randall Tier is the closest the TV audience gets to a Buffalo Bill stand-in for the series.[17] Lecter uses the language of gender diagnosis for Tier (calling the diagnosis "species dysphoria" rather than "gender dysphoria"), and Tier speaks openly about having an "identity disorder" (2.09). Though Tier is a pawn for Lecter to get closer to Graham (as Budge also was), by virtue of Tier's symbolic death—his body becoming literalized into the animal exoskeleton he has always wanted—Tier obtains a symbolic and sympathetic ending, something that Buffalo Bill never received in the book or film. In both of these characters, Budge and Tier, the lingering elements of Buffalo Bill—using human skin and wanting to be something else—are preserved in an attempt to keep the emotional core of the original source text while actively changing the political and cultural connotations of the tools used to express this core. In this way, Fuller manages to skirt around the major issue in adaptation theory—fidelity versus infidelity.[18]

Margot Verger is another character with queer or trans potential. Harris wrote her as a lesbian; in the *Hannibal* (1999) novel, she has a girlfriend named Judy, and the two of them long to have a child. Her sexuality is not treated as a joke but presented as an

---

17. Evelyn Deshane, "Gender/Animal Suits: Adapting Buffalo Bill from *The Silence of the Lambs* to NBC's *Hannibal*," in *Eating the Rude: Hannibal Lecter and the Fannibals, Criminals, and Legacy of America's Favorite Cannibal*, ed. Nicholas Yanes and Kyle Moody (Jefferson, NC: McFarland, forthcoming).

18. Carroll, "Affecting Fidelity," 36–40.

escape from the horrific abuse her brother inflicted upon her. Margot is described as extremely muscular owing to steroids, which have caused her to lose her ability to have children. Harris's depiction of her could have transgender potential, where Margot is starting the first process of gender transition from butch lesbian to transgender man, but because there is no confirmation or any other hint that she would like to transition (even less so than Buffalo Bill, who does apply for surgery and is called "transsexual" by several people in the books and films), Margot's potential trans identity is left aside. Harris's depiction of Margot has instead been interpreted as a fundamental misunderstanding about lesbian identity—that all lesbians really long to be men.[19]

Again, Fuller notices this discrepancy between his source material and the reality of LGBTQ life. Instead of removing the character of Margot entirely, as Ridley Scott does with in his film *Hannibal* (2001), Fuller changes Margot into a femme lesbian. Her brother Mason's brutality remains part of the story (because, like Gumb and Raspail, she was part of Lecter's practice before he was incarcerated, and it was her brother's violence that made her seek treatment), but the violation that becomes her main narrative arc in the second season involves her pregnancy and Mason's eventual removal of her uterus. The operation scene can be interpreted as both a way to explain Margot's later infertility (rather than having steroids/testosterone be the cause, as it is in the novel) and a way to show Mason's violation without having to represent the abuse scenes Harris describes in the original.

I rehash these queer characters and their adaptation processes to demonstrate how flawed some of Harris's depictions are and how Fuller demonstrates himself an adaptor who longs to fix these mistakes while still maintaining the emotional core of the source texts.

---

19. Todd VanDerWerff, "*Hannibal*'s Bryan Fuller on Rebooting Season Two Halfway Through," *AV Club*, Apr. 19, 2014, at https://tv.avclub.com/hannibal-s-bryan-fuller-on-rebooting-season-two-halfway-1798267889.

In the introduction to her edited collection *Adaptation in Contemporary Culture*, Rachel Carroll states that the act of adapting a text signals a "desire to return to an 'original' textual encounter; as such, adaptations are perhaps symptomatic of a culture's compulsion to repeat."[20] Needing to repeat a particular event is a hallmark of Freudian understanding of trauma, and to obtain a catharsis from the event and to heal, the event must be repeated.[21] Carroll's reading of adaptation as potentially healing, then, manages to skirt around the same issues of fidelity and infidelity that numerous adaptation theorists have taken up in the past (and that chapter 4 in this volume documents in fuller detail). Her adaptation theory comes after this intense focus on fidelity and instead invests in "affect[,] feeling, emotion, [and] identification [with a particular audience]."[22] When Fuller adapts, he picks and chooses for a particular audience and for a particular emotional reason—to demonstrate that although he enjoys the source material, he feels it has made mistakes that he seeks to fix. In other words, Fuller actively engages in a "transformative ecology" in his adaptation process, making his work akin to fanfiction, a comparison he has readily endorsed.[23] Fuller is wedded to the idea of *emotional* fidelity (rather than solely to textual fidelity) as a critical tool for adaptation, and he, as a fan of the original, does not want to leave behind certain textual elements. In some ways, I see Fuller's attempts to depict a transgender character as a fannish enthusiasm for something from the original Harris universe that Harris attempted to represent but failed; Fuller's need to repeatedly engage within a "transformative ecology" means that he engages

---

20. Rachel Carroll, "Introduction: Textual Infidelities," in *Adaptation in Contemporary Culture*, ed. Carroll, 1.

21. Much of Hannibal Lecter—in all the versions—also draws on Freudian techniques.

22. Carroll, "Affecting Fidelity," 40.

23. KT Torrey, "Love for the Fannish Archive: Fuller's *Hannibal* as Fanfiction," *Antenna*, Aug. 25, 2015, at http://blog.commarts.wisc.edu/2015/08/25/love-for-the-fannish-archive-fullers-hannibal-as-fanfiction/.

with Harris's source material, but he does so critically and therefore attempts to represent a trans person without engaging with the prior models of the deceptive/pathetic trans person.[24] But because Fuller has changed Buffalo Bill to Tier/Budge and has made Margot a femme lesbian who is a victim of reproductive violence, it means that there are no canon trans or queer characters left to adapt in the NBC version come the third season.

So Francis Dolarhyde becomes the next-best candidate. Dolarhyde is the obvious choice in part owing to his resemblance to Buffalo Bill in plotline and character construction; both hinge their identity on some metaphorical or mythological creature outside their own physical bodies, be it the death's head hawkmoth for Buffalo Bill or William Blake's red dragon for Dolarhyde. Because of these mythic associations, both characters are depicted as having queer skin in some manner or another: Buffalo Bill has a literal skin suit that he wears to become a woman, and Dolarhyde has a scarred cleft palate that makes him smash mirrors and long for escape in the body of a dragon. Even the name "Dolarhyde" emphasizes the eventual role that the literal hide will play for Buffalo Bill in the subsequent book. The physical way in which Dolarhyde eats pages of the William Blake book can also be seen in tandem with Jame Gumb's skin suit. Where Dolarhyde internalizes, Bill externalizes. Even when Dolarhyde relies on external accoutrements for his identity, tattoos and dentures, they are still very internal items; he must put the dentures inside his mouth for them to work, and the tattoo ink requires that needles puncture his skin. Both characters have different methods of transformation, but they ultimately have the same goal: to become someone—or something—else altogether.

Similarly, Dolarhyde's obsession with fitness and the tautness of his body (which is described in detail in the novel, through both Harris's narration and Reba McClane's reactions) can be read as a

---

24. Torrey, "Love for the Fannish Archive."

precursor to how Harris would portray Margot. The family trauma that permeates both Dolarhyde's and Margot's internal struggles also acts as the catalyst for physical transformation: both get stronger as a way to protect themselves from their abusers, and both subsequently find relief from their too-hard status in forming romantic relationships. After having adapted Margot in the second season and versions of Buffalo Bill in the first and second, Fuller has the perfect opportunity in the third season to develop Dolarhyde as a transgender character. Fuller does not evoke transgender identity outright—most likely not to evoke the "deceptive" transgender villain narrative. He instead returns to the original source material of *Red Dragon* and keeps the emotional core intact. He completes what Patricia White would call a "retrospectatorship" of his initial viewing experience through his adaptation process.

According to White, retrospectatorship is a viewing of an experience that "is transformed by unconscious and conscious past viewing experience" and utilizes the viewer's "subjective fantasy" of that experience to re-create the event.[25] In other words, retrospectatorship is watching a movie once but then thinking it is a different type of film when watching it again. White uses this term to analyze and validate queer readings of certain films, and it is these potential queer readings of characters who are not necessarily queer that I look at in particular here. Like Rachel Carroll, I believe that retrospectatorship "offers a valuable framework within which to conceptualize repetition, as a mode of cultural experience, and its relation to memory and affect,"[26] and I assert its use in understanding how Fuller adapts Francis Dolarhyde as a transgender man without actually acknowledging he has done so. He does this, first and foremost, by moving the latter half of the third season into Jack Halberstam's "queer time."[27]

---

25. White, *Uninvited*, 197.
26. Carroll, "Affecting Fidelity," 43.
27. Halberstam, *In a Queer Time and Place*, 1.

"In a Queer Time and Place"

At the start of episode 8 of season 3 in *Hannibal*, there is a time jump of several years. Hannibal Lecter is incarcerated; Will Graham is free and now in a relationship with Molly Foster; Margot and Alana have had their son; and Mason has now partnered with Cordell Doemling. The timeline jump brings the NBC series forward to match the timeline of the original books. Although some scenes from the later books have been moved up in the timeline—such as the standoff between Margot and her brother, along with Alana's (Judy's) pregnancy—this is the first time that the TV series embarks on well-established film territory.[28]

The third season is the third time the character of Francis Dolarhyde has been adapted for film or television, following the loosely based film *Manhunter* (1986) and the far more faithful "page-to-screen" adaptation[29] *Red Dragon* in 2002. Fuller's NBC series exists as a prequel, and the show takes place in the current day, thus moving the initial events in the novels (which take place in the 1980s) into 2013 and beyond. The adapted setting changes the characters and their reactions to events as well as the technology surrounding them. This alteration can be seen most clearly in the science team, the research Graham does for his lectures, and Freddie Lounds's reporting. Even the film *Red Dragon*, released in 2002, preserves the original novel's setting in the 1980s, including Graham's use of microfiche or the reliance on fingerprints and blood types in forensic science. Because Fuller has already adapted Harris's universe for the

---

28. Some of this moving around was done because of copyright issues. Because Fuller could not obtain the rights for Clarice and parts of *The Silence of The Lambs* but did have the rights to *Hannibal* and *Hannibal Rising*, he leaned on the events in the latter two books more in the adaptation process. Because *Hannibal Rising* is a prequel and doesn't disrupt the timeline of Hannibal's life as depicted in the series source material, and because the other changes in the timeline have more to do with copyright than with preference, I have for the most part excluded them from this analysis on queer time.

29. Carroll, "Affecting Fidelity," 36.

modern world, what the audience sees in the third season should look like the future—but that is not what happens at all.

The technology surrounding crime solving remains constant in the series (though in the third season it is de-emphasized considerably in comparison to its use in the earlier seasons), but everything surrounding Francis Dolarhyde seems to have gone back in time. In the novel *Red Dragon*, Dolarhyde finds the two families he murders through his job developing film—a detail Fuller retains in the NBC series; indeed, as Ellie Lewerenz notes in chapter 4 of this volume, the Dolarhyde story line is the one story line in almost all of the *Hannibal* TV series that remains an exact adaptation, exuding fidelity to its source material. Yet, according to a list compiled in 2012, there are only three photo labs in Maryland (where *Hannibal* is largely set) that still develop film, and it is likely that the number has gone down since then.[30] The dependency on film and photo developing should have been adapted to fit the updated setting, but the plotline around Dolarhyde's work, his fascination with infrared, and his scrapbooking remains the same as in the novels and the previous films.[31]

Furthermore, Freddie Lounds also seems to step backward in time. Before this point in the series, her reporting has always been via a blog, and she has always had an up-to-date phone in her hand. In the third season, however, her *TattleCrime* reporting has been relegated to print form, as seen in ". . . And the Woman Clothed with the Sun" (3.09) and "And the Woman Clothed in Sun" (3.10). In the original novel and film *Red Dragon*, Freddy Lounds is a plot device to make Dolarhyde engage with Will Graham via the newspaper.

---

30. "List of Photographic Labs in the US as of 2012," I Still Shoot Film, 2012, at http://istillshootfilm.org/post/24888047611/list-of-photographic-labs-in-the-us-as-of-2012.

31. One noted difference could be that in the NBC version Dolarhyde seems to display the ability to hack into phones when he talks to Hannibal, therefore rooting the scene in a more modern aesthetic. But this ability is not explained or developed in any way, so I treat this scene as an anomaly that affirms the fact that most of what Dolarhyde does in relation to technology is notably dated.

This plotline is repeated in the series almost exactly as it appears in both movies, right down to the printed forms of media. Dolarhyde's need to have a print copy of the paper can be attributed to his tactile personality and need to seek origination, so it makes sense that Fuller would still keep him in isolation and compiling scrapbooks—even in the age of Pinterest and Instagram—but it makes no sense for Lounds, who has already been accepted as a quick-fire blogger, to change to print media. The TV series (and Fuller) vaguely implies that owing to the time jump, her fame has allowed her to profit more, so perhaps this means a (re)turn to print media, but this change still does not hold the same type of allure or aesthetic value as the previous seasons. As a whole, the latter half of the third season seems to go backward.

Which seems to be precisely the point. Fuller has already demonstrated that he knows and understands these characters, so I must view the choice seemingly to go backward—while also going forward in time—as something fundamental to the plotline around Dolarhyde's character. Although it would be easy to simply say Fuller wanted to honor or maintain fidelity to the source material, examining this adaptation solely on its faithfulness to textual source—as Lewerenz also notes in chapter 4—means missing the queerness inserted into the act of the adaptation process. Whereas Lewerenz places this queerness onto the Will/Hannibal relationship (something I examine briefly later), I see Fuller's act of faithfulness to the *Red Dragon* story line in spite of showing other technological advances as queer in itself. Not only does it not really make much sense (as in *queer* in the original sense, meaning "strange" or "odd"), but the third season's construction of a time and place that follows Dolarhyde around like a second skin means that he has become queered according to Halberstam's logic.[32] This third adaption of Francis Dolarhyde and his story is faithful to the original, yet it queers the internal story logic at its core, thus retaining both textual and

---

32. Halberstam, *In a Queer Time and Place*, 1.

emotional fidelity to its source and ameliorating critics on both sides of the fidelity/infidelity divide in adaptation studies. It is faithful, yet it means something very different.

Dragon Hyde/Transgender Skin

Soon after Dolarhyde appears on screen, the audience knows he lives alone and is troubled by past abuse. Shrouding his world with the ephemera of the past—photo development, newspapers, and Mahjong tablets (rather than the online app-game version) locates him in a time-locked reality, which queers him. Queer time and places can be created by "disconnect[ing] queerness from an essential definition of homosexual embodiment" and instead focusing on a new way of understanding "non-normative behaviors."[33] Though Dolarhyde can and has been read as a gay character (especially with his designation as the "Tooth Fairy"), he can also be read as transgender through these same means of queering his time, space, and "non-normative behaviors" in those spaces.[34] Because Dolarhyde's memories do not allow him to develop beyond the small boy he views himself as, he transfers his energy into becoming the Great Red Dragon, which expresses a form of body dysphoria—of being uncomfortable in his own skin.

The terms *body dysmorphia* and *gender dysphoria* share similar Greek lexical roots and are often mistaken for one another, especially in eating-disorder treatment centers.[35] The image the West has of an anorexic patient viewing herself as fat in a mirror when she is really thin has become a trope to represent eating disorders; in the third season of *Hannibal*, it is also used to express Dolarhyde's dual identity. These symbolic elements—the mirror, bodily distrust, and a highly developed alter identity—also show up in transgender people, too, especially transgender men with eating disorders, who often diet

---

33. Halberstam, *In a Queer Time and Place*, 6.
34. Halberstam, *In a Queer Time and Place*, 6.
35. Evelyn Deshane, "The Other Side of the Mirror: Eating Disorder Treatment and Gender Identity," *Trans Rights: The Time Is Now* 6 (2015–16): 93–94.

or exercise excessively in order to shed unwanted femininity.[36] These "non-normative behaviors" have come to signal trans masculinity for certain audiences in the LGBTQ community, especially because depictions of transgender men in other media are so few and far between.

Julia Serano documents this disparity of representation as part of the effect of transmisogyny in culture; because feminine expression is what fuels sexism and misogyny, when transgender men transition into the dominant discourse and pass, they receive little friction and can easily live stealthily, so they aren't represented as often.[37] To make transgender men visible on the screen, then, the filmmaker must rely on the "transgender gaze" or "transgender look," wherein the audience—along with the transgender character—is "capable of seeing through the present to a future elsewhere."[38] In the third season of *Hannibal*, ephemera are used to demonstrate Dolarhyde's dysphoria—such as his tactile obsession with William Blake's painting of the red dragon and the smashing of mirrors—but it is in his embodiment of the Great Red Dragon through his voice and his imaginative moments rendered on the screen that we see the "transgender look" Halberstam describes. Dolarhyde longs to transform, and, thanks to Fuller, we get a glimpse into a "future elsewhere" in those moments when he grows a dragon tail. The fact that Dolarhyde holds up a dragon, not a cisgender man, as his ultimate identity does not disrupt the "transgender look" at all; in fact, it makes that look stronger.

The focus on a mythical creature cements Dolarhyde's trans connection not only to Buffalo Bill but also to the larger cultural narrative surrounding gender transition that consistently relies on the metaphor of the butterfly, phoenix, and other mythological creatures to express metamorphosis. As Casey Plett documents, gender transition is closely linked to mythology in our culture as a way to

---

36. Deshane, "Other Side of the Mirror," 93–94.
37. Serano, *Whipping Girl*, 70.
38. Halberstam, *In a Queer Time and Place*, 76–77.

give such transition "synchronicity and broad appeal."[39] The fact that Dolarhyde longs to change into a dragon rather than a man makes no difference to the trans reading of his body because trans people are often symbolically linked to myths (so much so that many of them internalize this narrative), and transgender men are often invisible from trans narratives after they transition. Furthermore, as Dolarhyde's relationship to Reba McClane develops in the third season of *Hannibal*, his relationship to his mirrored image becomes monstrous—which is, yet again, another association with transgender narratives.[40] The mythic and the monstrous work in the same way the pathetic/deceptive tropes work: as binaries that feed off one another in cissexist media. In this version of Dolarhyde's story line, however, Reba becomes a force that heals the monstrous associations with queerness.

Reba, like Dolarhyde, can be interpreted as having a Halberstam-like queer aura around her. Because she's blind, her body will never be treated with the same type of neoliberal "productive" narrative that Halberstam associates with his idea of "straight time."[41] Similarly, because Reba is in touch with her sexuality and takes on the dominant position in bed, she becomes even more in line with Dolarhyde's queer time. Fuller's adaptation reproduces their relationship with virtually all of the same milestones (waiting at the bus, the tiger, meeting her in the darkroom), but when Dolarhyde is viewed as a transgender man, their exchange in her kitchen in ". . . And the Woman Clothed with the Sun" takes on new meaning. Dolarhyde is initially excited by Reba because she cannot see his bodily queerness, a rarity for him. She does need to rely on listening, however, and in their meeting he does not speak much out of fear she will not accept him. Though he speaks only a few words to her, she effectively

---

39. Casey Plett, "The Rise of the Gender Novel," *The Walrus*, Mar. 18, 2015, at https://thewalrus.ca/rise-of-the-gender-novel/.

40. Joelle Ruby Ryan, "Reel Gender: Examining the Politics of Trans Images in Media and Film," PhD diss., Bowling Green State Univ., 2009, 180.

41. Halberstam, *In a Queer Time and Place*, 1–2.

"outs" him by commenting on his voice. She says in this episode, "I understand you because you speak very well and because I listen." Reba's comment, though small, manages to transform the transgender gaze into a kind of "transgender voice"[42] by which she is able to glimpse Dolarhyde's "future elsewhere." She knows everything about him—inside and out—and, more importantly, she doesn't seem to care. Though Dolarhyde initially leaves, it is after this moment that he begins to trust her. Simultaneously, it is also when Reba starts to break down all of his violent behaviors. By accepting his identity—his literal voice—she accepts who he is and manages to redeem him from his internalized cisgender gaze that depicts trans people as monster or myth, joke or villain, pathetic or deceptive. He can be human to her, something that he has never been in all the story lines in which his character has appeared and that becomes especially healing given Fuller's queer twist.

The main point of divergence in Fuller's adaptation of the *Red Dragon* story line occurs after Reba is no longer part of the story. Instead of having Will Graham see her in the hospital and then return to Molly and her son, where they will face off with Dolarhyde as a family unit (with Molly or the police prevailing in other depictions), Dolarhyde attacks Will Graham after Hannibal Lecter has escaped from custody in "The Wrath of the Lamb" (3.13). It is here that the queerness Fuller promised comes to fruition in the final "Hannigram" ending of the season.[43] Whereas the killing of Dolarhyde by Molly or the police or both in other versions of *Red Dragon* can be seen as a reestablishment of the neoliberal reproductive model of a successful family through the annihilation of the queer character, Fuller's version uses the death of a queer/trans character to facilitate the eventual union of two men. Through the act of hunting

---

42. Transgender people, both trans men and women, often have a difficult time with voice because the voice also acts as a way they are often "outed" on the phone or in person. Many trans women take voice lessons to lower their pitch, and many trans men rely on testosterone to finally deepen their voices.

43. Fuller, "I'M THINKING OF THE 10 EPISODES WE HAVE LEFT."

and killing Dolarhyde together, Hannibal Lecter and Will Graham understand one another on an intimate level, which Graham has been resisting since the beginning. In all of the previous versions of Graham's story line, he has been afraid of becoming just like Hannibal Lecter or the Red Dragon (including the facial scars that he must deal with at the end of the novel version), but in Fuller and NBC's version of events Graham's final line affirms the queer time and place where the NBC series has ended up: "It's beautiful."

Conclusion

Shortly before the last episodes in the third season were aired, NBC cancelled *Hannibal*. But I don't think that means failure—at least, not in the typical sense. As Jack Halberstam has written, failure is a type of queer art and embodiment that can attach itself to different objects, time periods, and people, thus changing the way we view what "success" really is.[44]

Throughout this chapter, I have argued that *Hannibal* showrunner Bryan Fuller has used his devotion to the original work as a fan and his role in the LGBTQ community to return to the original source material with both a critical eye turned toward the original author and an understanding of the need to preserve the same emotional core of the text. By evoking similar connections between the transgender or gender-nonconforming characters Margot Verger and Buffalo Bill as well as the cultural lexicon associated with transgender people, Fuller directs an alternative transgender reading of Francis Dolarhyde. By repeatedly trying to adapt the image of the trans person in Harris's universe, he manages to make the art of adaptation into something healing.

Excessive exercise to shed femininity, the different mirrored version of the self (even if it is a mythic version), and Fuller's previous awareness of the psychiatric language for "identity disorders"

---

44. See, for example, Judith Halberstam, *The Queer Art of Failure* (Durham, NC: Duke Univ. Press, 2011), 1–3.

(2.09)—all make me read Francis Dolarhyde as a transgender man. As the audience, however, we never get a confirmation—or denial—that Dolarhyde is transgender in any way. All we have is the past knowledge of Fuller's adaptation practices, the common narrative expression of trans identity, and a queer time and place in the series. In many ways, Patricia White's concept of retrospectatorship says that's enough.

Francis Dolarhyde does die at the end of NBC's *Hannibal*, as he does in every prior adaptation of Harris's novel *Red Dragon*. But by virtue of making his portrayal with Reba sympathetic and recasting the third season as part of Halberstam's notion of queer time, the series does not give Dolarhyde's death the same negative connotation. A queer character dies, but he is seen as human moments before he dies, in spite of his violent crimes, and he dies so that another queer relationship can begin between Will Graham and Hannibal Lecter. Though the two of them also die (perhaps) as they fall off the cliff, Fuller has his other queer family—Alana, Margot, and their son—survive, something that rarely happens to lesbian couples in prime-time television.[45]

In many ways, queerness in NBC's *Hannibal* means telling the typical story differently. Through an adaptation process devoted to retrospectatorship and an embracing of this overall queer art of failure, Bryan Fuller has managed to heal Thomas Harris's past mistakes and to give the LGBTQ audience something to connect with and, maybe sometime in the future, something else to look forward to.

Bibliography

Bersani, Leo. "Is the Rectum a Grave?" *AIDS: Cultural Analysis/Cultural Activism* 43 (Winter 1987): 197–222.

---

45. Heather Hogan, "Boobs on Your Tube: Every Queer Storyline of 2015, Ranked," *Autostraddle*, Dec. 31, 2015, at https://www.autostraddle.com/every-queer-tv-storyline-of-2015-ranked-322394/.

Broverman, Neal. "Violent Gay Protests at the Oscars: Could It Happen Again?" *The Advocate*, Feb. 27, 2016. At https://www.advocate.com/arts-entertainment/2016/2/27/violent-gay-protests-oscars-could-it-happen-again.

Carroll, Rachel. "Affecting Fidelity: Adaptation, Fidelity, and Affect in Todd Haynes's *Far from Heaven*." In *Adaptation in Contemporary Culture: Textual Infidelities*, edited by Rachel Carroll, 34–45. New York: Continuum, 2009.

———. "Introduction: Textual Infidelities." In *Adaptation in Contemporary Culture: Textual Infidelities*, edited by Rachel Carroll, 1–9. New York: Continuum, 2009.

Deshane, Evelyn. "Gender/Animal Suits: Adapting Buffalo Bill from *The Silence of the Lambs* to NBC's *Hannibal*." In *Eating the Rude: Hannibal Lecter and the Fannibals, Criminals, and Legacy of America's Favorite Cannibal*, edited by Nicholas Yanes and Kyle Moody. Jefferson, NC: McFarland, forthcoming.

———. "The Other Side of the Mirror: Eating Disorder Treatment and Gender Identity." *Trans Rights: The Time Is Now* 6 (2015–16): 89–101.

Fuller, Bryan. "I'M THINKING OF THE 10 EPISODES WE HAVE LEFT AND WHAT'S YET TO BE SEEN. #HANNIGRAM IS A THING AND IT'S COMING FOR THE #FANNIBALS!" @BryanFuller, @hoziered, Twitter, June 22, 2015.

Garber, Marjorie. *Vested Interests: Cross-Dressing and Cultural Anxiety*. New York: Routledge, 1997.

Halberstam, Jack/Judith. *In a Queer Time and Place: Transgender Bodies, Subcultural Lives*. New York: New York Univ. Press, 2005.

———. *The Queer Art of Failure*. Durham, NC: Duke Univ. Press, 2011.

Harris, Thomas. *Red Dragon*. New York: Dell, 1981.

———. *The Silence of the Lambs*. New York: St. Martin's Press, 1988.

Hogan, Heather. "Boobs on Your Tube: Every Queer Storyline of 2015, Ranked." *Autostraddle*, Dec. 31, 2015. At https://www.autostraddle.com/every-queer-tv-storyline-of-2015-ranked-322394/?all=1.

"List of Photographic Labs in the US as of 2012." I Still Shoot Film (website), 2012. At http://istillshootfilm.org/post/24888047611/list-of-photographic-labs-in-the-us-as-of-2012.

Pappadamas, Alex. "Q&A: Bryan Fuller on the End (for Now) of 'Hannibal,' the Future of Broadcast TV, and His Plans for Clarice Starling."

Grantland (blog), Aug. 31, 2015. At http://grantland.com/hollywood-prospectus/qa-bryan-fuller-on-the-end-for-now-of-hannibal-the-future-of-broadcast-tv-and-his-plans-for-clarice-starling/.

Plett, Casey. "The Rise of the Gender Novel." *The Walrus*, Mar. 18, 2015. At https://thewalrus.ca/rise-of-the-gender-novel/.

Romano, Aja. "'Hannibal' Is Subverting Everything We Know about Male Relationships." *Daily Dot*, Aug. 27, 2015. At https://www.dailydot.com/parsec/hannibal-series-finale-hannigram-queer-subtext/.

Ryan, Joelle Ruby. "Reel Gender: Examining the Politics of Trans Images in Film and Media." PhD diss., Bowling Green State Univ., 2008.

Serano, Julia. *Whipping Girl: A Transsexual Woman on Sexism and the Scapegoating of Femininity*. Berkeley, CA: Seal Press, 2007.

Torrey, KT. "Love for the Fannish Archive: Fuller's *Hannibal* as Fanfiction." *Antenna*, Aug. 25, 2015. At http://blog.commarts.wisc.edu/2015/08/25/love-for-the-fannish-archive-fullers-hannibal-as-fanfiction/.

VanDerWerff, Todd. "*Hannibal*'s Bryan Fuller on Rebooting Season Two Halfway Through." *AV Club*, Apr. 19, 2014. At https://tv.avclub.com/hannibal-s-bryan-fuller-on-rebooting-season-two-halfway-1798267889.

White, Patricia. *Uninvited: Classical Hollywood Cinema and Lesbian Representability*. Indianapolis: Indiana Univ. Press, 1999.

8 | Hannibal and the Cannibal

Tracking Colonial Imaginaries

Samira Nadkarni and Rukmini Pande

The success of the NBC series *Hannibal* (2013–15) has been theorized in various ways. Commentators have pointed to its use of aestheticized excess, its portrayal of sympathetic villainy, and its use of homosocial and homoerotic tension to engage audiences. In addition, scholars who are interested in the fandom around *Hannibal* have concentrated their analysis on its operationalization of "universal" tropes for horror, monstrosity, and cannibalism.[1] But such analysis has largely elided the fact that these tropes are deeply racialized.

What has not been registered is an acknowledgment of the fact that Hannibal Lecter's (Mads Mikkelsen) whiteness is at the heart of the narrative's ability to aestheticize the aforementioned taboos. Although there has not been a huge amount of scholarly work on the show so far, even in the popular-culture blogosphere, most discussion of race in *Hannibal* has revolved around the position and role of

---

1. Angela Ndalianis, "*Hannibal*: A Disturbing Feast for the Senses," *Journal of Visual Culture* 14, no. 3 (2015): 279–84; Lori Morimoto, "Outrageous Sirk-Umstances: Hannibal and the Aesthetics of Excess," paper presented at "Feasting on Hannibal: An Interdisciplinary Conference," Univ. of Melbourne, Nov. 29–30, 2016, at https://doi.org/10.17613/M6FM24; Jeff Casey, "Queer Cannibals and Deviant Detectives: Subversion and Homosocial Desire in NBC's *Hannibal*," *Quarterly Review of Film and Video* 32, no. 6 (2015): 550–67.

tertiary nonwhite characters within the narrative—such as Beverly Katz (Hettienne Park) and Jack Crawford (Laurence Fishburne)—instead of considering the whiteness that is necessary for the show's entire conceit and, further, for the fandom to function in the first place. This is quite a foundational misstep caused by what can be termed "theoretical whitewashing"—that is, scholarly disciplines' impulse to register the operations of race and racism only when there is a controversy that is *specifically* racial in character. That is to say, because of their status as minorities within Western media texts, nonwhite identities are seen to interrupt normative operations of such structures only in specific contexts when they *make themselves visible*. In this construction, race is viewed as a relevant factor only for theorizations about Western media texts when the issue under discussion specifically relates to a nonwhite character. Because whiteness is not considered a racialized identity with specific effects, its operations on interpretive structures can be presented as normative.

To interrupt this mode of theorization, this chapter therefore argues that *Hannibal*'s subversiveness fundamentally depends on the ways in which white crime and white evil are considered worthy of exploration and nuance in a way that is simply not available for nonwhite characters who might seek to inhabit similar archetypes. To put it bluntly, black and brown cannibalism cannot be aestheticized tropes to be explored in exquisitely detailed cinematography because it has already been operationalized against entire populations, wherein they are rendered *monstrous* to achieve significantly different ends—namely, imperialism and conquest.[2] That is,

---

2. Jeff Berglund, "Write, Right, White, Rite: Literacy, Imperialism, Race, and Cannibalism in Edgar Rice Burroughs' *Tarzan of the Apes*," *Studies in American Fiction* 27, no. 1 (1999): 53–76; Heather E. Martel, "Hans Staden's Captive Soul: Identity, Imperialism, and Rumors of Cannibalism in Sixteenth-Century Brazil," *Journal of World History* 17, no. 1 (2006): 51–69; Patrick Brantlinger, *Taming Cannibals: Race and the Victorians* (Ithaca, NY: Cornell Univ. Press, 2011); Jack D. Forbes, *Columbus and Other Cannibals: The Wetiko Disease of Exploitation, Imperialism, and Terrorism* (New York: Seven Stories Press, 2011).

although fetishization of nonwhite bodies performing cannibalism informs a significant history of colonial writing, it is rarely presented as intimate, seductive, or desirably powerful within the space of popular consciousness that *Hannibal* occupies. This is not to say that these tropes and their attractiveness are not still a worthy object of study, but to allow their whiteness to operate without being named as such allows race to be considered as merely an additional and incidental layer to any analysis rather than as a factor at the very core of such analysis. This chapter therefore sketches out the roots of the cannibal mythos and its links to colonialism before moving on to a close reading of *Hannibal* to demonstrate how these threads continue to inform cannibalism's contemporary articulations. Further, it also argues that the transition from cannibal as savage to cannibal as aesthete is one that is deeply rooted in the intertwined operations of whiteness and capitalism.

Cannibalism and the Colonial Project

It is critical to explicitly link *Hannibal* as a modern text to the etymology of the term *cannibal* precisely because it may be argued that Bryan Fuller mobilizes cannibalism's significatory tropes in ostensibly subversive ways. As sketched out earlier, the show purposely distances itself from the prototypical cannibal figure conjured up by the first breathless dispatches of various colonizing explorers in the New World. However, as this chapter argues, it is able to do so only because those originary tropes *cannot* be framed in aesthetically lavish excess for the titillation of its fan audiences. The metamorphosis of the primal scene of cannibalism from the apex of savagery and uncontrolled appetite to the finely crafted (and mouthwatering) presentation of haute cuisine by food stylists and master chefs for the show is therefore not a subversive choice because it links those tropes back to whiteness very explicitly. This is not to suggest that cannibalism itself lies outside of constructions of whiteness, but that its presentation within fields of popular culture is inevitably linked to morality and constructions of "the civilized." Therefore, when narratives of cannibalism and whiteness are expressed—for example, the cannibalism of Scotland's infamous Sawney Bean family in the sixteenth century or the cannibalism occurring among the survivors of the International Polar Expedition (1881–84)—they are created as outliers in a return to primal survival instincts or greed rather than as a symbol of their community and its cultural norms. In this manner, although both whiteness and nonwhiteness, when linked to cannibalism, are created as part of a colonial project where cultural values are expressed and connoted, the outcome is distinct in terms of cannibalism's use as aberration for white morality and culturally significant for nonwhite communities.

At this point, it is therefore necessary to contextualize the original primal scene of cannibalism in its historical specificity. As successive scholars have pointed out, the origin point of the term *cannibal* is a colonial encounter. On November 4, 1493, Dr. Diego Alvarez Chanca, a companion of Columbus on his second voyage to the Caribbean, wrote the earliest modern account of cannibalism in the Americas. Peter Hulme calls this description "one of the primal scenes of Early America: indigenous savagery observed and reported on by a European eyewitness, with Chanca's status as a medical doctor equipping him with the kind of knowledge and approach which supposedly mark him as an appropriate forerunner of the objective historian."[3] Dr. Chanca's (highly suspect) description was then further embellished by an influential scholar, Peter Martyr, who transformed it into an even more horrifying and exotic spectacle, complete with "pieces of human flesh broached on a spit ready for roasting."[4] This primal scene was reproduced innumerable times by various authors—often in the guise of "histories"—to establish the practice of cannibalism as fact and therefore to establish the

---

3. Peter Hulme, "Introduction: The Cannibal Scene," in *Cannibalism and the Colonial World*, ed. Frances Barker, Peter Hulme, and Margaret Iverson (Cambridge: Cambridge Univ. Press, 1998), 17.

4. Peter Martyr, *De Orbe Novo: The Eight Decades of Peter Martyr D'Anghiera*, trans. Francis Augustus MacNutt (New York: Library Reprints, 1912), quoted in Hulme, "Introduction," 18.

justification for the colonial project more generally. Although the cannibal figure first appeared in the context of the Caribbean, it was also associated with Cuba and significant parts of South America, including Brazil. The mythos was also popular with regard to the islands of the Pacific, including Fiji and New Zealand, as a veritable industry sprang up around the monetization of traveler's yarns (ostensibly nonfiction), postcards, exhibits of "freakish" human specimens, and missionary narratives.

As Gananath Obeysekere also observes in the context of the mobilization of the tropes mentioned earlier in Fiji, almost all of these accounts were fabricated in response to the fevered European demand for stories about savage cannibalism.[5] The primal scene, which initially revolved around the aftermath of the feast, then also expanded to include it. These episodes were always described in lurid detail with great focus on the disgusting savagery of spectacle. Not only did the natives of the European imagination exhibit their bestial nature by the act of cannibalism itself, but they were also proven to have no sense of etiquette in the act of consumption. This trope can also be seen in a passage from Jules Verne's novel *Among the Cannibals* (1876), wherein the Maori people of New Zealand are described in the following words: "Of the two hundred Maoris present at the sacrifice, each had a share of the human flesh; they disputed and fought over the least scrap, and drops of hot blood bespattered these horrible creatures."[6] This is an important aspect to consider when looking at the way *Hannibal* frames its primal scenes of cannibalism as well as at Hannibal's own motivations as something absolutely removed from this imagery of grasping greed.

Tracey Banivanua-Mar points out that it is certainly true that the act of anthropophagy (the eating of human flesh) features in diverse mythologies, including those of Greek and Roman origin. However,

---

5. Gananath Obeyesekere, "Cannibal Feasts in Nineteenth-Century Fiji: Seamen's Yarns and the Ethnographic Imagination," in *Cannibalism and the Colonial World*, ed. Barker, Hulme, and Iverson, 39–62.

6. Jules Verne, *Among the Cannibals* (London: Ward Lock, 1876), 105.

it is also vital to note the distinctiveness of the cannibal figure as *created* in colonial discourse. This discourse mobilized primarily a "brand of otherness or man-eating that was deeply entwined with and historically defined by colonial expansion. Discoveries of it signaled and shaped forthcoming conquest in spatial and later racial ways, which converged with the harder sophistry of colonialism's legal and moral footwork."[7] Hulme also underlines the importance of keeping this connection at the forefront of any analysis of the cannibal figure in modern contexts, maintaining that "cannibalism needs to be understood as a topic within the dialogue between Europe and its others, and therefore within the context of the colonial world."[8]

This dialogue has functioned in multiple ways. First, as outlined earlier, it offered an extremely convenient discursive function for the shaping of Europe's colonizing project in the Americas and the Pacific region. Banivanua-Mar further notes that in the case of Fiji this discursive regime in essence "racially profiled the Pacific effectively as the 'knitted-together strength' of any Orientalism. It marked the islands like surveyors' pegs as available for exploitation while also implying the paradigms of colonialism's moral commerce." Moreover, this framing, she argues, is not just something that can be consigned safely to the realm of historical record: "In a contemporary context where Cannibalism [sic] still has currency, it may yet alert us to the lingering dynamics of relations of power derived from a colonial era."[9] Second, this discursive scripting is also tied intimately to the production of the notion of modernity in Europe. As Hulme points out, when Montaigne wrote his famous essay *Des cannibales* in 1580, he engaged with an interpretive framework that was crucial not just for the development of colonialism but also for the intertwined project of capitalist modernity as well. Hulme observes that

7. Tracey Banivanua-Mar, "Cannibalism and Colonialism: Charting Colonies and Frontiers in Nineteenth-Century Fiji," *Comparative Studies in Society and History* 52, no. 2 (2010): 260.

8. Hulme, "Introduction," 5.

9. Banivanua-Mar, "Cannibalism and Colonialism," 259.

"the modern Cartesian subject of that capitalist modernity depends for its sense of self as independent entity on an image of a clearly differentiated 'other' who destroys boundaries [. . .] [and so] modernity enters the world's stage attached to its cannibal shadow."[10]

And, finally, it is also crucial to consider the effects of this discursive shaping on colonized cultures beyond the "othering" imposed on them. This thread of cannibalism as resistance therefore operates not by displacing the cannibal into and onto whiteness, as *Hannibal* does, but by examining the ways in which these postcolonial cultures have engaged with this overarching mythos in local contexts. Taking up the example of Cuba, Santiago Colás observes that artists and writers engaged with the European image of the cannibal in a fundamentally dialectical fashion:

> Confronting the European image of an aggressive, barbarous native, these writers saw not a threat but rather a word that summed up an equally long history of New World resistance to violent imposition of European norms upon the region. Where Europeans saw a savage threat, these writers recognized European fear and vulnerability. They found in cannibalism the limits to Europe's capacity to contain, assimilate, or indeed, destroy the resistant societies of the region.[11]

This mobilization of cannibalism as disruptive of European modes of cultural assimilation establishes its racialized otherness as foundational to that challenge. Traces of such resistance are also found at other points of colonial violence. In a Canadian context, Marlene Goldman has noted that the figure of the Wendigo (for the Native tribes of the Woodland Cree and the Ojibway) changed from an evil god to a creature with specifically cannibalistic features only

---

10. Hulme, "Introduction," 5–6.
11. Santiago Colás, "From Caliban to Cronus: A Critique of Cannibalism as Metaphor for Cuban Revolutionary Culture," in *Eating Their Words: Cannibalism and the Boundaries of Cultural Identity*, ed. Kristen Guest (New York: State Univ. of New York Press, 2001), 130.

after contact with European colonizers. So instead of as an example of a "fanciful product of an exotic culture," the Wendigo must be "read as [an aspect of] disaster narratives that register the impact of imperialism and colonization."[12] *Hannibal*'s repeated evocation of the Wendigo figure therefore not only functions within the show's contexts of Will and Hannibal's transgressions and Will's descent into madness but also situates Will's body as a site of colonization and resistance, culminating in the figure of what showrunner Bryan Fuller terms the "Willdigo."[13] In effect, the series deliberately evokes these narratives of colonial histories but uses them to frame white masculinity as central to its concerns.

As a result, the theories of consumption that underlie *Hannibal* present themselves on a nexus of multiple axes wherein food as a site of identity and culture intersects with cultural traditions of hospitality and power, racial and colonial histories, and cultural myths and narratives. Far from being a passive process, this intersection becomes a site of active change that functions as its own political and cultural agenda. As Michael Dietler argues,

> Progress in understanding the colonial experience and its unfolding consequences in the specific contexts examined here depends on recognizing that intercultural consumption of objects or practices, the process that instigated the initial entanglement of the colonial encounter, is not a phenomenon that takes place at the level of cultures, social formations, or other abstract structures. Nor is it a process of passive diffusion. It is an active process of creative appropriation, transformation, and manipulation played out by individuals and social groups with a variety of competing interests and strategies of action embedded in local political relations and cultural perceptions. [. . .] Hence, the colonial encounter

---

12. Marlene Goldman, "Margaret Atwood's Wilderness Tips: Apocalyptic Cannibal Fiction," in *Eating Their Words*, ed. Guest, 171.

13. Selena K. L. Breikss, "A Rare Gift," in *Hannibal Lecter and Philosophy: The Heart of the Matter*, ed. Joseph Westfall (Chicago: Open Court, 2015), 138.

must be very locally contextualized in the intersection of the different social and cultural logics of interaction of the specific parties involved.[14]

The show's use of aestheticized cannibalism and its creation of cultural objects and narratives on which to locate this interest are thus always already in conversation with these colonial histories, even as it turns these histories toward its own specific ends.

Cannibal Shadows: Colonial Traces in Fuller's *Hannibal*

One link between these colonial histories and the aesthetics of *Hannibal* might be the figure of the vampire. John Kraniauskas argues that vampirism can be seen as a reworking of the savagery of the cannibal scene in the colonial imagination into a more civilized sipping of blood.[15] Once again, this argument's connection to *Hannibal*, with both its overt (white) Europeanness and its obsession with civility and manners, is certainly evident. It is worth noting that popular-culture depictions of the white cannibal display a recognition of displaced and connoted power at a nexus where cannibalism's links to capitalism and the colonial project are then reappropriated as acts of resistance for whiteness. This analysis now takes up some of these threads in detail to demonstrate the continuing influence of the colonial dialogue about cannibalism in Fuller's text. Specifically, it focuses on the matrices of race, class, and gender—intersecting with capitalism, orientalism, colonialism, and so on—as expressed in the show's use of excess, language, modes of "civilized" behavior, and practices of feasting, hospitality, and consumption.

---

14. Michael Dietler, *Archaeologies of Colonialism: Consumption, Entanglement, and Violence in Ancient Mediterranean France* (Berkeley: Univ. of California Press, 2010), 55.

15. John Kraniauskas, "Cronos and the Political Economy of Vampirism: Notes on a Historical Constellation," in *Cannibalism and the Colonial World*, ed. Barker, Hulme, and Iverson, 142–57.

This resistance is often specifically a resistance framed by class and the violent excesses of capitalism. An example of this tendency is seen in the cult B-movie *Cannibal Women in the Avocado Jungle of Death* (J. F. Lawton, 1989), which describes a parodic white feminist resistance to capitalism located in cannibalism and tribalism, appropriating the seeming "savagery" of the cannibal as a means by which the (white) female Other can claim space. The film's intertextuality references multiple cultural texts, most significant of which are Joseph Conrad's *Heart of Darkness* (serialized in 1899, first published as a book in 1902) and Ruggero Diodato's Italian cult film *Cannibal Holocaust* (1980). With its reliance on narratives of cannibalism, whiteness, and the Other, *Cannibal Women* bases its climactic parodic moment on an acknowledgment of factions among the cannibalistic women—as supposed representations of divisions between radical feminists—through the act of consumption; that is, their differences are located in whether to eat the men they cook with guacamole or with clam sauce. This division over condiments is no doubt an intentionally sexist parody, but it relies purposefully on the association of whiteness, in particular white femininity, with cultural capital regarding manners and consumption. Although *Hannibal* is not parody of the same type, it shares this creation of cannibalistic consumption as mannered and resistant to the presence of a threatening legal apparatus, a feat it can accomplish only by its reliance on (seemingly invisible) whiteness. Both *Cannibal Women in the Avocado Jungle of Death* and *Hannibal* are concerned with constructions of class, gender, and the role of institutional and structural power in the way that anthropophagic consumption is framed, although the manner in which each presents this consumption remains distinct.

Richard C. King notes that theories of cannibalism function as a nexus for localized concerns of anthropophagy, consumerism, orientalism, racism, and eroticism: "Discussions of anthropophagy, whether classical or cross-cultural, then, have never been neutral, but rather have unfolded as charged contexts for the production of difference. [. . .] As a consequence, cannibalism, real and imagined, is best understood as a symbol, as a tool, as a weapon."¹⁶ These discussions not only function to create the orientalist imagery of the "savage cannibal" used to justify the false morality of European colonial expansion but are also deployed as contentious moral frameworks for theorizing the "civilized savage," who kills only what he consumes fully (versus the warfare, massacres, and genocide associated with the spread of [neo]colonialism). They also appear in context of the fears of "neocannibalism": European neoliberal global capitalism that consumes resources, markets, people, and more, processing them and leaving behind scads of waste.

King's essay implicitly undergirds Edward Said's notion of orientalism as a process that reveals far more about the colonizer than about the colonized, exposing the fears and moral questioning of a populace that exports these fears and questions onto "the other." As Kristen Guest states, "Traditionally used in colonial enterprises to justify acts of genocide or assimilation, then, the opposition between civilization and savagery also performs significant ideological work within western culture both by containing marginal groups and by helping to articulate the anxieties of their dominant social counterparts."¹⁷ Reappropriation of cannibalism as a way to center whiteness again suggests a ceasing of this exporting in favor of using the same ideology to undermine political, economic, or social power of marginalized groups or to locate an "other" for acts of differentiation, punishment, and/or assimilation, but it continues to direct the gaze toward European and North American whiteness in an effort to reengage with the same moral quandaries.

In effect, *Hannibal* participates in the choice to decouple the fears of cannibalism from its original colonial associations with race, nationality, and morality in an effort to display a more class-bound consciousness that indicates the uneasy neo/colonial relationship

---

16. Richard C. King, "The (Mis)Uses of Cannibalism in Contemporary Cultural Critique," *Diacritics* 30, no. 1 (2000): 109.

17. Kristen Guest, "Introduction: Cannibalism and the Boundaries of Identity," in *Eating Their Words*, ed. Guest, 2.

between the United States and its European past and neighbors. Thus, within the moral frameworks of the show, Garret Jacob Hobbs (Vladimir Jon Cubrt), or the "Minnesota Shrike" introduced in "Apéritif" (1.01), functions as a representation of North American blue-collar consumption, wherein he supposedly cares for and utilizes every part of his victims in order to properly "honor" their sacrifice. Hobbs's rural, blue-collar ethos is reflected in Will Graham's (Hugh Dancy) character and undergirds the association between Will and Hobbs alongside Will's empathic description of Hobbs as father and hunter. Will lives simply, fishes and creates his own lures (echoed in Hobbs's positioning and use of his daughter, Abigail [Kacey Rohl], as lure), and, at the close of the first season, is made to consume part of Abigail (thereby living out Hobbs's fantasy).

This representation of cannibalism is minimalist—an ethos that seemingly intends the minimum harm to the world around itself, while living out a fantasy of consumption that the cannibal (whether capitalist or anthropophagic) sees as inevitable. Although the viewers never see Garret Jacob Hobbs produce his victim's flesh as art for consumption, presumably preparing regular meals with it instead, they repeatedly see Hannibal do so. Hannibal goes so far as to mention that he is so careful about what he puts in his body that he does the majority of his own meal preparation (1.01). This practice gestures to his need for secrecy, but it also makes evident a certain implicit wealth and privilege regarding ingredients, preparation, and consumption: that is, Hobbs consumes *food*, whereas Hannibal consumes *cuisine*. Hobbs wastes nothing, whereas Hannibal wastes all but the choicest cut. The overt implication here is one wherein the rich are more wasteful, whereas the poor are more stringent and innovative with their habits of consumption, but there are also implicit implications regarding who survives the discoveries of these scenarios of power and immoral consumption.

In contrast, the character of Hannibal shows strong links to the European neo/colonial aspect of civilizing and civilized capitalist consumption. He chooses his victims for what he sees as breaches of etiquette, which results in their dehumanization in his eyes. Their death is therefore simultaneously punishment as well as an indication of their animality, and he is placed in the role of judge, jury, and executioner. As Dan Snow notes, Hannibal has a distinctive sense of style that is revealed variously through the architecture and furnishings of his office and home, his sartorial elegance, his musical tastes (underscored by the distinctive soundtracks that play during his kills), his love for the arts, and, most distinctively, his mobilization of culinary aesthetics and chosen cuisine.[18] His position as a white European Renaissance man, when coupled with his baroque aesthetics, adds to this notion of Hannibal as an embodiment of "the civilized man," even as his role as cannibal links him to the associated colonial roots of such a representation. This notion seems to have explicitly shifted the racial implications that would underlie such an assertion, but it continues implicitly to further colonial discourses within which the ideology that "only the truly civilized survive" in a world where "eat or be eaten" is increasingly reified.

Notably, Hannibal's consumption of bodies is suggested to have the violent and sardonic intent to make useful those who have offended him and shown themselves to be "pigs." The character of Tobias Budge in the season 1 episode "Fromage" (1.08), played by Demore Barnes and notably the only black serial killer on the show, mirrors Hannibal in his mobilization of a similar ethos of performance and violence justified as the creation of usefulness. Hannibal uses haute cuisine as a means by which to tie this savagery to displays of high culture, and Budge ties together the creation of catgut strings from the guts of his victims to the high-art performances of the symphony. As Hannibal serves his meals to those invited to his table, so, too, does Budge offer his students strings of gut rather than synthetic alternatives in a double layer of knowledge and transgression as he listens to them perform for him. Establishing these deliberate parallels suggests that the audience is meant to view Budge and Hannibal

---

18. Dan Snow, "Empathy for the Devil," in *Hannibal Lecter and Philosophy*, ed. Westfall, 201–5.

as similar figures in their role as serial killers. However, Budge's identity as a serial killer is quickly uncovered within the narrative, suggesting not only that Hannibal is more skilled at his deceptions and his social graces but also that Budge's inability to "play the game" more generally is what eventually leads to his death. Intentional or not, these parallels suggest a racial hierarchy wherein both ethnicities are sites of serial killing inherent to their expressions of art and culture, but whiteness (and consequently Hannibal) is shown as more likely to survive these encounters, and serial killing by white people is more likely to continue undiscovered.

Language use within the series is similarly weighted, with wordplay around knowledge of Hannibal's cannibalism producing both sites of knowledge and seeming ignorance. When speaking of the coinciding of humor and fear in *Hannibal*, Joseph Westfall argues that Hannibal's frequent wordplay within the series is a performance of power for both his un/knowing conversational partner and the viewer.[19] Westfall cites conversations with Jack Crawford and Tobias Budge as examples in which both Hannibal and his proposed victim are aware of his intent to eat them and in which the hunter and the hunted in question are in flux. Power in this situation therefore lies not only in the physical fight that follows (which Hannibal wins both times) but also in the ability to parry verbal jabs and barbs at the table with impeccable dinner etiquette, and it is thereby positioned as being on Hannibal's terms. Thus, cannibalism within this cultural construct is not positioned as outside the bounds of civility and morality in the same manner as it is in the film *The Hills Have Eyes* (Wes Craven, 1977, a transcultural Americanized version of the Sawney Bean narrative) or as a primal urge for survival, as in the film *Alive* (Frank Marshall, 1993); it remains a distinctly cerebral and aesthetic choice wherein even the attempts Hannibal's victims make

---

19. Joseph Westfall, "A Funny Thing Happened on the Way to the Dinner Party," in *Hannibal Lecter and Philosophy*, ed. Westfall, 183.

to reclaim power rely on an understanding of this wordplay and an ability to engage with Hannibal on his own terms.

According to Selena K. L. Breikss, the consumption of meat is an unwitting and at times unwilling bond between Hannibal and those dining at his table as well as a demonstration of Hannibal's superior position by weight of this knowledge, particularly in that he invites the very law enforcement officers who seek to capture him to eat at his table. With gift giving functioning in the series as a means by which to establish dominance, Hannibal's gifts establish the recipient's knowledge or ignorance and create additional systems wherein punishment for churlishness or bad manners when receiving such a gift is considered cause and justification for butchering.[20] Hosting dinner gatherings allows Hannibal a means by which not only to serve his allies and enemies with his creations, thereby turning them into inadvertent cannibals, but also to locate his own role as host of a feast. As Brian Hayden observes, feasts were a practical means by which to mobilize labor, create cooperation between certain groups and deliberately exclude others, enable alliances between certain social groups, compensate for transgressions, solicit favors and gain information, and attract desirable people by advertising the success of these gatherings.[21] This practical exertion of power is indicated in the series as Hannibal's actions consolidate his importance specifically through his role as host. His use of haute cuisine, his opulent surroundings, and an insistence upon urbane charm and gentility add specific connotations to the cultural hierarchies between Europe and its former colony (North America).

Thus, hosting not only locates Hannibal as a traditional figure of generosity but also creates him as powerful within structures of

---

20. Breikss, "A Rare Gift," 137.
21. Brian Hayden, "Fabulous Feasts: A Prolegomenon to the Importance of Feasting," in *Feasts: Archaeological and Ethnographic Perspectives on Food, Politics, and Power*, ed. Michael Dietler and Brian Hayden (Tuscaloosa: Univ. of Alabama Press, 2010), 29–30.

hospitality, wherein those at his table consequently owe him gratitude. This weaponization of hospitality and gift giving parallels colonial political enterprise, in which they were essential means by which to establish power imbalances and a need for reciprocation, eventually resulting in imperial incursion or, if they were refused, then the seeming justification for violent response as civilizing apparatus. Reciprocation within these settings becomes paramount—Hannibal creates situations in which characters such as Abigail Hobbs and Bedelia Du Maurier (Gillian Anderson) are forced to explicitly request his help ("Potage" [1.03], "Tome-wan" [2.12]), after which he assumes control over them by dint of this debt. His use of a colonial tableau wherein he has both created the problem and provided its solution thereby allows him to exert power not only through his knowledge of these characters' transgressions but through the structures of hospitality that emphasize the weight of this unpaid debt between them. In this manner, Hannibal's dominance extends to the ability to force his victims to consume preparations of their own limbs with seemingly urbane charm, as in the case of Abel Gideon (Eddie Izzard) in "Antipasto" (3.01), who has erred and assumed a debt by falsely assuming Hannibal's identity as the Chesapeake Ripper, as well as Bedelia Du Maurier, who spends the majority of her time with Hannibal in Italy being "prepared" by means of a careful diet for her eventual consumption ("Antipasto"), culminating in the postcredits scene of "The Wrath of the Lamb" (3.13), the series' final episode, in which her leg has been prepared and served to her. Neither Bedelia nor Abigail is created solely as a passive victim within this framing, and each exerts her own agency in an attempt to be a part of or resist Hannibal's final plans for her, and it is this resistance to Hannibal's dominance and their indebtedness that undergirds their narrative arcs.

The use of episode titles that shift from elements of French cuisine in the first season to elements of Japanese cuisine in the second and then elements of Italian cuisine in the first half of the third season appears to indicate an expansion of Hannibal's appetites and his reach, but it also suggests an implicit narrative of an unwitting culinary tourism. Food functions as a highly charged nexus for identity and culture, and culinary tourism in particular is a means by which a specific culture's authenticity and identity may be staged and consumed by an audience otherwise unfamiliar to it. With this understanding, it is possible to suggest that although Hannibal's meals imply on their surface a culinary tourism that locates itself in imperial cultures (French, Japanese, and Italian), with associated aesthetic effects, the use of human meat is intentionally disruptive, leading one to conclude that its use is to locate patrons of Hannibal's table within *his* specific culture and world. In this sense, Hannibal is both performing his identity for an unwitting audience as well as exerting violent control through his manipulation of the reality of the event, seemingly rewriting the history of his interpersonal engagements with his guests, who consume human flesh at his whim. He both creates and withholds truth, and this combination is essential to his system of intimidation and domination.

Hannibal's use of human flesh as haute cuisine functions as an updated version of the Sweeney Todd myth, wherein consumers of Mrs. Lovett's meat pies are unknowingly partaking in cannibalism, and thus re-creates cultural anxieties of oblivious yet seemingly immoral consumption. As Cynthia Baron, Diane Carson, and Mark Bernard note in *Appetites and Anxieties*, "Cannibal films reflect the fact that food consumption in consumer society is fraught with uncertainties; people do not know what they are eating; they do not know where their food comes from or where their disposed food will go."[22] That is, there is a sense of unease reflecting not only the contents of this food but also the methods used by those in power to provide it as sustenance for a society or for a chosen few.

However, this fear of consumption carries different connotations when applied outside structures of whiteness in the Global North,

---

22. Cynthia Baron, Diane Carson, and Mark Bernard, *Appetites and Anxieties: Food, Film, and the Politics of Representation* (Detroit: Wayne State Univ. Press, 2014), 131–32.

where marginalized identities and the creation and performance of regional cuisines are already exoticized, seemingly mysterious, and suspect in their use of offal or style of preparation. Cuisines in which offal is traditional and visible rather than hidden might therefore raise questions about their content within Euro-American settings, whereas haute cuisine prepared to seemingly universal aesthetics (themselves a function and lasting result of colonial histories) invisibilizes this hierarchy of cultural consumption. In the series *Hannibal*, the tension that arises in the eventual culinary denouement is therefore reliant not simply on the viewer's knowledge that the food being served has always been transgressive but also on the notion that Hannibal himself has always been viewed as a trustworthy figure by the other characters largely because of his refinement, his stature, and his aesthetics—all of which are strongly coded with whiteness alongside colonial and imperial legacies. In effect, this scenario reverses the colonial myth, so that the imperial "Renaissance man" is revealed as immoral consumer, but the shock and titillation the revelation produces are predicated on the distinction between his performance and identity, on the one hand, and those of the "traditional" (nonwhite) cannibal, on the other.

Food for Thought: Concluding Remarks

As Baron, Carson, and Bernard observe, "Films in which humans are the food product often comment on the symbolic but systemic cannibalism of imperial and economic ventures."[23] As this analysis has shown, *Hannibal* as a text is still intimately connected to the violent histories of imperialist fantasy that continue to function through various tropes in the present day. Indeed, it could be argued that within the transmedia economy of modern television, *Hannibal* implicates its fan audiences in these politics of consumption in an even deeper way. What does it mean when one of the most popular pieces of merchandise to come from the show is a cookbook that

---

23. Baron, Carson, and Bernard, *Appetites and Anxieties*, 130.

re-creates Hannibal's feasts? Clearly, part of what draws audiences to attempt to reproduce these tableaus is the spectacle of aesthetic excess that overlays the "barbarity" of the tableaus' true nature.

It is also important to note that the racialized fantasy of consumption—even in its most extreme form—is very much part of our contemporary culture. To recall just one case, in 2012 Sweden's minister for culture, Lena Adelsohn Liljeroth, caused controversy when she took part in a public art event that involved the cutting up and eating of a cake shaped like the torso of a black woman. When confronted with the horrendous racism of the entire program, the minister argued that it was the function of art to be "provocative."[24] North America's and Europe's simultaneous discomfort with and disavowal of its colonial past and present therefore must remain at the forefront when discussing how "art" builds its narratives on the foundation of such mythologies. It must also be acknowledged that fans of *Hannibal*—or Fannibals—actively consume these same tropes. Although fanwork is often lauded for its ability to pry open and interrogate the fault lines of texts such as *Hannibal*, it is notable that there has been little pushback or interrogation of the show's racial politics within fan reworkings. Fan authors don't just embrace the text's choice to center whiteness in its narrative but emphasize it even further.

This centering of whiteness has so far not received much attention by scholars who are interested in *Hannibal* as a cult television show and its audiences. This gap is indicative of a structural issue within the field as race and racism in fan studies are at once the topic of considerable discussion and the subject of considerable silence even though the problem was noted as early as 1992 in John Fiske's

---

24. Shockingly, the cake was created as an art installation to raise awareness about the practice of genital mutilation. The artist, Makode Aj Linde, was part of the installation, posing next to it with a blackened face and screaming every time someone cut off a piece. For more details, see Luke Harding, "Swedish Minister Denies Claims of Racism over Black Woman Cake Stunt," *Guardian*, Apr. 17, 2012, at https://www.theguardian.com/world/2012/apr/17/sweden-europe-news.

highly influential study.[25] That is not to say there is no work being done on this issue. Indeed, some of the most interesting recent scholarship in this area has emerged in the field of transnational/transcultural fandoms, where the source texts are non-Western and often in languages other than English.[26] This work is valuable, especially because it destabilizes the field's Anglophone focus. However, fan-studies scholars should be cautious of this impulse that seeks to displace the workings of racial identity as most relevant and "obvious" to something other than traditional media fandom studies, which is then free to tread largely familiar theoretical pathways.[27]

Although this tendency is registered as troubling in overviews, anthologies, and keynote addresses, this acknowledgment often

25. John Fiske, "The Adoring Audience: Fan Culture and Popular Media," in *The Cultural Economy of Fandom*, ed. Lisa A. Lewis (London: Routledge, 1992), 30–49.

26. See, for example, Aswin Punathambekar, "Between Rowdies and Rasikas: Rethinking Fan Activity in Indian Film Culture," in *Fandom: Identities and Communities in a Mediated World*, ed. Jonathan Gray, Cornel Sandvoss, and C. Lee Harrington (New York: New York Univ. Press, 2007), 198–209; Mark McLelland, ed., "Special Issue: Japanese Transnational Fandoms and Female Consumers," *Intersections: Gender and Sexuality in Asia and the Pacific* 20 (2009), at http://intersections.anu.edu.au/issue20_contents.htm; Bertha Chin and Lori Hitchcock Morimoto, "Towards a Theory of Transcultural Fandom," *Participations* 10, no. 1 (2013): 92–108, at http://www.participations.org/Volume%2010/Issue%201/7%20Chin%20&%20Morimoto%2010.1.pdf; and Irina Lyan and Alon Levkowitz, "From Holy Land to 'Hallyu Land': The Symbolic Journey Following the Korean Wave in Israel," *Journal of Fandom Studies* 3, no. 1 (2015): 7–21.

27. For alternative theoretical frameworks, see Rukmini Pande and Samira Nadkarni, "A Land Where 'Other' People Live," in *Fic: Why Fanfiction Is Taking Over the World*, ed. Anne Jamison (Dallas: BenBella Books, 2013), 342–52; Rukmini Pande, "Squee from the Margins: Racial/Cultural/Ethnic Identity in Global Media Fandom," in *Seeing Fans: Representations of Fandom in Media and Popular Culture*, ed. Paul Booth and Lucy Bennett (New York: Bloomsbury, 2016), 209–20; Rukmini Pande and Swati Moitra, "Yes! The Evil Queen Is Latina," in "Queer Female Fandom," ed. Julie Levin Russo and Eve Ng, special issue of *Transformative Works and Cultures* 24 (2017), at https://doi.org/10.3983/twc.2017.0908.

performs the rhetorical gesture of naming the problem, only so that it can be set aside once again. This rhetorical strategy is enabled by the continuing conceptualization of racial identity as an *additional* lens to be applied to the operations of fandom rather than as something that structures those operations in a fundamental and foundational manner. This strategy is also identified in critiques such as Rebecca Wanzo's, wherein she maintains that fan studies remains silent on issues of race and racism because these issues disturb some of the field's most dearly held truisms.[28] Therefore, although *Hannibal*'s rich intertextual and cerebral narrative is almost universally lauded, it is vital to note how it continues to participate in a distinctly neoimperial project.

Bibliography

Banivanua-Mar, Tracey. "Cannibalism and Colonialism: Charting Colonies and Frontiers in Nineteenth-Century Fiji." *Comparative Studies in Society and History* 52, no. 2 (2010): 255–81.

Barker, Frances, Peter Hulme, and Margaret Iverson, eds. *Cannibalism and the Colonial World*. Cambridge: Cambridge Univ. Press, 1998.

Baron, Cynthia, Diane Carson, and Mark Bernard. *Appetites and Anxieties: Food, Film, and the Politics of Representation*. Detroit: Wayne State Univ. Press, 2014.

Berglund, Jeff. "Write, Right, White, Rite: Literacy, Imperialism, Race, and Cannibalism in Edgar Rice Burroughs' *Tarzan of the Apes*." *Studies in American Fiction* 27, no. 1 (1999): 53–76.

Brantlinger, Patrick. *Taming Cannibals: Race and the Victorians*. Ithaca, NY: Cornell Univ. Press, 2011.

Breikss, Selena K. L. "A Rare Gift." In *Hannibal Lecter and Philosophy: The Heart of the Matter*, edited by Joseph Westfall, 135–45. Chicago: Open Court, 2015.

---

28. Rebecca Wanzo, "African American Acafandom and Other Strangers: New Genealogies of Fan Studies," *Transformative Works and Cultures* 19 (2015), at https://doi:10.3983/twc.2015.0699.

Casey, Jeff. "Queer Cannibals and Deviant Detectives: Subversion and Homosocial Desire in NBC's *Hannibal*." *Quarterly Review of Film and Video* 32, no. 6 (2015): 550–67.

Chin, Bertha, and Lori Hitchcock Morimoto. "Towards a Theory of Transcultural Fandom." *Participations* 10, no. 1 (2013): 92–108. At http://www.participations.org/Volume%2010/Issue%201/7%20Chin%20&%20Morimoto%2010.1.pdf.

Colás, Santiago. "From Caliban to Cronus: A Critique of Cannibalism as Metaphor for Cuban Revolutionary Culture." In *Eating Their Words: Cannibalism and the Boundaries of Cultural Identity*, edited by Kristen Guest, 129–48. New York: State Univ. of New York Press, 2001.

Dietler, Michael. *Archaeologies of Colonialism: Consumption, Entanglement, and Violence in Ancient Mediterranean France*. Berkeley: Univ. of California Press, 2010.

Fiske, John. "The Adoring Audience: Fan Culture and Popular Media." In *The Cultural Economy of Fandom*, edited by Lisa A. Lewis, 30–49. London: Routledge, 1992.

Forbes, Jack D. *Columbus and Other Cannibals: The Wetiko Disease of Exploitation, Imperialism, and Terrorism*. New York: Seven Stories Press, 2011.

Goldman, Marlene. "Margaret Atwood's Wilderness Tips: Apocalyptic Cannibal Fiction." In *Eating Their Words: Cannibalism and the Boundaries of Cultural Identity*, edited by Kristen Guest, 167–86. New York: State Univ. of New York Press, 2001.

Guest, Kristen, ed. *Eating Their Words: Cannibalism and the Boundaries of Cultural Identity*. New York: State Univ. of New York Press, 2001.

———. "Introduction: Cannibalism and the Boundaries of Identity." In *Eating Their Words: Cannibalism and the Boundaries of Cultural Identity*, edited by Kristen Guest, 1–10. New York: State Univ. of New York Press, 2001.

Harding, Luke. "Swedish Minister Denies Claims of Racism over Black Woman Cake Stunt." *Guardian*, Apr. 17, 2012. At https://www.theguardian.com/world/2012/apr/17/sweden-europe-news.

Hayden, Brian. "Fabulous Feasts: A Prolegomenon to the Importance of Feasting." In *Feasts: Archaeological and Ethnographic Perspectives on Food, Politics, and Power*, edited by Michael Dietler and Brian Hayden, 23–64. Tuscaloosa: Univ. of Alabama Press, 2010.

Hulme, Peter. "Introduction: The Cannibal Scene." In *Cannibalism and the Colonial World*, edited by Frances Barker, Peter Hulme, and Margaret Iverson, 1–38. Cambridge: Cambridge Univ. Press, 1998.
King, Richard C. "The (Mis)Uses of Cannibalism in Contemporary Cultural Critique." *Diacritics* 30, no. 1 (2000): 106–23.
Kraniauskas, John. "Cronos and the Political Economy of Vampirism: Notes on a Historical Constellation." In *Cannibalism and the Colonial World*, edited by Frances Barker, Peter Hulme, and Margaret Iverson, 142–57. Cambridge: Cambridge Univ. Press, 1998.
Lyan, Irina, and Alon Levkowitz. "From Holy Land to 'Hallyu Land': The Symbolic Journey Following the Korean Wave in Israel." *Journal of Fandom Studies* 3, no. 1 (2015): 7–21.
Martel, Heather E. "Hans Staden's Captive Soul: Identity, Imperialism, and Rumors of Cannibalism in Sixteenth-Century Brazil." *Journal of World History* 17, no. 1 (2006): 51–69.
Martyr, Peter. *De Orbe Novo: The Eight Decades of Peter Martyr D'Anghiera*. Translated by Francis Augustus MacNutt. New York: Library Reprints, 1912.
McLelland, Mark, ed. "Special Issue: Japanese Transnational Fandoms and Female Consumers." *Intersections: Gender and Sexuality in Asia and the Pacific* 20 (2009). At http://intersections.anu.edu.au/issue20_contents.htm.
Morimoto, Lori. "Outrageous Sirk-Umstances: Hannibal and the Aesthetics of Excess." Paper presented at "Feasting on Hannibal: An Interdisciplinary Conference," Univ. of Melbourne, Nov. 29–30, 2016. At https://doi.org/10.17613/M6FM24.
Ndalianis, Angela. "Hannibal: A Disturbing Feast for the Senses." *Journal of Visual Culture* 14, no. 3 (2015): 279–84.
Obeyesekere, Gananath. "Cannibal Feasts in Nineteenth-Century Fiji: Seamen's Yarns and the Ethnographic Imagination." In *Cannibalism and the Colonial World*, edited by Frances Barker, Peter Hulme, and Margaret Iverson, 39–62. Cambridge: Cambridge Univ. Press, 1998.
Pande, Rukmini. "Squee from the Margins: Racial/Cultural/Ethnic Identity in Global Media Fandom." In *Seeing Fans: Representations of Fandom in Media and Popular Culture*, edited by Paul Booth and Lucy Bennett, 209–20. New York: Bloomsbury, 2016.

Pande, Rukmini, and Swati Moitra. "Yes! The Evil Queen Is Latina." In "Queer Female Fandom," edited by Julie Levin Russo and Eve Ng, special issue of *Transformative Works and Cultures* 24 (2017). At https://doi.org/10.3983/twc.2017.0908.

Pande, Rukmini, and Samira Nadkarni. "A Land Where 'Other' People Live." In *Fic: Why Fanfiction Is Taking Over the World*, edited by Anne Jamison, 342–52. Dallas: BenBella Books, 2013.

Punathambekar, Aswin. "Between Rowdies and Rasikas: Rethinking Fan Activity in Indian Film Culture." In *Fandom: Identities and Communities in a Mediated World*, edited by Jonathan Gray, Cornel Sandvoss, and C. Lee Harrington, 198–209. New York: New York Univ. Press, 2007.

Snow, Dan. "Empathy for the Devil." In *Hannibal Lecter and Philosophy: The Heart of the Matter*, edited by Joseph Westfall, 199–216. Chicago: Open Court, 2015.

Verne, Jules. *Among the Cannibals*. London: Ward Lock, 1876.

Wanzo, Rebecca. "African American Acafandom and Other Strangers: New Genealogies of Fan Studies." *Transformative Works and Cultures* 19 (2015). At https://doi:10.3983/twc.2015.0699.

Westfall, Joseph. "A Funny Thing Happened on the Way to the Dinner Party." In *Hannibal Lecter and Philosophy: The Heart of the Matter*, edited by Joseph Westfall, 171–84. Chicago: Open Court, 2015.

———, ed. *Hannibal Lecter and Philosophy: The Heart of the Matter*. Chicago: Open Court, 2015.

9 | Bedelia Du Maurier

Hannibal's *Femme Fatale and Final Girl*

Kara M. French

The *Hannibal* episode "Sorbet" (1.07) opens with Hannibal Lecter listening, rapt with pleasure, to a soprano's full-throated aria from Handel's *Giulio Cesare* while cheekily attending a charity benefit for hunger relief. The unnamed diva commands Hannibal's full attention, bringing him to tears with her art. Though the opera singer is not seen again outside of this episode, later in "Sorbet" the narrative introduces the show's true prima donna, Hannibal's psychiatrist, Bedelia Du Maurier, played by Gillian Anderson. Bedelia is the only other woman Hannibal will openly weep in front of and perhaps the only other character besides Will Graham whose thoughts he will occasionally entertain.

As a character created exclusively for *Hannibal* (NBC, 2013–15), Bedelia Du Maurier has a unique relationship to the narrative. Bedelia is slippery and morally ambiguous and at different moments takes on the role of both perpetrator and victim. As the psychiatrist's psychiatrist, she is set up to serve an analytical function that endows her at times with a near fourth-wall-breaking insight, voicing the audience's concerns. The dilemma she faces as a participant-observer brings to the forefront questions of how complicit audiences may be in *Hannibal*'s violence and whether it is possible to enjoy the

I thank Allison Abra, Karolina Koczberska, and Olivia Tarcov for their support and feedback on this article.

show's lavish aesthetics without in some way condoning its horror-film ethics.

The arc of Bedelia's story evokes the femme fatale of film noir in a way that goes beyond her Veronica Lake hairstyle and chilly delivery. She is the quintessence of the mysterious woman who presents as a victim and is later revealed to be anything but. The character of Bedelia also represents Fuller's take on familiar horror motifs, such as Carol Clover's trope of the "Final Girl."[1] Bedelia is *Hannibal*'s Final Girl in a very literal sense—the last image in the show's finale, "The Wrath of the Lamb" (3.13), is the postcredits sequence where she is seated alone to feast on her own leg, poised to attack her mysterious host armed with nothing but a fork.

Bedelia both embodies and subverts these familiar female archetypes. As a camp figure, Bedelia disrupts the male gaze associated with the femme fatale as well as the male-centeredness of a series focused on Hannibal Lecter and Will Graham. In the postcredits sequence, Bedelia's status as Final Girl and audience surrogate comes together. The ambiguity of that final image invites the audience to engage in meaning making with the text, thus blurring the line between passive observers and active participants in the blood opera *Hannibal*.[2]

Author Anima, Audience Surrogate

Bedelia's role as prima donna in *Hannibal* is closely related to her character's ability to serve as a kind of winking author avatar, a status that sets her apart from the rest of the characters. In his memoir of gay life in twentieth-century New York City, author James McCourt suggests that opera cognoscenti worship the diva "because the diva is

---

1. Carol J. Clover, *Men, Women, and Chainsaws: Gender in the Modern Horror Film* (Princeton, NJ: Princeton Univ. Press, 1992), 35–39.

2. Hugh Dancy was the first to call *Hannibal* "a fever dream blood opera" (Hugh Dancy, interview on *Last Call with Carson Daly*, NBC, June 2, 2015), and I am borrowing his phrasing here, though the term *blood opera* often gets applied to films that combine crime drama with graphic depictions of violence.

the anima image of the composer": "Men project their animas. The diva reigns."³ To follow McCourt's camp train of thought, Bedelia is Bryan Fuller's anima, the feminine soul of the show. Fuller himself has seemingly encouraged this interpretation, referring to actress Gillian Anderson, arguably a television diva in her own right, as his muse.⁴ Anderson's performance, which over the course of three seasons transforms from chilly reserve to arch Grand Guignol, mirrors the narrative evolution of *Hannibal* itself, from its more conventional procedural origins in season 1 to what Fuller has openly described as a "pretentious art film" in season 3.⁵ It is no coincidence that Bedelia makes her debut midway through the first season just as the show begins to turn away from a procedural format to a more serialized story that foregrounds the developing relationship between Hannibal Lecter and Will Graham.

Bedelia's tie to authorship is symbolized by her last name, a nod to the novelist Daphne Du Maurier, renowned for suspense classics such as *Rebecca* and "The Birds." The name "Du Maurier" is synonymous with mystery and Hitchcockian thriller.⁶ Giving Bedelia the name of a suspense-genre author is an indication of her character's agency and ability to write herself a different ending than the one Hannibal has planned for her. This kind of authorial agency is shown in "Sakizuke" (2.02), when Hannibal arrives at Bedelia's home with the intention of killing her, only to find it abandoned, a bottle of her perfume left behind as a token postscript to their

---

3. James McCourt, *Queer Street* (New York: Norton, 2004), 347.

4. Michael Schneider, "Gillian Anderson's Second Revival, from the Scary *Hannibal* to the Sci-Fi *X-Files*," *TVInsider*, July 9, 2015, at http://www.tvinsider.com/26005/gillian-andersons-second-revival-from-the-scary-hannibal-to-the-sci-fi-x-files/.

5. Eric Thurm, "*Hannibal* Showrunner: 'We Are Not Making Television. We Are Making a Pretentious Art Film from the 80s,'" *Guardian*, June 3, 2015, at https://www.theguardian.com/tv-and-radio/2015/jun/03/hannibal-tv-showrunner-bryan-fuller.

6. Alfred Hitchcock adapted "The Birds" in 1963 and *Rebecca* in 1940.

relationship. It is also evident in Bedelia and Hannibal's parting exchange in "Dolce" (3.06). Hannibal tells Bedelia, "This isn't how I intended to say good-bye. I imagined it differently." To which Bedelia replies, "I didn't."

Bedelia implies that Hannibal's preferred ending for her would be a long, drawn-out feast with her as the main course, a chance to savor her. She uses his desire to savor her against him, choosing to make her departure at a moment when he would be denied his banquet. She further writes her own story in the latter half of season 3 in her decision to pose as "Lydia Fell," a brainwashed victim, instead of Hannibal's willing accomplice. The "Lydia Fell" story plays on the audience's own expectations about Bedelia's victimhood as many fans and media outlets speculated that she could not possibly accompany Hannibal to Florence of her own free will.[7] "Lydia Fell" also serves as both a reference and a rebuke to the ending of Thomas Harris's novel *Hannibal* (1999). In Harris's novel, Hannibal administers psychotropic drugs to Clarice Starling, putting her into a suggestible state in which she accepts him as her lover and abandons her career at the FBI to live a glamorous life by his side in Argentina.[8] In this way, Bedelia's authorship over "Lydia Fell" plays on audience expectations both within the confines of the NBC *Hannibal* universe and on a metalevel.

Bedelia's status as author avatar also bleeds into her role as an audience surrogate. Many of her remarks nearly break the fourth wall and are infused with dramatic irony. In season 1, Bedelia's knowledge of Hannibal's true nature is especially ambiguous, and the audience is never entirely clear if she possesses their level of knowledge about her patient's cannibalistic proclivities. In her first entrance in "Sorbet," Bedelia's insight cuts through Hannibal's charming

---

7. *Entertainment Weekly* critic Jeff Jensen repeatedly referred to Bedelia as Hannibal's "thrall." See Jeff Jensen, "*Hannibal* Review: Let's Save This Weird, Excellent Show," *EW*, July 16, 2015, at http://ew.com/article/2015/07/16/save-hannibal-review.

8. Thomas Harris, *Hannibal* (1999; reprint, New York: Bantam Dell, 2000).

gentlemanly persona, what she aptly terms his "person suit." While the other characters remain in the dark about Hannibal's murderous alter ego, Bedelia hints that she knows that the man who receives therapy from her is only a "version" of Hannibal and that there is some other, monstrous part of him hiding behind "a human veil." Hannibal does not entirely protest her assessment or correct her assumption that he is not being "perfectly honest" with her. During that first conversation, he instead asks, "Why do you bother?" To which Bedelia replies, "I see enough of you to see the truth of you. And I like you."

Bedelia in these therapy sessions not only allows Hannibal a space to voice his own concerns and wishes (although filtered through a human veil) but also voices the audience's concerns. Throughout seasons 1 and 2, Fuller and the other writers tease how much Bedelia actually sees behind Hannibal's veil as well as how she acquired this knowledge. In the season 1 finale, "Savoureux" (1.13), the narrative suggests that Bedelia may have known of Hannibal's cannibalistic appetites all along. As Hannibal serves Bedelia *tête de veau* in her residence, it is heavily implied that the "veal" is Abigail Hobbs, who, the audience is led to believe, has been sacrificed to frame Will and preserve Hannibal's secret. An exquisite tension vibrates throughout the entire scene, building to a crescendo as Bedelia takes that first bite of "veal." The audience questions if her hesitation is indicative of her knowledge that she is about to consume human flesh. Bedelia locks eyes with Hannibal as she takes a dainty, delighted bite; for a moment it seems as though she has seen through Hannibal's human veil as clearly as the audience has.

Bedelia's role as audience mouthpiece shifts in season 3 after Hannibal's true identity as the Chesapeake Ripper is revealed. Instead of voicing the audience's knowledge about Hannibal's violence, she becomes the primary commenter on Will and Hannibal's tempestuous relationship. She forces both men to confront a truth that they have hidden from themselves but that has become increasingly obvious to others, especially the legions of fans who self-identify as "Hannigram" shippers (i.e., those who hope for a romantic relationship between characters). In "Secondo" (3.03), Bedelia suggests that what Hannibal feels toward Will is not altogether different from what he once felt toward his beloved sister, Mischa, "a force of mind and circumstance," which Hannibal rephrases as "love." Later, in the penultimate episode, "The Number of the Beast Is 666" (3.12), Will asks Bedelia in a therapy session, "Is Hannibal in love with me?" Bedelia's ornate answer adds up to yes, that Hannibal finds nourishment at the very sight of him.

Hannibal employs the cinematographic technique of "suture" to further create empathy between Bedelia and the viewer at moments of high dramatic tension. Through a pattern of shot/reverse shot, suture uses the camera to portray Bedelia's point of view, aligning her perspective with that of the audience. This technique is seen most explicitly in the scene where Bedelia resigns as Hannibal's therapist. The camera cuts back and forth between Bedelia and Hannibal, "creating an imaginary unity between spectator and screen."[9] The audience wonders if her rejection of him will end in her death as he advances toward her, a lion stalking a gazelle. He looms over her, and for the first time the audience gets a sense of the visible size difference between the two characters. Seated during their therapy sessions, Hannibal and Bedelia appear on relatively equal footing, but in "Sakizuke" (2.02) the difference is magnified at a crucial moment, right when Bedelia proclaims to Hannibal's face, "You are dangerous," landing the pronouncement like a clinical diagnosis.

Suture is employed again in "Antipasto" (3.01), when the audience is introduced to Hannibal and Bedelia in medias res in Europe, where they are posing as a married couple. Familiar protagonists Will Graham, Alana Bloom, and Jack Crawford do not appear in "Antipasto," their fates uncertain. Bedelia instead takes on the role

---

9. Shohini Chaudhuri, *Feminist Film Theorists* (New York: Routledge, 2006), 48–50. In *The Subject of Semiotics* (New York: Oxford Univ. Press, 1983), Kaja Silverman was among the first to identify how suture builds identification between character and viewer, especially relevant for male viewers and female characters, the prime example being *Psycho* (Alfred Hitchcock, 1960).

of sympathetic audience surrogate, one whose life may be in danger. Metaphors of seeing and being seen echo throughout *Hannibal*, and in "Antipasto" much is made of Bedelia's gaze as she peers through the cracks of doors, looking upon Hannibal naked, without his "person suit" in the most literal way. The camera follows Bedelia's gaze later in the episode during a moment taut with suspense as Hannibal gives his lecture. He quotes Dante's *Inferno*, specifically the punishments to be inflicted upon traitors: "I make my own home be my gallows." The camera cuts between Hannibal and Bedelia in this sequence. The implication is that he is speaking directly to her and knows she has betrayed him and that he will make their home a place of execution.

Bedelia's status as audience surrogate is brought to the forefront again in "Antipasto" when Hannibal asks her, "Are you observing or participating?" Bedelia answers she is only observing and has no intention of participating in the murder of Anthony Dimmond or in any of Hannibal's cannibalistic activities. Hannibal concludes that there is no distinction between observing and participating, perhaps as in the discipline of anthropology: observation is participation.[10] But this speech also calls into question the audience's own duality as both participants and observers. It can be difficult to reconcile Fuller's insistence that Bedelia is the "smartest character on the show" with her decision to return to Hannibal's orbit—wouldn't it be smarter to stay as far away from him as possible?[11] And yet, like Bedelia, audience members see the truth of Hannibal and still like him, tuning in

---

10. On participant-observation methods, see Morris S. Schwartz and Charlotte Green Schwartz, "Problems in Participant Observation," *American Journal of Sociology* 60, no. 4 (1955): 343–53.

11. Fuller has referred numerous times to Bedelia as "the smartest character on the show" but most recently in a podcast where he explained that despite all her cleverness she can't resist "sticking her hand in the fire" (Rob Goluzzo, "For the Love of Horror, with Bryan Fuller!" interview, *Shock Waves*, podcast audio, Dec. 19, 2016, at http://www.blumhouse.com/2016/12/19/shock-waves-episode-31-for-the-love-of-horror-with-bryan-fuller).

week after week in spite of the suffering he inflicts on the protagonists and his victims. The audience can't resist the opportunity to observe him; Bedelia's fascination mirrors the viewers' own.

Twenty-First-Century Femme Fatale

Bedelia's narrative position as both author anima and audience surrogate is further filtered through the femme fatale archetype. Though other female characters (notably Alana Bloom and Margot Verger) may evoke a noir aesthetic in terms of hairstyle and costuming, the femme fatale is most evident in Bedelia's story arc, especially in her eleventh-hour reveal as an unrepentant killer.

Bedelia's resemblance to the femme fatale becomes more visually pronounced over the course of the series. It is no surprise that the character's evolution is communicated through costuming in a production so highly conscious of aesthetics. When Bedelia is first introduced in season 1, she is wearing elegant (if conservative) professional wear. Throughout much of seasons 1 and 2, she maintains a preference for long sleeves, her clothes well tailored but modest. However, in "Tome-wan" (2.12) she appears wearing a low-cut crimson blouse and a skirt with a pattern that resembles snakeskin. Her hairstyle likewise now has a vampy, 1940s twist.

The audience was previously led to believe that Bedelia had been attacked by a violent patient, an encounter so traumatizing that she took early retirement. It was heavily implied that Hannibal was responsible not only for referring the patient to Bedelia but also for killing him because the patient died by swallowing his own tongue. Fuller plays with the audience's knowledge of other Hannibal Lecter screen adaptations, alluding to the incident in which Hannibal forces an inmate, "Multiple Migs," to swallow his tongue after he is rude to Clarice Starling in the film *The Silence of the Lambs* (Jonathan Demme, 1991).

After Bedelia's revelation that she killed her patient, visual allusions to the femme fatale become increasingly more explicit. In her role as Hannibal's wife and accomplice in Florence, Bedelia adopts a much more provocative wardrobe. Demure separates are replaced

9.1. In the scene in "Tome-wan" (2.12) where Bedelia Du Maurier (Gillian Anderson) reveals that she murdered her patient, her costuming deliberately evokes the femme fatale. (© NBC/Gaumont)

by slinky dresses that reveal muscular forearms and draw attention to her décolletage. In one notable scene in "Antipasto," Bedelia undresses in front of Hannibal, her entire naked back to the camera like a nude still life. Like Hannibal, she has taken off her "person suit" to reveal a dark and predatory nature akin to Hannibal's own. Notably, the tailored skirt suits return in the latter half of season 3, when Bedelia tells half-truths about her relationship with Hannibal to a captivated lecture-hall audience.

For all that Bedelia's character embodies traits of authorship and agency, her story arc also reflects some of the misogyny associated with the femme fatale. Though femme fatale characters remain compelling for their overt sexuality and independence, in the noir narrative they suffer punishment for those same attributes, and *Hannibal*

9.2. Bedelia Du Maurier returns to professional wear in the latter half of season 3 when she is pretending to be Hannibal's victim, her own version of Hannibal's "person suit," as seen in ". . . And the Woman Clothed in Sun" (3.10). (© NBC/Gaumont)

is no exception. This is quite evident in the punishment meted out to Bedelia in the series finale's postcredits sequence. In what is arguably the most male-gaze-oriented shot in the entire series, Bedelia is seated alone at a candlelit dining table, dressed to the nines in an evening gown slit down to her navel.[12] The steaming roast on the table is strewn with roses and tropical fruits. The camera pans down, and we see that Bedelia's left leg has been amputated above the knee; the meat on the menu is hers.

As a punishment, cooking Bedelia's leg is specific both to the sins of her character against Hannibal and to the sins of the femme fatale more broadly. Janey Place argues that "the *femme fatale* is

---

12. Laura Mulvey was the first to coin the term *male gaze* to explain how film privileges a masculine perspective by sexualizing and objectifying women on-screen. See her article "Visual Pleasure and Narrative Cinema," *Screen* 16, no. 3 (1975): 6–18.

characterized by her long lovely legs."[13] Though we do not see in *Hannibal* the same male-gaze-inflected panning shots one might find of Cora in *The Postman Always Rings Twice* (Tay Garnett, 1946) or of Phyllis in *Double Indemnity* (Billy Wilder, 1944), Bedelia's elegant legs are prominently on display in her therapy scenes with Hannibal—indeed, she doesn't seem to own any trousers. As Hannibal says in the film *The Silence of the Lambs*, we covet "what we see every day," so it is possible that Hannibal may have long been tempted by this particular body part.

Bedelia's legs are more than just a symbol of her sexual power; they are also a symbol of her independence and agency. Part of the femme fatale's transgression is "ambition expressed metaphorically in her freedom of movement and visual dominance."[14] In one of their pseudotherapy sessions, Bedelia and Will discuss the way sinners are punished in Dante's *Inferno*, where the punishment mirrors the sin being punished, or *contrapasso*. Neither of them denies their sinfulness, though Will implies that Bedelia hasn't paid enough for her association with Hannibal. Bedelia's original sin against Hannibal is her decision to walk away from him in "Sakizuke," a sin that is later repeated in "Dolce" (3.06), when Bedelia tells him, "This is where I leave you. Or, more accurately, where you leave me." Bedelia is the only character capable of walking away from Hannibal, even if she does not walk very far.

As a visual motif, Bedelia's movement is associated with her resistance against Hannibal. Throughout season 1, when Bedelia is acting chiefly as Hannibal's psychiatrist and sympathetic ear, she hardly moves at all and is seen mostly seated across from Hannibal in the tête-à-tête of their therapy sessions. Her first moment of true movement dovetails with her resignation as his therapist in "Sakizuke," where he advances on her predatorily and she backs away, the

---

13. Janey Place, "Women in Film Noir," in *Women in Film Noir*, ed. E. Ann Kaplan (London: British Film Institute, 1998), 54.

14. Place, "Women in Film Noir," 56.

wobbling in her ankle suggesting fear and vulnerability. The third season features sequences of Bedelia striding across Florentine piazzas as she schemes to imprison Hannibal. Composer Brian Reitzel scores Bedelia's defiance with organ music, which percolates up from the cobblestones as Bedelia walks before a *Lonely Planet* guidebook's worth of attractions. The organ represents life, according to Reitzel, in contrast to Hannibal's favorite instrument, the harpsichord, which represents death, furthering establishing Bedelia as an antagonist to Hannibal.[15] In retrospect, knowing Bedelia's fate makes such sequences seem like tragic foreshadowing.

In film noir, "the *femme fatale* ultimately loses physical movement [. . .] and is often actually or symbolically imprisoned by composition as control over her is exerted and expressed visually."[16] In *Hannibal*, Bedelia loses physical movement in a very literal and grotesque way by having her left leg amputated and a meal made of it. It could also be read that Bedelia is not being punished because she has defied Hannibal with her abandonment but because she chose to ally herself with him. From Will's perspective, Bedelia has "played" Hannibal's game, and so she must also "pay" (3.12). In this reading, it is the leg that ran away with Hannibal to Florence, the one that waltzed with him, that is taken from her as punishment. And yet this interpretation still falls into the familiar trope where the femme fatale is punished for her dangerous sexuality.

However, it would be incorrect to interpret Bedelia's character strictly as a retro femme fatale stereotype. For all that her arc retains some of the misogynistic aspects of the femme fatale, *Hannibal* resists the temptation to make Bedelia solely an object of the male gaze.[17]

---

15. The organ, according to Reitzel, represents life because if pumped it can sustain a note indefinitely, whereas the sounds produced by a harpsicord quickly fade (Kate Kulzick, "*Hannibal*, Ep. 3.01: 'Antipasto,'" *Kate's Classical Corner* [blog], June 4, 2015, at http://www.popoptiq.com/kcc-hannibal-ep-3-01-antipasto/).

16. Place, "Women in Film Noir," 56.

17. Mulvey, "Visual Pleasure."

Bedelia as an author avatar disrupts both the male gaze and the male-centeredness of *Hannibal*'s story line. Even in the scene in which Bedelia undresses in "Antipasto," there is none of the panning, exploitative camerawork associated with the male gaze in cinema. If anything, the camera emphasizes Bedelia's musculature, suggesting she is as much of a predator as Hannibal. And, indeed, earlier in that same episode, Hannibal himself is naked under Bedelia's gaze; the camera shows the way her eyes roam appreciatively over his body, one of several instances in *Hannibal* in which male bodies are objectified.

Bedelia circumvents the male gaze metaphorically as well as visually. In a narrative that puts so much thematic emphasis on seeing and being seen by others in order to be known and loved, Bedelia is the character who sees without being seen, hidden from both other characters and the audience. She goes "behind the veil" with Hannibal and head to head with Will out of a "greed for edification," but she does not allow either man to truly see her or know her in return, feeding them both half-truths about herself.[18] Furthermore, for all that the visual imagery suggests that Bedelia has taken off her person suit with Hannibal in Florence, she later tells Will in ". . . And the Woman Clothed in Sun" (3.10) that she "wasn't herself" with Hannibal, that she was still wearing her "armor." This comment suggests that her couture person suit is well tailored enough to fool even Hannibal, who does not seem to suspect her enthusiasm for his murderous activities could be feigned. Bedelia holds the catbird seat in this Panopticon, where she can see and comment on Will and Hannibal's relationship without their looking back. And whereas their desire to see and be understood by one another will drive both of them to acts of self-destruction, Bedelia is tormented by no such impulse. Her motivations are likewise obscured to the audience.

18. Jesse McLean, *The Art and Making of "Hannibal: The Television Series"* (London: Titan Books, 2015), 58.

Hannibal's "Final Woman"

If Bedelia's punishment in the postcredits scene evokes the femme fatale's misogyny-laden downfall, her resistance in that same sequence pays homage to another feminine archetype: horror's "Final Girl." As Carol Clover defines this archetype in her landmark essay on gender in horror, the Final Girl is, like Stephen King's Carrie, a "victim-hero," potentially monstrous in her heroism. Clover argues that male horror audiences "identify with [. . .] screen females in fear and pain." Like a fairy tale, *Hannibal*'s version of horror invites the audience to be "both Red Riding Hood *and* the Wolf; the force of the experience, in horror, comes from knowing both sides of the story."[19]

On the one hand, Bedelia is *Hannibal*'s Final Girl in a very obvious sense; she is the only character in the show's last frame, still breathing and conscious enough to put up a fight as she slips a sharp-tined escargot fork into her lap. And although Bedelia's ultimate fate is unknown, creator Bryan Fuller envisions her surviving that dinner: "I think there's still kind of a funny moment in a future Hannibal story where you see a female figure walking down the road and you follow her home and she takes off her leg and you reveal it's Bedelia."[20] So, in the most basic sense, Bedelia meets Clover's criteria as "the distressed female [. . .] who did not die: the survivor, or Final Girl."[21]

By using her fork as a weapon, Bedelia meets another of Clover's criteria, what she dubs the "penetration scene," or the pivotal moment in which the victim, cornered and unable to flee, chooses instead to fight back. Bedelia is not running through a house of horrors as a slasher chases her with a machete, but it is clear that her

---

19. Clover, *Men, Women, and Chainsaws*, 5, 12, emphasis in original.
20. Oriana Schwindt, "*Hannibal* Finale: Bryan Fuller Reveals Will and Hannibal's Fate . . . and Explains That Chilling Last Dinner Scene," *TVInsider*, Aug. 29, 2015, at http://www.tvinsider.com/36936/hannibal-finale-bryan-fuller-reveals-will-and-hannibals-fate-and-explains-that-chilling-last-dinner-scene.
21. Clover, *Men, Women, and Chainsaws*, 35.

unknown host has penetrated the sanctuary of her home and violated the sanctity of her body. Bedelia has fled Hannibal more than once; now, literally immobilized, she has no choice but to attack—she has finally become the participant Hannibal always wanted her to be. If her host is indeed Hannibal, Bedelia's use of the escargot fork as a weapon is uniquely appropriate. Not only does it call to mind a moment in Ridley Scott's film *Hannibal* (2001) in which Clarice Starling (Julianne Moore) hides a fork in her napkin while at dinner with Hannibal Lecter (Anthony Hopkins), but it also is a hallmark of the Final Girl to use the killer's weapon against him. In Bedelia's case, the weapon is not a chainsaw or a machete or a scalpel, but a fork—sharp, sinister, and symbolic of Hannibal's cannibalism. Bedelia's choice of the fork could also be interpreted as indicative of her agency and desire to maintain an identity separate from Hannibal. Though she acknowledges she may share some of Hannibal's killer instincts, she will not partake in his cannibalism. As in their conversation in "Contorno" (3.05) on the nature of snails and fireflies, because of Bedelia's refusal to join him at his table, Hannibal would perhaps categorize her as a "snail" to be devoured rather than a firefly to be transformed. In claiming the escargot fork as her weapon, Bedelia turns the tool of her victimization against him.

Fuller's take on the Final Girl trope also updates it for a modern audience. For one, *Hannibal*'s Final Girl isn't a girl at all; she's a mature woman in a television landscape in which women older than forty make up only 26 percent of television characters despite being 47 percent of the US population.[22] It is significant that Bedelia is a Final Woman and not a Final Girl, defying the stereotype that survival instincts or heroism belong only to fresh-faced ingénues. Clover, in her original analysis of horror and suspense films of the late twentieth century, also notices that the Final Girl was frequently masculinized, often given a boyish name or androgynous appearance, from Ripley

---

22. Jennifer Siebel Newsom and Kimberlee Acquaro, dirs., *Miss Representation*, documentary (Greenbrae, CA: Girls' Club Entertainment, 2011).

in the *Alien* franchise to Stretch in *Texas Chainsaw Massacre 2* (Tobe Hooper, 1986).[23] More than simply boyish, the Final Girl of the 1970s and 1980s was virginal, her sexually active counterparts more likely to be the killer's victims. Even Clarice Starling embodies this aspect of the Final Girl as described by Clover: "masculine in both manner and career, uninterested in sex or men, and dead serious about her career."[24] The Final Girl trope, though empowering in some respects, also reflects a sexist double standard, wherein a female character must be masculine or virginal or both in order to be deemed worthy of survival. Bedelia as a Final Woman subverts this standard; she is quite obviously feminine, quietly so as Hannibal's psychiatrist, flagrantly so as a femme fatale in Florence. The suggestive scenes between Bedelia and Hannibal, including one that Bryan Fuller dubbed "post-coital,"[25] also indicate that Bedelia is unquestionably sexual.

Perhaps this transformation should be taken as a marker of how far the horror genre has come, that a woman need not be masculinized or de-sexualized in order to be empowered. Or it may also be a reflection of *Hannibal*'s largely female fanbase.[26] If, as Clover argues, the Final Girl is a way for the male horror viewer to identify with the female victim-hero, what happens when the horror viewer is female? No such translation is needed. Moreover, both Hannibal and Will take on many characteristics associated with the feminine. In this

23. Clover, *Men, Women, and Chainsaws*, 39–40.
24. Clover, *Men, Women, and Chainsaws*, 232–33.
25. Bryan Fuller, Twitter post, July 2, 2015, at https://twitter.com/BryanFuller/status/616789715526615040.
26. Fuller and journalists alike have remarked on *Hannibal*'s largely female and social-media-savvy fanbase. See Sarah Hughes, "The Power and the Gory: Why Women Love the New Wave of Violent TV," *Independent*, May 17, 2014, at http://www.independent.co.uk/arts-entertainment/tv/features/the-power-and-the-gory-why-women-love-the-new-wave-of-violent-tv-9384284.html; Allison McCracken and Brian Faucette, "Branding *Hannibal*: When Quality TV Viewers and Social Media Fans Converge," *Antenna*, Aug. 24, 2015, at http://blog.commarts.wisc.edu/2015/08/24/branding-hannibal-when-quality-tv-viewers-and-social-media-fans-converge/.

way, it is not Bedelia as Final Girl who is masculinized to appeal to a male viewer, but two male hero-monsters who are feminized for a female audience.

Conclusion: Observe or Participate?

The inherent ambiguity of the postcredits sequence lends itself to conflicting interpretations based on Bedelia's shifting status as author avatar, femme fatale, and Final Girl throughout the course of the series. If the ending is ambiguous, it is because Bedelia herself is ambiguous, both perpetrator and victim, "the smartest character on the show" yet still captivated by Hannibal's dark charisma. But it is the very ambiguity of Bedelia alone at the table in the final scene and the ability of this image to invite interpretation that ultimately break down the boundary between passive observation and active participation for the viewer, implicating the audience in *Hannibal*'s horror-film ethics.

In the aftermath of the season 3 finale, there has been much speculation among television critics and fans alike about the meaning of the final scene. Two distinct interpretations have prevailed. One is that Hannibal (and possibly Will) are Bedelia's host(s), that they survived their fall into the Atlantic, and that the scene is taking place at some future moment. The other is that the scene is happening simultaneously with the fall from the cliff and that Bedelia cooked her own leg in anticipation of Hannibal and Will's arrival. Creator Bryan Fuller and food stylist Janice Poon initially played up the mystery surrounding the identity of Bedelia's host, suggesting not only Hannibal and Will but also other characters from the Thomas Harris tetralogy as possible guests for the feast.[27] Fuller seems to have intended the postcredits "stinger" both to hint that Hannibal may have survived the fall but also to invite audience speculation and

---

27. Janice Poon, "Episode 13, 'The Wrath of the Lamb,'" *Feeding Hannibal* (blog), Aug. 30, 2015, at http://janicepoonart.blogspot.com/2015/08/episode-13-wrath-of-lamb.html.

critical conversation surrounding the mystery—the question "Who is eating Bedelia's leg?" functioning as the series' own version of "Who shot JR?" "We don't know if Hannibal is indeed serving her leg," Bryan Fuller comments and then asks, "Or is it Hannibal's uncle Robertus, or Lady Murasaki, or is it Will Graham?"[28]

However, when first presented with an alternate interpretation by noted television critic Alan Sepinwall, Fuller expressed incredulity that Bedelia eating her own leg could have been an intended reading.[29] Both Bryan Fuller and Gillian Anderson on the commentary track for the DVD edition of "Antipasto" admitted that Bedelia cooking her own leg was not an interpretation that even occurred to them while filming.[30] Fuller has become increasingly begrudging about this particular fan theory, appreciating its bizarre wackiness but pronouncing it a "false interpretation."[31]

There are several reasons why the "Bedelia cooked her own leg" interpretation may seem unsavory to Bedelia's creator. For one, it implies a finality to the narrative that was never intended—that Bedelia is eating her own leg alone because Will and Hannibal do not survive the fall and therefore the story is at its end. Despite low ratings, the cast and crew of *Hannibal* had been optimistic about a fourth season, and Fuller has expressed a desire to see the show continue on another network or platform. *Hannibal*'s abrupt cancellation by NBC midway through the third season may have encouraged some viewers to seek finality and closure in that final sequence rather than the continuity and mystery Fuller was hoping to communicate. More likely, however, is that Fuller sees Bedelia's autocannibalism as

---

28. Alan Sepinwall, "*Hannibal*'s Creator Explains That Dark, Twisted and . . . Romantic(?) Series Finale," Uproxx (website), Aug. 29, 2015, at http://uproxx.com/sepinwall/hannibal-creator-i-wanted-to-be-sure-we-had-an-ending-for-the-story.

29. Sepinwall, "*Hannibal*'s Creator Explains."

30. Gillian Anderson and Bryan Fuller, "'Antipasto' Audio Commentary," *Hannibal: Season Three*, DVD, disc 1 (Santa Monica, CA: Lionsgate, 2015).

31. Bryan Fuller, "'The Wrath of the Lamb' Audio Commentary," *Hannibal: Season Three*, DVD, disc 4 (Santa Monica, CA: Lionsgate, 2015).

being contradictory to his vision of the character and his understanding of her agency. For Bedelia to have mentally snapped in this way seems to be a weakness to him, "a crazier version" of Bedelia than he understands her to be.[32] He imagines Bedelia's agency in a very straightforward Final Girl sense: "No, somebody has got her, and will she or will she not survive[?] And what's so fun is that on the song that Siouxsie Sioux wrote, we hear her say, 'I will survive, I will survive,' as we're pushing in on Bedelia, and that could mean she's singing from Hannibal's perspective and it means he has survived and will eat this woman now, or Bedelia's point of view that it's like, 'You may have cut off this leg, but I've got this fork and I'm gonna do some damage before it's done.'"[33]

Those who interpret the final scene as Bedelia cooking her own leg are responding to another aspect of her character, one that places more emphasis on her agency as an author avatar to write her own ending. In this reading, Bedelia is her own victim rather than Hannibal's, and so the interpretation that she cooks her own leg maintains continuity with her actions regarding Hannibal throughout the course of the show; she "never considered herself in need of being rescued" from Hannibal, as she remarks in "Dolce" (3.06), despite her dangerous intimacy with him. Bedelia cooking her own leg does not necessarily mean she has accepted defeat or gone mad. Her actions can still be interpreted as rational and agentic. She knows Hannibal longs to savor her and that Will resents her lack of scars. If Bedelia is the hostess of this feast, she gives both men what they want but on her own terms, a strategic sacrifice so that she may save the rest of herself. This reading even accommodates the series' sense of *contrapasso*—the implication being that in trying to outsmart Hannibal one last time, Bedelia might have actually outsmarted herself. It also does not contradict Bedelia's status as Final Girl; cannibalism is of course Hannibal's weapon, and in cooking her own leg, Bedelia has seized it for herself.

32. Fuller, "'The Wrath of the Lamb' Audio Commentary."
33. Sepinwall, "*Hannibal*'s Creator Explains."

Other visual and audio cues give further credence to this more Bedelia-centered reading. The audio track "Love Crime" is sustained throughout the cliff sequence with Will and Hannibal, the final credits, and the postcredits scene with Bedelia in "The Wrath of the Lamb." Likewise, there is no visual interruption between the cliff sequence and the credits as they are superimposed over the waters that may (or may not) be Will and Hannibal's final resting place. Taken together, these cues suggest a unity of time, if not a unity of place, in this final sequence of events. In contrast, the postcredits sequence that ends the second season is composed quite differently, with interruptions in both image and soundtrack. At the end of "Mizumono" (2.13), the soundtrack and image change from Brian Reitzel's score "Bloodfest" and Hannibal alone in the rain to an image of fluffy clouds and a blue sky underscored by Bach's *Goldberg Variations*, Hannibal's theme. A plane shoots overhead, and from there the camera segues into the first-class cabin, where we find Hannibal and Bedelia, possibly days after the events of "Mizumono." Furthermore, the wide-panning shot of Bedelia at her dining table in the series' last scene makes the empty room look cavernous and Bedelia appear small and alone. Her expression as she grabs the fork could be read as apprehension or excitement—perhaps she is not afraid that Hannibal is there but afraid he is *not* coming and that she has irrevocably harmed herself for nothing.

In many ways, Bedelia's ambiguous ending parallels the situation of *Hannibal* fandom. Like Bedelia, who now waits for a guest who may never arrive, fans are left in fearful anticipation. In August 2017, producers reopened the conversation on a new season of *Hannibal*, but creator Bryan Fuller has cautioned fans it could take years for a fourth season to return to their screens.[34] Without definitive plans for more *Hannibal* in sight, fans will have to provide the "meat"—in the form of fanart and fanfiction, events such as Red Dragon Con

---

34. Dave Nemetz, "*Hannibal* Update: Bryan Fuller Says Revival 'Conversations' Are Underway," *TVLine*, Aug. 13, 2017, at http://tvline.com/2017/08/13/hannibal-season-4-bryan-fuller-revival.

and FannibalFest Toronto, and other forms of participatory culture. Indeed, "Fannibals" have already crossed the line from observation to active participation with online campaigns to save the show and even the production of two bound volumes of "Hannigram" fanfiction.[35]

Whatever one's preferred interpretation, the final scene dictates that the viewer must participate and engage in meaning making. Viewers who imagine Bedelia as a wedding feast for "Murder Husbands" Will and Hannibal see a femme fatale receiving her customary comeuppance, whereas those who root for her to pick up her fork and fight back are cheering on the Final Girl in a horror film's last act. Bedelia eating her own leg keeps the narrative focus on Bedelia and Bedelia's choices and resists the trope of "the damsel in distress" inherently baked into the premise of a show like *Hannibal*. Her autocannibalism becomes an act of authorship, a bizarre and gruesome grace note to this blood opera. As the camera pans back, it reveals a fourth place setting at this macabre feast—one for the viewer perhaps, an observer who has become a participant.

Bibliography

Anderson, Gillian, and Bryan Fuller. "'Antipasto' Audio Commentary." *Hannibal: Season Three*, DVD, disc 1. Santa Monica, CA: Lionsgate, 2015.

Chaudhuri, Shohini. *Feminist Film Theorists*. New York: Routledge, 2006.

---

35. Cynthia Littleton, "'Hannibal': Producers Stoke Fan Support with '#Save Hannibal' Twitter Campaign," *Variety*, June 22, 2015, at http://variety.com/2015/tv/news/hannibal-canceled-nbc-twitter-1201525727/. On the first anthology, see Alex E. Jung, "That Book of Hannibal Slash Fiction You Always Wanted Is Happening," *Vulture*, Nov. 17, 2015, at http://www.vulture.com/2015/11/there-will-be-a-book-of-hannibal-slash-fiction.html. A second fanthology was successfully crowdfunded and published in October 2017: see "*Radiance: A Fannibal Anthology* [compiled by Romina Nikolić and Germaine Bierbaum]" (description), Kickstarter, n.d., at https://www.kickstarter.com/projects/lovecrimecat/radiance-a-fannibal-anthology/description, accessed Aug. 19, 2017.

Clover, Carol J. *Men, Women, and Chainsaws: Gender in the Modern Horror Film*. Princeton, NJ: Princeton Univ. Press, 1992.

Dancy, Hugh. Interview on *Last Call with Carson Daly*. NBC, June 2, 2015.

Fuller, Bryan. Twitter post, July 2, 2015. At https://twitter.com/BryanFuller/status/616789715526615040.

———. "'The Wrath of the Lamb' Audio Commentary." *Hannibal: Season Three*, DVD, disc 4. Santa Monica, CA: Lionsgate, 2015.

Goluzzo, Rob. "For the Love of Horror, with Bryan Fuller!" Interview. *Shock Waves*, podcast audio, Dec. 19, 2016. At http://www.blumhouse.com/2016/12/19/shock-waves-episode-31-for-the-love-of-horror-with-bryan-fuller.

Harris, Thomas. *Hannibal*. 1999. Reprint. New York: Bantam Dell, 2000.

Hughes, Sarah. "The Power and the Gory: Why Women Love the New Wave of Violent TV." *Independent*, May 17, 2014. At http://www.independent.co.uk/arts-entertainment/tv/features/the-power-and-the-gory-why-women-love-the-new-wave-of-violent-tv-9384284.html.

Jensen, Jeff. "*Hannibal* Review: Let's Save This Weird, Excellent Show." *EW*, July 16, 2015. At http://ew.com/article/2015/07/16/save-hannibal-review.

Jung, Alex E. "That Book of Hannibal Slash Fiction You Always Wanted Is Happening." *Vulture*, Nov. 17, 2015. At http://www.vulture.com/2015/11/there-will-be-a-book-of-hannibal-slash-fiction.html.

Kulzick, Kate. "*Hannibal*, Ep. 3.01: 'Antipasto.'" *Kate's Classical Corner* (blog), June 4, 2015. At http://www.popoptiq.com/kcc-hannibal-ep-3-01-antipasto/.

Littleton, Cynthia. "'Hannibal': Producers Stoke Fan Support with '#Save Hannibal' Twitter Campaign." *Variety*, June 22, 2015. At http://variety.com/2015/tv/news/hannibal-canceled-nbc-twitter-1201525727/.

McCourt, James. *Queer Street*. New York: Norton, 2004.

McCracken, Allison, and Brian Faucette. "Branding *Hannibal*: When Quality TV Viewers and Social Media Fans Converge." *Antenna*, Aug. 24, 2015. At http://blog.commarts.wisc.edu/2015/08/24/branding-hannibal-when-quality-tv-viewers-and-social-media-fans-converge/.

McLean, Jesse. *The Art and Making of "Hannibal: The Television Series."* London: Titan Books, 2015.

Mulvey, Laura. "Visual Pleasure and Narrative Cinema." *Screen* 16, no. 3 (1975): 6–18.

Nemetz, Dave. "*Hannibal* Update: Bryan Fuller Says Revival 'Conversations' Are Underway." *TVLine*, Aug. 13, 2017. At http://tvline.com/2017/08/13/hannibal-season-4-bryan-fuller-revival.

Place, Janey. "Women in Film Noir." In *Women in Film Noir*, edited by E. Ann Kaplan, 47–68. London: British Film Institute, 1998.

Poon, Janice. "Episode 13, 'The Wrath of the Lamb.'" *Feeding Hannibal* (blog), Aug. 30, 2015. At http://janicepoonart.blogspot.com/2015/08/episode-13-wrath-of-lamb.html.

"*Radiance: A Fannibal Anthology* [compiled by Romina Nikolić and Germaine Bierbaum]" (description). Kickstarter, n.d. At https://www.kickstarter.com/projects/lovecrimecat/radiance-a-fannibal-anthology/description. Accessed Aug. 19, 2017.

Schneider, Michael. "Gillian Anderson's Second Revival, from the Scary *Hannibal* to the Sci-Fi *X-Files*." *TVInsider*, July 9, 2015. At http://www.tvinsider.com/26005/gillian-andersons-second-revival-from-the-scary-hannibal-to-the-sci-fi-x-files/.

Schwartz, Morris S., and Charlotte Green Schwartz. "Problems in Participant Observation." *American Journal of Sociology* 60, no. 4 (1955): 343–53.

Schwindt, Oriana. "*Hannibal* Finale: Bryan Fuller Reveals Will and Hannibal's Fate . . . and Explains That Chilling Last Dinner Scene." *TVInsider*, Aug. 29, 2015. At http://www.tvinsider.com/36936/hannibal-finale-bryan-fuller-reveals-will-and-hannibals-fate-and-explains-that-chilling-last-dinner-scene.

Sepinwall, Alan. "*Hannibal*'s Creator Explains That Dark, Twisted and . . . Romantic(?) Series Finale." Uproxx (website), Aug. 29, 2015. At http://uproxx.com/sepinwall/hannibal-creator-i-wanted-to-be-sure-we-had-an-ending-for-the-story.

Siebel Newsom, Jennifer, and Kimberlee Acquaro, dirs. *Miss Representation*. Documentary. Greenbrae, CA: Girls' Club Entertainment, 2011.

Silverman, Kaja. *The Subject of Semiotics*. New York: Oxford Univ. Press, 1983.

Thurm, Eric. "*Hannibal* Showrunner: 'We Are Not Making Television. We Are Making a Pretentious Art Film from the 80s.'" *Guardian*, June 3, 2015. At https://www.theguardian.com/tv-and-radio/2015/jun/03/hannibal-tv-showrunner-bryan-fuller.

10 | "Some Lazy Psychiatry, Dr. Lecter"

Teacups, Narrative, and Hannibal's *Critique of Psychoanalysis*

Karen Felts

When Bryan Fuller declared in the summer of 2015 that *Hannibal* (NBC, 2013–15) would refrain from using images of rape, particularly in the *Red Dragon* arc of season 3, he and the show were widely praised as feminist for distancing the show from the "rape-tainment" prevalent in prime-time drama, especially crime procedurals. Fuller stated that although he did not think "any of the crime procedural shows are actually 'glorifying' rape [. . .] it is certainly explored so frequently that it rarely feels genuine."[1] Rape on television, Fuller suggests, may raise awareness of such violence, but it does so in a manner that reduces it to a simple plot point or a ratings earner. In *Hannibal* episodes spun from Thomas Harris's novel *Red Dragon* (1981), in which the serial killer's crimes are sexually motivated rapes and murders, the decision to avoid depicting them is all the more politically significant considering the impetus to remain true to the source material. How does one faithfully adapt a novel about serial rape and murder without showing mutilated female bodies? More broadly, is it possible to have a genre-driven television show

---

1. James Hibberd, "'Hannibal' Showrunner Criticizes TV's Rape Scene Epidemic," *Entertainment Weekly*, May 28, 2015, at http://ew.com/article/2015/05/28/hannibal-rape-thrones/.

that breaks with the hallmarks of the genre? Although *Hannibal* was applauded for its conscientiousness regarding rape and its refusal to objectify rape victims, this particular assessment amounts mostly to positive-image criticism: we will represent women as agents and as heroes, not as victims. Though that criticism has merit, the real teeth of *Hannibal*'s gender critique lies in the way the series as a whole dismantles the familiar narrative structure of crime dramas and its discursive counterpart, psychoanalysis.

"Apéritif," *Hannibal*'s first episode, initially presents the series as a crime procedural, highlighting the generic conventions the show will eventually question and rewrite. The first shot is the aftermath of a crime: ambulances, police cars, a forensics team swarming a typical suburban house. Inside the house is a man, his eyes closed, pendulum swinging, time reversing itself in his mind, not simply reconstructing the crime from evidence but imaginatively reenacting it as he stares at the body of Mrs. Marlow in front of him. The beginning is familiar: a home invasion, a dead woman lying in her own blood, and a man in a khaki flak jacket staring at the scene. The man wears blue latex gloves, so the viewer knows he is with the police despite his lack of uniform. Forensic specialists gather evidence and place markers for crime-scene photos. Blood is pooled on the floor and splattered on the walls of an otherwise quintessentially middle-class home. This establishing scene is straight out of a crime procedural such as *CSI: Crime Scene Investigation* (2000–2015) or *Law and Order* (1990–2010).[2] And as in any procedural episode, the narrative begins with a disruption of normality—here epitomized by the safe, comfortable, heterosexual domestic world of the Marlow household. The home has been invaded, and the nuclear family destroyed. As a keenly insightful criminal profiler, the man in the opening scene, Will Graham, intends to identify the killer, expel him

---

2. The original promo pictures represent *Hannibal* as a crime procedural, with Hugh Dancy crouched over a dead body as if he were looking for clues, while team members stand behind him, ready to support his investigation.

from society via either imprisonment or death, and thereby reestablish the normative order of life.[3]

Many narrative conventions of detective fiction, as has often been noted, reinforce patriarchal gender roles and a heteronormative worldview, a tendency that is particularly troubling for feminist and queer critics—also, as "Apéritif" suggests, for the writers of *Hannibal*.[4] The gender dynamics represented through these narratives boil down to women as voiceless victims, much like the paralyzed Mrs. Marlow lying in her own blood;[5] the killer as a "sexual deviant," who is often coded as a repressed homosexual; and the detective as an active agent who uses his rationality to purge the world of the killer and the deviance the killer represents. Within this narrative framework, women are passive victims; they are not the agents of their own stories but merely the object of someone else's. Queer characters need to be expunged for balance to return. And the detective, who embodies rational, paternalistic masculinity, restores order and "traditional manly virtues" through his mastery of science and knowledge.[6] Yet while the opening of "Apéritif" suggests that *Hannibal* will adhere to this narrative model, the episode's conclusion calls that expectation into question. By the end of "Apéritif," imagination has trumped science, Will Graham has not penetrated or investigated Garret Jacob Hobbs so much as inhabited him, and Abigail Hobbs, a victim, is to be given her own story.

---

3. Nick Lacey, *Narrative and Genre: Key Concepts in Media Studies* (New York: St. Martin's Press, 2000), 234.

4. Richard Dyer, "Three Questions about Serial Killing," in *The Matter of Images: Essays on Representation* (London: Routledge, 1993), 114; Philip L. Simpson, *Psychopaths: Tracking the Serial Killer through Contemporary American Film and Fiction* (Carbondale: Southern Illinois Univ. Press, 2000), 75.

5. Mr. Marlow is also shot on his way down the stairs, but his death is merely incidental.

6. Mark Seltzer, *Serial Killers: Death and Life in America's Wound Culture* (New York: Routledge, 1998), 20.

Later in "Apéritif," *Hannibal* turns its attention to psychoanalysis, the discourse that underpins, legitimizes, and reinforces the gender norms on which the procedural narrative is based. Upon recognizing Hannibal Lecter's intention to penetrate the "bone arena of [his] skull," Will states, "Don't psychoanalyze me. You won't like me when I'm psychoanalyzed. Now if you'll excuse me, I have to go give a lecture on psychoanalyzing." Not only is Will pointing out the obviousness of psychoanalysis's approach and thus questioning its usefulness as a tool of detection, but he is also presenting it as something more theoretical—a topic for academic study and not a discourse with practical relevance to people in their real lives. Will's dismissal begins the three-season-long subversion of psychoanalysis both as a legitimate discourse for understanding human behavior and as an agent for enforcing gender and sexual norms. In its playful moments, the show suggests that psychoanalysis is a cliché that is not particularly helpful in understanding criminals, an empty grasping for "low-hanging fruit." This is most clearly evident in "Œuf" (1.04), when Hannibal asks Will about his mother, to which Will retorts, "That is some pretty lazy psychiatry, Dr. Lecter." More pointedly, however, the show reveals the dangers of investing in Freudian understandings of sexual desire and binary gender roles, as demonstrated in "Mizumono" (2.13) by the defenestration of Dr. Alana Bloom by Abigail Hobbs, Alana's former patient, whom she treated for "daddy issues." In "Mizumono," Hannibal also refers to the "dead religion of psychoanalysis," a line taken from Harris's novel *The Silence of the Lambs* (1988).[7] Both Harris and Fuller employ the line to show psychoanalysis's new role, particularly in the world of crime solving: much like Christianity, psychoanalysis has become a moral yardstick, yet instead of deciding who is saved and who is damned, it separates the healthy from the pathological,

---

7. Thomas Harris, *The Silence of the Lambs* (New York: St. Martin's Press, 1988), 163.

the phallic from the castrated, and the masculine from the feminine. And like a religion that seeks to explain the nature of the world, psychoanalysis, particularly as it is used in detective/serial-killer narratives, comprehends the world through its own necessarily reductive, psychosexual lens, in this case a phallocentric lens that worships and legitimizes the penis, privileges the heteronormative family, dismisses the feminine as absence, and valorizes a patriarchal, heterosexual masculinity.

Though psychoanalysis in general has been reclaimed by both feminist and queer communities, the particular brand of Freudian psychoanalysis on which the detective/serial-killer genre relies is neither feminist nor queer-friendly. As an interpretive tool for understanding and categorizing the serial killer, psychoanalysis presumes that the pathological is sexually motivated: for the killer, murder is a substitute for sex, and he kills to punish the feminine.[8] A failed Oedipus, whether because he is impotent, homosexual, or simply nonmasculine, he kills both to establish gender dominance and to achieve sexual satisfaction. His sexual deviance from the norm is the problem, the source of social and narrative disruption; this is what must be traced by both therapist and detective and what must be cured or contained in order to keep society safe. In this reductive form of psychoanalysis, childhoods are reconstructed, and the past is mined for the primal scene, the moment when the serial killer and his deviance were spawned. Hunting for this originating event is necessary both for understanding the killer's murderous impulses and for preventing the creation of future killers. With both Jame Gumb and Francis Dolarhyde in the Harris novels, the primal scene involves a non-gender-compliant mother and grandmother.[9] Hannibal, too, is given a primal scene in the novels, the cannibalization of his sister,

---

8. Carol J. Clover, *Men, Women, and Chainsaws: Gender in Modern Horror Film* (Princeton, NJ: Princeton Univ. Press, 1992), 29.

9. Harris, *Silence of the Lambs*, 282; Thomas Harris, *Red Dragon* (New York: Penguin, 1981), 244–72.

Mischa, which he discovers upon finding her baby teeth in the "stool pit" used by the German soldiers who ate her.[10]

Both Harris and Fuller are suspicious of primal-scene theory: Harris because it is reductive and Fuller because it is misogynist and homophobic. In primal-scene theory, the origin of the serial killer involves a traumatic and often sexualized event that occurs in the home during the killer's childhood; to solve the crime, the detective must discover this moment, which requires him to go to the killer's home. A line from the novel *The Silence of the Lambs*, later repeated in the television show, highlights Harris's and Fuller's similar distance from the going-home narrative while also revealing the critical difference between them: "Nothing happened to me. I happened," says Hannibal. In the novel, Hannibal employs the line to dismiss Starling, accusing her of trying to dissect him through psychoanalysis; he prefers that she view him as evil rather than use her insight to comprehend his past. It is a rebuff that allows him to remain impenetrable and authoritative.[11] In the television show, the line is spoken in "Secondo" (3.03) between Hannibal and Bedelia Du Maurier as he sensuously washes her hair. In a moment of intimacy and fragile trust, when Hannibal could easily drown Bedelia, she probes his past: "Why can't you go home, Hannibal? What happened to you there?" In part, Bedelia's question is motivated by jealousy. Will Graham, her rival, is at that moment sitting in Hannibal's childhood home, drinking Lecter estate wine with the servant Chiyoh, a spatial connection denied to Bedelia. Yet her question is more an attempt at intimacy than a dissection of Hannibal. Hannibal's response is tender rather than angry. He pauses while lathering her hair and says, "Nothing happened to me. I happened." Hannibal is not the victim of a primal scene (as compared to the novel's version of him);

---

10. Thomas Harris, *Hannibal* (1999; reprint, New York: Bantam, 2006), 291; see also Brian Baker, *Contemporary Masculinities in Fiction, Film, and Television* (New York: Bloomsbury, 2015), 208.

11. Harris, *Silence of the Lambs*, 21; see also Baker, *Contemporary Masculinities*, 208.

he *is* the primal scene. In Fuller's adaptation, the line suggests that Hannibal was "born this way," not made. His tender washing of his naked lover's hair undercuts the psychoanalytic assumption that serial killers kill because of sexual pathology, a pathology grounded in misogyny and homophobia. Neither is Hannibal impotent, nor is his masculinity threatened; he simply kills. He can wash hair, cook, attend to his clothing, and be in love with Will Graham, and his masculinity remains firmly intact.[12]

The television show goes to great lengths to challenge the trope of the serial killer's primal scene. Eldon Stammets, Eliot Budish, Katherine Pimms, James Gray, Randal Tier, Matthew Brown, Tobias Budge, and Georgia Madchen all kill for reasons that have nothing to do with sexual pathology. They are driven to kill by alienation or aesthetics. The psychosexual killers Clark Ingram (the social worker in the horse) and Larry Wells (the totem-pole constructionist) are not given creation stories. Neither is Francis Dolarhyde, perhaps the most psychosexually driven killer in the series, though the novel *Red Dragon* goes to great lengths to explain his creation myth. The series as a whole has a surprising dearth of families as well. The presence of a backstory is problematic for two reasons. First, the killer's origin myth is frequently laced with misogyny. One bad mother or grandmother not toeing the gender line is the source of all this public mayhem and violence. The implication is that if women would just behave, then they would not be killed, nor would they produce murderous sons.[13] Second, the backstory assumes that deviance is

---

12. Unlike the problematic linear narrative central to both detective fiction and psychoanalysis, where there is a central (primal) point from which the self emerges, "Secondo" offers an interesting alternative: the mosaic. Hannibal and Will have an imagined therapy session shot entirely with prisms, suggesting that vision and self are not a linear but a "geometric progression," much like "painted shards of glass." The use of the mosaic suggests that the self is infinitely more complex and cannot be explained or dismissed with a single moment.

13. The one family-focused episode, "Œuf," presents an interesting spin on stories that blame mothers for their own deaths, so common in shows such as *Law*

violent, thus eliding the violence inherent in normalcy. The problem here is twofold: it assumes that the nonnormative is a threat that must be rehabilitated or expelled, and it assumes normalcy (read: traditional masculinity) is not predicated on violence.[14] Hence, Garret Jacob Hobbs's importance. According to "Apéritif," Hobbs is by all appearances normal: he is a white, married, heterosexual father who "fits pipe" for a living and hunts doe for fun. He is unmarked, the embodiment of white male masculinity. And, critically, he is never given an origin story. We know only that he wants to "honor every part" of the women he kills. By denying him an excuse, by refraining from narrativizing his psychology, the show refuses to let normative masculinity off the hook.

To fully critique the gender politics of the crime procedural, *Hannibal* must also undermine the discourse on which the procedural's gender roles are predicated: psychoanalysis. In the *Entertainment Weekly* interview quoted earlier, Fuller describes rape imagery and narratives as "low-hanging fruit"; similarly, Will Graham dismisses therapeutic conversations about his mother as "low-hanging fruit" in "Œuf." Though this might simply be a coincidence or a turn of phrase Fuller is fond of, it does link this essay's twin concerns: the ways in which the show challenges the mated conventions of the procedural drama and psychoanalysis and these two discourses' reinforcement of heteronormative gender roles. Although Fuller's *Hannibal* echoes Harris's own ambivalence about psychoanalysis, the show's attack on it is relentless, exercised through multiple characters and through all three seasons.[15]

Though parallels drawn between the detective in crime narratives and the Freudian psychoanalyst may be tired clichés, they bear repeating for their relevance to *Hannibal*'s Will Graham. The

---

and Order: Criminal Intent (2001–11) and *Law and Order: Special Victims Unit* (1999–).

14. Dyer, "Three Questions about Serial Killing," 112.

15. Simpson, *Psychopaths*, 82.

detective and the therapist, both born in the nineteenth century thanks to Victorian preoccupations with otherness and classification, share many traits: both are men; both are hired to hunt the cause of pathology; both cling to minutiae as evidence of crime or disease; both are scholars of human desire; and both assemble signs to reconstruct narratives of the past in order to restore normalcy. Figures of knowledge and vision, the detective and the therapist seek to penetrate the human psyche, see into its secrets, and use rationality to explain and contain the irrational. As embodiments of phallic rationality, the detective and the therapist serve as enforcers of binary difference, patrolling the boundary between normal and abnormal, self and other, masculine and feminine.

In *Hannibal*, as in most serial-killer narratives, the distinctions between detective and therapist are erased. There are only therapists who happen to do the work detectives do (Alana Bloom, Hannibal Lecter, Frederick Chilton) and detectives who do the work therapists do (Jack Crawford, Will Graham). Even Abigail Hobbs considers becoming a psychiatrist. Perhaps the most direct representation of *Hannibal*'s critical view of psychoanalysis is Neil Frank's death in Bedelia's office in ". . . And the Woman Clothed in Sun" (3.10). He is in the process of dismissing psychotherapy as "culty and weird," a racket run by therapists and ultimately not helpful, when he chokes on his own tongue. In an attempt to "help," Bedelia shoves her fist into his throat, a psychoanalytic fisting/blowjob of sorts. She penetrates him and, in so doing, silences him. It does not take much effort to read this moment: therapy is a phallic fist that we are forced to swallow, leading to the death of the self. The scene's symbolism is relatively obvious; the sustained critique of psychoanalysis is subtler. It is through the characters that most often resort to psychoanalytic discourse, Frederick Chilton and Alana Bloom, that *Hannibal* points to the gender-related problems stemming from such a phallic-oriented approach. If one uses "penetration" as a means of understanding, the show suggests, one will ultimately be penetrated in return.

In the Harris novels, Frederick Chilton is a bad psychiatrist who "fumbles" around in Lecter's head and a sexist who objectifies

Clarice Starling.[16] Chilton resents Lecter for his intelligence and notoriety in the psychological community, and he resents Starling for being a woman who has garnered more respect than he has from Lecter and the FBI. By the time Lecter eats Chilton in Haiti, Chilton's fate seems justified: a man who treats women like meat will become meat. As played by Raúl Esparza in the series *Hannibal*, Chilton is less of a letch and much more of an opportunist. Rather than corner Alana Bloom and pressure her for dates, as would the Chilton of the novels, he instead dismisses her intelligence and credentials by implying that her success is entirely owing to her looks, as in "Mukōzuke" (2.05): "What is it about you, Dr. Bloom? The most sinister neurochemistry in the field can't help percolating in your presence. The interesting ones just fall at your feet. . . . You're like catnip for killers." Esparza delivers this line with a hint of gay shade; it is her desirability to these men, not her skills as a psychiatrist, that brings all the psychopaths to her yard. The comment does more than dismiss Alana Bloom as an intellectual and professional; it highlights a form of heterosexual dynamic demanded by psychotherapy. Chilton implies that men do not want to be opened up or penetrated by other men—though the Will Graham/Hannibal Lecter dynamic seems to belie this point. Chilton is left out in the psychoanalytic cold because he is an unlikable opportunist who lacks grace and intelligence.

Chilton spends three seasons attempting to penetrate men's minds, yet his psychosexual impotence compels him to resort to other penetrative means: he invasively records Will Graham's conversations; in "Takiawase" (2.04), he injects both Will and Abel Gideon with drugs to make them amenable to his "fumbling"; and he subjects Abel to psychic driving in order to convince him that he (Abel) is the Chesapeake Ripper. Although Hannibal commits similar acts, the punishments Chilton receives in the narrative—he is dissected in an observatory and made to hold his own bowels, framed for a crime

---

16. Harris, *Red Dragon*, 80; Harris, *Silence of the Lambs*, 8.

and then shot in the face while handcuffed to a table, glued naked to a wheelchair to have his lips bitten off and then to be set on fire—suggest that his acts of psychic invasion are much more reprehensible. More so than Hannibal Lecter, Chilton is invested in the Freudian, and his analyses of both Gideon and Dolarhyde are stereotypical profiles of castrated males acting out against women. Yet Chilton's investment in Freud runs deeper: he wants to become Freud, the sire of a new psychological legacy. Indeed, Chilton is transparent in his ambitions: discover the Chesapeake Ripper and dissect his mind; explore the "rare" disorders of Will Graham's empathy pathology; and penetrate the mind of Hannibal Lecter, killer cannibal. By mastering these feared and phallic men, Chilton would make himself the master of phallic men. The phrase "psychic driving," first used in "Entrée" (1.06), clearly implies that he drives his patients the way he does his sporty Jag—as an expression both of his compensation and of himself. If therapy is about helping the patient find himself, Chilton uses therapy so that the patient will find not himself but the self that Chilton desires for him. It is significant that when Gideon dissects Chilton, he slices him open as if he were performing a cesarean section. For impregnating Gideon with the seed of Chilton's ambitions in "Rôti" (1.11), Chilton is delivered of his bowels. Chilton's legacy is a shit baby.

Unlike Chilton, who is punished season after season, Alana Bloom is properly schooled in season 2 about the perils of investing in psychoanalysis, and by season 3 she has moved beyond its penetrative and gender-prescriptive discourse, a change illustrated by her wardrobe shift from wrap dresses to pantsuits. Alana's beer drinking and skirt wearing in the earlier seasons suggest that she subscribes to a particular version of male-identified femininity: she is smart and independent, but she is also desirable and nonthreatening. In "Apéritif," Will Graham has already established her as Dr. Bloom, an authority in the field, but in her first meeting with Jack Crawford, Alana wears her hallmark patterned wrap dress. Alana's feminine attire enables her to downplay her authority. The dress presents her as classically feminine, despite her masculine credentials,[17] but it is the dress's Rorschachian pattern that suggests her psychoanalytic alignment with binary gender roles. The Rorschach pattern of Alana's dresses is a form of animal-like Lacanian mimicry used to camouflage and protect her, while also serving to mimic her predators.[18] The patterns are dizzying, and their colors correspond, at least in her few scenes in "Apéritif," to the same colors worn by Jack Crawford. The Rorschach pattern adds to Alana's protective disguise by providing her with a visual appearance that invites her interlocutors to project their own desires onto her. Is that a Pac-Man? A dog? Much like the test itself, Alana appears to be whatever the viewer desires. Her need for camouflage is made clear when we first see pictures of the Minnesota Shrike victims, all of whom look strikingly similar to Alana: long dark hair, blue eyes, pale skin, lithe. Abigail and Alana even wear the same-size clothing. The implication is clear: Alana has survived because of her capacity to conceal herself, her desires, and her abilities in the shape of patriarchal desires—an unthreatening and desirable woman.

In the first season, Alana respects boundaries when it comes to male minds. She admits to Jack that although she would love to penetrate the secrets of Will Graham's mind, she refrains from doing so out of respect for their friendship, which she manages by never being alone with him in the same room. Although this respect may be merely one of binary gender roles, the show links Alana's femininity to her psychological practices and particularly to her investment in

---

17. To be clear, I do not believe that the role of the doctor is inherently masculine, though the novel and the film adaptations do make this association. Both the books and the films present doctors as conventionally masculine; indeed, in Harris's *Red Dragon*, Dr. Bloom is a man, Dr. Alan Bloom. Fuller's *Hannibal* continually undoes this convention.

18. Jacques Lacan, "The Mirror Stage as Formative of the Function of the I as Revealed in Psychoanalytic Experience," in *Écrits: A Selection*, trans. Alan Sheridan (New York: Norton, 1977), 3.

a strain of Freudian psychology. Early on, Alana encourages Abigail to embrace her victim status in group therapy with other victimized women, a narrative that Abigail finds confining and alienating. Seeing only Abigail's "daddy issues," Alana fails to consider the possibility that Abigail might not be reducible to a victim, as psychotherapy so often encourages in women. Alana attempts to dress Abigail in her own psychic clothing, an effort she literalizes in "Potage" (1.03) by shopping for Abigail and encouraging her to dress in the same camouflage apparel that she wears. Alana does much the same to Will in season 2, suggesting that he was broken by Jack, his FBI father figure. To Alana, Will, though himself a victim, is like all men, a victimizer. In preparing for his defense in "Sakizuke" (2.02), Alana tells him: "You have an incomplete self. We are who we are in the now, and we are the sum of our memories. There are pieces of you you can't see." Alana pressures Will to play his Freudian part and access repressed memories, to see that he has become Abigail's father and committed horrific atrocities. Yet despite Alana's attempts to outfit Abigail and Will in the clothing of psychoanalysis, both characters reject their assigned roles. Like Chilton, Alana can see only through the narrow lens of psychoanalysis and her own investment in its gendered binary truth: women are victims, men are victimizers.

Blinded by daddy issues, Alana's attachment to Freudianism holds the key to her relationship with Hannibal, Alana's phallic father, and it is through this relationship that she is narratively punished. In "Sorbet" (1.07), we witness Alana cooking with Hannibal. She wields a knife and drinks his beer, a special blend he fermented just for her. He was once her mentor when she was a graduate student, and she wonders why they never had an affair. Much like the mimicry of her dress, Alana begins to imitate and reflect back to Hannibal his own desires: she can handle a knife, she shows her own delicate palate for the wine-barrel beer, and she is happy to cook with him. Like Abigail, Alana becomes the object of killer daddy's desires. Their affair begins in earnest in "Futamono" (2.06), when she plays "Chopsticks" on his pianoforte, laying her hands on his instrument. Her choice of music becomes emblematic of her relationship with

Hannibal; she is merely a child playing his game, unable to master either the piano or his mind. "Chopsticks," all puns of chopping aside, is a rudimentary composition that involves the banging of a few keys, analogous to Alana's one-note analysis of Will and Abigail. She dissects (or "chops"), but she does so with the same repetitive notes, the same Freudian ideas. Whereas Hannibal composes and penetrates, Alana dabbles and "swallows."

It is fitting that Alana breaks her pelvis when Abigail, her daddy-issue doppelgänger, pushes her out a window. Though it is easy to make jokes about Hannibal's prowess—he is so massively phallic that he breaks her pelvis—it is more useful to look at this breakage as a prophetic Freudian punishment. To invest in psychoanalysis is to invest in a theory that reads Alana as absence, as castrated. Alana's skirts and her identification with male hegemony find their violent complement in the shattered bones of her pelvis. Freudian psychoanalysis regards her as broken, and she has become so. Freudian psychoanalysis regards her as castrated, and her fractured pelvis embodies this absence. Moreover, Alana's defenestration[19] involves not only the act of being thrown from a window but also the destruction of the window itself. The psychoanalytic window through which Alana views Hannibal proves to be both a blind and a means for her punishment. It obscures rather than reveals his true nature, and it is her willingness to go to the window in "Mizumono" that puts her in such danger. Alana has run up the stairs to the bedroom, fleeing Hannibal, who has dropped his knives and intends to kill her with his bare hands instead. While Alana is concentrating on the door that bars Hannibal from entering, Abigail appears, like a shimmering reflection of Alana herself. Back from the dead, the return of Alana's "repressed," Abigail has replaced one killer daddy, Garret Jacob Hobbs, with another, Hannibal. The patient Alana pegged as an eternal victim, Abigail, now forfeits her agency to Hannibal,

---

19. I also have to add that "defenestration" sounds a great deal like "de-penis-stration"—as if Alana has had the phallus removed from her.

mirroring Alana's own loss of self. Abigail becomes the Freudian oedipal daughter, opting to destroy another woman, a version of herself, rather than the father who victimized her.[20] As a result, it is Alana who falls victim to her therapeutic allegiances, and her devotion to psychoanalysis, along with its patriarchal gender binary, is thrown out the window with her.

The defenestration scene proves to be a watershed moment in Alana's evolution beyond Freudianism, and the narrative rewards her subsequent transformation. When Alana first confronts Hannibal in the kitchen, she tries to shoot him using Will Graham's gun, only to find that Hannibal has removed the bullets. The phallus is useless to protect her. Similarly, Alana's therapeutic approach lacks firepower as well; relying on the father's tools to dismantle him is useless. Mason Verger's death reinforces this symbolism. Alana and Margot Verger could easily stab him, shoot him, poison him, but instead he is thrown into his own vat of eels and choked by a symbolic phallus in "Digestivo" (3.07). While recovering from her injuries in "Aperitivo" (3.04), Alana tells Chilton that bone marrow from her pelvis has seeped into her blood, causing her to "think differently." This new thinking suggests a break from psychoanalysis, a movement beyond the gender binary of man as victimizer and woman as victim. We see the first indication of Alana's altered thinking in her wardrobe change. Discarding the apotropaic dresses and skirts of the first two seasons, Alana now rocks the pantsuit. Early in the season, she dons bold, solid colors, but by the time she becomes a mother, she is papered in striped patterns more reminiscent of an animal than a Rorschach blot. Her suits are strikingly similar to Hannibal's—black-and-white plaids, paisleys, and checks—and it could be argued that Alana has not so much rejected the Freudian father as she has

---

20. In Abigail's therapy, her mother's death is mentioned only in passing and is thus rendered insignificant. Abigail recalls in "Relevés" (1.12) that on her mother's birthday they were going to hike Eagle Mountain, the not-so-high "highest place in Minnesota." From both Freddie Lounds's and Alana's perspectives, Abigail is entirely defined as her father's daughter.

become him. Yet Alana's pantsuits as well as her relationship with Margot do not suggest a masculinized predator. Her shoulder-length hair and her boldest suits make an appearance only after she has become a mother, hinting that she is not so much a hunter as a protector, who, like a striped jungle cat, will defend both her young and Will Graham.

Alana's relationship with Margot could be read as a psychological backlash against men, but this reading, too, is reductive. Alana and Margot do not bond solely over their mutual victimhood by patriarchy, even though both of them bear the scars of patriarchal "affection" on their bodies. Mason counts on Alana and Margot accepting this victim narrative; they are to be subsumed into his story of masculine revenge, his Zeus-like consumption of the cannibal father who made him. Indeed, Mason is the beneficiary of both his biological father's teachings and his will, and the ideas that he espouses reflect the worst of psychoanalytic thinking: women are meant for breeding, mere empty vessels to be filled. Women, to Mason, are no more useful than pigs, and they are equally as expendable, while motherhood is no more significant than a slab of bacon (3.07). In many respects, Mason is the perfect symbol of phallic power: he is nearly bodiless, and his power is entirely symbolic, sustained by the word of the father. Unsurprisingly, he fails to see the power in female union, in "Naka-choko" (2.10) relegating lesbian relationships to "button stitching"—something quaint, cute, and ultimately inessential. In extracting Mason's sperm with a cattle prod, Margot and Alana reduce Mason to a mere breeding stud, showing that male bodies and hence the phallus they symbolize are equally dispensable. The removal of the biological father as well as of the symbolic one through a feminine unity rewrites the Freudian narrative of the expendable womb. In Alana's transformation, pelvis triumphs over penis.

The character who both links and destabilizes the procedural narrative and the psychoanalytic discourse that supports it is Will Graham. Compared to Chilton and Alana, who embrace the psychoanalytic gender binary, Will represents the straddling of binaries.

It is particularly appropriate that in "Apéritif" Jack says to Will, "I need you in the saddle," to which Will replies, "I'm in the saddle. Just confused which direction I'm pointing." Will never quite inhabits one position or one self; he is simultaneously detective and therapist, therapist and patient, detective and killer, masculine and feminine, self and other. The character Will Graham originates in Harris's novel *Red Dragon*, in which he is a married boat mechanic and FBI profiler who, while antisocial, nevertheless relies on his empathy to solve unusual cases. Yet in the novel and in its film adaptations, *Manhunter* (Michael Mann, 1986) and *Red Dragon* (Brent Ratner, 2002), his empathy apparently extends only to men. In all three versions, Will Graham is only ever asked to assume the mind of male serial killers—that is, Hannibal Lecter and Francis Dolarhyde. Will's empathy, although feminizing, has its masculine limits: various forms of butchness must be added to show that he is not too feminine, too "open." For example, in *Manhunter* Will Graham (William Peterson) hurls reporter Freddy Lounds into a car for taking a picture of him while he is in the hospital, a brutish gesture that counteracts any effeminacy suggested by Will's empathetic abilities. Unsettling this binary logic, the Will Graham of the series *Hannibal*, as played by Hugh Dancy, is neither effeminate nor butch, but a composite of both, just as he is a composite of both Graham and Starling in the Harris novels.[21] Dancy's Graham can empathize with female killers, such as Georgia Madchen, without needing compensatory acts of masculine aggression. Hugh Dancy physically embodies this duality: he is both manly and beautiful, strong and delicate, like a GI Joe made of porcelain.

It is tempting to read Will Graham's empathic connections to killers as feminizing, in contrast to the conventionally phallic detective who penetrates the minds and secrets of those he investigates—or so

---

21. The easiest example of this hybridization appears in "Digestivo" (3.07), when Hannibal carries Will out of Muskrat Farm like his bride. The scene pays homage to a scene in the novel *Hannibal* where Hannibal carries Clarice in the same manner (Harris, *Hannibal*, 476).

the film adaptations and the preponderance of Will-bottom fanfiction suggest. But such a reading would reinforce the opposition between the masculine penetrator and the feminine penetrated, a Freudian binary that the Will of Fuller's *Hannibal* consistently disrupts. In this binary, much like Mason's views discussed earlier, the feminine is a passive vessel, waiting to be penetrated and filled, a lack waiting to be made whole. This scenario privileges penetration and reduces the feminine to a merely passive receptacle, demeaning the feminine as a void and attenuating the power of empathy to little more than a hole in the self. Again, if we return to Mason as the epitome of Freudian binary thinking, vessels are there to be filled with masculine legacy; they are defined entirely as a void and rendered powerless. But Will neither rejects the feminine nor accepts it as a void waiting to be filled. As early as the first episode, Will is compared to a teacup, a piece of delicate china that Jack brings out for special occasions. Though Hannibal initially dismisses this characterization in "Apéritif" suggesting instead that Will is the "mongoose I want under the house when the snakes slither by," a conspicuously phallic comparison—the teacup metaphor nevertheless persists, particularly for Hannibal, who begins to see his life with Will and Abigail as a broken teacup to be remade (2.13).[22] In the novel *Hannibal*, the teacup is a metaphor for entropy and Hannibal's desire to turn back time, a placeholder for Mischa, a symbol for the cannibalized girl.[23] But in Fuller's *Hannibal* the teacup is Will, as most clearly visualized in "Primavera" (3.02) when the shattered teacup is cast as Will's broken face.

Domestic and fragile, the teacup initially seems like a dismissive metaphor, a yonic symbol whose purpose is to be filled, but this would be a narrow Freudian reading of its symbolism, one that

---

22. Marc Almond's song "Snake Charmer" in the soundtrack for "Antipasto" is mistakenly (I think) applied to Hannibal, primarily because Will is not in that episode. But as this conversation from "Apéritif" points out, Hannibal is the snake, but Will is the mongoose and "snake charmer."

23. Harris, *Hannibal*, 411.

Fuller's *Hannibal* implicitly calls into question. In "Apéritif," Mrs. Marlow's security password is *tea kettle*, a detail that immediately establishes Will's metaphorical counterpart, a crime scene and a murder that will be "poured" into him. Yet a teacup, like Will, is not a void, nor is it penetrated, and to see it as incomplete is to misunderstand it, to project an absence onto it. Just as fluid is poured into a teacup, killers are poured into Will; he takes them in and sweats them out. But in doing so the teacup is neither altered nor made complete by anything that it happens to hold—no matter what is poured into it, the teacup will remain as it has always been. To the contrary, the teacup defines and gives shape to the fluid it holds; without it, the fluid is just that, fluid, shapeless, unconsumable. Giving the lie to Mason's Freudian belief that vessels that have not been filled are incomplete, teacups can and do exist separately from what they contain at any given moment. They are not lacking in and of themselves. To turn this metaphor back to Will, he can "fill himself" with others via his empathy, but he still fundamentally remains Will. Like the teacup, he can be both a fully distinct self and a container of the other, simultaneously static and fluid, active and feminine. Empathy in this metaphor is neither feminine nor masculine, but both.

Will's gender fluidity reveals itself again in his ability to fish. Just as his empathy upends the penetrator/penetrated dynamic so often relied upon in the detective character, his fishing also "straddles" the active/passive binary. Hunting is a common trope for the relationship between detective and killer, as in the title *Manhunter*.[24] Hunters spy their prey, track them, and then kill them with (usually) a gun. It is significant that Will is never very good with a gun: it takes him several shots at close range to bring down Garret Jacob Hobbs; he only manages to shoot Tobias Budge in the ear; he cannot bring himself to shoot Clark Ingram or Hannibal; and in his dream of hunting the

---

24. Adding to the preponderance of the hunting-themed detective series is the Netflix series *Mindhunter* (2017–), produced by David Fincher and Charlize Theron.

nightmare ravenstag, he symbolically hunts himself. As Abigail points out in "Relevés" (1.12), fishing is a form of hunting, but it differs from hunting in the balance between active and passive. The hunter actively stalks and pursues his prey; the fisher, too, is active in creating a lure, casting his line, and taunting the fish into being caught. But whereas the hunter violently forces his desire onto his quarry, the fisher waits for the prey to act on its own desire—as Will says in "Su-zakana" (2.08), a fisher should "use live bait that moves and excites them to action." Straddling the rational and the emotional, the fisher is a creator of desire, not a perpetrator of it. Armed with his "rod," the fisher must wade into the fluids, exist in the stream with the fish; he is both part of the stream and separate from it.

Will's straddling of binaries manifests itself less metaphorically in his resistance to and rejection of psychoanalysis. Though he may teach it, he does not subscribe to it, either in his work with the FBI or in his therapy sessions with Hannibal and Bedelia. Over the course of thirty-nine episodes, Will never categorizes the killers he identifies in terms of pathology or sexual motivation.[25] Even in the penultimate episode, "The Number of the Beast Is 666" (3.12), when he attempts to humiliate the Tooth Fairy in the tabloid *Tattle-Crime*, remarking that the Tooth Fairy is "a vicious, perverted sexual failure" and the "product of an incestuous home," it is clear he is delivering an empty script, one he knows that Chilton will support and that Freddie Lounds's readers will find appealing. He thinks less of Alana and Chilton for their reliance on such interpretations, which to Will are demeaning, inaccurate, and ultimately reprehensible. When faced with Lecter's psychoanalytic tactics, Will routinely deflects them with mirroring comments such as "How does that make you feel?" It could be argued that Will's recalcitrance is provoked by his therapists' fascination with him as an object of study.

---

25. If dreams are the bedrock of psychoanalytic truth and therapy, granting access to the subject's most hidden desires, then even Will's dreams resist Freud in that they are more prophetic than libidinal.

Both Alana and Chilton admit to wanting to get inside his head: both see him as fundamentally unstable, and both refer to his empathy as a "disorder." More than just a lack of order or classification, the term *disorder* implies a problem and a disruption; to analyze Will successfully would be to "cure" him, contain him, remake him based on an image of what is normal. It is precisely the logic and persuasive power of the psychoanalytic version of Will as "disordered" that enables Hannibal to frame Will for multiple murders. Despite Will being right about every single serial killer up to "Relevés," Jack and the Sassy Science team are more inclined to believe, without any sense of irony, that "pure empathy made him kill." A ridiculous theory about repressed memories of the trauma he inhabited and then inflicted is more believable than Will himself. The problem with psychoanalysis, Will's false incarceration implies, is that classification and overly simplistic concepts produce believable distortions—complex individuals are reordered into pathologized subjects.

Will finds Hannibal appealing as a therapist because Hannibal does not see him as a disorder in need of rehabilitation. Hannibal is a Nietzschean therapist, encouraging his patients to become who they are. His therapy, like his murders, rejects the language of paraphilia. Even in his discussion with Franklyn Froideveux in "Sorbet" (1.07), when Hannibal suggests that Franklyn may be erotically interested in Tobias, he does not use the word *homosexual*. Franklyn's desire is simply that: a desire. It does not make Franklyn who he is, nor does labeling him help his therapy.[26] It goes without saying that Hannibal is not a therapeutic saint, for he, too, uses therapy as a means to penetrate Will with needles, light, his voice, even a stomach tube containing Abigail's ear. Like Chilton and Alana, Hannibal is punished when his therapy becomes too phallic, when he practices too devotedly the "dead religion of psychoanalysis." In "Mukōzuke"

---

26. The term *homosexual* was historically used to pathologize love and attraction between men, labeling these acts of desire as deviant. *Hannibal* notably omits this terminology. In interviews, Bryan Fuller also refrains from using this term to describe Will and Hannibal's relationship.

(2.05), Will sends Matthew Brown to crucify and hang Hannibal in a swimming-pool alcove, suggesting that Hannibal is both Jesus, Will's savior, and Judas, his betrayer. In the punishment of Hannibal, the series nevertheless reiterates his Nietzschean approach: become yourself and do not make a false god of your therapist.

Rejection and opposition do not offer the most destabilizing of critiques. One does not eliminate victimhood by becoming a victimizer instead, just as one does not undermine the discourse of femininity by becoming more masculine. As Neil Frank's death suggests, embracing the oppositional, such as rejecting psychoanalysis altogether, serves only to reinforce it. And just as Will Graham straddles the masculine and the feminine, *Hannibal* straddles the discourses of psychoanalysis and aesthetics. In their last supper together in "Mizumono," Will and Hannibal discuss imagos, a psychoanalytic concept of ego formation in which the child internalizes an image of himself in the mirror while being held by a loved one, typically the mother, whom the child regards as an inseparable part of himself. The theory blurs the boundaries of self and other, masculine and feminine, real and imagined.[27] In their discussion, Hannibal asks Will if he knows what an imago is. Ever the fisherman, Will responds, "A flying insect." Hannibal combines Will's answer with his own: "An imago is an image of a loved one buried in the unconscious . . . the concept of an ideal always searching for an objective reality to match." Psychoanalysis is insect and bait; swallow it, and you will find yourself hooked, ensnared, trapped by someone else's desire. But it is also an ideal version of the self and a loved one, a self that, once realized, as the final word of the series reminds us, is "beautiful."

Bibliography

Baker, Brian. *Contemporary Masculinities in Fiction, Film, and Television*. New York: Bloomsbury, 2015.

27. Lacan, "The Mirror Stage," 3.

Clover, Carol J. *Men, Women, and Chainsaws: Gender in the Modern Horror Film.* Princeton, NJ: Princeton Univ. Press, 1992.
Dyer, Richard. "Three Questions about Serial Killing." In *The Matter of Images: Essays on Representation*, 110–17. London: Routledge, 1993.
Harris, Thomas. *Hannibal.* 1999. Reprint. New York: Bantam Dell, 2006.
———. *Red Dragon.* New York: Penguin Group, 1981.
———. *The Silence of the Lambs.* New York: St. Martin's Press, 1988.
Hibberd, James. "'Hannibal' Showrunner Criticizes TV's Rape Scene Epidemic." *Entertainment Weekly*, May 28, 2015. At http://ew.com/article/2015/05/28/hannibal-rape-thrones/.
Lacan, Jacques. "The Mirror Stage as Formative of the Function of the I as Revealed in Psychoanalytic Experience." In *Écrits: A Selection*, translated by Alan Sheridan, 1–7. New York: Norton, 1977.
Lacey, Nick. *Narrative and Genre: Key Concepts in Media Studies.* New York: St. Martin's Press, 2000.
Seltzer, Mark. *Serial Killers: Death and Life in America's Wound Culture.* New York: Routledge, 1998.
Simpson, Philip L. *Psychopaths: Tracking the Serial Killer through Contemporary American Film and Fiction.* Carbondale: Southern Illinois Univ. Press, 2000.

11 | "Do You See?"
Clues, Reasoning, and Connoisseurship
Michelle D. Miranda

First appearing in the 1980s, Hannibal Lecter has become one of the most famous fictional serial killers in literature and cinema alike. Credited with having an impact on real-world criminal investigations and the field of forensic psychology, this character has endured for more than thirty years, continually reincarnated through cinematic psychological thrillers and procedural dramas, which subsequently reinvigorate pop-culture fandom. NBC's series *Hannibal* (2013–15) is the most recent adaptation of the exploits of Hannibal Lecter, receiving critical acclaim and rapidly spawning a substantial fanbase. *Hannibal* captivates its audience through the presentation of horrific crimes and the subsequent forensic methods that are the hallmark of criminal investigations. Placed into the crime scene and into the minds of killers, viewers of *Hannibal* have an intimate perspective of forensic science and forensic psychology and how they apply to criminal investigation.

Through the examination and analysis of crime scenes and related physical evidence as well as the use of the techniques of criminal profiling, the investigators in *Hannibal* track a series of killers and eventually uncover a cannibal killer among them. Nothing is what it seems, as Hannibal Lecter manipulates physical and psychological evidence and deliberately misdirects investigations—challenging the reliability of what is real—to keep him one step ahead of the investigators. Observation as a critical component of reasoning plays a central role in *Hannibal*. Observation through experience and attention to seemingly insignificant details are the skills necessary to truly see, and these skills evolve differently in the characters as *Hannibal* progresses. The series effectively uses signs to draw attention to the detection of clues, a concept that can be linked to the continuum of art, science, and psychology that characterizes *Hannibal* and blends the aesthetic with the grotesque.

This chapter begins by introducing the concepts of scientific method, observation, and reasoning, drawing attention to their presence throughout the *Hannibal* narrative. An introduction to forensic science, specifically crime-scene investigation and criminalistics, follows. The chapter then introduces elements of forensic psychology, specifically criminal profiling, and considers the role of observation and reasoning in the profiling of serial killers. It then examines the intersection of art and crime, demonstrating how techniques used in art connoisseurship can be compared to the techniques of offender profiling, crime-scene investigation, and forensic-evidence analysis as portrayed in *Hannibal*. And, finally, it discusses Hannibal Lecter's ability to effectively manipulate the physical and psychological evidence throughout *Hannibal*.

Clues: Forensic Science

"Observing Is What We Do": Observation and Reasoning

Observation is a critical part of forensic investigations, specifically the utilization of the scientific method in the interpretation of evidence.[1] The scientific method is characterized by making inquiries, collecting facts through observation and experimentation, and then interpreting the resultant data. This method includes all principles and procedures utilized throughout the process, including reasoning. And it is characterized by its goal of developing a theory based on

---

1. The quotation in the subhead is from "Apéritif" (1.01).

the initial observations of some phenomena.² Information obtained through observation becomes significant when reasoning is used to interpret and assign relevance to such data or facts. Throughout *Hannibal*, observation is a central tenet to gaining knowledge and finding facts. Killers Garret Jacob Hobbs and Georgia Madsen instruct Will Graham to "see"; the severed arm of Miriam Lass found in the observatory holds a note reading, "What do you see?"; Agent-in-Charge Jack Crawford frequently asks Graham to help him "see"; and while showing photographs of victims, Frances Dolarhyde asks a captive Frederick Chilton, "Do you see?" This *seeing* goes beyond visual acuity, requiring understanding and consideration of the killer's viewpoint as well as focused attention to often overlooked details. According to Johann Wolfgang von Goethe, "we have eyes and ears only for what we know," which implies that the ability to observe is controlled by our knowledge and experience. "He who merely enjoys nature sees nothing but the broad expanse of a green and flowery meadow, while the botanist is struck with the infinite details of each separate little plant."³

This link between knowledge, observation, and detail is important to understanding Graham's ability as a profiler in that the vastness of his knowledge and empathy allow him to see the details of a scene as well as the scene as a whole. Unlike the botanist or nature lover as described by Goethe, Graham can see with a visual acuity that is not limited. Although the ability to observe and understand is inherently limited by one's own experiences and what one is able to comprehend, Graham possesses additional cognitive gifts.

---

2. Michelle D. Miranda, "Forensic Silence: Identification, Individualization, and the Power of Observation," in *"The Silence of the Lambs": Critical Essays on a Cannibal, Clarice, and a Nice Chianti*, ed. Cynthia Miller (London: Rowman and Littlefield, 2017), 94.

3. Johann Wolfgang von Goethe, *Goethe's Opinions on the World, Mankind, Literature, Science, and Art*, trans. Otto Wenckstern (London: Parker and Son, 1853), 68, 69.

Having pure empathy and the ability to understand the motivations of others, Graham is able to *see* owing to a combination of his intuition, active imagination, and interpretation of facts. According to the nineteenth-century Irish physicist John Tyndall, imagination, armed with knowledge and reason, is the "mightiest instrument of the physical discoverer."[4] Graham's imagination becomes a powerful tool that allows him to see a killer's motivations and actions as depicted in a crime scene, a tool that sets him apart from other investigators and enables him to provide the investigative leads needed to catch the killer.

According to C. S. Peirce, all of our acquired knowledge may be said to rest on observed facts.[5] Peirce distinguishes three types of reasoning as they relate to obtaining knowledge and drawing conclusions about observed phenomena: deductive, inductive, and abductive. The deductive method of reasoning begins with a theory from which a hypothesis is developed, which can be tested with experimentation and additional observation. By making an inference from a general principle, deduction provides certainty in reaching a conclusion. Inductive reasoning begins with observations from which a hypothesis is developed. Through comparison, experimentation, and data interpretation, a measure of probability can be assigned to the resultant conclusion. Abductive reasoning requires creativity, intuition, and imagination to generate new ideas about observed phenomena and is the process of forming hunches about the world based on observation and perception.[6] Peirce describes the method of abductive reasoning as including an element of guesswork, or speculation,

---

4. John Tyndall, *Scientific Use of the Imagination and Other Essays* (London: Longmans, Green, 1872), 6.

5. C. S. Peirce, "Abduction and Induction," in *Philosophical Writings of Peirce 1940*, ed. Justus Buchler (New York: Dover, 1955), 150.

6. Thomas Sebeok and Jean Sebeok, "'You Know My Method': A Juxtaposition of Charles S. Peirce and Sherlock Holmes," in *The Sign of Three: Dupin, Holmes, Peirce*, ed. Umberto Eco and Thomas Sebeok (Bloomington: Indiana Univ. Press, 1983), 18.

11.1. *See?* Recurring scenes at the observatory—the discovery of Miriam Lass's arm holding a note for Crawford; the "surgery" of Frederick Chilton by Abel Gideon while Freddie Lounds is forced to watch and assist; and the display of Beverly Katz's body by the Chesapeake Ripper—draw attention to the significance of observation and detail throughout *Hannibal*. (© NBC/Gaumont)

adding that abduction provides the best explanation in reaching a conclusion, an assessment based largely on the idea that the majority of human reasoning comes from conjecture.[7] Nancy Harrowitz describes the process of critical thinking and problem solving as moving from abduction, which suggests, to induction, which shows, and, finally, to deduction, which proves.[8] Such critical thinking is necessary when conducting a criminal investigation and reconstructing a crime scene. At the onset of an investigation, Graham utilizes abductive reasoning. As the case progresses and more information is obtained through the introduction of new evidence and analysis

---

7. Peirce, "Abduction and Induction."
8. Nancy Harrowitz, "The Body of the Detective Model: Charles S. Peirce and Edgar Allan Poe," in *The Sign of Three*, ed. Eco and Sebeok, 181.

of physical traces in the laboratory, Graham refines his profiles and reconstructions, moving through the three different types of reasoning as facts are established.

Although abductive reasoning is based on guesswork (i.e., Graham's "leaps"), the conclusions an investigator draws from such reasoning methods during the preliminary stages of an investigation can prove useful in providing leads and guiding the investigation. As the evidence is analyzed in the laboratory and the victimology is presented, Graham refines his hypotheses to further the investigation and eventually come to meaningful conclusions with an increased emphasis on objectivity. This subjective-to-objective interpretation runs in tandem with the movement from abduction to deduction. Starting with a seemingly infinite number of possibilities at the onset of an investigation, Graham makes abductive leaps, and as the investigation progresses, the evidence decreases the possibilities until the best or only scenario presents itself.

By establishing the importance of the scientific method and the process of reasoning, Graham and his fellow investigators can effectively analyze and reconstruct the crime scene and develop meaningful offender profiles. These fundamental tools are critical to successful criminal investigations and to ultimately identifying the perpetrator.

"I Pull Apart, Layer by Layer, Like She Would a Crime Scene": Crime Scene Investigation

Crime-scene investigation is characterized by the systematic examination of the location of a suspected criminal act.[9] The technical aspect of crime-scene investigation is concerned with the recognition, documentation, collection, and preservation of physical traces within the location. Crime-scene reconstruction utilizes the scientific method and reasoning to determine the sequence and manner of events that took place before, after, and during the crime. It involves

---

9. The quotation in the subhead is from "Mukōzuke" (2.05).

considering all aspects of the event, including analysis of the physical evidence and scientific interpretation of the resultant data; interpretation of information generated from witnesses (e.g., through interviews and interrogations); recovery of forensic technologies (e.g., data recovered from surveillance cameras and global positioning systems); examination of the victim (e.g., autopsy and toxicology results as well as the victim's profile); and any photos or additional information obtained throughout the course of the investigation. By moving from apparently insignificant facts gathered by observation to the ordering of the facts to provide a narrative sequence, the observer can reconstruct a sequence of events to provide a meaningful interpretation of a crime scene.[10]

The basis for crime-scene investigation is the ability to detect and recognize the significance of minute details the perpetrator has left behind at the scene. Detection and recognition have historical significance, and their application to criminal investigation has gained importance over time. As Carlo Ginzburg notes,

> Man has been a hunter for thousands of years. In the course of countless chases, he learned to reconstruct the shapes and movements of his invisible prey from the tracks on the ground, broken branches, excrement, tufts of hair, entangled feathers, stagnating odors. He learned to sniff out, record, interpret, and classify such infinitesimal traces as trails of spittle. He learned how to execute complex mental operations with lightning speed.[11]

Interestingly, Ginzburg's hunting analogy can be directly linked to the dichotomy of hunter and fisherman that plays out throughout the *Hannibal* series, both literally and figuratively. As with locating prey, attention to traces is critical to making connections between the scene, the perpetrator, and the victim.

---

10. Carlo Ginzburg, "Morelli, Freud, and Sherlock Holmes: Clues and Scientific Method," *History Workshop Journal* 9 (1980): 13.
11. Carlo Ginzburg, *Myths, Emblems, Clues* (London: Hutchinson Radius, 1986), 102.

"The Evidence Explains": Criminalistics and Physical Evidence

Forensic science, specifically criminalistics, relies on trace and transfer evidence to provide clues to identify and aid in the reconstruction of events. Forensic science is the application of natural sciences to legal matters, and criminalistics is a branch of forensic science concerned with the recognition, collection, identification, individualization,[12] and evaluation of physical evidence (e.g., blood, hairs, fibers) and pattern evidence (e.g., fingerprints, shoe prints, bloodstains) with the primary goal of reconstructing the events central to an investigation. According to Paul Kirk, accurate identification must rest on a proper basis of training, experience, technical knowledge, and skill as well as on an understanding of the fundamental nature of the identity itself.[13] A central tenet in the examination and comparison of physical evidence is that no two objects are alike—relationships can be established between common objects, but each of those objects ultimately has some uniqueness that sets it apart from all other objects. Physical traces transferred between the perpetrator(s), victim(s), and scene(s) can be located and classified based on visual, microscopic, and instrumental analysis, which is usually done in a crime laboratory. Even though Graham has the ability to use his empathy and imagination to profile, he is careful to note the importance of and need for evidence to support his conclusions. He makes this assertion on two particular occasions, the first in "Apéritif" (1.01) during a conversation with Jack Crawford, in which Crawford alludes to Graham's conjectural process of making inferences to move from the unknown to the known without clear explanation:

---

12. Individualization is characterized by features or properties exclusive to a single person or object that allows for the demonstration that a particular sample is unique. See Peter De Forest, Robert Gaensslen, and Henry Lee, *Forensic Science: An Introduction to Criminalistics* (New York: McGraw-Hill, 1983), 6–7.

13. Paul Kirk, *Crime Investigation: Physical Evidence and the Police Laboratory* (New York: Interscience, 1953), 17.

CRAWFORD. You have a very specific way of thinking about things. . . . You make jumps you can't explain.
GRAHAM. No . . . the evidence explains.
CRAWFORD. Then help me find some evidence.

The importance of evidence to support intuitive investigative methods is addressed again in a brief conversation between Graham and FBI investigator Beverly Katz in "Entrée (1.06), specifically regarding the similarity of his method to the investigatory work of FBI agent-in-training Miriam Lass. Katz protests that Lass "made a jump somewhere they couldn't explain. You make those jumps," to which Graham replies, "The evidence has to be there."

Although objects' physical attributes can be compared to demonstrate similarity or a common source, exclusions can be just as valuable to an investigation. Being able to find differences that effectively rule out a possible source or scenario can reduce the pool of contributors or provide a more significant likelihood of possibilities. "It is possible to indicate a probable occupation or to describe a habitat with remarkable accuracy from careful examination of some apparently trifling object found at the scene of the crime. Such facts do not necessarily constitute proof of guilt of any particular person, but they may give background which is of greatest value."[14]

This concept is crucial in the investigation of the Minnesota Shrike serial-killer case in "Apéritif." The detection and analysis of the metal turnings Katz finds during an examination of garments from the crime scene provide an investigatory lead that narrows down the source of the trace metal particles and the occupation to which they are connected, which directs the investigation to the specific construction site where Garret Jacob Hobbs is employed.

The importance of locating physical traces and determining their value in criminal investigations is paramount to developing leads and progressing from abductive reasoning to more definitive conclusions.

14. Kirk, *Crime Investigation*, 7.

In the investigation of serial murders, facts derived from evidence analysis and crime-scene reconstruction can form the basis for well-developed criminal profiles.

Signs: Forensic Psychology and Criminal Profiling

Criminal profiling is the process of using behavioral and physical evidence to draw inferences about a perpetrator's traits through examination and interpretation of the crime scene, including the victim. Profiling is based on the concept that a criminal will exhibit consistencies across a series of similar criminal acts, allowing for the acts to be linked to a particular perpetrator or type of perpetrator. Serial offenders, often the focus of profiling techniques, are described in terms of their motive, or reason, for committing the crimes; their modus operandi (MO) or methodology, which addresses how they commit their crimes; and their signature, or a unique, extraneous feature of the crime. Cases are often linked based on attributes of the MO and the signature.[15] Utilizing theoretical concepts and clinical experience from the fields of psychology, psychiatry, psychoanalysis, and sociology, criminal profiling applies scientific methodology and reasoning to aid in forensic investigations in an effort to determine an offender's physical and psychological features in order to reduce the size of the pool of suspects. Profiling is not necessarily intended to specifically identify one particular suspect to the exclusion of all others. In this way, the profiling method is similar to methods used in the forensic sciences, in which exclusions can prove quite meaningful in an investigation through the process of elimination. Much like crime-scene reconstruction, criminal profiling is based on consideration and evaluation of several facets of the crime—the crime scene, including the identification of the MO and signature; the victim, including identification, physical characteristics, medical history,

---

15. For additional information, see John Douglas, Ann Burgess, Allen Burgess, and Robert Ressler, *Crime Classification Manual*, 2nd ed. (San Francisco: Jossey-Bass, 2006).

psychological history, victimology, and information obtained during autopsy; and related forensic evidence.

Profiling, often described as using either inductive or deductive reasoning, can be more accurately aligned with abductive and inductive reasoning. Preliminary methodologies employed in profiling are based largely on guesswork, and the profile is refined as the case progresses, traces are analyzed and interpreted, and facts are established. This process is characterized by the profiler moving from abductive to inductive reasoning when developing probabilities through consideration of prior cases and personal experience. A criminal profile evolves as the case progresses and more information is discovered, and preliminary hypotheses may be discarded or refined as new facts present themselves. For example, in "Apéritif" Graham exhibits certainty in his repeated assertions that Hobbs hunts alone for his victims. This assertion is discarded when Graham later becomes aware of Abigail Hobbs's involvement in her father's crimes. In this case, Graham's original assertion of Abigail's lack of involvement is likely biased and clouded by his emotional attachment to the case and to Abigail herself.

Although the practice of offender profiling has evolved and many different methods have been developed for approaching best practices of criminal profiling, early methods used by the FBI Behavioral Science Unit (BSU) are often the benchmark for profiling strategies employed in film and television. Traditional profiling is described as a process consisting of data collection, reconstruction, hypothesis formulation, profile development and testing, and reporting.[16] This methodology bears resemblance to the scientific method applied to problem solving in the natural sciences. When profiling, investigators use "brainstorming, intuition, and educated guesswork" along with "years of accumulated wisdom, extensive experience in the field, and

---

16. John Douglas, Robert Ressler, Ann Burgess, and Carol Hartman, "Criminal Profiling from Crime Scene Analysis," *Behavioral Sciences and the Law* 4 (1986): 405.

familiarity with a large number of cases"—in short, both abductive and inductive reasoning.[17] In general, case information and investigator experience are the primary sources of profile development. The first stage, or the profiling-inputs stage, is concerned with the collection of facts and data related to the incident, including but not limited to police reports, crime-scene reports, victim information (including victim background and behaviors), forensic information (medical and autopsy reports, traces collected and evaluated), and photographs. In the second stage of profiling, the decision-process-model stage, the investigator organizes the data in a manner to develop patterns. This stage utilizes "decision points" to organize information and "form an underlying decisional structure for profiling."[18] During the crime-assessment stage, a reconstruction of events is conducted. In addition, evaluations of victim and offender behaviors, the elements of the crime scene, and classification of the crime are conducted. These evaluations aid in determining the motivation behind the crime. This stage leads to the criminal-profile stage, in which a profile is generated and investigatory information for the identification, apprehension, and interviewing of the offender is developed. It is important to keep in mind that both scene reconstructions and offender profiles are only as robust as the facts applied and the biases avoided.

The Dichotomy of Art and Science: Forensic Connoisseurship

In the series *Hannibal*, a subtle narrative links the evaluation of art, crime-scene investigation, and criminal profiling, connecting all three through their need for skills of observation and attention to detail. The observation of minute details to determine the value and provenance of works of art parallels crime-scene investigation, with the artwork in the same position as the crime scene, the artist in the same position as the killer, and the art connoisseur or critic in the position of the criminal investigator. *Hannibal* effectively brings this

---

17. Douglas et al., "Criminal Profiling," 405.
18. Douglas et al., "Criminal Profiling," 408.

forensic connoisseurship to light by intersecting the assessment of fine art and criminal investigation.

Giovanni Morelli was an art historian and critic known for questioning and studying the originators of Italian artwork during the nineteenth century.[19] According to Morelli, most works displayed in museums at the time were incorrectly attributed to a painter (often a master painter): the forgers had missed certain details necessary to achieve a true reproduction, and the evaluator had overlooked those same details in determining authenticity.[20] Edgar Wind explains that "Morelli believed that the inadvertent expressions of the painter would reveal his character, and such expressions, displayed in minute details such as the hands, ears, fingernails, and toes of the artwork, could be attributed to an individual artist." To identify the hand of the master and distinguish it from the hand of the copyist, states Wind, "we must rely on small idiosyncrasies which seem inessential[,] [. . .] features which look so irrelevant that they would not engage the attention of any imitator [. . .] or forger."[21] By identifying what details were overlooked or impossible to duplicate exactly, adds Carlo Ginzburg, Morelli "would achieve his aim of telling originals from fakes, the hand of the master from that of the copyist or the follower."[22]

19. See Giovanni Morelli, *Italian Painters: Critical Studies of Their Works—the Borghese and Doria-Pamfili Galleries in Rome*, trans. Constance Ffoulkes (London: John Murray, 1900), and *Italian Painters: Critical Studies of Their Works—the Galleries of Munich and Dresden*, trans. Constance Ffoulkes (London: John Murray, 1907).

20. Although numerous scientific and technological advances have been made in the art world, such as instrumental techniques and imaging technologies, the reliance on subjective expert opinion using intuition and experience (through acquired knowledge gained by observing other works of art by a given artist) is still practiced in assigning attribution to a work of art.

21. Edgar Wind, *Art and Anarchy*, 3rd ed. (Evanston, IL: Northwestern Univ. Press, 1985), 38, 36.

22. Carlo Ginzburg, "Clues: Morelli, Freud, and Sherlock Holmes," in *The Sign of Three*, ed. Eco and Sebeok, 96.

Armed with historical knowledge and intuition, the connoisseur has the ability to distinguish originals and forgeries through observation. Attributions are made by the ability to see, and the same holds true for crime-scene investigation. Will Graham is able to see both the details and overall whole of a crime scene to correctly assign it to its creator. Much like the art connoisseur, Graham combines his knowledge, experience, and imagination to draw connections between the crime scene (work of art) and the killer (artist).

Alphonse Bertillon, a French criminologist, developed anthropometry in the late nineteenth century, which was one of the first biometric techniques used for the identification of criminals. Like Morelli, Bertillon focused on physical details; certain physical features of an individual, such as ear shape and size, could be utilized as tools of identification in criminal investigations. Even as biometric identification techniques advanced—for instance, through the introduction of fingerprint analysis and comparison—physical traits, specifically the ear, remained a distinctive, readily visible feature of the human body with unique attributes.[23] Bernhard Berenson, art historian and connoisseur, further developed Morelli's ideas in the twentieth century, remarking, "The ear is [. . .] very characteristic of the painter, more characteristic [. . .] than any other detail of the human figure." Berenson added that although the ear is an excellent test of authenticity, it alone is not sufficient to assign authorship.[24] This assertion highlights that although the details are critical, they must be considered along with the whole painting (crime scene).

Ear imagery appears throughout *Hannibal*, evoking connections to criminal identification (Bertillon) and art connoisseurship (Morelli and Berenson): Graham coughs up Abigail Hobbs's ear, which Lecter had forced down his esophagus during a seizure; Lecter's ear figures prominently during an opera singer's performance; and the ear of

---

23. Harry Söderman and John O'Connell, *Modern Criminal Investigation* (New York: Funk and Wagnalls, 1935), 49.

24. Bernhard Berenson, *Study and Criticism of Italian Art*, 2nd series (London: Bell and Sons, 1902), 130.

11.2. Scene from "Amuse-Bouche" (1.02) in which plate 57 of Alphonse Bertillon's photo album corresponding to his text on anthropometry is prominently displayed on the wall in Lecter's office. (© NBC/Gaumont)

the murdered and mutilated bailiff is sent to Graham's lawyer during Graham's trial as the Copycat Killer. In Lecter's office, adjacent to the ladder on the second floor hangs a framed image of ear patterns developed by Bertillon.[25] This plate, exhibiting the peculiarities of the ear, draws attention to the importance of detail in identification sciences, details that did not go unnoticed by Bertillon and Morelli in their investigations to determine identity. Bertillon believed visual examination and measurement of the details and unique characteristics of the ear could lead to identification of an individual, just as Morelli believed the details of an ear in a painting could indicate

25. Plate 57 in Alphonse Bertillon, *Identification anthropométrique: Instructions signalétiques par Alphonse Bertillon, album* (Melun, France: Imprimerie Administrative, 1893), 94.

forgery and aid in the identification of who had created a certain work of art.[26]

"The Devil Is in the Details": The Crime Scene as a Work of Art

Lecter's early attachment to Botticelli's painting *Primavera* (1482), which he would routinely observe and sketch while at the Uffizi Gallery in Florence before relocating to the United States, serves as the inspiration for his earlier crimes as the Florentine killer Il Mostro.[27] In "Primavera" (3.02), Inspector Rinaldo Pazzi directly links Lecter's crime scenes and posing of remains to fine art, explaining that "it was his custom to arrange his victims like a beautiful painting. [. . .] Exactly like a Botticelli." On a few other occasions throughout *Hannibal*, crime scenes are described as works of art. When investigating the murders of the Turner family in "Œuf" (1.04), as they are found seated around the dining-room table, crime-scene investigator Jimmy Price describes the scene as "Norman Rockwell with a bullet."

The Wound Man illustration, which recurs multiple times in *Hannibal*, further demonstrates the intersection between art and crime. This artistic anatomical guide to wounds featured in various medical treatises of the late fifteenth century serves in the series as a signature for the Chesapeake Ripper (Hannibal Lecter) before being copied or forged by Abel Gideon. First appearing in the pilot episode, "Apéritif," the Wound Man illustration appears in several versions throughout *Hannibal* and further serves as the model for the postmortem display of human remains.

---

26. The ear and its distinctive features prove to be a substantial clue in Arthur Conan Doyle's story "The Cardboard Box," featuring famous fictional detective Sherlock Holmes. See Arthur Conan Doyle, "The Cardboard Box," in *The Annotated Sherlock Holmes*, 2 vols., ed. W. Baring-Gould (New York: Clarkson, 1967), 2:193–208.

27. The quotation in the subhead is from "Apéritif."

The body of Ronald Umber is viewed and treated as a work of art throughout "Sakizuke" (2.02). Having originally been placed in the killer's mural of human remains located in a silo with an oculus, Umber's body represents a fragment of a larger work of art. Much like the observatory serves as a symbol of sight and *seeing*, the arrangement and color palette of the human mural as well as its location in the silo draw attention to the importance of observation and detail as an overarching theme in *Hannibal*. Specifically, the mural must be viewed from above, through the silo's oculus, to reveal the eye design. During examination of Umber's body at the FBI lab, Lecter likens the remains to a painting and highlights the importance of trace-evidence retention: "There may be trace evidence preserved in the craquelure . . . the cracks that appear in an oil painting as it dries and becomes rigid with age." Accordingly, corn dust found in the "craquelure" of Umber's body leads the investigators to the eye mural composed of human remains arranged as a palette of skin tones, of which Umber had originally been a part. Here, the eye mural, with its composition of human bodies, is a work of art, its artist James Gray, the Eye Mural Killer. Although Lecter alters the crime scene (and thus the work of art and the artist's vision) by inserting Gray into his own "painting," Graham "Morellizes" and is able to detect the forgery in the artwork—concluding that Gray was not intended to be in the mural and that therefore another killer has added to the crime scene. Graham's empathy and imagination enable him to see the original artist's (Gray's) vision and therefore to detect the inconsistency in the color palette as well as in the placement and posing of the artist's body within the mural. Additional evidence (DNA in Gray's vehicle, which is found near the scene) eventually provides the facts to support Graham's reasoning, demonstrating the transition he makes from abduction to induction (and deduction).

Morelli's influence extends beyond the art world to Sigmund Freud and the field of psychoanalysis. Freud reasoned that Morelli was able to distinguish copies from originals and attribute works to a specific artist "by insisting that attention should be diverted from the general impression and main features of the picture, and by laying stress on the significance of the minor details." Comparing Morelli's ideas about art to psychoanalysis, Freud added, "[Psychoanalysis,] too, is accustomed to divine secret and concealed things from despised or unnoticed features, from the rubbish-heap, as it were, of our observations."[28] Freud reasoned that by studying such trivial details, it would be possible to gain insight into the artist's thoughts and determine the motivation behind the work of art.[29] This process parallels Graham's studying a crime scene to understand and ultimately identify the killer. For example, when the body of Cassie Boyle is found impaled on a stag head in "Apéritif," Graham attributes this crime scene to a copycat, not to the Minnesota Shrike: "Whoever tucked Elise Nichols into bed didn't paint this picture." Recognizing the killer assumed to be the Chesapeake Ripper as the artist and forger in "Entrée (1.06), Graham similarly asserts, "I see the Ripper, but I don't feel the Ripper.... Plagiarism." Even when in "Sorbet" (1.07) the investigators are certain that a body found in a bathtub is another victim of the Chesapeake Ripper, Graham again "Morellizes" and correctly attributes the scene to another killer:

> ZELLER. ... he was interrupted before he could paint his picture ...
> GRAHAM. The Ripper wasn't painting a picture in the hotel ... someone else was ...
> KATZ. The Ripper painted this picture for sure, in big, broad strokes.

The correlation between art and crime is demonstrated throughout *Hannibal*'s narrative. Connoisseurship and applications of art history mirror detection and profiling—from observation follows

---

28. Sigmund Freud, "The Moses of Michelangelo," in *The Standard Edition of the Complete Psychological Works of Sigmund Freud*, vol. 13: 1913–1914, ed. James Strachey (London: Hogarth Press, 1955), 222.

29. Jack Spector, "The Method of Morelli and Its Relation to Freudian Psychoanalysis," *Diogenes* 66 (1969): 69.

interpretation and description, which lead to determining the motivations of the artist/perpetrator and, finally, attribution. By viewing crime scenes as works of art, Graham is able to use Morelli's maxims to assign correct attribution to the artist/perpetrator responsible for creating the crime masterpiece. He can thus detect forgery in the work of the Copycat Killer and eventually identify Lecter as a serial murderer.

Forgers and Forgeries: Misdirection and Manipulation of Clues

Hannibal Lecter's knowledge of crime and the human mind enables him to manipulate people, evidence, and crime scenes in order to remove himself from suspicion of murder. Effectively steering investigations and implicating other individuals in his crimes, he is often secretly in control. As the Copycat Killer, Lecter stages crime scenes through the postmortem display of victim's remains, misleading Graham and Crawford by directing attention away from the real killers and toward other suspects, including Graham himself. Much like works of art attributed to masters that are later found to be forged, these crime scenes and displays of human remains are forged throughout *Hannibal*.

Upon examination of the crime scene displaying the body of Cassie Boyle, originally believed to be another victim of the Minnesota Shrike, Graham profiles both the murder and the display as having been committed not by the Minnesota Shrike but by a copycat, an intelligent psychopath and sadist who is mocking the investigators. Graham concludes in "Potage" (1.03) that "this copycat was an intelligent psychopath.... There would be no traceable motive, no pattern. He wouldn't kill again this way." Later, when the body of Marissa Schurr is found posed and mounted in the Minnesota Shrike's hunting cabin in a manner consistent with the display of Cassie Boyle, Graham's initial profile of the Copycat Killer is brought into question. Not only is Lecter able to raise doubt about Graham's profiling abilities, but he is also able to place physical traces on Marissa Schurr's body that implicate Cassie Boyle's brother in Schurr's murder.

Although Graham's profile appears incorrect to Crawford, and although the physical evidence points elsewhere (both of which Lecter intended), Graham remains certain that Cassie Boyle and Marissa Schurr were murdered by the same individual—the Copycat Killer (Lecter), not the Minnesota Shrike. While Graham is uncovering the truth about Lecter and seemingly unraveling before Crawford and his colleagues, Lecter is able to place physical evidence from Cassie Boyle, Marissa Schurr, Dr. Sutcliffe, and Georgia Madchen into Graham's fishing lures to make it appear as though Graham is the Copycat Killer. While Beverly Katz is examining the overwhelming evidence against Graham (planted by Lecter) in "Kaiseki" (2.01), Lecter remarks, "The duty of what you do . . . is in its certainty. It'll be your evidence that convicts Will." Katz's response, perhaps foreshadowing her eventual suspicion of Lecter, is that there is "no need to infer, or intuit."[30] Here, abduction has transitioned to deduction because there is no longer any speculation on the part of the FBI regarding the assertion that Graham is the Copycat Killer.

With his knowledge of pattern evidence, specifically bloodstain patterns, Lecter is able to collect and distribute Abigail Hobbs's blood throughout a crime scene to make it appear as if her throat has been slit. He is able to manipulate Abigail into giving him one of her ears, which he then force-feeds to Graham. Both the staging of Abigail's death and the presence of her ear make it appear as if Graham has

---

30. Lecter adds, "So much simpler than psychiatry." Echoing this conclusion in a different case, Chilton states in "Futamono" (2.06) that the "simplest explanation as to why [Abel Gideon] can describe Hannibal Lecter's home is that he was in Hannibal Lecter's home." This concept is addressed in the novel *The Silence of The Lambs*, when Lecter assists Clarice Starling in her investigation of serial killer Buffalo Bill: "First principles, simplicity. Of each particular thing, ask: what is it in itself? What is its nature? What does he do, this man you seek?" (Thomas Harris, *The Silence of the Lambs*, 25th anniversary ed. [New York: St. Martin's Press, 2013], 208; see also the film *The Silence of the Lambs* [Jonathan Demme, 1991]). In "Futamono," a similar conversation occurs between Crawford and Graham regarding the Chesapeake Ripper. Graham asks, "What is the first and principal thing that he does? What need does he serve by killing?"

killed her (along with Cassie Boyle and Marissa Schurr). Lecter also manipulates Graham's mental deterioration from encephalitis. Using his position as Graham's therapist, he is able to control Graham, Crawford, and Dr. Sutcliffe, which enables him to stage the death of Dr. Sutcliffe and direct Crawford's suspicion to Graham owing to the latter's physical and psychological decline. As Lecter manipulates the physical and psychological evidence and leaves crime scenes in his wake, Graham is able to empathize and remember, allowing him to *see* clearly and finally determine that Lecter is both the Chesapeake Ripper and the Copycat Killer. Lecter also eventually and ironically manipulates events to release Graham, planting elsewhere fishing lures containing physical evidence from murders committed during Graham's institutionalization.

In an effort to help Graham while he is institutionalized, Matthew Brown, the orderly at the Baltimore State Hospital for the Criminally Insane, stages the scene of the bailiff's murder in an effort to copy the Chesapeake Ripper murders, remarking to Graham in "Mukōzuke" (2.05) that it was "easy to re-create your work. It was so specific." The copyist, or forger, will focus on the reproduction of the most obvious, apparent features of a work of art (or crime scene) in an effort to reproduce the master's work. The untrained observer may overlook the details that indicate a forgery, leading to an incorrect attribution. Lecter's ability to masterfully manipulate crime scenes, physical traces, and people permit him to remain undetected for an extended period of time. His extensive knowledge and experience allow him to craft crime scenes that are wrongly attributed to other individuals. Incorrect interpretation of crime scenes as well as the skillful manipulation of the scenes and the posing of human remains make it difficult for investigators to ascertain what is real and what is fake in the initial stages of an investigation.

"What Do You See?"

Hannibal grips the viewer with powerful imagery and complex dialogue, both of which portray forensic science and criminal profiling as critical aspects of fact finding in the investigation of vivid murders and grotesque crime scenes throughout the series.[31] By drawing on the importance of observation, reasoning, and the detection of traces, *Hannibal* takes the viewer through criminal investigations and scene reconstructions to identify murderers driven by their psychological motivations. Challenging the integrity of cases and the sanity of the investigators is the continuous manipulation by Hannibal Lecter, an intelligent psychiatrist and serial killer driven by cannibalism and the twisted desire to see what happens when his victims are driven to survive by any means possible. Just as *Hannibal* brings attention to the importance of physical and psychological evidence, it also demonstrates the limitations of such evidence and the potential for misdirection in criminal investigations. Moreover, *Hannibal* effectively brings together crime and art to portray the crime scene as a work of art that can be attributed to its creator by attention to and interpretation of minute details. *Hannibal* emphasizes throughout the importance of the scientific method in problem solving and focuses on the importance of observation to truly see into a killer's mind and motivations.

Bibliography

Berenson, Bernhard. *Study and Criticism of Italian Art*. 2nd series. London: Bell and Sons, 1902.

Bertillon, Alphonse. *Identification anthropometrique: Instructions signaletiques par Alphonse Bertillon, album*. Melun, France: Imprimerie Administrative, 1893.

De Forest, Peter, Robert Gaensslen, and Henry Lee. *Forensic Science: An Introduction to Criminalistics*. New York: McGraw-Hill, 1983.

Douglas, John, Ann Burgess, Allen Burgess, and Robert Ressler. *Crime Classification Manual*. 2nd ed. San Francisco: Jossey-Bass, 2006.

Douglas, John, Robert Ressler, Ann Burgess, and Carol Hartman. "Criminal Profiling from Crime Scene Analysis." *Behavioral Sciences and the Law* 4 (1986): 401–21.

---

31. The quotation in the subhead is from *Sakizuke* (2.02), among other episodes.

Doyle, Arthur Conan. "The Cardboard Box." in *The Annotated Sherlock Holmes*, 2 vols., edited by W. Baring-Gould, 2:193–208. New York: Clarkson, 1967.

Eco, Umberto, and Thomas Sebeok, eds. *The Sign of Three: Dupin, Holmes, Peirce*. Bloomington: Indiana Univ. Press, 1983.

Freud, Sigmund. "The Moses of Michelangelo." In *The Standard Edition of the Complete Psychological Works of Sigmund Freud*, vol. 13: 1913–1914, edited by James Strachey, 211–36. London: Hogarth Press, 1955.

Ginzburg, Carlo. "Clues: Morelli, Freud, and Sherlock Holmes." in *The Sign of Three: Dupin, Holmes, Peirce*, edited by Umberto Eco and Thomas Sebeok, 81–118. Bloomington: Indiana Univ. Press, 1983.

———. "Morelli, Freud, and Sherlock Holmes: Clues and Scientific Method." *History Workshop Journal* 9 (1980): 5–36.

———. *Myths, Emblems, Clues*. London: Hutchinson Radius, 1986.

Goethe, Johann Wolfgang von. *Goethe's Opinions on the World, Mankind, Literature, Science, and Art*. Translated by Otto Wenckstern. London: Parker and Son, 1853.

Harris, Thomas. *The Silence of the Lambs*. 25th anniversary ed. New York: St. Martin's Press, 2013.

Harrowitz, Nancy. "The Body of the Detective Model: Charles S. Peirce and Edgar Allan Poe." in *The Sign of Three: Dupin, Holmes, Peirce*, edited by Umberto Eco and Thomas Sebeok, 179–97. Bloomington: Indiana Univ. Press, 1983.

Kirk, Paul. *Crime Investigation—Physical Evidence and the Police Laboratory*. New York: Interscience, 1953.

Miranda, Michelle D. "Forensic Silence: Identification, Individualization, and the Power of Observation." in *"The Silence of the Lambs": Critical Essays on a Cannibal, Clarice, and a Nice Chianti*, edited by Cynthia Miller, 91–102. London: Rowman and Littlefield, 2017.

Morelli, Giovanni. *Italian Painters: Critical Studies of Their Works—the Borghese and Doria-Pamfili Galleries in Rome*. Translated by Constance Ffoulkes. London: John Murray, 1900.

———. *Italian Painters: Critical Studies of Their Works—the Galleries of Munich and Dresden*. Translated by Constance Ffoulkes. London: John Murray, 1907.

Peirce, C. S. "Abduction and Induction." In *Philosophical Writings of Peirce 1940*, edited by Justus Buchler, 150–56. New York: Dover, 1955.

Sebeok, Thomas, and Jean Sebeok. "'You Know My Method': A Juxtaposition of Charles S. Peirce and Sherlock Holmes." In *The Sign of Three: Dupin, Holmes, Peirce*, edited by Umberto Eco and Thomas Sebeok, 11–54. Bloomington: Indiana Univ. Press, 1983.

Söderman, Harry, and John O'Connell. *Modern Criminal Investigation*. New York: Funk and Wagnalls, 1935.

Spector, Jack. "The Method of Morelli and Its Relation to Freudian Psychoanalysis." *Diogenes* 66 (1969): 63–83.

Tyndall, John. *Scientific Use of the Imagination and Other Essays*. London: Longmans, Green, 1872.

Wind, Edgar. *Art and Anarchy*. 3rd ed. Evanston, IL: Northwestern Univ. Press, 1985.

12 | Fannibals Are Still Hungry

Feeding Hannibal *and Other Series Companion Cookbooks as Immersive Fan Experience*

Amanda Ewoldt

The very first episode of *Hannibal* (NBC, 2013–15), "Apéritif" (1.01), beautifully sets the tone for what we can expect of the rest of the series' treatment of food as a part of the narrative and an important part of community building between characters. We meet Will Graham, conscripted by Jack Crawford of the FBI to help hunt a serial killer who abducts young women and, as we find out, consumes them. We also meet Hannibal Lecter halfway through the episode, as the camera first focuses on a beautifully plated meal and then pans out to show a man in a suit eating it by himself in a darkened dining room. Both Will and Hannibal are introduced in ways that highlight their isolation: Will's sweating, tortured pure empathy sets him apart even in a crowded crime scene, and he prefers the society of dogs to other human beings; Hannibal prepares and consumes his own gourmet meals usually in solitude instead of in company, although he does occasionally have a dinner party. In this episode, we get the first of many cooking montages as well as the first of many social meals and the accompanying witty conversation that characterizes Hannibal's dinner parties. Hannibal, intrigued with Will's empathic abilities and social isolation, brings a home-cooked egg-and-sausage scramble to Graham's hotel room to share an impromptu breakfast. It is an overture of interest and what passes for friendship in Hannibal's world, and Will accepts both the food and Hannibal's offer of assistance for the rest of the episode. "Apéritif" also sets the stage for the naming of each episode after courses of meals. Season 1 utilizes elements of French cuisine, season 2 Japanese, and the first half of season three Italian. Finally, the first episode sets the table for the rest of the series by featuring not one but two cannibals who personally hunt and prepare their own meals from their victims and then feed those meals to their friends or family: the psychopath of the week who becomes known as the Minnesota Shrike, and Hannibal.

Most scholarly criticism about NBC's *Hannibal* has focused almost exclusively on cinematography, violence, and horror. Surprisingly, considering that food (or food porn) is a visceral and constant aspect of the show, little has been written about *Hannibal* and food or about food as a Fannibal fan practice. In one of the few discussions of food and *Hannibal*, Michael Fuchs argues that food is a means of storytelling in the show as well as a method of disturbing typical boundaries of class and society and that Hannibal's cannibalism defies easy characterization.

> Conceptually, cannibalism is intricately related to barbarism, which stands at the beginning, or opposite, of civilization. [...] Lecter's introduction in "Apéritif," however, problematizes this connection, for the character is both linked to the cultured taste of classical music and that barbaric taste of human meat; he is simultaneously a connoisseur of fine art and a brute driven by instincts, and neither of the two.[1]

In other words, in *Hannibal* food is the best medium to illustrate the blurred boundaries between art and barbarism. The show and its title character take a cheerfully macabre view of the intersection of grisly, brutal murder and art. The overall theme of the show is becoming or being true to one's own nature, so Hannibal helps his victims reach whatever potential he believes they possess. With his murder victims,

---

1. Michael Fuchs, "Cooking with Hannibal: Food, Liminality, and Monstrosity in *Hannibal*," *European Journal of American Culture* 34, no. 2 (2015): 99.

he transforms rude material into beautiful and artistic meals for himself and his guests, and he helps his patients unlock their own darker natures thus far repressed by society. Hannibal uses the preparation and consumption of food as a tool to facilitate that *becoming* in himself and others. In their study of the cinematic representation of food, Cynthia Baron, Diane Carson, and Mark Bernard argue that "individual food choices are fraught with ideological implications. Representations of eating and drinking are charged with dense connotations that arise from culturally and socially determined meal systems that identify 'correct' versus 'incorrect' food behaviors."[2] Fannibals thus face a conundrum in terms of foodways[3] and the show, where the acceptable/taboo and civilized/uncivilized dichotomies are blurred at Hannibal's dinner table. Throughout the series, *Hannibal* presents viewers with human meat in the most civilized of fashions: multiple courses served on fine china in a proper dining room, classical music accompanying the preparation montages, allusions to fine art, and carefully selected wine pairings. The food is reflective of Hannibal himself: savagery and Darwinian amorality wrapped in the trappings of the cultural and financial elite and elevated by art beyond his own base nature. For Hannibal, even his unwitting dinner guests are elevated by their consumption of beautifully prepared human meat because it proves that underneath the veneer of polite society and culture, they all are cut from the same apex-predatory cloth. At his dining table, the strong eat the weak, the one percent eat the other 99 percent, and everyone eats the rude.

In sum, there has been little research on food and *Hannibal* even though food is a centerpiece of the show. This chapter aims to fill in

---

2. Cynthia Baron, Mark Bernard, and Diane Carson, *Appetites and Anxieties: Food, Film, and the Politics of Representation* (Detroit: Wayne State Univ. Press, 2014), 28.

3. *Foodways* is a term used in the social sciences, including the study of folklore. *Merriam-Webster Dictionary* defines *foodways* as "the eating habits and culinary practices of a people, region, or historical period." In the scope of this chapter, we may also widen the definition to include fandoms.

this gap, albeit in a different way than perhaps expected. Rather than critically analyze the representation of food in the show, it examines the way companion cookbooks, including Janice Poon's book *Feeding Hannibal*,[4] offer fans an immersive experience in their favorite texts via foodways shared with the characters. After all, official and unofficial series companion cookbooks have been published for decades, and no one can deny the popularity of cozy mystery novels that include recipes for their readers to try.

Second, this chapter discusses the foodie fascination inspired by *Hannibal*. The fans of the show not only have an amicable and ongoing relationship with the show's creative team years after its cancellation but are also riveted by the work of the show's food stylist, Janice Poon. The insatiable curiosity about her food-styling methods eventually led Poon to publish a cookbook titled *Feeding Hannibal*, which encourages readers to identify with Hannibal on the visceral level of food preparation and presentation. The show invites viewers to observe Hannibal's remarkable foodways, but the cookbook invites them to participate. Food is a way to build a sense of community and identity not only between Hannibal and his dinner guests but also between Hannibal and the fans through an interest in the show's food styling as well as among the fans through the opportunity to create and partake of food featured in the show.

Fandom and Food

Fandom is inherently communal. Incidentally, so is food. Connections between food and fandom are not new. One need only browse the mystery section of the library to find countless mystery novels centered on coffee shops or bakeries that include recipes either in the text or in appendices for fans of the book or series to try. And although the *Harry Potter* series does not include recipes, the foodways of the wizarding world captured the imagination of fans

---

4. Janice Poon, *Feeding Hannibal: A Connoisseur's Cookbook* (London: Titan Books, 2016), 114.

worldwide. This means that in addition to the immersive rides of the Wizarding World of Harry Potter and Diagon Alley at Universal Studios, the attractions also host a *Harry Potter*–themed restaurant and the Honeydukes candy shop. Fans can sample famous treats from the series, such as butterbeer and Bertie Botts' Every Flavor Beans.[5] These opportunities to experience the *Harry Potter* foodways are every bit as exciting as being able to buy a wand.

Many franchises have official and unofficial cookbooks connected to them. *Star Wars, Downton Abbey* (2010–15), *The Hunger Games, True Blood* (2008–14), *Alice in Wonderland, Harry Potter,* and even *Anne of Green Gables* have companion cookbooks. At last count, the *Game of Thrones* series (2011–) has two companion cookbooks, including an official one with George R. R. Martin's personal approval. In an article on cookbooks and franchise licensing, Karen Raugust interviews Lorena Jones, publishing director of the companion cookbook for *True Blood*, a series set in Louisiana, where culture revolves around food. Jones affirms the immersive quality of such cookbooks: "You have a cuisine that's perennially popular, paired with a show where food and foodways are an important part of it. It's very much in-world, but it's also authentic bayou cooking."[6] Companion cookbooks offer fans another layer of immersion into their favorite worlds and a more personal identification with their heroes through the opportunity to share foodways.

At the time of writing, there is very little published research on fandom and companion cookbooks, although a recent article, "Eat Your Favorite TV Show: Politics and Play in Fan Cooking" by Madison Magladry also engages with the way such cookbooks offer an

---

5. Having been to Honeydukes, I can report that the butterbeer tastes like cream soda and the name "Bertie Botts' Every Flavor Beans" does not lie: some of these jelly beans really do taste like vomit, grass, earwax, and, allegedly, earthworm. (I have not eaten an earthworm for comparison, but, based on the accurate flavors of the other beans, I take Bertie Botts's word for it.)

6. Karen Raugust, "Licensed Characters Add Spice to Cookbooks," *Publishers Weekly*, July 30, 2012.

immersive fan experience as well as opportunities to create fan identities. Magladry examines two different types of series companion cookbooks to uncover how fans use food to negotiate their experience as both fans and consumers: the "'cookbook for fans[,]' which is *first* a fan product and a cookbook second," and the "'fan text for cooks,' which is more representative of a cookbook than a fan text."⁷ *Feeding Hannibal* falls into the latter category of companion cookbooks because it is first and foremost a cookbook, with the added benefit of also being an officially recognized paratext to the TV show.

Certainly, it would be a worthwhile task to further examine companion cookbooks, their publication histories, and their place in their respective fandoms and audiences. I have a few different companion cookbooks in my possession, including *The "Anne of Green Gables" Cookbook*, first published in 1985, featuring recipes for meals, snacks, and drinks that appeared in the best-selling series by L. M. Montgomery in the early twentieth century. The target audience for the cookbook is young girls who are fans of the series and novice cooks. The cookbook offers sections on cooking tips and terminology and features black-and-white sketches of scenes and characters as well as relevant quotes from the novels.⁸ In my literary travels, I have also found *Sneaky Pie's Cookbook for Mystery Lovers*. The cookbook is written "by" Sneaky Pie, Rita Mae Brown's feline coauthor of her best-selling mystery series, and features recipes for humans and their pets alike (dogs, cats, and horses).⁹ Clearly,

---

7. Madison Magladry, "Eat Your Favorite TV Show: Politics and Play in Fan Cooking," *Continuum: Journal of Media and Cultural Studies* 32, no. 2 (2018): 111, 112, emphasis in the original.

8. Kate McDonald, *The "Anne of Green Gables" Cookbook*, illus. Barbara de Lella (Toronto: Seal Books, 1988), 6–7.

9. Sneaky Pie Brown, *Sneaky Pie's Cookbook for Mystery Lovers* (New York: Bantam Books, 1999), "Author's Note." (I wish I could say that citing a book allegedly written by a cat is weird, but in a chapter like this anything goes.)

the audience of this cookbook includes not only mystery lovers but animal lovers as well.

Such companion cookbooks also offer another level of literary analysis. *The Unofficial "Hunger Games" Cookbook* by Emily Ansara Baines, for example, prefaces each recipe with a brief and relevant passage from one of the novels or a discussion of what the food signifies in the source text. Baines connects each recipe to characters, locations, and events in the *Hunger Games* trilogy. For example, the cookbook's recipe for "Springtime Soup" offers a short analysis of the symbolism of the soup followed by a parenthetical citation from the source text: "Katniss describes this soup as 'tasting like springtime,' a season that represents hope, fertility, and rebirth or rebellion after the long, cold winter of the Capitol's reign. The vegetables in this soup are indeed in season in the spring (*Catching Fire*, Chapter 6)."[10] The cookbook's introduction briefly discusses food as an instrument of power, communication, and identity in the three books of the series, respectively. It offers readers and aspiring young chefs "a portal into Katniss's two worlds—one of luxury and pampering, and one of hardship and labor."[11] The overall idea of the cookbook—and of others like it—is to use food to allow fans a glimpse into the fictional world they admire while remaining safely entrenched in their own.

Furthermore, the communal aspect of food means that fans do not prepare feasts to eat by themselves but often incorporate such themed food into gatherings, including birthday parties and premiere- or finale-watch parties, activities that have slowly gained media attention, as seen in an article from 2012: "As hordes of viewers tune in to HBO's *Game of Thrones* to see what's up with those dragons, fantasy geeks are kicking their fandom up a notch. The

---

10. Emily Ansara Baines, *The Unofficial "Hunger Games" Cookbook* (Avon, MA: Adams Media, 2012), 69.
11. Baines, *Unofficial "Hunger Games" Cookbook*, xiii, xiv.

much-anticipated April 1 premiere of the show's second season has hard-core fans preparing viewing parties with games, costumes and even medieval grub."[12] Food, then, has officially if quietly entered fandom celebrations and culture, alongside the more traditional fan practices. A quick Internet search unearths numerous websites and blogs dedicated to fandom food. For example, Tara Theoharis, who runs *The Geeky Hostess* blog, sells geeky baking paraphernalia and often posts themed recipe and party ideas for myriad fandoms.[13] The James Bond fandom has the Bond Lifestyle website, which identifies products featured in the books and films, including food and drinks, for fans who wish to emulate the infamous spy's habits.[14] More recently crafted is the fan-moderated Tumblr blog *MI6 Café Recipe Exchange*, which features food-themed quotes from Ian Fleming's Bond novels as well as themed recipes created or submitted by the online fan community. These recipes are periodically compiled into online *MI6 Café Cookbook* volumes.[15]

Since food has found its way into the fan practices of countless fandoms, it comes as no surprise that the food featured in *Hannibal* has gained its own dedicated following. *Sugared Nerd*, a food blog and website for a Los Angeles catering company that specializes in fandom food and recipes, planned a dinner party for the second season finale of *Hannibal* in 2014. The writer defended the unusual theme choice:

> [Showrunner Bryan] Fuller and food stylist Janice Poon have done an amazing job making every meal Hannibal prepares look so

---

12. Rosemary Counter, "A Feast Fit for Dragon Slayers: *Game of Thrones* Fans Are Preparing Elaborate Meals Full of Heart for the Premiere," *Maclean's*, Apr. 2, 2012, at http://archive.macleans.ca/article/2012/4/2/a-feast-fit-for-dragon-slayers.

13. Tara Theoharis, "The Geeky Hostess," *The Geeky Hostess* (blog), 2010, at http://www.geekyhostess.com/about/the-geeky-hostess/.

14. See, for example, Remmert Van Braam, "Food and Drinks," Bond Lifestyle (website), 2005, at http://www.jamesbondlifestyle.com/food-drinks.

15. *MI6 Café Recipe Exchange* (blog), Tumblr, n.d., at https://mi6caferecipes.tumblr.com/, accessed Jan. 15, 2018.

good, you can't help but want to eat it, despite knowing what the secret ingredient is. In fact, between Hannibal's cooking and artfully arranged formations of dead bodies left behind by some of the most creative and crafty killers on tv [sic], the entire show seems designed to make the grotesque into something so beautiful you can't look away.[16]

Hannibal delights in unconventional aesthetics, and the show's menu proves it. "The food is people" might be a common tongue-in-cheek tag for Tumblr Fannibal posts, but as Gavia Baker-Whitelaw argues, "The depth of discussion in *Hannibal* fandom suggests everyone is well aware of the horrifying nature of the show. All this cooking and weaving of flower crowns is done with self-awareness and a healthy element of gallows humor—which fits perfectly with the show's morbidly funny tone."[17] If the overall fandom personality reflects the show's dark whimsy and playful pretentiousness, then it makes sense that Fannibals are not queasy about the food. They are instead fascinated by the preparation, morality, attention to detail, and presentation of the dishes within the show. Food becomes its own character in *Hannibal*, perhaps in part because sometimes the food served was in fact a character at some point. Although the menu changes from episode to episode, food is a constant presence throughout all three seasons, and rare is the episode that lacks a decadent dinner scene or artistically rendered foodstuff.

Feeding Fannibals: Janice Poon

The relationship between Fannibals and the show's creative team has generally been amicable, each party expressing mutual affection for the other over social media. The actors still discuss the show and their

---

16. "Party Time: *Hannibal* Finale Dinner," *Sugared Nerd*, May 24, 2014, at http://www.sugarednerd.com/recipes-and-how-tos/2015/7/18/party-time-hannibal-finale-dinner.

17. Gavia Baker-Whitelaw, "'Hannibal' Inspired Fans to Turn Cannibalistic Art into Real-World Dinner Parties," *Daily Dot*, Sept. 2, 2015, at http://www.dailydot.com/parsec/hannibal-recipes-cooking-fandom-fannibals/.

willingness to return to make another season—even when they are being interviewed for their other current work. Most of Mads Mikkelsen's interview for *Collider* in 2015 is about *Hannibal*, despite his major roles in the upcoming films *Doctor Strange* (Scott Derrickson, 2016) and *Rogue One: A Star Wars Story* (Gareth Edwards, 2016). When asked about a fourth season of the show, Mikkelsen replied, "If it comes to a point where we can actually make a full season, I think we will all make it happen because we've enjoyed it so much. If it doesn't happen, we are very pleased and proud that NBC chose to air this, in the first place, as it's a radical show in their world."[18] His costar Hugh Dancy echoed this idea in a separate interview for *Collider* a year later: "All I can say is that Bryan is very busy, Mads is busy, I'm busy right now, but I know that all of us would happily come back in the future."[19] Fannibals have taken these sentiments to heart, keeping the home fires burning with a steady stream of fanworks, including two Kickstarter anthologies. The first was *RAW: A Hannibal/Will Fanthology* (2015), described as "an anthology tribute to the relationship between Will Graham & Hannibal Lecter, featuring over 200 pages of art, comics, and fiction."[20] The second was *Radiance: A Fannibal Anthology* (2017), described as half love letter, half proof that the fandom is still alive:

> RADIANCE is not only a love letter to an inspiring TV-show and its creators but also a declaration of love to a devoted and wonderful fandom that, even (almost) two years after the cancellation of

---

18. Christina Radish, "Mads Mikkelsen on 'Hannibal,' Season 4 Rumors, 'Doctor Strange,' 'Rogue One,' and More," *Collider*, Dec. 8, 2015, at http://collider.com/mads-mikkelsen-doctor-strange-star-wars-rogue-one-hannibal-interview/.

19. Allison Keene, "*Hannibal* Season 4 Would Have Returned to First Season in 'Unexpected' Way," *Collider*, Jan. 9, 2016, at http://collider.com/hannibal-season-4-story-hugh-dancy-interview/.

20. "*RAW: A Hannibal/Will Fanthology* [edited by Aimee Fleck and Tea Fougner]" (description), Kickstarter, n.d., at https://www.kickstarter.com/projects/badinfluencepress/raw-a-hannibal-will-fanthology/description, accessed Nov. 20, 2016.

their show, is here, living and thriving, and answered enthusiastically when we called for them to show us their visions of Will Graham's transformation, creating incredible and breathtaking new art and fiction.[21]

Bryan Fuller, Hannibal's showrunner, was delighted with the *Radiance* anthology and even donated at one of the highest levels to fund it.[22] Although the Hannibal fandom is hardly unique in getting along with the creative producers, the level of mutual interest and affability is notable even three years and counting after the show's cancellation. Interaction persisted while the fandom waited for the rights on the show to expire in hopes that it might be picked up by another network or platform. Perhaps the shared outrage between Fannibals and the creative team over the show's cancellation is what has helped maintain this relationship instead of allowing it to disintegrate naturally.

The ongoing relationship between showrunners and fans is also interesting in terms of traditional fandom boundaries. Fans typically see fandom as a private–public space, according to Kristina Busse and Karen Hellekson: "Plenty of fans who post publicly still expect certain forms of privacy: they consider themselves part of a closed subculture that has traditionally existed under the radar and whose members have followed specific privacy rules."[23] In other words, most fans expect that whatever fanwork they produce will be kept in-house, out of sight of mainstream audiences and the producing team alike, and enjoyed only by other fans. Those who are not in the fandom have little reason to seek out their work, and there is

---

21. "*Radiance: A Fannibal Anthology* [compiled by Romina Nikolić and Germaine Bierbaum]" (description), Kickstarter, n.d., at https://www.kickstarter.com/projects/lovecrimecat/radiance-a-fannibal-anthology, accessed Aug. 2, 2017.

22. Bryan Fuller, Twitter post, June 18, 2017, 8:54 a.m., at https://twitter.com/BryanFuller/status/876468223406821376.

23. Kristina Busse and Karen Hellekson, "Identity, Ethics, and Fan Privacy," in *Fan Culture: Theory/Practice*, ed. Katherine Larsen and Lynn Zubernis (Newcastle upon Tyne, UK: Cambridge Scholars, 2012), 46.

an unspoken rule about fans not "outing" other fans.[24] In exploring boundaries in the *Supernatural* fandom, the relationships within fandom, and the relationships between the show's creative team and the fans, Katherine Larsen and Lynn Zubernis examine the ways boundaries are negotiated in the digital age, where contact with a show's creative team is often little more than a tweet away. Larsen and Zubernis echo Busse and Hellekson's idea of fan privacy: "However much fan practices are celebrated within fandom (and within academia), many fans do not want those practices noticed—not by producers, or actors, or the mainstream media."[25] Even today, although fans can interact freely with the Powers That Be over social media, fandom prefers mostly to remain an open secret. Although fellow fans and aca-fans (i.e., academics who identify as fans) know better than to characterize fandom practices such as cosplay (costume play), "shipping" (the hope that characters in a show or real people connected to it will form a relationship), and fanfiction as deviant, the same understanding cannot be counted on from the mainstream audiences or even from the production teams if a fan or journalist breaks the First Rule of Fandom.[26] In terms of the Fannibals specifically (and in my own many experiences of trying to discuss the show with non-Fannibals), their gallows humor and fond attachment to one of fiction's most notorious cannibals is not usually understood or approved of by mainstream audiences. Regardless, the rules of interaction between showrunners and fans seem to be more flexible in the *Hannibal* fandom, with the production team as enthusiastic about the show as the fans are. This relationship blurs the borders of the fandom and who appears to be in it.

In addition to the production team and actors, Fannibals have also formed a rather unprecedented relationship with the show's food

24. Busse and Hellekson, "Identity, Ethics, and Fan Privacy," 40.
25. Katherine Larsen and Lynn S. Zubernis, *Fandom at the Crossroads: Celebration, Shame, and Fan/Producer Relationships* (Newcastle upon Tyne, UK: Cambridge Scholars, 2012), 144.
26. First Rule of Fandom: Don't talk about fandom outside of fandom.

stylist, Janice Poon. In an interview for *SciFiNow*, Poon mentions that her job as a food stylist usually goes unnoticed: "The food has to be really sensational to draw the director's attention, otherwise you just see it in the establishing shot or the long shot. You get no feedback whatsoever, you're lucky if you get a credit."[27] Fannibals noticed. Hannibal's tantalizing dinner parties, cannibal puns, and elaborate presentations are hard to ignore, and Poon's interaction with the Fannibal community spurred her on to integrate the food into the narratives:

> But when you see that the Fannibals are so interested and they're looking at everything and wanting to know the meaning of things, it's very gratifying and it does make you try harder. I always liken [the process] to writing, because every word has to contribute to the piece or you get rid of it. It either gives information or atmosphere or it moves the plot ahead, it has to do something, and that's the approach that I was taking to food. It came across as very elaborate because there are a lot of metaphors in food. Food has a great deal of meaning, and eating a home cooked meal with somebody is really an exercise in faith, because you're saying this could be mother's milk or it could be polonium tea![28]

In other words, the food in the show functions as more than just food porn or an inside joke between Hannibal and viewers. Food contributes to the narrative process and adds new and deeper layers of meaning to the show. The visceral fascination with the show's menu and the creative mind behind it started with Poon's food blog *Feeding Hannibal*, where she archived sketches of her work and provided behind-the-scenes commentaries about the food she designed for each episode, as well as set photos, poetry, snapshots of scripts, fan art, images of paintings, and explanations of her artistic

---

27. Jonathan Hatfull, "Janice Poon Talks Feeding Hannibal, Cannibals, and Fannibals," *SciFiNow*, Oct. 19, 2016, at https://www.scifinow.co.uk/interviews/janice-poon-talks-feeding-hannibal-cannibals-and-fannibals/.

28. Hatfull, "Janice Poon."

decisions.[29] The blog was comments enabled, allowing fans to interact directly with her. The comments ranged from admiration of her work and the way she inspired fans to broaden their own cookery horizons to troubleshooting discussions regarding the successes and failures of the recipes Fannibals tried for themselves. Poon also posted pictures of Fannibals' *Hannibal*-inspired food and dinner place settings, encouraging fans to email her the pictures of their culinary adventures and to send her links to their foodie blog posts.

The blog's popularity among foodie Fannibals eventually paved the way for the official *Feeding Hannibal* cookbook. Published in October 2016, the cookbook is a glossy, gorgeous love note to the show's food and includes a mischievous foreword penned by Mads Mikkelsen. Replete with stunning photography, the book features set stills, Poon's work sketches, and close-ups of various dishes, ingredients, and presentations. I can happily report the cookbook functional, although aesthetically it belongs on my coffee table or bookshelf rather than lumped in with my other cookbooks. *Feeding Hannibal* echoes the show's darkly whimsical tone and includes recipes used in the show (adjusted to use nonhuman ingredients, of course) as well as recipes inspired by various characters. Although the cookbook has the traditional sections dedicated to appetizers, meat, seafood, dessert, and so on, there are also chapters entitled "Achieving the Hannibal Look," which provides tips and tricks of a food stylist, and "How to Hannibalize Your Table," which includes ideas about macabre garnishes, presentation, and table settings.

However, the cookbook does not merely focus on food preparation but also looks at food in terms of metaphor and aesthetics. Poon gleefully delivers advice on engaging in Hannibalesque dinner conversation. One method is to explicate a recipe's particularities,

---

29. Janice Poon, entry on *American Gods*, *Janice Poon: Art and Food-Styling* (blog), Blogspot, June 25, 2017, at http://janicepoonart.blogspot.ca/. This blog used to be known as *Feeding Hannibal*, but because Poon has maintained it while working on other projects such as *American Gods* (2017–), it is more generally titled now.

as she demonstrates with her recipe for Ravenstag Stew: "Gin, not people, is my secret ingredient in this stew but don't keep it a secret from your guests [. . .] regale them, Hannibal-style, with the saucy information that wild venison eat juniper berries and this improves their flavor. Gin is made with juniper berries. [. . .] Hence, the addition of gin to the stew accents this woodsy richness."[30]

Poon encourages her readers to assume Hannibal's mantle as a debonair, gracious, mysterious host. She also challenges them to take an ordinary dinner party and elevate it both in aesthetics and meaning. Discussing a recipe is one way to capture that image of the amateur chef with a flair for the dramatic. Poon also coaches her readers on the conversation formula that reflects Hannibal's uniquely pretentious way of communicating with his guests:

1. Make a wordy, overblown remark about an element of the dinner.
2. Refer this back to your guest by adding, "tell me, Will, what . . ."
3. Finalize with a random phrase excerpted from (1).
Example: "The plastic tablecloth is a thin superstratial layer of hydrophobic material. In the event of liquid spillage or overthrow, it protects the chatoyancy and grain of my priceless mahogany table. Tell me Will, what will protect your brain—I mean, grain?"[31]

In the cookbook's overall narrative, the Fannibal foodie-chef is invited to identify with Hannibal—to essentially *become* Hannibal by inhabiting his mannerisms and adopting his dramatic method of speech, even if only in play.

In fact, Hannibal dinner parties and other show-related food and décor activities are a form of cosplay. In her essay "Stranger Than Fiction," Nicolle Lamerichs writes, "Fan costumes involve four elements: a narrative, a set of clothing, a play or performance before spectators, and a subject or player. [. . .] [C]osplay motivates

---

30. Poon, *Feeding Hannibal*, 114.
31. Poon, *Feeding Hannibal*, 210.

fans to closely interpret existing texts, perform them, and extend them with their own narratives and ideas."[32] A *Hannibal*-themed or inspired dinner party is an opportunity for the hosting amateur chef to cosplay the Hannibal character. As in the show, food becomes an instrument of the dinner party's cosplay/narrative, and by adopting Hannibal's careful attention to macabre detail and twisting speech patterns, the Fannibal-chef inhabits Hannibal's role. Of course, the host's foray into cosplay allows the guests to join the game as well: they may choose to mimic a character and engage the host with elaborate word-play. The dinner party is elevated; the occasion becomes dinner, a show, and a role-playing game all in one.

Conclusion

Comparatively little research has been done about food and fandom. If food is discussed at all, it tends to be in the context of the meaning that food or hunger has in a particular text, not about what the fandom (if any exists) does with the food. There are considerable gaps in research involving series companion cookbooks and fandoms, and very little research has been done regarding the ways specific fandoms utilize foodways as a fan practice. Yet food is being increasingly incorporated into mainstream fan practices, as evidenced by the growing popularity of series companion cookbooks, themed-party ideas, and amateur food photography found on Instagram (which presents yet another research gap). Even the most basic search of Pinterest will reveal thousands of fandom-themed party ideas and recipes. Themed food adds a fun touch to ordinary gatherings celebrating season premieres and finales. As for myself, I will admit to throwing a fandom party with themed food on occasion. Granted, usually those watch parties revolve around the infrequent season premieres of *Sherlock* or *Doctor Who* because every time I tried to

32. Nicolle Lamerichs, "Stranger Than Fiction: Fan Identity in Cosplay," *Transformative Works and Cultures* 7 (2011): 1.2.

plan a *Hannibal*-themed dinner party, my friends and acquaintances (who are not Fannibals) began looking nervous and suddenly found other very important things to do on a Wednesday night. Alas. However, in the *Hannibal* fandom, food has a special importance as a fan activity because of food's relation to the show's narrative and characters. Janice Poon's blog offers fans a direct conduit to the creative mind behind the show's elaborate foodways, and her official cookbook, *Feeding Hannibal*, gives readers a guide to creating *Hannibal*-inspired dishes, table décor, and mannerisms. Taken together, the blog and cookbook function to immerse fans more deeply into the show by allowing them to step into the kitchen with Hannibal and try out his recipes (sans people).

I have a couple of confessions: watching *Hannibal* has made me more adventurous in the kitchen, more discriminating in my selection of ingredients, and more conscious of food presentation. Binge-watching the show also makes me hungry. To be clear, I am not a cannibal, nor do I have any immediate plans to become one. Yet *Hannibal* delights in taboo foodways and art, and to engage with the show is to engage with our own perceptions and ethics regarding what we eat and what we find beautiful. In the third-season opener, "Antipasto" (3.01), Hannibal gives Bedelia Du Maurier a choice: "Observe or participate?" This same ultimatum is given to the show's audience from Hannibal's first appearance in the pilot episode, "Apéritif." Fan practices traditionally involve cosplay, fanfiction, fan videos, or fan art. However, with *Hannibal*, food itself becomes a fan practice. Not satisfied with mere voyeuristic observation and being drawn "behind the veil" with Hannibal, fans participate by creating and consuming food. With the *Hannibal* food stylist Janice Poon's blog and her official cookbook *Feeding Hannibal*, participation becomes even more pointed as fans can try actual recipes from the show. Granted, we are not participating in real cannibalism, but we are participating in metaphorical cannibalism, or at least thinking about it. On some level, we weigh our own morals against Hannibal's even as we use "his" recipes and knowingly substitute other meats for human flesh.

Bibliography

Baines, Emily Ansara. *The Unofficial "Hunger Games" Cookbook*. Avon, MA: Adams Media, 2012.

Baker-Whitelaw, Gavia. "'Hannibal' Inspired Fans to Turn Cannibalistic Art into Real-World Dinner Parties." *Daily Dot*, Sept. 2, 2015. At http://www.dailydot.com/parsec/hannibal-recipes-cooking-fandom-fannibals/.

Baron, Cynthia, Mark Bernard, and Diane Carson. *Appetites and Anxieties: Food, Film, and the Politics of Representation*. Detroit: Wayne State Univ. Press, 2014.

Brown, Sneaky Pie. *Sneaky Pie's Cookbook for Mystery Lovers*. New York: Bantam Books, 1999.

Busse, Kristina, and Karen Hellekson. "Identity, Ethics, and Fan Privacy." In *Fan Culture: Theory/Practice*, edited by Katherine Larsen and Lynn Zubernis, 38–56. Newcastle upon Tyne, UK: Cambridge Scholars, 2012.

Counter, Rosemary. "A Feast Fit for Dragon Slayers: *Game of Thrones* Fans Are Preparing Elaborate Meals Full of Heart for the Premiere." *Maclean's*, Apr. 2, 2012. At http://archive.macleans.ca/article/2012/4/2/a-feast-fit-for-dragon-slayers.

Fuchs, Michael. "Cooking with Hannibal: Food, Liminality, and Monstrosity in *Hannibal*." *European Journal of American Culture* 34, no. 2 (2015): 97–112.

Fuller, Bryan. Twitter post, June 18, 2017, 8:54 a.m. At https://twitter.com/BryanFuller/status/876468223406821376.

Hatfull, Jonathan. "Janice Poon Talks Feeding Hannibal, Cannibals, and Fannibals." *SciFiNow*, Oct. 19, 2016. At https://www.scifinow.co.uk/interviews/janice-poon-talks-feeding-hannibal-cannibals-and-fannibals/.

Keene, Allison. "*Hannibal* Season 4 Would Have Returned to First Season in an 'Unexpected' Way." *Collider*, Jan. 9, 2016. At http://collider.com/hannibal-season-4-story-hugh-dancy-interview/.

Lamerichs, Nicolle. "Stranger Than Fiction: Fan Identity in Cosplay." *Transformative Works and Cultures* 7 (2011). At https://journal.transformativeworks.org/index.php/twc/article/view/246/230.

Larsen, Katherine, and Lynn S. Zubernis. *Fandom at the Crossroads: Celebration, Shame, and Fan/Producer Relationships*. Newcastle upon Tyne, UK: Cambridge Scholars, 2012.

Magladry, Madison. "Eat Your Favorite TV Shows: Politics and Play in Fan Cooking." *Continuum: Journal of Media and Cultural Studies* 32, no. 2 (2018): 111–20.
McDonald, Kate. *The "Anne of Green Gables" Cookbook*. Illustrated by Barbara de Lella. Toronto: Seal Books, 1988.
MI6 Café Recipe Exchange (blog). Tumblr, n.d. At https://mi6caferecipes.tumblr.com/. Accessed Jan. 15, 2018.
"Party Time: *Hannibal* Finale Dinner." *Sugared Nerd*, May 24, 2014. At http://www.sugarednerd.com/recipes-and-how-tos/2015/7/18/party-time-hannibal-finale-dinner.
Poon, Janice. *Feeding Hannibal: A Connoisseur's Cookbook*. London: Titan Books, 2016.
———. Entry on *American Gods*. *Janice Poon: Art and Food-Styling* (blog), Blogspot, June 25, 2017. At http://janicepoonart.blogspot.ca/.
"*Radiance: A Fannibal Anthology* [compiled by Romina Nikolić and Germaine Bierbaum]" (description). Kickstarter, n.d. At https://www.kickstarter.com/projects/lovecrimecat/radiance-a-fannibal-anthology. Accessed Aug. 2, 2017.
Radish, Christina. "Mads Mikkelsen on 'Hannibal,' Season 4 Rumors, 'Doctor Strange,' 'Rogue One,' and More." *Collider*, Dec. 8, 2015. At http://collider.com/mads-mikkelsen-doctor-strange-star-wars-rogue-one-hannibal-interview/.
Raugust, Karen. "Licensed Characters Add Spice to Cookbooks." *Publishers Weekly*, July 30, 2012.
"*RAW: A Hannibal/Will Fanthology* [edited by Aimee Fleck and Tea Fougner]" (description). Kickstarter, n.d. At https://www.kickstarter.com/projects/badinfluencepress/raw-a-hannibal-will-fanthology/description. Accessed Nov. 20, 2016.
Theoharis, Tara. "The Geeky Hostess." *The Geeky Hostess* (blog), 2010. At http://www.geekyhostess.com/about/the-geeky-hostess/.
Van Braam, Remmert. "Food and Drinks." Bond Lifestyle (website), 2005. At http://www.jamesbondlifestyle.com/food-drinks.

13 | *Hannibal*

Adaptation and Authorship
in the Age of Fan Production

Lori Morimoto

In the opening credits of "Apéritif" (1.01), the first episode of the NBC series *Hannibal* (2013–15), comes the acknowledgment that the show is based on *characters* from the Thomas Harris novel *Red Dragon* (1981). This is an unexpected deviation from "based on the book" acknowledgments typical of text-to-screen adaptations—one that, even at this early point, signals *Hannibal*'s difference from how we typically understand such texts. As Anna Krawczyk-Łaskarzewska writes, the "circular nature" of *Hannibal* at once "encourage[s] and resist[s] attempts at theorization" as adaptation.[1] It borrows dialogue, story, and characters from both Harris's Hannibal Lecter novels and their film adaptations, creating a television text whose intertextual pleasures at once invite a return to the beginning and back in something of a textual ouroboros and unmoor the show in such a way that issues of fidelity are rendered secondary at best. As described by creator Bryan Fuller, the series is "my fan fiction,"[2] a familiar enough

---

1. Anna Kwrawczyk-Łaskarzewska, "Translation Theory vs Film Adaptation Studies: Taxonomies of Recycling and Bryan Fuller's *Hannibal*," in *Komunikacja międzykulturowa w świetle współczesnej translatologii*, vol. 2: *Kultura i język* (Olsztyn, Poland: Institute of Slavic Eastern Europe, 2015), 50.
2. Laura Prudom, "'Hannibal' Finale Postmortem: Bryan Fuller Breaks Down That Bloody Ending and Talks Revival Chances," *Variety*, Aug. 29, 2015,

claim on the part of "fanboy auteurs"[3] who want to demonstrate their fannish bona fides to an increasingly fan-centered media marketing demographic. Yet such uses of the term notwithstanding, a fanfiction lens does in fact enable us to understand *Hannibal*'s palimpsestic text in ways that exceed the general scope of adaptation studies.

Emerging scholarship of what Thomas Leitch provisionally calls "Adaptation Studies 3.0"[4] attends to Lawrence Lessig's "Read/Write (RW) culture" in its theorization of, in particular, media texts characterized by remix, appropriation, repurposing, and transformation.[5] In contrast with "Read/Only (RO) culture,"[6] which "fetishizes the text as a solitarily, pristinely autonomous object,"[7] RW culture is inherently dialogical, its franchises, reboots, and narrative universes always in conversation with what has come before. This distinction in fact mirrors the distinction separating "affirmational" and "transformative" fanworks,[8] in which the latter take their own intertextual liberties in ways that, like RW culture, foreground "'amateur' creativity" and the limits of copyright law.[9] As Leitch describes it, this is the vanguard of current adaptation studies, yet scholarship of fanfiction, almost since its inception, has centered on "remix" culture

---

at http://variety.com/2015/tv/news/hannibal-finale-season-4-movie-revival-ending-spoilers-1201581424/.

3. Suzanne Scott, "Who's Steering the Mothership? The Role of the Fanboy Auteur in Transmedia Storytelling," in *The Participatory Cultures Handbook*, ed. Aaron Alan Delwiche and Jennifer Jacobs Henderson (New York: Routledge, 2013), 44.

4. Thomas Leitch, introduction to *The Oxford Handbook of Adaptation Studies*, ed. Thomas Leitch (Oxford: Oxford Univ. Press, 2016), 5.

5. Lawrence Lessig, *Remix: Making Art and Commerce Thrive in the Hybrid Economy* (New York: Penguin, 2008), 28.

6. Lessig, *Remix*, 28.

7. Jonathan Gray, *Watching with "The Simpsons": Television, Parody, and Intertextuality* (New York: Routledge, 2006), 19.

8. Obsession_inc, "Affirmational Fandom vs. Transformational Fandom," *Dreamwidth*, June 1, 2009, at http://obsession-inc.dreamwidth.org/82589.html.

9. Lessig, *Remix*, 33.

and dialogical texts. Of course, fanfiction has had its own struggles with the original/copy binary, albeit less in terms of fidelity than in terms of derivation and appropriation within a legal framework.[10] Indeed, it is because of the complicated relationship of fanfiction to copyrighted texts that fanworks in the United States are widely considered iterations of "transformative works," legally defined as those that "add [. . .] something new, with a further purpose or different character, altering the [original creation] with new expression, meaning, or message."[11] Moreover, as scholars of fanfiction argue, the dialogical nature of RW culture is equally native to fan-created transformative works.

Given *Hannibal*'s own intensely dialogical relationship with both its antecedent texts and its transformational fans, this essay explores the show through a fanfiction studies lens, considering both how it functions as adaptation and how its narrative reflects an attitude toward RW culture at odds with Hollywood's intellectual property–driven media industry. Fanfiction is by nature inextricably linked to the communities that read, recommend, critique, and reward its authors. So I first examine Fuller's and the production's relationship with *Hannibal*'s community of fans as a prelude to and qualification for consideration of the show as fanfictional adaptation. I further explore how *Hannibal*'s three-season narrative acts as a commentary on a broader shift from RO culture to RW culture and then offer a consideration of the material contexts and implications of transformative adaptation in media.

Fanfiction and the Fanboy Auteur

As noted earlier, in describing *Hannibal* as "fanfiction," series creator Bryan Fuller seems to align himself with a comparatively small

---

10. Abigail Derecho, "Archontic Literature: A Definition, a History, and Several Theories of Fan Fiction," in *Fan Fiction and Fan Communities in the Age of the Internet*, ed. Kristina Busse and Karen Hellekson (Jefferson, NC: McFarland, 2006), 72.

11. Campbell v. Acuff-Rose Music, 510 US, at 569.

group of "fanboy auteurs," including J. J. Abrams and Steven Moffat, who also characterize their remakes and reboots of favorite stories and characters as such. Yet insofar as "fanfiction" is written overwhelmingly by women, the term *fanfiction* is also used pejoratively in writing by (often male) fan critics and media commentators as a way of foregrounding such texts' feminized excesses and infidelities. As invoked by media creators, claims of writing fanfiction typically signal an attempt to gain "close proximity to [. . .] fans [through] an understanding of their textual desires and practices,"[12] arguably helping to establish creators' fannish credibility within a fandom economy that prizes authenticity. The effect is paradoxical. Fanboy auteurs' works often do confound original/copy binary distinctions in textually innovative ways that suggest, if not exemplify, fanfiction. At the same time, as Suzanne Scott notes, they blur the dividing line between "'official' and 'unauthorized' forms of narrative expansion" in such a way that the fanboy auteur, as "creator/figurehead of a transmedia franchise who attempts to navigate and break the conventional boundaries between producers and consumers," becomes a critical cog in corporate marketing targeted at a demographic of "fellow" fans—a demographic that in practice rarely seems to respect female fans or their works.[13]

Fanboy auteurs are thus implicated in an often gendered clash between fan cultural and media industrial imperatives that might be considered a key problematic of fan studies, albeit one that can account for *Hannibal* and Fuller only imperfectly. Fan studies emerged in the 1990s from cultural studies' legitimization of popular-culture consumption, largely on the basis of its perceived oppositionality to hegemonic media industries—Michel de Certeau's "tactics of the disempowered."[14] In English-language fanfiction studies and communities alike, this counterhegemony is embodied

12. Scott, "Who's Steering the Mothership?" 44.
13. Scott, "Who's Steering the Mothership?" 44.
14. Jonathan Gray, Cornel Sandvoss, and C. Lee Harrington, "Introduction: Why Study Fans?" in *Fandom: Identities and Communities in a Mediated World*,

in the "gift economy" of fanfiction production and consumption.[15] Originating in "fans' fear that they [would] be sued by producers of content for copyright violation," the gift economy is a circle of reciprocity between writers who gift (rather than sell) their stories to fans and readers who in turn (re)pay them with feedback, fan art, and so on.[16] Today, when the "fan demographic" is the target of frontline marketing at such events as San Diego Comic Con and Disney's D23 Expo, and when promotional fanfiction and fan art contests threaten to reinscribe fanworks within frameworks of copyright and commerce, we might also understand the gift economy as an often politicized fandom bulwark against media-industry mobilization of fan affect and labor. Against this background, the figure of the economically and culturally privileged fanboy auteur and his claims of writing "fanfiction" seem understandably, even rightly, cynical and galling. As Matt Hills writes of the BBC series *Sherlock* (2010–17), "In order to discursively secure their status as professional, autonomous creatives, [creators Steven Moffat and Mark Gatiss] are required to (re)segregate production and 'fandom,' symbolically distancing themselves from certain [. . .] readings," thereby "validat[ing] gendered fan*boy* knowledge, but at the expense of implicitly disciplining and devaluing fan passion/affect."[17] However, in the case of *Hannibal*, this is precisely where Fuller and his team warrant consideration outside the strictly oppositional framework of gift/commercial economies that typically characterizes fan-producer relations within fandom and fan studies.

---

ed. Jonathan Gray, Cornel Sandvoss, and C. Lee Harrington (New York: New York Univ. Press, 2007), 1.

15. Karen Hellekson, "A Fannish Field of Value: Online Fan Gift Culture," *Cinema Journal* 48, no. 4 (2009): 114.

16. Hellekson, "A Fannish Field of Value," 114.

17. Matt Hills, "*Sherlock*'s Epistemological Economy and the Value of 'Fan' Knowledge: How Producer-Fans Play the (Great) Game of Fandom," in *"Sherlock" and Transmedia Fandom: Essays on the BBC Series*, ed. Louisa Ellen Stein and Kristina Busse (Jefferson, NC: McFarland, 2012), 37, 39, italics in the original.

Critical to any understanding of fanfiction is an awareness of its fundamentally *social* nature, an awareness Fuller demonstrates when he explains, "I feel like it was a unique experience of myself as a fannibal [sic], writing the show as I imagined it [. . .] and then sharing it with other fan fiction writers who then elaborated on it in their own ways. It was a wonderful communal experience."[18] The production's skilled use of social media to communicate directly with fans was instrumental in creating and sustaining this community. Although Anglo-American television has increasingly turned to such outlets as Twitter to promote shows and connect with audiences, there is no clear consensus on how exactly these outlets should be used. At best, production-side social media can "forge a sense of aspirational intimacy with [an] audience,"[19] but as Bertha Chin observes, "attempts at engagement [. . .] do not prevent controversies from occurring."[20] Creators' insistence on a definitive, "correct" interpretation of their text; actors' weighing in, uninvited, on fanworks and cultures; hints of "fanagement" practices that police and contain fan reactions and readings as a means of "protect[ing] brand value"[21]—each is a potential point of friction between fan and producer cultures that has the potential to quickly devolve from social media skirmish to conflagration.

This was the minefield of possible missteps and misunderstandings within which *Hannibal* established its fan-centered social media presence: not only Fuller but also producers Martha De Laurentiis

---

18. Prudom, "'Hannibal' Finale Postmortem."

19. Louisa Ellen Stein, *Millennial Fandom: Television Audiences in the Transmedia Age* (Iowa City: Univ. of Iowa Press, 2016), 112.

20. Bertha Chin, "Social Media, Promotional Culture, and Participatory Fandom," in *Public Relations and Participatory Culture: Fandom, Social Media, and Community Engagement*, ed. Amber Hutchins and Natalie T. J. Tindall (London: Routledge, 2016), 11.

21. Matt Hills, "*Torchwood*'s Trans-transmedia: Media Tie-ins and Brand 'Fanagement,'" *Participations: Journal of Audience and Reception Studies* 9, no. 2 (2012): 425.

and Loretta Ramos, director David Slade, food designer Janice Poon, secondary cast members, the official NBCHannibal Twitter account, and others involved with the show actively tweeted about *Hannibal* throughout its run, engaging with one other and fans alike in playful banter about the show. In particular, Fuller famously live-tweeted during both East and West Coast broadcasts of new *Hannibal* episodes, revealing behind-the-scenes trivia and instances of homage to his own media fan favorites through characteristically exuberant CAPSLOCK posts. Such outreach was unquestionably part of *Hannibal*'s overall marketing strategy, but in fulfilling a corporate imperative through recognizably fannish voices and dialogical engagement with fans, *Hannibal* largely avoided the kinds of disjuncture that often sow oppositionality between producers and fans.

Notable within this strategy was the show's presence on the female-fandom-centric site Tumblr. The official NBCHannibal tumblr (blog) was established prior to the series premiere, and at first it unidirectionally blogged promotional stills and trailers to generate interest in the show. Concurrently and outside the purview of NBC, a largely female *Hannibal* fandom was also emerging from within the existing fan cultures of Tumblr. In response, NBCHannibal began to engage with fans on their own terms. "#HOW DO YOU TALENT"[22] or "10/10 would install this stained glass in own house,"[23] appended to reblogged fanart, at once demonstrated relatively rare production-side affirmation of slash (male/male) fanworks and deftly performed authentic familiarity with and belonging in Tumblr fan culture. Ostensibly organizational hashtags on NBCHannibal posts equally reflected the kinds of memetic commentary through which fans communicated. In posts that mixed marketing and fan languages, fluency commingled with corporate logic in such a way as to avoid the taint

22. "This Is My Design," NBCHannibal, Tumblr, last modified June 30, 2013, at http://nbchannibal.tumblr.com/post/54277038529.

23. "Confutatis," NBCHannibal, Tumblr, last modified May 18, 2014, at http://nbchannibal.tumblr.com/post/86116330157/alessiapelonzi-confutatis-some day-perhaps.

of fanagement: "On a scale from 1 to a disemboweled Dr. Chilton, how empty do you feel during the HeAteUs?"[24] Ultimately, then, the success of the NBCHannibal tumblr lay in its ability not only to engage with fans but also to do so on fandom terms.

It can be argued that such uses of fan language (and, I would add, culture) constituted a "seduction," the performed "reappropriat[ion of] fan language as producer language."[25] But in successfully appropriating *women*'s commonly maligned fan culture to promote *Hannibal*, the production simultaneously affirmed that culture. Within the gendered hierarchy of media fandoms,[26] where fanart is thrust at unsuspecting actors by television talk-show hosts for a laugh and women's interest in supposedly "masculine" genres is derisively dismissed as mere love of pretty boys, this kind of appropriation seems a small price to pay for such validation. Like other fanboy auteurs, Fuller is a self-professed avid fan of both Harris's novels and their film adaptations. But I would argue that *Hannibal*'s fanfiction bona fides begin in Fuller's and the production's careful enactment of fan reciprocity, setting the stage for a blurring of boundaries that reflects fanfiction's unruly, dialogical approach to both text and authorship.

Hannibal the Cannibal

The first episode of *Hannibal* introduces us to a mysterious "copycat killer," whose murder tableaux at once reflect and exceed those of Garret Jacob Hobbs (Vladimir Cubrt), the notorious Minnesota

---

24. "On a Scale from 1 to a Disemboweled Dr. Chilton," NBCHannibal, Tumblr, last modified Aug. 31, 2013, at http://nbchannibal.tumblr.com/post/59878939766/on-a-scale-from-1-to-a-disemboweled-dr-chilton. #HeAteUs was the official NBC hashtag used during the series' two hiatuses.

25. Jingyi Li, "Gone Fishing: New Participatory Cultures in & out of *Hannibal*," paper presented at the Society of Cinema and Media Studies Undergraduate Conference, Northampton, MA, Apr. 24–25, 2015.

26. Kristina Busse, "Geek Hierarchies, Boundary Policing, and the Gendering of the Good Fan," *Participations: Journal of Reception and Audience Studies* 10, no. 1 (2013): 73.

Shrike. Lecturing on this copycat to his class of FBI trainees, profiler Will Graham (Hugh Dancy) observes, "He had intimate knowledge of Garret Jacob Hobbs's murders, motives, patterns—enough to recreate them and, arguably, elevate them to art" ("Apéritif," 1.01). By this reckoning, we might understand the copycat (Hannibal Lecter [Mads Mikkelsen], of course) as both fan and creator, transforming Hobbs's own materials (dead girls and antlers) in such a way that the intertextual contrast of original to copy helps Will see the Shrike's "tells" more clearly. *Hannibal*, too, engages in such copying, cannibalizing both novels and films for their parts in ways that simultaneously reflect and exceed them. This cannibalization occurs as early as our introduction to Hannibal Lecter: immediately following the first appearance of Hannibal, a popular-culture icon closely associated with Anthony Hopkins's portrayal of him in Jonathan Demme's film *The Silence of the Lambs* (1991), is a scene where Will says of Hobbs, "He's eating them," cutting to a close-up of cooked meat being transported from serving dish to plate, sliced, and eaten by a shadowed man. The (implied) cannibalism synonymous with Hannibal Lecter's popular-culture persona here attunes us to his identity, aurally reinforced for fans of the film through Bach's *Goldberg Variations*, recalling its diegetic use in *The Silence of the Lambs*. In this way, Mikkelsen is established as a Hannibal both recognizable and unfamiliar, which is to say the show narratively "enter[s] the archive of other works by quoting them consciously, by pointedly locating [itself] within the world of the archontic text."[27]

As described by Abigail Derecho, archontic fanfiction at once draws from and adds to a textual archive in ways that all but nullify original/copy hierarchies in favor of a multitextual palimpsest—one that in fact characterizes *Hannibal*. In Harris's original novel *Red Dragon*, Graham and Lecter (as they are referred to in the novel) are connected solely through Graham's offstage identification of

---

27. Derecho, "Archontic Literature," 65.

Lecter as the serial killer the Chesapeake Ripper and Lecter's retaliatory stabbing of Graham. That is, they barely know each another, Lecter's assertion that he and Graham are *"alike"*[28] notwithstanding. Their more intimate relationship in the NBC series instead draws inspiration from Brett Ratner's film adaptation of the novel in 2002, effectively closing any distance between novel and film as originary texts. Similarly, the way Lecter is recognized as the Ripper in the film is echoed in *Hannibal*, although the discovery is given not to Will but to an original character, FBI trainee Miriam Lass (Anna Chlumsky), both a Clarice Starling surrogate and an intertextual callout to the protagonist of Fuller's series *Dead Like Me* (2003–4), Georgia Lass (Ellen Muth). Thus, although *Hannibal*'s textual genealogy is clear, like fanfiction it evinces an archontic orientation "that allows or even invites writers to enter [the archive], select specific items they find useful, make new artifacts using those found objects, and deposit the newly made work back into the source text's archive."[29] Nor is *Hannibal*'s archive confined to the world of Harris's Lecter: Ellen Muth also plays unwitting killer Georgia Madchen ("lass" in German) in *Hannibal*, her casting and character a playful reflection of "that tendency toward enlargement and accretion"[30] characteristic of archontic texts.

Hannibal's archontic orientation is particularly discernible where it repurposes exposition, dialogue, and aesthetics from both novels and films. Throughout the series, prose from the novels is appropriated as dialogue:

> Graham had a lot of trouble with taste. Often his thoughts were not tasty. There were no effective partitions in his mind. What he saw and learned touched everything else he knew [. . .]. His learned

---

28. Thomas Harris, *Red Dragon* (1981; reprint, New York: Berkeley, 2009), 83, italics in the original.
29. Derecho, "Archontic Literature," 65.
30. Derecho, "Archontic Literature," 64.

values of decency and propriety tagged along, shocked at his associations, appalled at his dreams; sorry that in the bone arena of his skull there were no forts for what he loved.[31]

In *Hannibal*'s opening episode, "Apéritif," this passage is remixed as Will and Hannibal's first conversation:

> WILL. Tasteless.
> HANNIBAL. Do you have trouble with taste?
> WILL. My thoughts are often not tasty.
> HANNIBAL. Nor mine. No effective barriers.
> WILL. I build forts.
> HANNIBAL. Associations come quickly.
> WILL. So do forts.
> [. . .]
> HANNIBAL. I imagine what you see and learn touches everything else in your mind. Your values and decency are present yet shocked at your associations, appalled at your dreams. No forts in the bone arena of your skull for things you love.

Will's recognition of himself in Hannibal's assessment lays the foundation for a uniquely sympathetic (for being appropriated from Graham's novelized sense of self) rapport between them, one that is both nonexistent in the book and possibly the single greatest source of dramatic tension in the series.

Book and film dialogue is similarly repurposed in *Hannibal*, often independent of its original contexts: "Nothing happened to me, Officer Starling," Lecter says in the novel *The Silence of the Lambs* (1988). "I happened. You can't reduce me to a set of influences. You've given up good and evil for behaviorism, Officer Starling. You've got everybody in moral dignity pants—nothing is ever anybody's fault."[32] The monologue here is in the series divided between two characters across three different episodes: when Hannibal says

---

31. Harris, *Red Dragon*, 18.
32. Thomas Harris, *The Silence of the Lambs* (1988; reprint, New York: St. Martin's Press, 1998), 21.

to Bedelia Du Maurier (Gillian Anderson), his psychiatrist, "Nothing happened to me. I happened" ("Secondo," 3.03); when Will tells him, "You can't reduce me to a set of influences. I've given up good and evil for behaviorism" ("Naka-choko," 2.10); and when Hannibal complains to fellow psychiatrist and jailer Alana Bloom (Caroline Dhavernas), "You've got Will dressed up in moral dignity pants. Nothing is his fault" (". . . And the Woman Clothed with the Sun," 3.10). Although each line suitably informs its context in the show, such uses equally evoke the "unspeakable bliss"[33] of being intertextually hailed by such dialogue for a fan (and thus co-creator of textual meaning). This pleasure is particularly (if subjectively) acute when *Hannibal* liberates dialogue from the Ridley Scott film (2002) of the same title to explicitly romantic ends. In the film, Hannibal, played again by Anthony Hopkins, is expounding, under an alias, on a passage from Dante for the wife of a doomed Italian inspector:

HANNIBAL. "He woke her then, and trembling and obedient she ate that heart out of his hand. Weeping, I saw him then depart from me."
ALLEGRA PAZZI. Dr. Fell, do you believe a man could become so obsessed with a woman from a single encounter?
HANNIBAL. Could he daily feel a stab of hunger for her and find nourishment in the very sight of her? I think so. But would she see through the bars of his plight and ache for him?

Transposed to a "quantifiably bitchy" therapy session between Will and Bedelia in "The Number of the Beast Is 666" (3.12), these lines retain Lecter's subtle confession of love (for Clarice Starling) but imbue them with more pointed significance:

WILL. Is Hannibal in love with me?
BEDELIA. Could he daily feel a stab of hunger for you and find nourishment in the very sight of you? Yes. But do you ache for him?

---

33. Roland Barthes, *The Pleasure of the Text*, trans. Richard Millar (New York: Hill and Wang, 1975), 21.

Bedelia's appropriated dialogue is singularly pleasurable to the knowing fan. At the same time, translated from the film's heteronormative text to Will and Hannibal's decidedly queer, if not explicitly gay, relationship, her words affirm its romantic nature with a frankness seldom expressed in codified television "bromance." As in slash (same-sex) fanfiction, the archive here is a starting point for something new and transformative that evokes its origins without being constrained by them.

If archival dialogue and exposition are fair game for *Hannibal*, so too are the films' musical soundtracks, witnessed in the use of both Bach's *Goldberg Variations* as well as the aria "Vide cor meum." Composed for Scott's film *Hannibal* by Patrick Cassidy and Hans Zimmer as part of an opera performance Hannibal attends, in the series it is the musical backdrop to the last scene of season 1, which follows Hannibal's successful realization of his goal to shield young killer Abigail Hobbs (Kacey Rohl) from FBI investigation by framing Will for both Hannibal's crimes and the presumed murder of Abigail. As a triumphant Hannibal arrives at Will's cellblock (a visual citation of the iconic cellblock of Demme's *The Silence of the Lambs*), he pauses and closes his eyes to the opening strains of the song, which follows him through the short walk to Will's cell ("Savoureux," 1.13). This palimpsest of the show's decontextualized use of the song and Hannibal's self-satisfied gravitas ensures that fans familiar with the film are "really reading two texts at once."[34] Mafalda Stasi describes the fanfictional palimpsest as "a nonhierarchical, rich layering of genres" that augment the archive rather than supplant an originary text.[35] In this sense, the show's use of "Vide cor meum" further reinforces *Hannibal*'s transformative, rather than derivative, habitus.

---

34. Derecho, "Archontic Literature," 73.

35. Mafalda Stasi, "The Toy Soldiers from Leeds: The Slash Palimpsest," in *Fan Fiction and Fan Communities*, ed. Busse and Hellekson, 119.

"This Is *My* Design"

If *Hannibal* can be described as a "state sanctioned"[36] transformative work, gleefully and *legitimately* ignoring the boundaries of individual works within the Hannibal Lecter archive, consideration of its story as commentary on authorship in an age of "writerly" fan production suggests a more transgressive will at work. "The writerly text is *ourselves writing*," Roland Barthes asserts, wherein "the reader [is] no longer a consumer, but a producer of the text."[37] By this definition, as Kristina Busse and Karen Hellekson argue, the serialized television series around which fan communities often coalesce might equally be considered writerly, their narrative open-endedness "invit[ing] [. . .] the viewer to enter, interpret, and expand the text."[38] *Hannibal*, too, engages in seriality, both narrative and (literally) embodied in serial acts of murder through which artistic and semiotic intent is expressed. Of course, this interpretation of both Hannibal's serial manipulations of other characters and the show's grotesque murder tableaux as symbolically equivalent to the act of writing requires a degree of blindness to the actual violence they overlay. Nonetheless, insofar as murder is consistently characterized in *Hannibal* as a metaphorical expression of love—a "serenade" ("Fromage," 1.08), a "poem" ("Hassun," 2.03), a "courtship" ("Kō No Mono," 2.11)—such equivalence seems narratively, if not morally, justified. Particularly at a time when, "even in the context of social media and its connotations of collaboration, the myth of

---

36. Liz Shannon Miller, "For Shows Like 'The Handmaid's Tale' and 'American Gods,' Literary Adaptations Are the New Fan Fiction," *IndieWire*, June 1, 2017, at http://www.indiewire.com/2017/06/handmaids-tale-american-gods-fan-fiction-1201834371/3/.

37. Roland Barthes, *S/Z*, trans. Richard Miller (New York: Hill and Wang, 1974), 4–5, italics in the original.

38. Kristina Busse and Karen Hellekson, "Introduction: Work in Progress," in *Fan Fiction and Fan Communities*, ed. Busse and Hellekson, 6.

individual genius and creative vision persists,"[39] and when television creators engage in the "discursive containment" of transformative fandoms through narratives that "display [...] the fan to herself in controlling forms,"[40] the audacity of *Hannibal*'s narrative challenge to the sanctity of authorial integrity cannot be overstated.

Early in season 1, Will and Hannibal settle into a seemingly harmonious and complementary relationship as reader and writer, respectively, of the "readerly" (or RO) text. Will reads crime scenes, although it is his writerly "pure empathy" ("Apéritif") that enables him to stand in the shoes of killers to interpret motives and meaning. In this sense, Will embodies at least the potential for textual transgression from the start. Hannibal, in contrast, "writes" singularly auteurist murder tableaux, cruelly asserting the sanctity of his vision in the face of "plagiarism" ("Entrée," 1.06) and wresting (narrative) autonomy from those around him through manipulation. In his discussion of "fan-tagonistic" television narratives, in which creators purposely write counter to fan desires and expectations in order to contain unruly textual transgressions, Derek Johnson argues that in so doing they "inhibit fandom's discursive productivity by disarticulating fans from storytelling practice and rearticulating them to compliant consumption."[41] Hannibal, too, inhibits Will's dangerously insightful acts of crime-scene interpretation by using Will's undiagnosed encephalitis as a means of disarticulating him from his writerly imagination in order to frame him for Hannibal's crimes. Yet, rather than "compliant consumption," this betrayal is ultimately so egregious to Will that it "has the opposite effect,"[42] inciting him

---

39. Derek Johnson, "Participation Is Magic: Collaboration, Authorial Legitimacy, and the Audience Function," in *A Companion to Media Authorship*, ed. Jonathan Gray and Derek Johnson (West Sussex, UK: Wiley, 2013), 146.

40. Judith May Fathallah, *Fanfiction and the Author: How Fanfic Changes Popular Cultural Texts* (Amsterdam: Amsterdam Univ. Press, 2017), 14.

41. Derek Johnson, "Fan-tagonism: Factions, Institutions, and Constitutive Hegemonies of Fandom," in *Fandom*, ed. Gray, Sandvoss, and Harrington, 297.

42. Fathallah, *Fanfiction and the Author*, 14.

to authorship of his own text. By season 2, following hospitalization and imprisonment for Hannibal's crimes, Will has reread his interactions with Hannibal, both remembered and recovered, for evidence of Hannibal's guilt. In so doing, he draws back the curtain on the mechanics of Hannibal's "writing," breathlessly admiring Hannibal's artistry and command of the narrative in "Yakimono" (2.07) even as they pave the way for Will's own authorial "becoming."

Once exonerated of the Copycat Killer's—that is, the Ripper's—crimes, Will begins in "Naka-choko" to test his "fledgling" skills by repurposing Hannibal's own corporeal materials in what he claims as "*my* design" against countless other "designs" he has read to this point. For his part, Hannibal seems satisfied to slip into the role of mentor to but not author of Will's growing savagery, as he admits in "Su-zakana" (2.08): "I can feed the caterpillar, I can whisper through the chrysalis, but what hatches follows its own nature and is beyond me." He recognizes in Will's "design" similarities to his own and in his hubris mistakenly assumes a shared purpose and perspective. When at the end of season 2 Will rewrites Hannibal's happily-ever-after intentions of killing Jack Crawford (Laurence Fishburne) and absconding together to Europe by instead arriving at Hannibal's home armed and ambivalently prepared to turn Hannibal into the FBI ("Mizumono" 2.13), Hannibal quickly reasserts "the patriarchal, traditional authority of the author"[43] by murdering the heretofore-assumed dead Abigail Hobbs before Will's eyes, pitilessly disciplining Will's authorial presumptuousness.

Here authorial integrity seems restored to its previously inviolate position. Yet, as Judith Fathallah writes in the context of George R. R. Martin and the HBO series *Game of Thrones* (2011–), where adaptation is involved, "the highly traditional and patriarchal discourse of sole authority [. . .] seems to break down and fragment."[44] In *Hannibal*, this fragmenting is reflected in the series' narratively

---

43. Fathallah, *Fanfiction and the Author*, 115.
44. Fathallah, *Fanfiction and the Author*, 117.

fractured third season (which Dancy has coincidentally described as the "best realization of Bryan's *writerly* mind"[45]), in which those who have survived Hannibal attempt, with varying degrees of success, to fill the authorial void he has left behind. Grasping psychiatrist Frederick Chilton (Raúl Esparza) attempts to cash in on Hannibal's midseason capture through a wildly fanciful exposé, *Hannibal the Cannibal: The Savory Mind of Dr. Lecter*. The book establishes Chilton as enough of an author/ity on serial killer psychology that when Will comes looking for someone to profile serial killer Francis Dolarhyde (Richard Armitage) for an online tabloid in order to flush Dolarhyde out of hiding, Chilton is more than happy to oblige. Yet because Chilton's profile coincides with Will's own self-preserving authorial ascendance, Will ends up rewriting Chilton's version of events in real-time during Chilton's interview with reporter Freddie Lounds (Lara Jean Chorosteki) in "The Number of the Beast Is 666":

> CHILTON. The Tooth Fairy's actions indicate a projective delusion compensating for intolerable feelings of inadequacy. Smashing mirrors ties these feelings to his appearance.
> WILL. Not only is the Tooth Fairy insane; he is ugly and impotent.

Will's ghostwritten text ends up provoking Dolarhyde to discipline Chilton as the apparent author of these insults by immolating him at the hands of his alter ego, the Tooth Fairy/Red Dragon.

Freddie, for her part, is interested in her more salacious version of events, as she admits in ". . . And the Woman Clothed with the Sun":

> WILL. You came into my hospital room while I was sleeping, flipped back the covers, and took a picture of my temporary colostomy bag.
> FREDDIE. I covered your junk with a black box. A big black box. You're welcome.

45. Hugh Dancy, Q&A talk at Behold the Red Dragon Con 3, London, Feb. 24, 2017, my italics.

WILL. You called us "murder husbands."
FREDDIE. You did run off to Europe together.

The term *murder husbands* originated in *Hannibal* fandom and, as such, might seem at first glance to be emblematic of what Fathallah terms "textual provocation,"[46] invalidating fans' romantic notions through, in this case, their association with Freddie's debased writing. Yet Will is unable or unwilling to correct Freddie here, having in fact pursued Hannibal to Europe *on his sailboat*, independent of any official investigation. We might thus just as equally understand Freddie's actions as neither patriarchal rejection of nor permission for alternative interpretations of "official" show canon, but instead as the show's participation in fans' transformative storytelling.

This sense of participation is reinforced by Will's own growing awareness "that every text contains infinite potentialities."[47] Will begins the third season by "posit[ing] the question 'what if' to every possible facet of [the] source text [. . . ,] explor[ing] situations that the makers of the source text simply cannot, because of the need for continuity and chronological coherence in the source text's universe."[48] When we first encounter Will in this season, he is in the hospital, returning to consciousness after Hannibal's attack to find Abigail, unexpectedly alive, arriving at his bedside from a hazy shadow. She encourages him to follow Hannibal to Europe, and the pair travel to Italy in a journey that culminates in a conversation at the Norman Chapel in Palermo, Sicily, in "Primavera" (3.02):

WILL. What if no one died? What if . . . what if we all left together? Like we were supposed to? After he served the lamb . . . where would we have gone?
ABIGAIL. In some other world?
WILL. In some other world.

46. Fathallah, *Fanfiction and the Author*, 164.
47. Derecho, "Archontic Literature," 76.
48. Derecho, "Archontic Literature," 76.

Abigail, it transpires, is little more than a figment of Will's imagination at this point, his talks with her both inner monologue and the story he tells himself about what might have happened had things gone differently. In "Aperitivo" (3.04), two episodes later and self-liberated from the constraints of continuity and chronology, the show returns to that same moment at Will's bedside. This time, it is Chilton who emerges from the shadows, prodding Will to seek revenge on Hannibal in a scene that makes manifest the ways "*Hannibal* treats the repetitive nature of fanfic—stories that 'play out' a multiplicity of variations of the same basic story—as a source of narrative strength."[49]

Both manipulated and manipulative throughout season 3, Will comes into his writerly own early in the final episode by transforming how Hannibal (and we) understand Hannibal's midseason act of surrendering to the FBI after he has been devastatingly rejected by Will. Handcuffed and kneeling on the snowy ground, Hannibal looks up at Will as he says to Jack, "I want you to know exactly where I am and where you can always find me" ("Digestivo," 3.07), attempting to control his and Will's story even in apparent defeat. Three years later, however, Will rewrites this moment in his (presumed) parting words to Hannibal in the final episode, "The Wrath of the Lamb" (3.13): "You turned yourself in so I would always know where you were. But you'd only do that if I rejected you." Ultimately, it is Will's penultimate act that definitively establishes both himself and *Hannibal* as transformative storytellers. Will proposes to Jack a new plan to capture Dolarhyde by pretending Hannibal has escaped federal custody to meet him—a plan that, as Harris writes, "sounded weak to Graham even as he said it." In *Red Dragon*, Graham is serious, if skeptical, about it:

> "The obvious thing is to try to get him to come to a mail drop," Graham said. "Bait him with something he'd like to see." [. . .]

---

49. K. T. Torrey, "Love for the Fannish Archive: Fuller's *Hannibal* as Fanfiction," *Antenna: Responses to Media & Culture*, Aug. 25, 2015, at http://blog.commarts.wisc.edu/2015/08/25/love-for-the-fannish-archive-fullers-hannibal-as-fanfiction/.

"He'd be an idiot to go for it."
"I know. Want to hear what the best bait would be?"
"I'm not sure I do."
"Lecter would be the best bait," Graham said. [. . .]
"Why in God's name would anybody want to meet Lecter? I mean, even the Tooth Fairy?"
"To kill him, Jack. . . . See the Tooth Fairy could absorb him that way, engulf him, become more than he is."[50]

On their surface, these lines evince little transformational potential when they appear in the final episode of *Hannibal*:

> WILL. The obvious thing is to get him to come to us. Bait him with something he wants more than me.
> JACK. He'd have to be an idiot to go for it.
> WILL. Oh, I know. Want to hear what the best bait would be?
> JACK. I'm not sure I want to.
> WILL. Hannibal would be the best bait.
> JACK. Why in God's name would anyone want to meet Hannibal Lecter?
> WILL. Well, to kill him, Jack. The Dragon could absorb him that way, engulf him, become more than he is.

Dialogue from the novel is used almost verbatim here; what attunes us to its transformational *inversion* of meaning here is performance. Francesca Coppa writes, "One could define fan fiction as a textual attempt to make certain characters 'perform' according to different behavioral strips [. . .] acting independently of the works of art that brought them into existence."[51] Understood in this way, Dancy's wry delivery and minute eye roll at an oblivious Jack bear an almost synesthetic relationship to the dialogue, inflecting it in such a way that we realize *this* Will has every intention of authoring Hannibal's

---

50. Harris, *Red Dragon*, 144.
51. Francesca Coppa, "Writing Bodies in Space: Media Fan Fiction as Theatrical Performance," in *Fan Fiction and Fan Communities*, ed. Busse and Hellekson, 230.

escape. When, in the end, Will pulls Hannibal over a cliff following their "pack" murder of Dolarhyde, the visual reveal of empty and unbloodied rocks and sea below seems to affirm nothing so much as the open-ended possibilities of the writerly text.

Conclusion

The transformative work *Hannibal* performs was enabled in no small part by the material contexts of its production. A story about a cannibalistic serial killer-psychiatrist, however iconic, was always going to appeal primarily to a niche audience of Hannibal Lecter fans and horror aficionados, and it was given a remarkable degree of creative latitude, for network television, to do just that. Much has been written about what *Hannibal* "got away with" on NBC: gore, cannibalism, even a kaleidoscopic lesbian sex scene. Yet considered against much of the media around which English-language online fandoms coalesce, I would argue that *Hannibal* is perhaps most audacious in its challenge to the sanctity of producer/fan and writer/reader binaries, particularly through its narrative and textual transformations of a multiply licensed (by both MGM and the De Laurentiis Company) intellectual property in an industry predicated on the ownership and management of such property.

Anglo-American fans today are valued by industry above all as a new marketing demographic, albeit a potentially unruly one that typically must be both materially and narratively contained when textual play crosses boundaries of ownership and interpretation. Women's transformative fan practices are particularly vulnerable to such tactics not only by industry but by gendered fandom and the mass media as well. In slipping outside this disciplining frame through its fanfictional embodiment and performance of RW culture, *Hannibal* meets its viewers as fellow fans and storytellers in a shared love of the writerly text that may hint at adaptations to come.

At the same time, as of this writing the possibility of a fourth season of *Hannibal* hangs in the air and with it some fans' voiced concerns about the narrative direction it might take. Fuller has floated several ideas in interviews since the show was canceled, among them his desire to incorporate *The Silence of the Lambs* into *Hannibal*. This idea has been welcomed by some fans eager to see Mikkelsen's enactment of the novel's and film's story line and, in particular, the Clarice/Hannibal dynamic, but it has also been a source of tension for those fans who desire a continuation of Will and Hannibal's story insofar as the two story lines are perceived to be mutually exclusive. Given the almost wholly transformational nature of *Hannibal*, I cannot help but think that there is no anticipating what a fourth season might bring. But all these reactions, my own included, ultimately attest to the continued resilience of the figure of the god-author, albeit less in terms of being the last word on textual meaning[52] than in the sense that Fuller's industrial privilege—his right to unilaterally decide how *Hannibal* will progress and with whom—necessarily affords him the (possibly unwanted) ability both to make dreams come true and to shatter them to pieces. The "god" of this iteration quite literally has the power to giveth and taketh away, and fans who remain affectively invested in *Hannibal* are at the mercy of this god's whims, regardless of their own capacity for transformational fan production. Here, then, may be where we locate the limitations of even the most sympathetic fanboy auteur: he (always he) may not simply be open to but also welcome writerly fan production. He may perceive his own work as an entirely analogous endeavor. His adaptation may itself be transformational. But to the extent that *his* transformative work is understood as—*felt* to be—the definitive text around which fan production coalesces, author/ity and canonicity remain.

Bibliography

Barthes, Roland. *The Pleasure of the Text*. Translated by Richard Miller. New York: Hill and Wang, 1975.

---

52. Judith May Fathallah, "'Except That Joss Whedon Is God': Fannish Attitudes to Statements of Author/ity," *International Journal of Cultural Studies* 19, no. 4 (2014): 460–61.

———. *S/Z*. Translated by Richard Miller. New York: Hill and Wang, 1974.

Busse, Kristina. "Geek Hierarchies, Boundary Policing, and the Gendering of the Good Fan." *Participations: Journal of Reception and Audience Studies* 10, no. 1 (2013): 73–91.

Busse, Kristina, and Karen Hellekson, eds. *Fan Fiction and Fan Communities in the Age of the Internet*. Jefferson, NC: McFarland, 2006.

———. "Introduction: Work in Progress." In *Fan Fiction and Fan Communities in the Age of the Internet*, edited by Kristina Busse and Karen Hellekson, 5–32. Jefferson, NC: McFarland, 2006.

Chin, Bertha. "Social Media, Promotional Culture, and Participatory Fandom." In *Public Relations and Participatory Culture: Fandom, Social Media, and Community Engagement*, edited by Amber Hutchins and Natalie T. J. Tindall, 8–12. London: Routledge, 2016.

"Confutatis." NBCHannibal, Tumblr, last modified May 18, 2014. At http://nbchannibal.tumblr.com/post/86116330157/alessiapelonzi-confutatis-someday-perhaps.

Coppa, Francesca. "Writing Bodies in Space: Media Fan Fiction as Theatrical Performance." In *Fan Fiction and Fan Communities in the Age of the Internet*, edited by Kristina Busse and Karen Hellekson, 225–44. Jefferson, NC: McFarland, 2006.

Dancy, Hugh. Q&A talk at Behold the Red Dragon Con 3, London, Feb. 24, 2017.

Derecho, Abigail. "Archontic Literature: A Definition, a History, and Several Theories of Fan Fiction." In *Fan Fiction and Fan Communities in the Age of the Internet*, edited by Kristina Busse and Karen Hellekson, 61–78. Jefferson, NC: McFarland, 2006.

Fathallah, Judith May. "'Except That Joss Whedon Is God': Fannish Attitudes to Statements of Author/ity." *International Journal of Cultural Studies* 19, no. 4 (2014): 459–76.

———. *Fanfiction and the Author: How Fanfic Changes Popular Cultural Texts*. Amsterdam: Amsterdam Univ. Press, 2017.

Gray, Jonathan. *Watching with "The Simpsons": Television, Parody, and Intertextuality*. New York: Routledge, 2006.

Gray, Jonathan, Cornel Sandvoss, and C. Lee Harrington, eds. *Fandom: Identities and Communities in a Mediated World*. New York: New York Univ. Press, 2007.

———. "Introduction: Why Study Fans?" In *Fandom: Identities and Communities in a Mediated World*, edited by Jonathan Gray, Cornel Sandvoss, and C. Lee Harrington, 1–18. New York: New York Univ. Press, 2007.

Harris, Thomas. *Red Dragon*. 1981. Reprint. New York: Berkeley, 2009.

———. *The Silence of the Lambs*. 1988. Reprint. New York: St. Martin's Press, 1998.

Hellekson, Karen. "A Fannish Field of Value: Online Fan Gift Culture." *Cinema Journal* 48, no. 4 (2009): 113–18.

Hills, Matt. "*Sherlock*'s Epistemological Economy and the Value of 'Fan' Knowledge: How Producer-Fans Play the (Great) Game of Fandom." In *"Sherlock" and Transmedia Fandom: Essays on the BBC Series*, edited by Louisa Ellen Stein and Kristina Busse, 27–40. Jefferson, NC: McFarland, 2012.

———. "*Torchwood*'s Trans-transmedia: Media Tie-Ins and Brand 'Fanagement.'" *Participations: Journal of Audience and Reception Studies* 9, no. 2 (2012): 409–28.

Johnson, Derek. "Fan-tagonism: Factions, Institutions, and Constitutive Hegemonies of Fandom." In *Fandom: Identities and Communities in a Mediated World*, edited by Jonathan Gray, Cornel Sandvoss, and C. Lee Harrington, 285–300. New York: New York Univ. Press, 2007.

———. "Participation Is Magic: Collaboration, Authorial Legitimacy, and the Audience Function." In *A Companion to Media Authorship*, edited by Jonathan Gray and Derek Johnson, 135–57. West Sussex, UK: Wiley, 2013.

Kwrawczyk-Łaskarzewska, Anna. "Translation Theory vs Film Adaptation Studies: Taxonomies of Recycling and Bryan Fuller's Hannibal." In *Komunikacja międzykulturowa w świetle współczesnej translatologii*, vol. 2: *Kultura i język*, 48–63. Olsztyn, Poland: Institute of Slavic Eastern Europe, 2015.

Leitch, Thomas. Introduction to *The Oxford Handbook of Adaptation Studies*, edited by Thomas Leitch, 1–22. Oxford: Oxford Univ. Press, 2016.

Lessig, Lawrence. *Remix: Making Art and Commerce Thrive in the Hybrid Economy*. New York: Penguin, 2008.

Li, Jingyi. "Gone Fishing: New Participatory Cultures in & out of *Hannibal*." Paper presented at the Society of Cinema and Media Studies Undergraduate Conference, Northampton, MA, Apr. 24–25, 2015.

Miller, Liz Shannon. "For Shows Like 'The Handmaid's Tale' and 'American Gods,' Literary Adaptations Are the New Fan Fiction." *IndieWire*, June 1, 2017. At http://www.indiewire.com/2017/06/handmaids-tale-american-gods-fan-fiction-1201834371/3/.

Obsession_inc. "Affirmational Fandom vs. Transformational Fandom." *Dreamwidth*, June 1, 2009. At http://obsession-inc.dreamwidth.org/82589.html.

"On a Scale from 1 to a Disemboweled Dr. Chilton." NBCHannibal, Tumblr, last modified Aug. 31, 2013. At http://nbchannibal.tumblr.com/post/59878939766/on-a-scale-from-1-to-a-disemboweled-dr-chilton.

Prudom, Laura. "'Hannibal' Finale Postmortem: Bryan Fuller Breaks Down That Bloody Ending and Talks Revival Chances." *Variety*, Aug. 29, 2015. At http://variety.com/2015/tv/news/hannibal-finale-season-4-movie-revival-ending-spoilers-1201581424/.

Scott, Suzanne. "Who's Steering the Mothership? The Role of the Fanboy Auteur in Transmedia Storytelling." In *The Participatory Cultures Handbook*, edited by Aaron Alan Delwiche and Jennifer Jacobs Henderson, 41–52. New York: Routledge, 2013.

Stasi, Mafalda. "The Toy Soldiers from Leeds: The Slash Palimpsest." In *Fan Fiction and Fan Communities in the Age of the Internet*, edited by Kristina Busse and Karen Hellekson, 115–33. Jefferson, NC: McFarland, 2006.

Stein, Louisa Ellen. *Millennial Fandom: Television Audiences in the Transmedia Age*. Iowa City: Univ. of Iowa Press, 2016.

"This Is My Design." NBCHannibal, Tumblr, last modified June 30, 2013. At http://nbchannibal.tumblr.com/post/54277038529.

Torrey, K. T. "Love for the Fannish Archive: Fuller's *Hannibal* as Fanfiction." *Antenna: Responses to Media & Culture*, Aug. 25, 2015. At http://blog.commarts.wisc.edu/2015/08/25/love-for-the-fannish-archive-fullers-hannibal-as-fanfiction/.

14 | Rei(g)ning Lecter

An Interview with Series Writer Nick Antosca on Hannibal

Matthew Sorrento

A glimpse at Nick Antosca's background would suggest him to be a writer of what Stephen King describes as "sensitive literary fiction."[1] An Ivy League graduate who revealed literary talents early—he wrote his first published novel, *Fires* (2006),[2] while an undergraduate at Yale—Antosca would appear to be a member of the Jonathan Safran Foer school. And yet Antosca's fiction is dedicated to the speculative, in the tradition of Harlan Ellison and the early work of Jonathan Lethem, and decidedly veers away from the "slick-magazine" style of many young writers and masters of fine arts graduates. Should one of the narratives begin in the everyday, Antosca's fiction reveals a fissure in reality—both realistic and antireal—that offers much more than a high-concept conceit. In the title

---

1. Stephen King, *Carrie*, with a new introduction by Stephen King (New York: Simon and Schuster, 1999), 1.
2. Nick Antosca, *Fires* (2006; reprint, New York: Civil Coping Mechanisms, 2011). See also Nick Antosca, *Midnight Picnic* (New York: Word Riot, 2009), *The Obese* (New York: Lazy Fascist Press, 2012), and *The Hangman's Ritual* (New York: Civil Coping Mechanisms, 2013), as well as Matthew Sorrento, "Where the Dead Can't Bury Their Dead: A Review of *Midnight Picnic* by Nick Antosca," *PopMatters*, Feb. 9, 2009, at http://www.popmatters.com/review/69910-midnight-picnic-by-nick-antosca/.

14.1. *Hannibal* writer Nick Antosca on the set of his series *Channel Zero*, 2016. (Syfy, © Nick Antosca)

story of his collection *The Girlfriend Game* (2013, cleverly adapted into a short film in 2015 by Armen Antranikian),[3] a young couple tests their relationship through a pickup game at bars, and when the girlfriend takes the game further than planned, latent aggression plays out. Evidenced by many other works, Antosca's is a unified style that offers varied results.

His knack for vivid description and precise dialogue led him to writing for the screen. He wrote for the series *Teen Wolf* (2012) before serving as story editor and writer of episodes of the military series *Last Resort* (ABC, 2012–13) and Alfonso Cuarón's series *Believe* (NBC, 2014). When joining the *Hannibal* writers' team for season 3 (2015), Antosca found material ideal for his sensibility. In the series, menace is everywhere, with psychopath Hannibal Lecter initially working with the FBI and characters such as Abigail Hobbs, daughter of the Minnesota Shrike and an accomplice in her father's killings. In a series featuring procedural investigation of extreme crimes,

---

3. Nick Antosca, *The Girlfriend Game* (New York: Word Riot, 2013). See also Matthew Sorrento, "Games We Play: Nick Antosca and Armen Antranikian on *The Girlfriend Game*," *Film International*, Feb. 10, 2015, at http://filmint.nu/?p=14518.

Antosca contributed to the suspenseful narrative of the search for creators of visually poetic violence and murder. Always committed to developing character, Antosca wrote for the show's strong leads, some frail and some culpable, and cowrote the series closing episode, "The Wrath of the Lamb" (3.13).

I spoke with Antosca in December 2016 as he was editing the second season and preparing the third of *Channel Zero* (2016–), the dark fantasy series he created for the SyFy Network. He is currently at work on *The Act*, a true-crime series, for Hulu.

Can you discuss your first exposure to Hannibal Lecter? I assume it was viewing Silence of the Lambs *[Jonathan Demme, 1991].*

When I was a kid, there were certain specific movies that my parents would kind of taunt me with as being too scary for me to watch or too adult or whatever. *The Shining* [Stanley Kubrick, 1980] was one example, and *Silence of the Lambs* was another. They let me see *The Shining* when I was eleven or so. *Silence of the Lambs* a bit later, probably because of the more disturbing themes of sexual violence. But I found it mesmerizing and terrifying. Later, when the novel *Hannibal* came out [in 1999],[4] I pretended to be sick on the day it was released and stayed home from school so I could read the whole book in a day.

How did Harris's writing style inspire you?

I had read the first three Hannibal Lecter novels when I was a kid.[5] Even then I noticed how *Red Dragon* has a very workmanlike, procedural style, and by the time you get to *Hannibal*, it's sort of florid and grand. Which, funnily enough, is also the progression of storytelling style from season 1 of *Hannibal* to

---

4. Thomas Harris, *Hannibal* (New York: Delacorte Press, 1999).

5. Thomas Harris, *Red Dragon* (New York: Putnam, 1981), *The Silence of the Lambs* (New York: St. Martin's Press, 1988), and *Hannibal*.

season 3. It pretended to be a procedural at first. I also reread the first three Harris novels when I was trying to get a job on the *Hannibal* staff. I had finished another job and had lunch with an executive from De Laurentiis, Lorenzo de Maio, who said they'd be hiring. So I begged my agents to get me an interview and quickly reread all the books.

It's fascinating how Hannibal Lecter has such limited screen time in Silence *but is still so powerful—how did this version of the character inspire you, and how was the investigator role, Clarice Starling, inspiring?*

The Anthony Hopkins version didn't really inspire us, actually. I came into the *Hannibal* writers' room on season 3, so Bryan [Fuller] and Mads [Mikkelsen] had created the show version of Hannibal Lecter long before I was involved. It's much more drawn from the books but also elevated in a way; Bryan has said that in the show Lecter is Lucifer. Starling didn't influence the show at all because we didn't have the rights to *Silence of the Lambs*! We only had the rights to characters created in the other three books.

How did you respond to the different screen adaptations of Harris's Red Dragon*? It's fascinating to see how Michael Mann handled the material, before Anthony Hopkins "became" Lecter and starred in [Brett] Ratner's version of the story [2002], scripted by Ted Tally [who also adapted* Silence*].*

Yes, absolutely. I loved the Mann version, and honestly I don't remember seeing the other one; I know I have seen it, but I don't remember when. I cowrote both the first and last episodes of the *Red Dragon* arc in season 3, so I watched *Manhunter* [Michael Mann, 1986] a bunch of times when I was working on "The Great Red Dragon" [3.08].

I imagine you are in tune with serial-killer cinema. Would you say the Hannibal *franchise was the biggest inspiration to you? More so than the films by David Fincher [Se7en, 1995; Zodiac, 2007], perhaps?*

Overall I would say the movie *Silence of the Lambs* is a big influence on me, just in general. In terms of the show, stylistically, I think Ridley Scott's *Hannibal* [2001] might be the strongest influence, in its sense of grand gestures and magnificent architecture and imagery.

I wonder how important classics in serial-killer, true-crime literature are to you, like Robert Graysmith's book Zodiac.[6] *Was Fincher's film version inspirational to you?*

I've never read Graysmith's book. I've read a ton of true-crime serial-killer writing, though, separately. Ann Rule and Vincent Bugliosi and a million lesser-known, disposable books.[7] The Fincher film was influential to me on projects other than *Hannibal*. Stylistically and in terms of storytelling, I don't think *Zodiac* was connected at all to what Bryan had in mind for the TV version of *Hannibal*.

Are you a fan of themed serial-killer films, like Se7en? *The series seems very interested in them.*

I don't necessarily like the serial-killer subgenre more than I like horror films overall. I also feel like *Hannibal* the series is sort of its own beast, much more impressionistic and florid than movies like *Se7en* or even *Silence of the Lambs*. We tended to reference movies like *Don't Look Now* [Nicolas Roeg, 1973], *Diabolique* [Henri-Georges Clouzot, 1955], *The Talented Mr. Ripley* [Anthony Minghella, 1999], and *The Cook, the Thief, His Wife, & Her Lover* [Peter Greenaway, 1989] in the [writers'] room.

---

6. Robert Graysmith, *Zodiac* (New York: St. Martin's Press, 1986).

7. See, for example, Vincent Bugliosi and Curt Gentry, *Helter Skelter: The True Story of the Manson Murders* (New York: Norton, 1974), and Ann Rule, *The Stranger Beside Me: Ted Bundy, the Shocking Inside Story* (New York: Norton, 1980).

Have you found the connection of the crime-film genre and horror in the story of Hannibal Lecter to be inspiring?

Yeah, it's really the gold standard in that regard, isn't it? Particularly the Demme film. It's this perfect hybrid of the real and grounded with this sense of predatory otherness. And it's also great cinematic storytelling.

How important do you find research of real serial killers, or are you inspired mainly by fictional representations?

Specifically for *Hannibal* the series, at least while I was there, research on real serial killers wasn't really a thing. It's not *American Psycho* [Mary Harron, 2000], where we're reading FBI case files and writing up the stomach-turning things that real serial killers do to people. *Hannibal* was more about psychology and philosophy. We would study painting and classical art. The death tableaus were about visual aesthetics and psychological metaphors.

You joined the writing team for season 3. What situation brought you to the series?

I did not watch season 1 when it was on the air. I heard about it afterward. My late friend Ned Vizzini had been watching it and said it was great. So I'd binge-watched it over Christmas break. When season 2 started, I was watching as it aired. I begged my agents to get me a meeting on it. Nobody seemed to think it was coming back. They got me a meeting with an executive named Lorenzo de Maio at the De Laurentiis Company, and he told me it *was* coming back and suggested I meet. So I had a series of meetings, first with the studio, then [with series writer and executive producer] Steve Lightfoot. The last one was with Bryan Fuller, and it was very short. He was really hard to read. After about fifteen minutes, he said, "I have to go feed my dogs. Someone will get in touch soon." So that was that.

Did one work of yours, either fiction or a script, get the attention of the Hannibal *producers?*
Steve Lightfoot read my short-story collection *The Girlfriend Game* and recommended me to Bryan. Steve's a voracious reader. Most producers would not read a short-story collection as a writing sample.

Can you walk us through how an episode is planned and written? Are all of them outlined together by the writing team and then handed out for scripting to separate writers or small teams?
Bryan Fuller comes in with a rough but solid idea of what the episode is. And also what it isn't. Then the writers' room sits around with the idea and fleshes it out, with Bryan or Steve Lightfoot guiding the conversation. We write the scenes up as bullet points on a whiteboard. Once we have the general structure and order of scenes, we get more detailed on each scene and break it down. Usually we have a couple really cool scenes or key visuals planned. Other scenes are more vague. Then the outline gets assigned to a writer, who goes off and writes it up as a fifteen- or twenty-page outline. The writer gets notes from Bryan and Steve. The writer rewrites the outline. The writer gets some more notes and gets sent off to write the script. Then Bryan and Steve give notes on the script, and the writer does a second draft. Then Bryan usually does a third draft and continues rewriting and polishing as we go into production.

Some writers speak of how it's fairly easy to channel suspense when a crime is proposed on-screen. Do you find such a setup similar?
Well, sure, I guess so. But suspense is in the execution, less so in the conception, although certainly you can set up a premise that lends itself to a suspenseful unfolding of events. *Hannibal* was never really about suspense, though. That's why no one ever cared about spoilers. Bryan would give interviews at the beginning of the season where he would basically just describe

everything that was going to happen in the season. It was about the experience and the aesthetic.

To your mind, what did Lawrence Fishburne bring to series, besides the obvious connections as a mentor figure in other roles?
In addition to being a tremendous actor, he brings authority. For whatever reason, like Michael Caine or Morgan Freeman, he's just one of those actors who brings a cloak of believability and gravity to any role.

Investigator Will Graham is especially frail with his gift—did you find this inspiring when joining as writer?
His psychological fragility is a big part of the series, something Bryan always emphasized. It's an opportunity to make the show more cinematic because there's a more elastic kind of subjectivity to play with. His mind is falling to pieces, and the visuals of the show should reflect that, so Bryan always encouraged us to write toward that.

From what you've experienced, would you say that you and other series writers were largely motivated by trying to undo any established conceptions of Hannibal Lecter and the same for investigator Graham?
No, not at all. If anything, the spirit in the room was that we were trying to make glorious fanfiction. Bryan has a great deal of reverence for the first three Lecter novels and for Harris as a writer. A lot of the dialogue in the show is taken directly from Harris's prose in the books—not the dialogue from the books, but the actual prose itself, used as dialogue for the screen.

Have you ever focused on food this much before in your writing? I know consumption has been a theme in your short fiction.
No—I have never focused as much on food in my writing as I did when I was writing for* Hannibal.*

14.2. Nick Antosca: "The series is focused on the emotional, intellectual, psychological love affair between Will Graham and Hannibal Lecter. We blurred the lines between investigator and criminal as a necessary consequence." Will Graham (Hugh Dancy) and Hannibal Lecter (Mads Mikkelsen) in "The Number of the Beast Is 666" (3.12). (© NBC/Gaumont)

I feel as if the series deliberately focuses on blurring lines between investigator and criminal, even more than the films did. How do you think the series tried to do so?

> The series is focused on the emotional, intellectual, psychological love affair between Will Graham and Hannibal Lecter. We blurred the lines between investigator and criminal as a necessary consequence of that—that's not what the show's about. That's my feeling at least, speaking only for myself. It's not a show about crime and investigation; it's a show about two lonely and deeply disturbed people who are magnetically, destructively drawn toward each other on a psychological level.

Are there any specific writers from season 1 or 2 who inspired you?

> All of them! The only one—other than Bryan and Steve—who I worked with directly was Jeff Vlaming, who remained on for season 3. The other season 3 writers—Don Mancini and Helen

Shang and Angelina Burnett and Tom Deville—were also new to the season.

When coming on board, were you struck by the cleverness of the show? An example: the Minnesota Shrike is a cannibal who feeds the evidence away by honoring every part of his murdered corpse, making it into something.

Of course! Bryan is an ingenious writer. The show has some of the most clever dialogue and construction I've read.

Do you see Fishburne's portrayal of [Jack] Crawford as inspired by the rogue-cop tradition, like Dirty Harry?

No, not at all. I think Crawford is much more of an institutional figure. He tries to play by the rules. He's not really a loner, I don't feel. I couldn't see Harry Callahan as an authority figure in an office, like Jack is.

Do you have a favorite episode from season 1 or 2, and can you discuss why?

It would be "Tome-wan" [2.12] from season 2, where Mason [Verger] feeds his face to the dogs. It's one of my favorite scenes in the whole series. It's also the funniest scene of the series—so deranged. I couldn't believe I was seeing that on TV. What a magnificent scene. I had just gotten hired to write for season 3 when I saw that episode on the air, but the [writers'] room [for season 3] hadn't started yet. I was so psyched to be in that room.

How do you feel about Graham going insane and becoming murderous, which Red Dragon *flirts with but doesn't go to?*

That's not exactly how I would characterize it, but I get what you mean. I love it!

Were there any concerns about portraying mental illness, especially in Graham, since he works as an audience surrogate?

No, but you have to be careful. Subjectivity is elastic. You don't want to go too far—the audience comes out of alignment with the protagonist, and a bond is broken.

The fight at the beginning of season 2 is a great opening for viewers—it shows that the season will go in a new direction with attention to Lecter and Crawford. Are you a fan of cyclical narrative structures like this one, and did such an opening inspire the beginning of season 3 in a different way?

I'm a fan of narrative structures that challenge me to become a more active viewer, as long as they have a purpose and a payoff. As to the inspiration of the season 2 opening, I can't speak to that because that one is pure Fuller. We came into the room on the first day, and he pretty much knew what the first episode of season 3 was.

Were you ever concerned that the series caters to gorehounds who are thrilled by the poetic visuals of murder and oversee the probing psychology of crime and investigation?

No, because the pace and tone of the show tend to repel viewers who love schlock.

Do feel there is any connection between the show and the body-horror tradition of [David] Cronenberg? I feel that some of the episodes, especially in season 2 with the escaped silo "mural" victim, use this style.

Oh, absolutely! I know Bryan has an appreciation for body horror. The death tableaux in *Hannibal* are risky propositions. They could easily become tiresome and kitschy, but somehow they hold up as art.

The body-horror element reminds me of the show's use of director Vince Natali—any comments on his contributions? What did you like about working with the directors of your episodes?

Vincenzo is great. I barely interacted with the episodic directors. I spent most of my time in the writers' room. When I *was* on location, I was mostly in the production office with Bryan and Steve, writing and rewriting.

Do you feel that the truly novelistic scope of this series, which has unity of effect per show but builds into a greater narrative, is challenging viewers and, as some television critics like to say, making them smarter?

I wouldn't dare to suggest that it is making anyone smarter. I hope that it is challenging them, and I hope it is preparing their palate for more shows in the same artistic spirit.

Some concepts of the show, like pigs trained to kill and victims stuffed in animal fetuses, sound a bit goofy on the page, though they are executed on screen brilliantly and tie into the murder-consuming theme well. Did you ever feel that some of the concepts sounded goofy, perhaps on the scenario level, and [that you] really needed to trust the execution?

Jesus, yes. So often. There were so many arguments in the writers' room about "pig baby"—the fetus being grown inside the sow. I was strongly in favor of it, I'd like to note. Some of the writers argued vehemently against it. I can see how it could play silly. But I had a feeling it would come out exquisitely grotesque in the execution. Later, doing *Channel Zero*, we had the same concerns with the Tooth Child. It really could've been utterly silly.

You mentioned that Greenaway's The Cook, the Thief, His Wife, & Her Lover *came up a lot during writers' meetings. Do you recall for which episodes it came up and how it motivated the narrative?*

I don't recall, exactly, but it may have come up in reference to Abel Gideon being fed his own limbs. But more I think the reference was just aesthetic. It's a movie that's both beautiful and sickening.

14.3. Nick Antosca: "I think the reference [to *The Cook, the Thief, His Wife, & Her Lover* (Peter Greenaway, 1989)] was just aesthetic. It's a movie that's both beautiful and sickening." (© Palace Pictures)

In conceiving season 3, did the writing team set out to portray Lecter doing things he's never done? For example, I'm sure he's acted as an impostor, but not to the extent [he is] at the start of the season.

What I recall was more a decision to expand our own palette. Taking it out of Baltimore, making it more florid and European. References became *Don't Look Now* and *Diabolique*. I think there was an awareness that we wouldn't get a fourth season, so there was a desire to go for broke. Season 3, I think, is closest to what Bryan always dreamed of for the show.

[Bedelia] Du Maurier [Gillian Anderson] is a very interesting character. How did she motivate your work and contributions on the season?

I think most writers on the staff would agree she's the hardest character to write. She's such a cipher, intentionally so. In part because going with Dr. Lecter to Europe is such a perverse decision. We had to write a character for whom that was simply her nature. And also—she's as smart as Hannibal. It's tough to write a show where *every* character is the smartest character in the room.

Episode 8, "The Great Red Dragon," in season 3, which you scripted, is pretty fascinating. Can you discuss how you approached transforming Lecter's character from the striking presence he had in the previous episodes, a charismatic if dark professional working with the FBI, to a man in custody? I'm also curious about how you conceived the effective transition sequence, with Lecter seemingly penitent in church to the imagery of him in lockup, which appears subjective to him, before he's actually in custody.

It was a relief to put him in a cage—an exciting challenge. A challenge because of course you have to keep him active while he's incarcerated. But there's so much capital with the character by that point, both in popular culture and the show itself, that it's kind of a moment the audience has been waiting for, so it was exciting to get there. The transition is just one of those things the show does really well—cinematic storytelling. I always liked writing sequences without dialogue.

[In season 3, Dr. Frederick] Chilton's [Raúl Esparza] new book is about a "Tooth Fairy" killer—it's probably a coincidence that Channel Zero, *your follow-up show, is about a "tooth fairy," too, or is there more of a connection?*

It's a coincidence—sort of. The Tooth Child in *Channel Zero* came from a dream that I had while writing on *Hannibal*. I tried to get the Tooth Child in *Hannibal*, and it even did appear in a vision in one script, but then it was cut, fortunately.

It's interesting to see Chilton turn to crime writing, and judging from his unflattering portrayal in Silence of the Lambs, *his move could be read as a condemnation. Plus, since [Francis] Dolarhyde [Richard Armitage] forces Chilton to refute his claims about him [in episode 12], this could also be read as negative critique. What are your thoughts on true-crime writing in general? Do you feel that the show critiques it, or was there any importance to it in your writing for the show?*

14.4. Nick Antosca with Fiona Shaw and Craig William Macneill on the set of *Channel Zero*, 2016. (Syfy, © Nick Antosca)

To my knowledge, there was never an intended critique of true-crime writing overall. I love good true-crime writing, like *Helter Skelter*. It's one of my favorite books.

I'm sure writing Dolarhyde, who originated in Harris's Red Dragon *and in the film versions [*Manhunter *and* Red Dragon*], is a real treat for a writer. Can you reflect on this aspect?*

Oh yeah, that was fun. I'm really happy to have cowritten his first and last appearances in the series. The intent was to always write him as human, driven by pitiable and very human impulses. I love the opening of "The Great Red Dragon"—with Dolarhyde getting the tattoo. I love visual stuff there and the insane music. It feels like this pure, weirdly beautiful pathology captured on film.

Reba McClane [Rutina Wesley] seems like another treat to write for. When scripting, what was your impression of her? She is wonderfully ambiguous to viewers.

In the book, she's very strong and very smart. We wanted to preserve that and make sure she didn't feel like a victim. Like everyone else, she wants love and human connection.

Leading to the final showdown in the series closer, episode 13, must have been fun. Can you discuss how you handled scripting this episode? Was it like "holding onto the reins," as Andre Dubus used to say, with the impending showdown, or did it require gentle handling?

I went up to set in Toronto to work on the final episode with Bryan and Steve. At the end of the season, the schedule always gets brutally crammed up, so we were racing to get it done and make it worthy of the lead-up. Bryan came up with all these beautiful images he wanted to include, moments that could feel like a great end of the story for each character. So I don't know—to me, it felt like "holding onto the reins" because there wasn't any time for gentle handling. I love how the episode turned out—it's one of my favorite episodes of the show.

In moving to your own show, Channel Zero [CZ], *for which you also serve as showrunner, it's interesting to see you move from a human boogeyman in* Hannibal, *if you will, to a supernatural one in CZ. Can you comment on this?*

It's all creating a world. The world of *Hannibal* is no closer to reality than the world of CZ.

Can you discuss the origin of the story [as "creepypasta"] and your interest in it? Also, how do you feel about the "creepypasta" trend in general? For example, do you see it as a benefit to the literary world?

Creepypastas are just short stories. Some short stories are well written and effective, and some aren't. For CZ, we look for creepypastas with an effective and arresting core idea that we can build a season around. Something that is inherently exciting and ingenious but leaves room for elaboration and invention. "Candle Cove" and "No-End House"—the first two stories/seasons we've adapted—are great examples of that.

How did you find it to work with a lesser-known cast on CZ, *in contrast to the mostly well-known players in* Hannibal?
Good actors are good actors. Fiona Shaw is a legend in [the] theater world. I didn't work with the cast on *Hannibal* anywhere near as much as I work with the cast on *CZ*, where I spend countless days on set with them. But on both shows, everyone is a genuinely wonderful person to work with.

The strong premise really stays with me when viewing CZ: *a children's show that kids remember from the '80s but may have never really existed. I think of all the trademark film projects that had a strong premise that pulled in their directors—*Psycho *[Alfred Hitchcock, 1960], with its midnarrative killing off of the main character, or [Otto] Preminger's* Laura (1944), *in which the missing title character [Gene Tierney], after returning to her apartment, suddenly turns into a murder suspect. Was the premise [of* CZ] *a draw that shaped your interest and approach to the show?*
Yeah, that's what I'm getting at. It's easy to gauge whether a premise is striking a chord in people. "Classic" creepypastas build cult audiences, and you can see which ideas resonate. Best-case scenario is we find a creepypasta with a really striking or unique idea, which then gives us ideas. Building a season is kind of a conversation with the original idea, to take it further.

Has writing about serial killers or mad mentors, like Lecter, come into your own fiction [not written for the screen]? Also, has CZ *inspired anything?*
I've been so busy since *Hannibal* ended that I haven't written any prose fiction! I have just been writing and producing TV

shows. I have too many ideas. You can only do so many things at once, but TV is a healthy medium for writers now. Fiction, not so much. It's hard to justify pouring a story I love into another novel right now, although I don't think I'll be able to stop myself from sitting down to write a short story just for fun sometime soon.

Bibliography

Antosca, Nick. *Fires*. 2006. Reprint. New York: Civil Coping Mechanisms, 2011.

———. *The Girlfriend Game*. New York: Word Riot, 2013.

———. *The Hangman's Ritual*. New York: Civil Coping Mechanisms, 2013.

———. *Midnight Picnic*. New York: Word Riot, 2009.

———. *The Obese*. New York: Lazy Fascist Press, 2012.

Bugliosi, Vincent, and Curt Gentry. *Helter Skelter: the True Story of the Manson Murders*. New York: Norton, 1974.

Graysmith, Robert. *Zodiac*. New York: St. Martin's Press, 1986.

Harris, Thomas. *Hannibal*. New York: Delacorte Press, 1999.

———. *Red Dragon*. New York: Putnam, 1981.

———. *The Silence of the Lambs*. New York: St. Martin's Press, 1988.

King, Stephen. *Carrie*. With a new introduction by Stephen King. New York: Simon and Schuster, 1999.

Rule, Ann. *The Stranger Beside Me: Ted Bundy, the Shocking Inside Story*. New York: Norton, 1980.

Sorrento, Matthew. "Games We Play: Nick Antosca and Armen Antranikian on *The Girlfriend Game*." *Film International*, Feb. 10, 2015. At http://filmint.nu/?p=14518.

———. "Where the Dead Can't Bury Their Dead: A Review of *Midnight Picnic* by Nick Antosca." *PopMatters*, Feb. 9, 2009. At http://www.popmatters.com/review/69910-midnight-picnic-by-nick-antosca/.

Willoquet-Maricondi, Paula, and Mary Alemany-Galway, eds. *Peter Greenaway's Postmodern/Poststructuralist Cinema*. Lanham, MD: Scarecrow, 2008.

APPENDIX

CONTRIBUTORS

INDEX

Appendix
Hannibal *Episodes*

Season 1

1.01. "Apéritif." Written by Bryan Fuller. Directed by David Slade. Apr. 4, 2013.
1.02. "Amuse-Bouche." Written by Jim Danger Gray. Directed by Michael Rymer. Apr. 11, 2013.
1.03. "Potage." Written by David Fury, Chris Brancato, and Bryan Fuller. Directed by David Slade. Apr. 18, 2013.
1.04. "Œuf." Written by Jennifer Schuur. Directed by Peter Medak. Not aired in the United States.
1.05. "Coquilles." Written by Scott Nimerfro and Bryan Fuller. Directed by Guillermo Navarro. Apr. 25, 2013.
1.06. "Entrée." Written by Kai Yu Wu and Bryan Fuller. Directed by Michael Rymer. May 2, 2013.
1.07. "Sorbet." Written by Jesse Alexander and Bryan Fuller. Directed by James Foley. May 9, 2013.
1.08. "Fromage." Written by Jennifer Schuur and Bryan Fuller. Directed by Tim Hunter. May 16, 2013.
1.09. "Trou Normand." Written by Steve Lightfoot. Directed by Guillermo Navarro. May 23, 2013.
1.10. "Buffet Froid." Written by Andy Black, Chris Brancato, and Bryan Fuller. Directed by John Dahl. May 30, 2013.
1.11. "Rôti." Written by Steve Lightfoot, Bryan Fuller, and Scott Nimerfro. Directed by Guillermo Navarro. June 6, 2013.
1.12. "Relevés." Written by Chris Brancato and Bryan Fuller. Directed by Michael Rymer. June 13, 2013.

1.13. "Savoureux." Written by Steve Lightfoot, Bryan Fuller, and Scott Nimerfro. Directed by David Slade. June 20, 2013.

Season 2

2.01. "Kaiseki." Written by Bryan Fuller and Steve Lightfoot. Directed by Tin Hunter. Feb. 28, 2014.
2.02. "Sakizuke." Written by Jeff Vlaming and Bryan Fuller. Directed by Tim Hunter. Mar. 7, 2014.
2.03. "Hassun." Written by Jason Grote and Steve Lightfoot. Directed by Peter Medak. Mar. 14, 2014.
2.04. "Takiawase." Written by Scott Nimerfro and Bryan Fuller. Directed by David Semel. Mar. 21, 2014.
2.05. "Mukōzuke." Written by Ayanna A. Floyd, Steve Lightfoot, and Bryan Fuller. Directed by Michael Rymer. Mar. 28, 2014.
2.06. "Futamono." Written by Andy Black, Bryan Fuller, Scott Nimerfro, and Steve Lightfoot. Directed by Tim Hunter. Apr. 4, 2014.
2.07. "Yakimono." Written by Steve Lightfoot and Bryan Fuller. Directed by Michael Rymer. Apr. 11, 2014.
2.08. "Su-zakana." Written by Scott Nimerfro, Bryan Fuller, and Steve Lightfoot. Directed by Vincenzo Natali. Apr. 18, 2014.
2.09. "Shiizakana." Written by Jeff Vlaming and Bryan Fuller. Directed by Michael Rymer. Apr. 25, 2014.
2.10. "Naka-choko." Written by Steve Lightfoot and Kai Yu Wu. Directed by Vincenzo Natali. May 2, 2014.
2.11. "Kō No Mono." Written by Jeff Vlaming, Andy Black, and Bryan Fuller. Directed by David Slade. May 9, 2014.
2.12. "Tome-wan." Written by Chris Brancato, Bryan Fuller, and Scott Nimerfro. Directed by Michael Rymer. May 16, 2014.
2.13. "Mizumono." Written by Steve Lightfoot and Bryan Fuller. Directed by David Slade. May 23, 2014.

Season 3

3.01. "Antipasto." Written by Bryan Fuller and Steve Lightfoot. Directed by Vincenzo Natali. June 4, 2015.
3.02. "Primavera." Written by Jeff Vlaming and Bryan Fuller. Directed by Vincenzo Natali. June 11, 2015.

3.03. "Secondo." Written by Angelina Burnett, Bryan Fuller, and Steve Lightfoot. Directed by Vincenzo Natali. June 18, 2015.
3.04. "Aperitivo." Written by Nick Antosca, Bryan Fuller, and Steve Lightfoot. Directed by Marc Jobst. June 25, 2015.
3.05. "Contorno." Written by Tom de Ville, Bryan Fuller, and Steve Lightfoot. Directed by Guillermo Navarro. July 2, 2015.
3.06. "Dolce." Written by Don Mancini, Bryan Fuller, and Steve Lightfoot. Directed by Vincenzo Natali. July 9, 2015.
3.07. "Digestivo." Written by Steve Lightfoot and Bryan Fuller. Directed by Adam Kane. July 18, 2015.
3.08. "The Great Red Dragon." Written by Nick Antosca, Steve Lightfoot, and Bryan Fuller. Directed by Neil Marshall. July 25, 2015.
3.09. ". . . And the Woman Clothed with the Sun." Written by Jeff Vlaming, Helen Shang, Bryan Fuller, and Steve Lightfoot. Directed by John Dahl. Aug. 1, 2015.
3.10. ". . . And the Woman Clothed in Sun." Written by Don Mancini and Bryan Fuller. Directed by Guillermo Navarro. Aug. 8, 2015.
3.11. ". . . And the Beast from the Sea." Written by Steve Lightfoot and Bryan Fuller. Directed by Michael Rymer. Aug. 15, 2015.
3.12. "The Number of the Beast Is 666." Written by Jeff Vlaming, Angela Lamanna, Bryan Fuller, and Steve Lightfoot. Directed by Guillermo Navarro. Aug. 22, 2015.
3.13. "The Wrath of the Lamb." Written by Bryan Fuller, Steve Lightfoot, and Nick Antosca. Directed by Michael Rymer. Aug. 29, 2015.

Contributors

JESSICA BALANZATEGUI is a lecturer in cinema and screen studies at Swinburne University of Technology. Jessica's research examines childhood and national identity in global film and television; the impact of technological and industrial change on screen genres and entertainment; and vernacular storytelling and aesthetics in digital cultures (in particular the digital gothic). She is the author of *The Uncanny Child in Transnational Cinema* (2018), and her work has been published in numerous edited collections and journals (including *Studies in Australasian Cinema*, the *Quarterly Review of Film and Video*, and the *Journal of Visual Culture*). She coedited the *Quarterly Review of Film and Video* special issue "Hannibal Lecter's Forms, Formulations, and Transformations" (2018) and co-convened the conference "Feasting on Hannibal" in 2016 with her coauthors in this collection, Naja Later and Tara Lomax. Jessica is the founding editor of Amsterdam University Press's book series Horror and Gothic Media Cultures and an editor of *Refractory: A Journal of Entertainment Media*.

EVELYN DESHANE has written articles on transgender identity and politics for the *Atlantic*'s Tech Channel, *Plenitude*, *Briarpatch*, and Hoax Zine. Evelyn (pron. Eve-a-lyn) received an MA from Trent University in transgender narratives and is now attending Waterloo for a PhD on transgender representation in American road novels and adaption theory. See evedeshane.wordpress.com for more on Evelyn's writing projects and speaking events.

AMANDA EWOLDT received her PhD in English from the University of Louisiana at Lafayette. She studied medieval literature and folklore, which led to her interest in pop culture and fandom studies.

KAREN FELTS did graduate work in English literature at the University of California at Riverside as well as at Indiana University, Bloomington, where her dissertation research focused on film adaptations of Victoriana and racial and gender nostalgia. Her current teaching and research interests include discourses of gender and sexuality, popular culture, narrative, and genre fiction. She has been teaching English full-time at Orange Coast Community College in Costa Mesa, California, for the past eighteen years and is a devoted Fannibal.

KARA M. FRENCH is assistant professor of US women's history and program director for gender and sexuality studies at Salisbury University. She received a joint PhD in history and women's studies from the University of Michigan. Her forthcoming book, currently titled "Against Sex: Identities of Sexual Restraint in Early America," concerns the development of celibacy as a distinct sexual identity in early nineteenth-century America. Dr. French pursues an interdisciplinary research agenda and teaches courses on US women's history, gender studies, and LGBTQ studies.

EVAN HAYLES GLEDHILL completed their PhD in the English Literature Department at the University of Reading, with a thesis examining the interrelations of monstrosity and the family within the gothic. Their research interests include representations of anomalous corporeality, masculinities, and intertextual audience engagement. Their published work includes chapters on fascism in the *X-Men* film franchise, gothic posthumanism in the *Star Trek* and *Alien* franchises, embodiment in the CW series *Arrow* (2012–), and gothic fandom in romantic-era women's periodicals.

LEANNE HAVIS is professor of criminal justice in the Division of Arts and Sciences at Neumann University. She earned her BA in political science from the University of Kansas, her MA and PhD in comparative criminology and criminal justice from the University of Wales, Bangor, and, most recently, her MBA from Holy Family University. Her professional and research interests include metacognitive pedagogy, assessment methods, and student-engagement techniques.

NAJA LATER is an academic at the Swinburne University of Technology, Australia. She teaches intersections between pop culture and politics, with a focus on superheroes and horror. She is a cofounder of the All Star Women's Comic Book Club.

ELLIE LEWERENZ received a bachelor's degree in English literature and media studies from the University of Bonn in 2015. She went on to study film at the University of Edinburgh, where she graduated with distinction in 2016. Ellie's postgraduate dissertation focuses on masculinity and male homosocial desire in superhero films.

TARA LOMAX is a sessional lecturer in the School of Film and TV at the Victorian College of the Arts. She is completing a PhD in screen studies at the University of Melbourne, with research on the transtextual poetics of franchise cinema. Her research has been published in the journals *Quarterly Review of Film and Video* and *Senses of Cinema* as well as in the edited collections *The Superhero Symbol* (2019) and *"Star Wars" and the History of Transmedia Storytelling* (017). She also co-convened the conference "Feasting on Hannibal" (2016) with her chapter coauthors, Jessica Balanzategui and Naja Later.

MICHELLE D. MIRANDA holds a PhD in criminal justice, with a concentration in forensic science, from the Graduate Center of the City University of New York, an MS in forensic science from John Jay College of Criminal Justice, an MPhil in criminal justice from the Graduate Center of the City University of New York, and a BS in biology from Manhattan College. She is a diplomate with the American Board of Criminalistics and a member of the American Academy of Forensic Sciences. Miranda worked as a criminalist in the Trace Evidence Section of the New York City Police Department Crime Lab and as both a medical photographer and a death investigator for regional medical examiner's offices in New York State. She is currently employed as an associate professor in the Department of Security Systems and Law Enforcement Technology at Farmingdale State College of the State University of New York. Miranda is the author of the book *Forensic Analysis of Tattoos and Tattoo Inks* (2015).

LORI MORIMOTO received a PhD in media and film studies from Indiana University and now writes as an independent researcher. Her work centers on transcultural fan cultures and transnational film and media. Her writing is featured in *A Companion to Media Fandom and Fan Studies* (2018), *The Routledge Companion to Media Fandom* (2017), and *Fandom: Identities and Communities in a Mediated World*, 2nd ed. (2017). She has also published on transcultural fandom in *Transformative Works and Cultures*, *Participations*, *East Asian Journal of Popular Culture*, and *Mechademia Second Arc*. She is currently writing a monograph about the Japanese female fandom of Hong Kong stars in the 1980s and 1990s.

KAVITA MUDAN FINN is an independent scholar who has taught medieval and early-modern literature at Georgetown University, George Washington University, Simmons College, Southern New Hampshire University, and the University of Maryland, College Park. She earned her DPhil from the University of Oxford in 2010 and published her first book, *The Last Plantagenet Consorts: Gender, Genre, and Historiography 1440–1627*, in 2012. Her work has also appeared in *Shakespeare*, *Viator*, *Critical Survey*, the *Journal of Fandom Studies*, *Medieval and Renaissance Drama in England*, and *Quarterly Review of Film and Video*, and she has edited several collections, including *Fan Phenomena: "Game of Thrones"* (2017) and *The Palgrave Handbook of Shakespeare's Queens* (2018).

SAMIRA NADKARNI's publications trace her interests in postmodern poetry and performance, pop culture, postcolonialism, ethics, fan studies, and digital texts. She sits on the editorial board for the undergraduate journal *Watcher Junior*; writes reviews for the speculative fiction and fantasy magazine *Strange Horizons*; contributes to the digital poetry project *i <3 e-poetry*; and has had her creative writing published in *New Writing Dundee*, *Grund Lit*, and *Causeway Magazine*. Alongside teaching, she works as a journalist and copy editor for various national and international publications. She is currently collaborating with Ensley F. Guffey to coedit and contribute to a collection of critical essays currently titled "War in the Whedonverses," forthcoming in 2019.

EJ NIELSEN is a PhD candidate in communication at the University of Massachusetts, Amherst, with an MFA in studio art (printmaking) from New Mexico State University. Their research focuses on popular media, particularly with regards to monstrosity, gender, and fan studies.

In addition to several book chapters, they have recently published articles in *Journal of Fandom Studies*, *Transformative Works and Cultures*, and *Quarterly Review of Film and Video*.

ANDREW OWEN received an MA and a PhD in sociology from Bangor University in Great Britain. His main area of research focuses on the social history and role of both horror and humor in popular culture. Owen has been an instructor of sociology at the university level for more than fifteen years. He has presented on the topic of film in several countries, including Great Britain, Norway, China, and the United States. He regularly teaches classes on film for historical theaters, especially the Bryn Mawr Film Institute and the Colonial Theatre, Pennsylvania.

RUKMINI PANDE has recently completed a PhD dissertation titled "Intersections of Identity in Media Fandom Communities" at the University of Western Australia. She is on the editorial board of the *Journal of Fandom Studies* and has been published in multiple edited collections, including *Seeing Fans: Representations of Fandom in Media and Popular Culture* (edited by Paul Booth and Lucy Bennett, 2016) and *Fic: Why Fanfiction Is Taking Over the World* (edited by Anne Jamison, 2013). In addition, she coauthored the article "'Yes, the Evil Queen Is Latina!': Racial Dynamics of Online Femslash Fandoms" for a special issue of *Transformative Works and Cultures* (June 2017). Her first book, *Squee from the Margins: Fandom and Race*, was published in 2018.

GABRIEL A. RIEGER is an associate professor of medieval and Renaissance literature at Concord University, where he serves as faculty adviser to the Concord University Newman Club, the Concord University Film Society, and the Concord University chapter of Amtgard. He is also the executive director of the Appalachian Shakespeare Project and served as editor of the journal *The Selected Papers of the Ohio Valley Shakespeare Conference* from 2013 to 2017. His research has appeared in the *Journal of the Fantastic in the Arts*, *The Upstart Crow*, and *Early Modern Literary Studies*. He is also the author of the monograph *Sex and Satiric Tragedy in Early Modern Literature: Penetrating Wit* (2009). A longtime fan of the *Hannibal* canon, he lives in Athens, West Virginia, with his wife and two children.

MATTHEW SORRENTO is film studies lecturer at Rutgers University in Camden, New Jersey. He is interview and book review editor of the journal *Film International* (filmint.nu), to which he contributes regularly. The author of *The New American Crime Film* (2012), Sorrento is currently editing (with David Ryan) a collection on David Fincher's film *Zodiac* and has recently contributed to *A Companion to the War Film* (2016), *The New Western* (2016), *Framing Law and Crime* (2016), and *The Encyclopedia of the Lost Generation* (2019). He is on the advisory board of the Law, Culture, and the Humanities book series for Fairleigh Dickinson University Press.

Index

adaptation: as fanfiction, 8, 58–59, 79, 131, 259–60; fidelity in, 8, 40, 54–56, 58, 66, 71–72, 129, 131, 135–37, 258, 260; film, 2, 65, 76, 126, 128, 134, 267, 286; of Thomas Harris novels, 2, 7–8, 27, 37, 55–56, 58–59, 65–66, 71, 75, 79, 93, 124, 126, 128, 130–31, 133–36, 140, 142, 176, 203n17, 215, 258, 265, 267, 286; as remix, 259; studies, 137, 259; theory, 54, 56, 129, 131; therapeutic, 7, 130–33, 140, 141; as transformative, 58–59, 131, 133, 260, 277

aestheticizing: cannibalism, 145–47, 153, 158, 162; excess, 145, 163; seriality, 41; violence, 3

aesthetics, 4, 38, 71, 99, 120, 198, 213, 216, 252, 267, 294; cuisine and, 16, 157, 161, 247, 253; gothic, 75; of *Hannibal*, 6, 135n31, 136, 153, 170, 288, 290; noir, 176; and seriality, 27–29, 37, 41

Alighieri, Dante, 19, 23, 175, 179, 269

Anderson, Gillian, 93, 160, 169, 171, 177, 186, 269, 295. *See also* Du Maurier, Bedelia

". . . And the Beast from the Sea" (3.11), 67

". . . And the Woman Clothed in Sun" (3.10), 60, 135, 178, 181, 200

". . . And the Woman Clothed with the Sun" (3.09), 56–57, 69, 107, 109, 120, 135, 139, 269, 274

anthropophagy. *See* cannibalism

"Antipasto" (3.01), 41, 47–48, 160, 174–75, 177, 181, 186, 209n22

Antosca, Nick: *The Act*, 301; *Channel Zero*, 294, 296, 298–300; and creepypastas, 298–99; film influences on *Hannibal* 285–87, 292, 294–95; *The Girlfriend Game*, 284, 289; *Last Resort* 284

"Apéritif" (1.01), 17, 40, 110, 156, 193–95, 199, 202–3, 208–10, 216n1, 222–23, 225, 230, 232, 239–40, 255, 258, 266, 268, 272

"Aperitivo" (3.04), 8, 206, 276

art: connoisseurship, 8, 216, 226–28, 232, 240; food presentation as, 2, 16, 240–41, 246–47, 252, 255; murder as, 8, 114, 230–33, 240, 265–66, 272, 293

author: Bedelia Du Maurier as, 170–72, 176–77, 181, 185, 187, 189; fans as 5, 45–50, 79, 163, 260–63; Bryan Fuller as, 5–6, 46, 141; Will Graham as, 273–78; Hannibal Lecter as, 271–73

authorship, 45, 228, 261, 265, 271; and authority, 273–74, 279; collaborative, 77; and colonialism, 148–53; and criminal investigation, 226–28; and whiteness, 81

Barthes, Roland, 269, 271
becoming, 67–69, 129, 137, 141, 240–41, 273
Behavioral Science Unit (BSU). *See* Federal Bureau of Investigation (FBI)
Bloom, Alana, 3, 58, 60, 63; bisexuality, 134–42; pregnancy, 134; as psychiatrist, 195, 200–207, 211–12
Brontë, Charlotte, 75–80, 85–91
Budge, Tobias, 129, 157–58, 198, 210, 212
Buffalo Bill. *See* Gumb, Jaime
Burnett, Angelina, 292

Caleb Williams (novel), 74–86, 90–92
cannibalism, 7, 27, 34, 102, 117, 183, 266, 278; and adaptation, 55, 58–59, 65, 265; anthropophagy, 19, 21–23, 149, 154, 156; auto-, 186–87, 189; and capitalism, 13–15, 20, 24, 147, 153–54, 162; and colonialism, 147–53, 155; and consumption, 16, 20–21, 149, 152–54, 156, 159, 161–62; and homosexuality, 65; as metaphor, 15, 20, 255; as monstrous, 22, 27, 145; and power, 18, 21, 25, 147, 150, 152–56, 159, 161; and race, 145–57; as rebellion, 22, 24, 64; as satire, 18; as savage, 147–49,

151, 153–55; as synthesis, 117; and transgression, 55, 152, 157
capitalism, 10–16, 18, 20–22, 24, 147, 150, 153–54, 156
Chesapeake Ripper. *See* Lecter, Hannibal
Chilton, Frederick, 21, 55, 58, 66, 200–202, 204, 207, 211–12, 274, 296
Chiyoh, 118, 197
clue. *See* evidence; forensic science
collaboration, x, 271
colonialism, 147, 150, 153, 155
consumerism, 19–20, 22, 24, 154, 161–63
"Contorno" (3.05), 183
cookbooks, 252; as fan merchandise, 162–63, 239, 242–46, 254–55. *See also Feeding Hannibal*
Cook, the Thief, His Wife & Her Lover, The (1989 film), 18, 287, 294–95
"Coquilles" (1.05), 17
Crawford, Jack, 84, 89, 113, 158, 200, 203, 273; John Douglas as model for, 30; Laurence Fishburne as, 3, 58, 146, 292; and Will Graham, 111–12, 114–15, 204, 208–9, 212, 217, 222–23, 276–77; as mentor, 114; and Clarice Starling, 99, 102–3, 105, 114. *See also* Fishburne, Laurence
Crawford, Phyllis (Bella), 89
crime procedural, 3, 5, 171, 192–93, 195, 199, 207, 215, 284–86
crime scene investigation. *See* forensic science
criminal profiling, 28–30, 33–36, 215–20, 224–26, 235–36
Cronenberg, David, 293

Index 315

Dancy, Hugh, 9, 170n2, 193, 208, 248, 274, 277. *See also* Graham, Will
De Laurentiis, Martha, 263
De Laurentiis Company, 278, 286, 288
Demme, Jonathan. *See Silence of the Lambs, The* (1991 film)
detective: as character, 35–36, 60–61, 78, 194, 197, 199–200, 208, 210; as genre, 35–36, 75, 194, 198; Will Graham as, 208; in serial killer genre, 196. *See also* crime procedural
"Digestivo" (3.07), 88, 119, 206, 208, 276
Dimmond, Anthony, 116, 175
Dolarhyde, Francis, 61, 136, 217, 274, 276, 278, 296–97; adaptation of, 56–58, 65–72, 126–27, 135–36, 198; and Will Graham, 62, 69–72; pathology of, 196, 198; and psychoanalysis, 202; and queerness, 126–27, 133, 135, 139; as transgender, 137–42
"Dolce" (3.06), 49, 91, 117–18, 172, 179, 187
Douglas, John, 4, 30–31, 224n15
Dracula, 102–3
dreams, 2–3, 211n25, 268, 296
Du Maurier, Bedelia, 65, 69, 106, 117, 269–70, 295; as audience surrogate, 169–76, 185; as author anima, 170–76, 185; as femme fatale, 170, 176–81, 185; as Final Woman, 170, 182–85; and Will Graham, 63–64, 68–69, 211, 269; and Hannibal Lecter, 117, 160, 197, 255; as psychiatrist, 63–64, 68, 106, 116, 200; series finale and, 41, 93, 178–81, 185–89

"Entrée" (1.06), 17, 202, 223, 232, 272
evidence, 92, 105, 115, 233–36; forensic, 74, 99, 193, 200, 215–16, 219–26, 231, 292; psychological, 215, 235–36, 273
executioner's humor, 18. *See also* gallows humor

fandom, xi, 5–6, 8, 164–65, 215, 241n3; and authenticity, 261; and food, 242–47, 254–55; gendered, 278; and *Hannibal*, 145–46, 188; moral panics about, 46, 48; practices, 188, 255; and race, 146, 164–65; relationship with production, 249–50, 261–62, 272, 278; transformative, 272; and whiteness, 146. *See also* Fannibals
fanfiction, 47–49, 189, 209, 248, 259–65, 270; archontic, 8, 260, 266–67; as deviant, 49–51, 250; *Hannibal* as, 5, 7–8, 28, 45–47, 58, 79, 260, 265, 275, 278, 290; and race, 163; and repetition, 28, 47–48, 276
Fannibals, xi, 5, 7, 9, 124, 145, 163, 188, 255; and fan practices, xi, 7, 162–64, 189, 240, 247, 248–49, 251–52; and food, 8, 162–64, 189, 240–41, 247, 251–54; relationship with production, 249–52, 264–65, 278
fan studies, 163–65, 260–62

fanworks, 249; and community, 262–63; and race, 163; fanart, xi, xiii, 5, 188, 251, 255, 262, 264–65
Federal Bureau of Investigation (FBI), 3–4, 29–31, 33, 74, 99–100, 104, 113, 288; Behavioral Science Unit (BSU), 30, 99, 225, 231; in *Hannibal*, 61, 71, 76, 81, 84, 99–100, 103, 117, 119, 204, 211, 223, 239, 267, 270, 276, 284; in Thomas Harris's novels, 172, 201, 208, 296
Feeding Hannibal: blog, x, 251–53, 255; book, 239, 242, 244, 253, 255. *See also* Poon, Janice
femme fatale, 24, 170, 176–82, 184–85, 189
film noir: *Hannibal* as, 3, 170, 176–77, 180
Final Girl, 24, 93, 170, 182–89. *See also* Final Woman
Final Woman, 182–84
Fincher, David, 201n24, 287
Fishburne, Laurence, 3, 74, 146, 273, 290, 292
foodways, 241–43, 241n3, 254–55
forensic psychology, 215–16, 224–26
forensic science, 6, 134, 215–16, 222, 235
forgery, 229–31, 233, 235
Freud, Sigmund, 18, 131, 202, 211n25, 231–32
Freudian analysis, 195–213, 231–32
"Fromage" (1.08), 128, 157
Fuller, Bryan, x–xi, 9, 35, 44–45, 49, 51, 80, 105, 138, 147, 175, 175n11, 199, 288; and adaptation, 55, 79, 96–98, 112, 121, 126–36, 139–42, 176, 192, 198, 203n17, 209–10; as creator, 4, 7–8, 28, 75, 83, 111, 147, 170–71, 173, 182–83, 185–86, 195, 197, 286, 289, 293; *Dead Like Me*, 2, 267; as fan author, 45–46, 58, 79, 258; as fanboy auteur, 259–62, 279; and *Hannibal*'s cancellation, 6, 41; *Pushing Daisies*, 2; and queerness, 65, 74–75, 110, 124, 127, 140, 212n26; relationship with fans, 5, 186, 188, 260–65; as showrunner, 2–3, 6, 102, 246, 267, 278–79; on social media, 124, 184, 249; and television narrative, 28, 35–36, 39–40, 42; and whiteness, 152–53; *Wonderfalls*, 2
"Futamono" (2.06), 17, 41, 117, 204, 234
futurity, 43–44, 48, 50; queer, 125–26, 125n4

gallows humor, 18, 247, 250
gaze: Bedelia's, 175; colonialist, 155; male, 170, 178–81, 178n12; transgender, 138, 140
gender: assumptions, 93, 111–12; binary, 195, 200, 203–4, 206–7; critique in *Hannibal*, 193; dynamics, 75–76, 78, 82, 84, 111, 194, 200; dysphoria, 127, 129; and fanfiction, 49; and fans, 262, 265, 278; femininity, 8, 81–82, 86, 99–100, 138; fluidity, 210; and horror, 182; and marriage, 92; masculinity, 81, 84, 93, 138; and mentorship, 98, 100–101, 108, 110; nonconforming, 125, 137–38, 196, 198, 199; norms, 82, 84, 93, 195, 200, 202; politics, 199, 261; and power, 75, 78–80, 82,

85, 88, 90, 94, 97, 105, 196; and queerness, 63; roles, 93, 194–95, 199, 203–4; studies, 6. *See also* transgender

genre, 39, 75, 80, 265, 270; -bending, 2; crime procedural, 3, 192–93, 288; detective, 35, 196; fantasy, 38; gothic romance, 7, 74–77, 93–94; horror, 38, 41, 184, 288; science fiction, 38; serial killer, 287; slash as, 79; suspense, 171; television, 8, 94, 192

Gideon, Abel, 41, 120, 160, 201–2, 230, 234, 294

gift economy, 261–62

Godwin, William, 75, 77–85, 88, 90–91

gothic, 7, 75–76, 93; melodrama, 3; romance, 7, 74–77, 80, 84, 91, 94

Graham, Will, ix, 1, 4, 17, 40, 98, 170, 174, 186, 199, 203, 206–7, 228–29, 239, 290; in adaptation, 7, 60, 62, 71, 110, 121, 134–35, 141, 208, 266–67, 276–77; as blue collar, 156; as detective, 134, 193–94, 199–200, 217–20, 222–23, 225, 228, 231–32; and Francis Dolarhyde, 67; and empathy, 4, 111, 202, 217–18, 222, 231, 239; in fanfiction, 46, 49, 248; and fishing, 156; and gender, 81, 86, 111, 208, 213; in Thomas Harris's novels, 7, 34, 58–59, 61–62, 71, 76, 101–2, 135, 140, 208, 266–67, 276–77; mental health of, 62, 235, 292–93; relationship with Hannibal Lecter, 4, 35, 44, 46, 49, 55, 59, 63–65, 69–72, 76, 81, 84, 91, 98, 110–11, 116, 124, 127, 129, 136, 141–42, 169–71, 198, 201, 235, 248, 266, 291; as unreliable narrator, 48, 277

Grand Guignol, 2, 19, 171

"Great Red Dragon, The" (3.08), 8, 60, 66–67, 286, 296–97

Grendel, 23

Gumb, Jaime, 2, 31, 65, 127–30, 132–33, 138, 141, 196, 234n30

Halberstam, Jack, 124–25, 127, 133, 136–39, 141–42

Hannibal (novel), 1, 105, 113, 116, 120–21, 126, 129–30, 172, 208n21, 209, 285–86, 290; treatment of Clarice Starling in, 97–103, 106, 109–11, 117–18, 120, 172

Hannibal (2001 film), 1, 97, 130, 183, 269, 270, 287

Hannibal Rising (novel), 1, 116n35, 134n28

Hannibal Rising (2007 film), 1–2

Harris, Thomas, 1, 4, 6, 56, 71, 75, 97–103, 185, 258, 265–68, 276–77, 285–86, 290, 297; and binarism, 55, 196; criticisms of, 65, 127–34, 141–42, 192; research for books, 30–31; and serial killer novel, 28, 50

"Hassun" (2.03), 113, 271

heteronormativity, 44, 196; rejection of in *Hannibal*, 8, 45, 49–50, 74, 194, 199

Hobbs, Abigail, 112, 115, 160, 173, 194–95, 200, 203, 206n20, 209, 229, 284; as mentee, 7, 98, 103–10, 112; as murderer, 104, 106–9, 225; relationship with Hannibal Lecter, 160, 205, 234, 270;

Hobbs, Abigail (*cont.*)
relationship with Will Graham, 156, 204, 225, 275–76; as surrogate daughter, 44, 60, 110, 116, 204, 206
Hobbs, Garret Jacob, 101, 110, 113–15, 156, 194, 210, 217, 223, 265–66; as father, 199, 205
Hopkins, Sir Anthony, 2, 183, 266, 269, 286
horror, 9, 38, 42, 145, 182–85, 189, 240, 278, 287–88; aesthetics, 170; body, 103, 293; in Grand Guignol, 19; Hannibal Lecter texts as, 2, 27–28; of seriality, 39, 41–42; television, 40, 42

identity: blurred, 183; cultural, 161; disorder, 129, 141; dual, 137; and food, 152, 242, 245; indeterminate, 60, 82; queerness and, 83; racialized, 146, 162, 164–65; repetition, 32; sexual, 125; transgender, 130, 133, 138, 142
intertextuality, 4, 30, 154, 165, 258–59, 266–67

Jane Eyre (novel), 74–80, 85–94
Jenkins, Philip, 27–34, 36–37, 39, 42–43, 50

"Kaiseki" (2.01), 16, 91, 112, 234
Katz, Beverly, 3, 146, 219, 223, 234
Kickstarter, 5, 189; Radiance, 189n35, 248–49; RAW, 189n35, 248
King, Stephen, 102, 182, 283

"Kō No Mono" (2.11), 89, 271
Kubrick, Stanley, 285

Lacan, Jacques, 203
Lecter, Hannibal: in adaptation, 27–37, 40, 44, 96, 98, 102, 128, 258, 266, 268–69, 285; as author, 271–78; as cannibal, xi, 1–4, 7, 14, 20, 27, 34, 59, 64–65, 75, 117, 119, 145–47, 149, 154, 156–62, 172–75, 183, 187, 196, 202, 215, 236, 240–41, 247, 250, 255, 266; as colonizer, 103; and Francis Dolarhyde, 67–70, 276, 278; in fanfiction, 46, 49, 248; and gender, 63, 76, 81–82, 84, 86, 97–101, 111–12, 208, 213; as gourmand, xiii, 64–65, 149, 156–62, 239, 241–42, 251–55; as infection, 23, 102, 107, 112; as mentor, 97–121; power and, 20, 37, 43, 75, 77, 79, 81–82, 97, 100, 105, 147, 156–62, 187, 270; as psychiatrist, 129, 195–96, 200–206, 209, 211–13, 234, 270; and queerness, 45–46, 49, 59–60, 63–64, 82, 93, 136, 140–41, 270; relationship with Abigail Hobbes, 7, 44, 60, 98, 104–10, 112, 160, 234; relationship with Alana Bloom, 60, 63, 105, 202–6; relationship with Bedelia Du Maurier, 64, 116–17, 160, 169, 171–81, 183–89, 197, 255, 268–69, 295; relationship with Clarice Starling, 97–118, 120–21, 172, 176, 183, 208n21, 234n30, 269, 279; relationship with Jack Crawford, 102, 158, 273, 276; relationship with Will

Graham, 4–5, 7, 35, 44, 46, 49, 55, 59, 63–65, 69–72, 75–76, 81, 84, 91, 98, 110–11, 116–21, 124, 127, 129, 136, 141–42, 169–71, 198, 201, 208–9, 212–13, 234–35, 239, 248, 266, 268, 270, 291; as serial killer, 4, 27–37, 50, 196–98, 201, 215, 230, 233–35, 240; and vampirism, 102–3, 153; whiteness and, 8, 82, 93, 145, 146–47, 151–55, 157–58, 161–63. *See also* Hopkins, Sir Anthony; Mikkelsen, Mads
Lecter, Mischa, 101, 116–17, 174, 197, 209
Lightfoot, Steve, 288–89
Lounds, Freddie, 3, 58, 106, 134–35, 206, 211, 219, 274–75
"Love Crime" (song), 188

Maio, Lorenzo de, 286, 288
Mancini, Don, 291
Manhunter (1986 film), 1, 4, 126, 134, 208, 210, 286, 297
mentorship, 7, 97–101, 103–6, 108, 110, 112, 114–15, 120–21, 204, 273, 290, 299
metaphor: cannibalism as, 18–21, 24, 151, 255; food as, 251–52; in *Hannibal*, x, 175, 179, 181; murder as, 271, 288; in science fiction/fantasy, 38; sexual, 100, 110; teacup as, 209–10; transformation and, 132, 138
Mikkelsen, Mads, ix, 2, 4, 9, 76, 145, 248, 252, 266, 279, 286
Mindhunter (book), 4, 210
Minnesota Shrike. *See* Hobbs, Garret Jacob

"Mizumono" (2.13), 47–48, 108, 114, 188, 195, 205, 273
monsters, 1, 22, 41–45, 47, 91, 102, 185
monstrosity, 29, 32, 36, 49, 51, 74, 145; of Hannibal Lecter, 7, 27–28, 37–38, 40, 42–47, 50
"Mukōzuke" (2.05), 201, 212, 220, 235
Muth, Ellen, 267

"Naka-choko" (2.10), 63, 114, 129, 207, 269, 273
nakama, xi, 118
Natali, Vincenzo, 293–94
neoliberalism, 10, 13–14, 22, 139–40, 155
Nietzsche, Friedrich, 14, 22, 212–13
"Number of the Beast Is 666, The" (3.12), 63, 174, 211, 269, 274

observation, 175, 185, 215–17, 221, 226, 231–32, 236, 255
"Œuf" (1.04), 16, 104, 109, 195, 198–99, 230
offal, 22, 162

patriarchy, 74, 77, 80, 83, 85, 88–90, 194, 196, 203, 206–7, 273
pig, 12, 15, 17, 24, 117, 157, 207, 294
Poon, Janice, ix–xi, 2, 185, 242, 246–47, 251–53, 255. *See also Feeding Hannibal*
porcine, 17, 24
"Potage" (1.03), 105–6, 160, 204, 233
"Primavera" (3.02), 116, 209, 230, 275

psychiatry, 60, 89, 224, 234n30
Psycho (1960 film), 174n9, 299
psychoanalysis, 8, 192–213, 224, 231–32
psychopathy, 98, 201, 233, 240, 284

queer, 126–30, 136, 140–42, 194, 196, 270; counterpublics, 125; futurity, 125; reading, 126, 133; skin, 132; space, 125, 137; time, 44, 125, 127, 133, 134n28, 137, 139, 141–42. *See also* queerness
queering, 7, 49, 54–55, 59, 66, 71, 75–76, 80, 82, 92–93, 124, 136–37
queerness, 8, 36, 44–46, 48–49, 60, 62–66, 70, 71–72, 76, 78–79, 82–83, 93–94, 124, 126, 136, 139–40, 142. *See also* queer

race, 8, 13, 145–47, 153, 155, 163, 165
Ratner, Brett, 1, 117, 126, 208, 267, 286
Red Dragon (novel), 1–2, 8, 30, 34, 54–63, 65–66, 70–71, 96, 97n2, 98, 101–2, 124, 126, 133, 135–36, 140, 142, 192, 198, 203n17, 208, 258, 266–68, 276–77, 285–86, 297
Red Dragon (2002 film), 1, 4, 117, 134–35, 208
Reitzel, Brian, 180, 188
"Relevés" (1.12), 106, 206, 211–12
repetition, 27–28, 32, 36–37, 39–40, 42–44, 47–48, 50, 133
resistance, 37–38, 160, 179, 182, 211; cannibalism as, 151; and whiteness, 152–54

retrospectatorship, 126, 122, 142
romance: between Hannibal and Will, 46, 110, 270; heterosexual, 78, 85, 91; gothic, 7, 74–77, 80, 84, 91, 94; queer, 46
"Rôti" (1.11), 202

"Sakizuke" (2.02), 88, 171, 174, 179, 204, 231, 236
satire, 18
"Savoureux" (1.13), 173, 270
Scott, Ridley, 1, 97, 130, 183, 269, 287
"Secondo" (3.03), 116, 118, 174, 197, 198, 269
seriality, 7, 34, 38, 51; criminal, 36, 47, 271; in fanfiction, 46, 50; monstrous, 27, 35, 37–42, 44, 47, 50; and television, 28, 39–42, 44, 48, 271
serial killing, 27, 29–34, 36, 38–39, 48
"Shiizakana" (2.09), 114, 129
Silence of the Lambs, The (novel), 1, 30, 65, 96–99, 102–3, 105, 121, 134n28, 195–97, 201, 234, 268, 285–86
Silence of the Lambs, The (1991 film), 1, 4, 97, 103, 127, 176, 234n30, 266, 270, 285
Siouxsie Sioux, 187
social media, 5, 184n26, 247, 250, 263, 271
"Sorbet" (1.07), 16, 89, 169, 172, 204, 212, 232
spoilers, 3, 289
Starling, Clarice, 1, 122, 128, 134, 184, 200–201; adaptation in *Hannibal*, 7, 96, 98, 103–5, 107–18, 120–21, 183, 267, 286;

relationship with Hannibal
  Lecter, 97–118, 120–21, 172, 176,
  208n21, 234, 269, 279
"Su-zakana" (2.08), 113, 115, 273
Swift, Jonathan, 18

"Takiawase" (2.04), 112, 201
Tally, Ted, 102, 286
Tantalus, 20, 23
television, 13, 258, 263, 265, 272;
  fandom, 6, 243–44; genre, 163,
  192; *Hannibal* as network, x, 44,
  142, 278, 292; narrative, 39, 57,
  272; prestige, 5; queerness on, 48,
  270; reality, 22; and seriality, 7,
  28, 37, 39–40, 42, 54, 271; and
  social media, 263; transmedia
  economy of, 162; women on, 171,
  183, 192
temporality, 32, 37, 40–41, 43–44,
  46, 49, 127
theoretical whitewashing, 146
Tier, Randall, 114, 129, 132, 198
"Tome-wan" (2.12), 87, 160, 176–77,
  292
transformative work, 278–79. *See
  also* fanworks

transgender, 46n47, 125, 127–28,
  130–31, 133, 137–42
transgression, 49, 54–55, 152, 157,
  159–60, 179, 272
"Trou-Normand" (1.09), 107

Verger, Margot, 63, 89, 127, 129–30,
  132–34, 141–42, 176, 206–7
Verger, Mason, 119, 130, 134, 206–7,
  209–10, 292
violence, 13, 27–30, 32–35, 37, 41,
  43–44, 48, 50, 55, 65, 92, 119,
  169, 170n2, 173, 192, 198–99;
  aesthetics of, 2–3, 285; colonial,
  151; domestic, 86, 88–89, 130;
  metaphorical, 271; reproductive,
  132; and whiteness, 8, 157

whiteness, 8, 145–48, 151, 153–55,
  158, 161–63
"Wrath of the Lamb, The" (3.13), 41,
  68, 70–71, 91, 119, 140, 160, 170,
  188, 276, 285

"Yakimono" (2.07), 273

www.ingramcontent.com/pod-product-compliance
Lightning Source LLC
Chambersburg PA
CBHW060942230426
43665CB00015B/2030